MW01487188

A Modern Guide to the Multiple Streams Framework

ELGAR MODERN GUIDES

Elgar Modern Guides offer a carefully curated review of a selected topic, edited or authored by a leading scholar in the field. They survey the significant trends and issues of contemporary research for both advanced students and academic researchers.

The books provide an invaluable appraisal and stimulating guide to the current research landscape, offering state-of-the-art discussions and selective overviews covering the critical matters of interest alongside recent developments. Combining incisive insight with a rigorous and thoughtful perspective on the essential issues, the books are designed to offer an inspiring introduction and unique guide to the diversity of modern debates.

Elgar Modern Guides will become an essential go-to companion for researchers and graduate students but will also prove stimulating for a wider academic audience interested in the subject matter. They will be invaluable to anyone who wants to understand as well as simply learn.

For a full list of Edward Elgar published titles, including the titles in this series, visit our website at www.e-elgar.com.

A Modern Guide to the Multiple Streams Framework

Edited by

Nikolaos Zahariadis

Mertie Buckman Chair and Professor of International Studies, Rhodes College, USA

Nicole Herweg

Research Fellow, Ruprecht-Karls-University, Heidelberg, Germany

Reimut Zohlnhöfer

Professor of Political Science, Ruprecht-Karls-University, Heidelberg, Germany

Evangelia Petridou

Associate Professor of Political Science, Mid Sweden University, Sweden, and Senior Researcher, NTNU Social Research, Norway

ELGAR MODERN GUIDES

Edward Elgar
PUBLISHING

Cheltenham, UK • Northampton, MA, USA

Published by
Edward Elgar Publishing Limited
The Lypiatts
15 Lansdown Road
Cheltenham
Glos GL50 2JA
UK

Edward Elgar Publishing, Inc.
William Pratt House
9 Dewey Court
Northampton
Massachusetts 01060
USA

A catalogue record for this book
is available from the British Library

Library of Congress Control Number: 2023945353

This book is available electronically in the **Elgar**online
Political Science and Public Policy subject collection
http://dx.doi.org/10.43379781802209822

ISBN 978 1 80220 981 5 (cased)
ISBN 978 1 80220 982 2 (eBook)

Printed and bound in Great Britain by
TJ Books Limited, Padstow, Cornwall

To my brother Soto,
For helping me appreciate the element of art in public policy

To Claus and Petra

To my wife Martina and my children Rebekka and Benjamin,
For making the sun shine

To Mikie and Sasha

Contents

Figures

Tables

Contributors

Gertrud Alirani is a senior researcher in Political Science at Risk and Crisis Research Centre, Mid Sweden University. Her research focuses on governance and policy processes with a specific interest in sustainability, urban development and crisis management.

Thomas A. Birkland is a Professor of Public Policy in the Department of Public Administration at NC State University. His research focuses on the politics and policy process in natural hazards, crises, and industrial accidents.

Sonja Blum is currently Acting Associate Professor for Comparative Political Science and Public Policy at Bielefeld University, Germany. She is also Affiliate at the FernUniversität in Hagen, Germany, and at the KU Leuven Public Governance Institute, Belgium. Sonja is founding Co-Chair of the EGPA Permanent Study Group Policy Design & Evaluation. She has published in journals such as Policy and Society, European Policy Analysis, Evidence & Policy, International Review of Administrative Sciences, and Social Policy & Administration.

Stephen Ceccoli is the P.K. Seidman Professor of Political Economy at Rhodes College, Memphis, TN, where he teaches in the International Studies Department. His research interests include domestic and comparative aspects of regulation, public opinion and policymaking. He is the author of *Pill Politics: Drugs and the FDA* (Lynne Rienner) and has published in various journals, including *International Studies Quarterly, Social Science Quarterly, Political Behavior, Presidential Studies Quarterly,* and *Policy Studies.*

Xinran Andy Chen is a senior analyst at Trivium China, a China-focused policy consulting firm headquartered in Beijing. He is a graduate of Rhodes College, Memphis, TN, where he obtained his B.A in Economics and International Studies and later earned an M.A. in Asian Studies from Georgetown University's School of Foreign Service. He has published in the Virginia Review of Asian Studies.

Rob A. DeLeo is an Associate Professor of Public Policy at Bentley University. His research examines policy change in anticipation of emerging hazards.

Dana A. Dolan is a Policy Fellow and Adjunct Faculty with the Schar

School of Policy and Government at George Mason University, USA, and a Professorial Lecturer in International Affairs at The George Washington University Elliott School of International Affairs where she teaches graduate courses in policy process theories and qualitative methods. She has published in Policy Studies Journal, Ambio, Carbon and Climate Law Review, Journal of Planning Education and Research, and (in a prior life) IEEE Software and is currently completing her first book on Slow Emergencies.

Kerstin Eriksson is senior researcher at RISE Research Institutes of Sweden and affiliated researcher at Mid Sweden University, Sweden, Her research focuses on crisis management and climate adaptation with a specific interest in the roles of local public authorities and volunteers.

Theofanis Exadaktylos is Professor of European Politics at the University of Surrey, UK. His research interests focus on European public and foreign policies, Europeanization, the politics of austerity and crises, political trust and policy implementation, policy styles and Greek politics. He recently co-edited the book "Policy styles and trust in the age of pandemics: Global threat, national responses" (Routledge) with Nikolaos Zahariadis, Evangelia Petridou and Jörgen Sparf. He is the co-editor of the Journal of Common Market Studies Annual Review and the convenor of the ECPR Standing Group on Political Methodology.

Nicole Herweg is a postdoctoral Research Fellow in the Department of Political Science at the University of Heidelberg, Germany. Her research interests are in comparative public policy with a focus on policy processes. She is the author of *European Union Policy-Making: The Regulatory Shift in Natural Gas Market Policy* (2017) and has published in academic journals, including the *European Journal of Political Research*, *Journal of Comparative Policy Analysis*, *Policy Sciences*, and *Policy Studies Journal*.

Roger Hildingsson is a Senior Researcher in Political Science at Lund University, Sweden, holding a PhD on the state and climate politics. His research focuses on environmental politics, green state theory, climate policy-making, and urban sustainability. Currently, he is conducting research on carbon pricing policies, on industrial decarbonisation, and on narratives of the transition to post-fossil futures.

Nathan Jeschke is a PhD candidate in the School of Public Affairs at the University of Colorado Denver. His work focuses on local agenda setting and policy learning after disasters.

Roine Johansson is Professor of Sociology at Risk and Crisis Research Centre, Mid Sweden University. His main research interests lie within organization studies, more specifically organizational aspects of crisis management.

During recent years he has focused mainly on volunteerism during disaster response operations.

Vassilis Karokis-Mavrikos is a PhD Candidate in European Public Policy at the University of Surrey. His PhD thesis studies agenda-setting and policy formulation dynamics at the European Union level through a new EU-MSF lens. His research interests include Public Policy Change Drivers, Policy Entrepreneurship, Policy Styles, Public Health, and Digital Governance. He has published in prominent peer-reviewed journals and contributed to various edited volumes.

Åsa Knaggård is Associate Professor in Political Science at the Department of Political Science, Lund University, Sweden. She is also affiliated with the Centre for Environmental and Climate Science at Lund University. Her interests include political decision making and policy processes in particular pertaining to environmental problems and the interaction of science and politics. She has published in journals such as European Journal of Political Research, Policy Studies, Environmental Science and Policy, Climate Policy, and Sustainability.

Maria Mavrikou is a Research Fellow in Management and Administration of Health Services and Social Care at the University of West Attica. Her research interests centre around Public Health, Health Systems Evaluations, Public Policy Analysis and Public Administration. Her work has been featured in in prominent international journals and she has contributed to books and edited volumes in English and Greek.

Vilém Novotný is an Assistant Professor at the Department of Public and Social Policy, Faculty of Social Sciences, Charles University, Prague, Czech Republic. His major research interests include policy process research, especially the Multiple Streams Framework, policy-politics relations, and climate change policy.

Lacin Idil Oztig (PhD) is Associate Professor at Yıldız Technical University, Istanbul. She is the editor of Alternatives: Global, Local, Political. She teaches Middle East politics and international organizations. She does research on border politics, democratization, human rights, secularism, and populism. Her work has appeared in various journals including Environment and Planning C: Politics and Space, Territory, Politics, Governance, Third World Quarterly, European Policy Analysis, Government and Opposition, Public Health, Middle East Policy, the Social Science Journal, Cambridge Review of International Affairs, Journal of Borderlands Studies, and Journal of Balkan and Near Eastern Studies.

Evangelia Petridou is Associate Professor at Mid Sweden University,

Sweden, and senior researcher at NTNU Social Research in Norway. She is co-editor of the International Review of Public Policy (IRPP). Her research interests center on policy process theories and specifically policy entrepreneurship, collaboration mechanisms in bureaucracies, and crisis management as a policy sector. She has published in leading journals, including the *Policy Studies Journal, Policy Studies, European Policy Analysis, Politics and Policy.*

Katharina Rietig is Professor of Sustainability and International Politics at Newcastle University, UK. Her research focuses on the role of learning, non-state actors and multilevel governance dynamics between countries and the United Nations, and how these dynamics facilitate policy change for more effective environmental and climate change governance. She holds a PhD and MSc from the London School of Economics and published a monograph with MIT Press.

Diego Sanjurjo holds a PhD in political science from the Autonomous University of Madrid and Master degrees in public policy and international development. He specializes in security policies and is currently the Coordinator of the Citizen Security Program of the Uruguayan Ministry of Interior (Montevideo, Uruguay). He also teaches at the Uruguayan Catholic University and his main areas of research include public policy theories, Latin American policies and security, gun, and drug policies.

Kristin Taylor is an Associate Professor in the Department of Political Science at Wayne State University. Her research focuses on the public policy process, specifically agenda setting, policy learning and change after a crisis.

Stefanie Thurm graduated from Kaiserslautern University with a Master's degree in social sciences. She is currently working at Saarland University in the project *Linking Borderlands* which is funded by the German Federal Ministry of Education and Research. Her PhD research focuses on cross-border cooperation, policy learning and language policy.

Annette Elisabeth Töller is Professor of Public Policy and Environmental Politics at FernUniversität in Hagen. Her research interests focus on public policies and policy processes in the areas of air pollution control, waste management, climate protection and bioeconomy. Recent work has been published in Environmental Politics, Environmental Policy and Panning, Journal of Environmental Studies and Sciences, and Sustainability. Since 2020, she has been serving as a member of the German Advisory Council on the Environment.

Annemieke van den Dool is an Assistant Professor in the Social Sciences Division at Duke Kunshan University in China. Her research focuses on policymaking, policy process theories, and crisis management in China, especially in the areas of health and the environment.

Lotta Vylund is a PhD student at Division of Fire Safety Engineering Lund University, Sweden. Her research focus on problem solving networks in the fire and rescue service.

Georg Wenzelburger is Professor of Comparative European Politics at Saarland University. His research interests include the comparative analysis of public policies in areas like the politics of welfare state reform, law and order policies and the effects of digitalization on politics. Recent work has been published with *Oxford University Press* (The partisan politics of law and order) and in leading political science journals such as the *British Journal of Political Science*, the *European Journal of Political Research*, *Party Politics* and *West European Politics*.

Nikolaos Zahariadis is the Mertie Bukman Chair and Professor of International Studies at Rhodes College, Memphis, TN, USA.

Stephanie Zarb is a Visiting Assistant Professor in the Department of Political Science at Albion College. Her research focuses on local government implementation of disaster mitigation strategies and the politics of environmental hazards.

Reimut Zohlnhöfer is Professor of Political Science at the University of Heidelberg, Germany. His research interests include the advancement of the Multiple Streams Framework, Comparative Policy Analysis and German Politics. He has published in many leading journals, including British Journal of Political Science, Comparative Political Studies, European Journal of Political Research, European Political Science Review, Policy Studies Journal, Socio Economic Review and West European Politics.

Acknowledgments

Every book is a journey replete with fluctuating emotions, dead ends, amazing discoveries, adventure, and friendship. This book was no exception. The editors and contributors took a relatively simple idea, ambiguity, and explored the implications of its presence in the complex environment of public policymaking, using different issues and in many different national contexts. In some cases, a few of us felt like modern-day Pythias, peeking through the fog of policy to understand the politics of choice. In the process, we uncovered glimpses of rationality, signs of strategic behavior, and lots of rituals and instances of meaning making. The framework we have used, the Multiple Streams Framework (MSF), has proven to be a valuable guide in this journey by shedding light on how to interpret the process and explain the outcomes.

Having been edited and co-authored by a mixture of seasoned and young academics, the book contains explorations of the MSF across developed (the United States, Sweden, Greece, Germany, and Australia among others) and developing countries (Brazil, China, and Turkey), using diverse issue areas ranging from migration policy to crises caused by forest fires. We took the MSF one step further to explain sub-national and international policies. Being astute students of public policy, we realize and freely acknowledge that the MSF does not explain all decisions equally well. But where the framework's assumptions hold, conditions of organized anarchies, the explanations and even predictions supported the main thrust of the argument. Policy choice is often the result of interacting three elements – policies, problems, and politics – during open policy windows by policy entrepreneurs. While the core elements of the MSF are simple, they number only five, their interaction is highly complex and contingent. But the theoretical extensions and empirical applications in this volume point to the same conclusion. The process appears to be similar whether one talks of agenda setting, policy formulation, or policy implementation.

Each of the editors could not have taken the journey alone. Rather, we each needed the other for expertise, advice, and the occasional push to get things done. Nikos Zahariadis wants to thank his co-editors and contributors for graciously agreeing to share this journey with him, keeping him on target when needed, and constantly pushing forward. Experience has proven he needed it. Although he is no wiser now, this experience has also taught him that it does, indeed, take a village. He wants to thank his colleagues and students at Rhodes

College who have had to endure his lectures and occasional tirades on public policy. He is thankful that they were polite enough not to ask him to stop or show signs of boredom. Nikos also wants to thank his wife, Ellen, and daughter, Zoë, for letting him finish the manuscript even though it often came at the cost of spending less time with them.

Nicole Herweg would like to thank her academic companions. First and foremost, her thanks go to her co-editors for their passion and valuable input in making this edited volume fly. Furthermore, she would like to thank the contributors for their cooperation and thought-provoking chapters. Also, the seed for this book was sowed over the years at different meetings and in personal communications with researchers interested in the MSF and policy process theories in general. Therefore, Nicole wishes to thank these companions for the scientific exchanges that sparked her scientific curiosity and have been a constant source of inspiration.

Reimut Zohlnhöfer would also like to thank his co-editors for intellectual surprises, a great collaboration and a lot of fun. Similarly, he owes a lot to the people at his chair, particularly Andrea Ficht, Frederic Kohlhepp and Fabian Engler. Moreover, without the exciting discussions with Moshe Maor, Reimut's contribution to this book would not have been possible. Finally, he wishes to thank his wife Martina and his children, Rebekka and Benjamin, for everything.

Evangelia Petridou is grateful to her fellow co-editors for sharing their considerable experience with her and doing it with pleasure and kindness. Evangelia would like to acknowledge funding from FORMAS, Sweden, FR-2019/0002 (Putting out Fires: A Multiple Streams Analysis) for the work that has gone into this volume.

The editors also wish to thank the commissioning editor, Harry Fabian, and the rest of the team at Edward Elgar for their professionalism and support for this project. It was the right project at the right time, and we appreciate the opportunity that you provided to make this happen. Finally, we hope analysts and more importantly younger scholars and students find this volume useful in their work. We don't expect them to agree with everything we say but even if our work makes them think harder about why they disagree, we will have accomplished our objective to offer a valuable and informative explanation of the policy process.

1. Advancing the Multiple Streams Framework

Nikolaos Zahariadis, Nicole Herweg, Reimut Zohlnhöfer, Evangelia Petridou, and Vilém Novotný

INTRODUCTION: PYTHIA'S CAVE AND THE MULTIPLE STREAMS FRAMEWORK[1]

How do policy makers decide what issues to attend and which choices to make or implement? This question is especially puzzling because policy makers themselves often do not have the requisite information and do not know what they want. They cannot possibly attend to all issues or even educate themselves on what they consider to be the most important problems. Prioritizing issues is a process that contains doses of political power, perception, potency and proximity in different quantities at different times (Zahariadis 2016b, 7–8). It makes the goal of the all-attentive, omniscient, or even satisficing, policymaker largely an idealized myth. In this book, we present and discuss a framework of the policy process, the Multiple Streams Framework (MSF), that provides an answer to the above question by side-stepping this myth (Kingdon 2011; Zahariadis 2003). Exploring systematically MSF's suitability in various issues across subnational, national, and international contexts, we conceptualize public policy somewhat like a Delphic oracle, a process replete with bias, language and symbols among interacting policy actors who generate conflicting messages in staged settings of political power. Drawing on the wisdom and cunning of the ancients, we look for answers in the ritualized context within which issues are raised and decisions are made, stressing two important elements of the process: ambiguity and time (see Zohlnhöfer and Rüb 2016). Ambiguity points to the need to interpret policy facts and time highlights the dynamics of change and shifting priorities. These concepts together help us explain the why and when of public policymaking.

Travelling back to Delphic times in ancient Greece, we observe that Pythia, Apollo's priestess, delivered prophecies in a highly ritualized environment inside a cave by uttering incomprehensible words that only priests could interpret to anxious pilgrims who sought the god's favor. At one level, interpretation of the oracle was critical to the process because of the need to turn pilgrims into a steady stream of god-fearing believers while rituals and symbols, as in all religious ceremonies (Turner 1995), helped anchor the known and the familiar to the uncertain and the spiritual. At another level, priests understood that their role was not to change but to reinforce the established political order. Their position and wealth depended on the good will of ruling kings and emperors who sought advice that suited, not undermined, their political stature. Speaking truth to power was not an option. In this way, the oracle strove to strike a balance between the mystical – the ambiguous, ritualistic, and symbolic meaning-making process – and the instrumentalist – the political and material components of decision-making. But balance did not imply equal doses of each component; just some combination depending on who was asking and when.

Policy makers operate as if they find themselves in Pythia's cave. They similarly provide their interpretations of events to generate support or opposition, to suppress or direct attention to important issues, or perhaps in the extreme to discredit opponents or institutions with "alternative facts" or "fake news." Pythia's cave and the whole process of delivering the oracle were spectacles with ambiguous symbols and occasionally shifting meanings; so is politics and public policymaking today (Edelman 1988). The process is conceptualized in dramaturgical terms "as sequences of staged performances of conflict and conflict resolution" (Hajer 2005, 624). In this world of policymaking, Pythia's cave is not a place but a staged sequence of events; a temporal occasion to mix participants and processes, problems and solutions, meaning and interest. Policymaking is not mainly rational but largely contextual in that what decisions are made depends largely on when they are made. What are the mechanisms by which ambiguous messages become public policy and how do actors accomplish policy change (or not)?

We are mindful that policymaking is also about allocating resources to define and address public problems, however imperfectly; what March and Olsen (1984, 735) call instrumentalist politics. The process involves shaping, exercising and reproducing current configurations of political power. When possible, policy makers calculate costs, anticipate benefits, build sensible coalitions and estimate consequences that serve their own political future. Meaning-making and strategic behavior, which may also involve coercion, are but two components of the same logic of political manipulation (Zahariadis 2003).

To circle back to Pythia, ambiguity served both sides well: it played the useful role of enriching the priests, while it provided meaning and divine inspiration to pilgrims (Zahariadis 2016a). Applying the MSF, we make a similar point in this book. Public policy is as much about clarity, cost/benefit analysis and strategic calculations, as it is about deception, meaning, and symbols. We aim to explain the co-existence of these contradictory elements, model their complex interaction, systematically gather useful information, and articulate the consequences for choice in public policy.

A BRIEF SUMMARY OF THE MULTIPLE STREAMS FRAMEWORK

The core idea of the MSF since the first publication of Kingdon's seminal book in 1984 is that agenda-setting and policy making are not exercises in rational problem-solving in the sense that policy-makers identify political problems and then pick the policies that are best suited to solve the given problems. Rather, problems and policies, in addition to the political climate, develop independently of one another. Hence, it might just as well be the case that a pre-existing solution is attached to a newly arising problem than the other way around. And sometimes, the politics are just right and something may be put on the agenda that can, but does not have to solve a particular problem. In sum, the MSF offers a different perspective on the policy-making process than is familiar from many other frameworks. There are many policies that can be considered solutions for one problem, but also many problems that can be attached to one policy. The match between problem and solution/policy needs to be actively established by political actors (called policy entrepreneurs) who will try to frame problems in a way that makes their policies seem to fit the problem. This matching can only happen at specific points in time, however, so-called policy windows, when there is agenda-space available for a specific issue.

Assumptions

This unconventional way of thinking about the policy process rests on the garbage can model of organizational choice (Cohen, March and Olsen 1972), with which it also shares assumptions. We will briefly discuss these assumptions in turn. One core premise of both the garbage can model and the MSF is that the policy process is characterized by ambiguity, "defined as the presence of multiple, conflicting, and irreconcilable interpretations [of] public events, situations, and processes" (Zahariadis 2016a, 4).[2] Hence, policy problems may be understood in different ways by different people. As a result, more than one solution may be suitable for the same problem, depending on how it is framed (Kingdon 2011). Second, and drawing from Simon (1997), MSF assumes that policy-makers operate under time constraints and due to limited time as well as limited cognitive capacity can only consider a limited number of possible alternatives to a policy problem. Third, and as a result of the ambiguity of policy problems and time constraints, the policy preferences of the actors involved in the process are not fixed, but rather depend on how the problem is framed. As Herweg, Huß, and Zohlnhöfer (2015, 437) note, this does not mean that policy-makers do not have preferences; rather, it means that they may be unclear. That is to say that policy-makers do not know which specific policies they want at the onset of policy processes. A fifth assumption is unclear technology that concerns institutional ambiguity. This is manifested in turf disputes or jurisdictional overlap, which may hinder the work of actors in bureaucracies or governmental departments. Unclear technology is further complicated by fluid participation in the sense that policy experts and actors in the policy making process move from the public to the private sector. A final assumption is that the streams that flow through the political system – problems, policies, and politics – are independent, at least in principle. That is to say that policies are not (only) developed in response to problems but independently of them and that political majorities are independent from political problems and potential solutions.

Core Analytical Elements

The three independent streams are also the core analytical elements of the MSF, together with the policy window and the policy entrepreneurs (for the following, see Herweg, Zahariadis, and Zohlnhöfer 2018). The assumption of stream independence implies that each stream has a life of its own and can (and must) be analyzed independently.

In the *problem stream*, conditions compete for policy-makers' attention. In MSF thinking, problems are not objective facts. Rather, they are defined by so-called problem brokers (Knaggård 2015). Nonetheless, some conditions are more likely to be considered as problems. If problem brokers can convince policy-makers or the public that the current condition substantially diverges from some ideal state, that the country is falling behind in comparison with other states, or if they succeed in changing the context in which a condition is understood, policy-makers might come to consider a condition a public problem that necessitates political action. At the same time, conditions that in principle could be considered problems need to come to policy-makers' attention. According to MSF thinking, there are three ways this can happen. First, indicators like the inflation rate or budget deficit can signal that a condition needs to be dealt with, particularly, if the indicator significantly changes for the worse. Second, feedback on extant policies can indicate that a condition might need attention. Third, focusing events like disasters and crises, but also personal experiences of policy-makers can direct attention to these issues.

In the *policy stream*, policy ideas are developed independently of the problems that are currently relevant in the problem stream. The actors in the policy stream are experts in a given issue area that can come from government and bureaucracy, parties, interest groups, academia, media etc. These actors interact in policy communities (Herweg 2016). Some members of the policy community are so-called policy entrepreneurs, i.e., "advocates who are willing to invest their resources – time, energy, reputation, money – to promote a position in return for anticipated future gain in the form of material, purposive, or solidary benefits" (Kingdon 2011, 179). Policy entrepreneurs present their proposals at various occasions and seek to find support for them among the other members of the policy community. These other experts discuss and criticize these proposals and policy entrepreneurs modify their proposals in response or several proposals are merged to eventually emerge as a worked-out policy alternative. This process is called softening-up. The members of the policy community tend to assess proposals on the basis of the so-called criteria for survival. Hence, proposals that are technically feasible, that reflect the values of the experts in the policy community, that are anticipated to find political support, and the costs of which are considered tolerable stand a better chance to be considered a viable alternative for future coupling of the streams.

While in the policy stream deliberation prevails, in the *political stream* powering and negotiation dominates. Three elements make up this stream: the national mood, interest groups, and government. The national mood mirrors public opinion. It is important to note that this concept is a social construct. The national mood is something policy-makers sense from various sources. Opinion polls are likely one of these sources but others can also be relevant like media reporting or personal contacts. Interest groups are also considered relevant. If all relevant or at least very powerful interest groups oppose a proposal and launch campaigns against it, it becomes unlikely that this proposal will be pursued further. At the same time, the national mood can trump interest group opposition under certain conditions. Finally, it makes a difference who the responsible minister and the relevant members of parliament are and which party controls the government and parliament. For agenda-setting, the political entrepreneur, an actor who holds a formal leadership position like the responsible minister (Roberts and King 1991), becomes important. At this stage, it is not yet required that the necessary majorities for a policy are already available. Rather, if the policy entrepreneur can convince a political entrepreneur that her policy project will solve an important problem or will otherwise be politically expedient and the political entrepreneur takes over the proposal, the political stream is ready for coupling (Zohlnhöfer 2016). If majorities are not forthcoming at this point, the political entrepreneur can try and find them during decision-making.

While the streams develop independently, at specific points in time, which are called policy windows, they can be coupled together. Policy windows can open in two of the streams, the problem and the political stream. In the political stream a window can open as new members enter parliament, the government changes or a minister is replaced. Similarly, a swing in the national mood can open a policy window. Some windows also open more routinely. For example, budget negotiations can be used as policy windows for a substantial number of issues. In the problem stream, windows open as disasters or worsening indicators make the status quo unsustainable, for example. It has been argued that conditions that may endanger government stability or the government's re-election are particularly likely to open policy windows in the problem stream (Herweg, Huß, and Zohlnhöfer 2015; Herweg, Zahariadis, and Zohlnhöfer 2022).

Once a window opens, the policy entrepreneur will try to couple her solution to the problem that opened the problem window or will argue that her proposal fits nicely with the developments in the political stream that opened the politics window. This will work more likely if the streams are ready for coupling, that is if the problem is defined in a way that suits the policy entrepreneur, if a viable policy alternative exists and if a political entrepreneur is willing to back the proposal and seek for majorities for it during decision making.

Again, policy windows do not objectively open for specific projects. Rather, policy entrepreneurs will look out for developments in the problem and politics streams and try to couple their preferred policy to developments they deem favorable for their purpose. Of course, there are limits to what can be coupled, as proposals cannot be framed as solutions to all problems and certain constellations in the political stream are more favorable to specific proposals than to others. Nonetheless, there is a broad array of policies that can be coupled to any one problem and similarly the same proposal can often be attached to a large number of problems.

If the policy entrepreneur succeeds in coupling the three streams, their preferred proposal gets on the agenda. Coupling success to some degree depends on external factors, e.g., the number of competing issues that also seek agenda access. As argued above, agenda space is limited. Hence, an issue might not make it onto the agenda even though there is a well-defined problem, a viable policy alternative, a willing political entrepreneur and a development that could in principle be used as a policy window, if other more pressing issues block the agenda. At the same time, success also depends on the policy entrepreneurs themselves. The more access they have to key policy-makers, the more resources (in terms of time they can spend on their activities, reputation and material resources) they control and the more persistent they act, the greater is the likelihood of success.

While Kingdon's original argument only dealt with agenda-setting, more recent contributions have extended the MSF to decision making and even policy implementation and termination, as also evidenced by some of the contributions to this volume. One prominent example of how the MSF can be extended to decision making is Herweg, Huß, and Zohlnhöfer's (2015; also Herweg 2013) suggestion of a second policy window. The idea is that if an issue gets on the agenda, this opens a decision window in the policy stream. During this second phase, called decision coupling, political entrepreneurs seek to find majorities for their proposal. Here, institutions play an important role because the institutional setting defines which actors need to agree to the policy change (see Zohlnhöfer, Herweg, Huß 2016). Political entrepreneurs have a number of instruments at their disposal, which they can employ to get approval for their proposal. For example, they can go back to the policy stream and combine other proposals with their own to increase support for the overall package (package deals). Similarly, the political entrepreneur can try to get the proposal adopted in a watered-down version this time around (and hope to get further steps enacted in the future). Finally, the political entrepreneur can try to manipulate the veto actors. For example, she can paint the problem that the proposal is supposed to deal with as particularly grievous or increasing in size. This might incite these actors to give their approval. In this way, the MSF logic remains intact and the framework can be applied to stages beyond agenda-setting, too. In similar ways, the MSF can be and has been adapted to political systems for which it has not been originally developed.

CONCEPTUAL ADAPTATION AND CHANGE IN EMPIRICAL APPLICATIONS

Conceptual adaptation comes in two varieties: temporal and comparative. As theories are applied in diverse settings, core hypotheses are confirmed or qualified while secondary hypotheses are added or discarded. This is important because policy theory development, as Sabatier (2007) informs, needs to be systematic in order to gain cumulative explanatory power and paradigmatic stature. It should be "used by a variety of scholars" to develop "increasing coherence and scope" (p. 324). In this section, we examine each adaptation in turn to point out that MSF approximates what Lakatos (1970) called a "progressive scientific research program". The program's aim is to accumulate knowledge by 1. systematic specification of the MSF's "hard core" assumptions and concepts that cannot be altered without abandoning the program and 2. testing, adaptation, and respecification of the "protective belt" of auxiliary hypotheses, which may be adjusted or even completely replaced to defend the "hard core" (cf. Lakatos 1970, 132).

Table 1.1   *The hard core of the MSF*

MSF element	Hard Core
Problem stream	Process of problem recognition and definition
Political stream	Processes determining the political climate
Policy stream	Process of forming and refining policy alternatives, resembling a process of natural biological selection
Policy entrepreneur	"Advocates who are willing to invest their resources – time, energy, reputation, money – to promote a position in return for anticipated future gain in the form of material, purposive, or solidary benefits" (Kingdon 2011, 179)
Policy (or Agenda) Window	Opportunity for policy entrepreneurs to push their favorite policy

Conceptual Adaptation over Time

The MSF "hard core" consists not only of basic structural elements such as the three streams (problem, politics, and policy), policy windows, (policy) entrepreneurs and their basic features, but also of MSF core assumptions concerning ambiguity, time constraints, elements of organized anarchy (problematic policy preferences, unclear technology, and fluid participation), and stream independence. The "hard core" component manifests in the following hypothesis for the framework as a whole: "Agenda change becomes more likely if (a) a policy window opens, (b) the streams are ready for coupling, and (c) a policy entrepreneur promotes the agenda change" (Herweg et al. 2018, 31). Of course, the hypothesis applies to all stages of the policy process with reasonable adaptations. Table 1.1 provides an overview of the MSF "hard core" elements based on Kingdon (2011) and Herweg, Zahariadis, and Zohlnhöfer (2018).

In contrast, the "protective belt" represents the component of a scientific program that should be challenged, confirmed, or amended. Performed in a cumulative fashion, this has enabled some subsequent research – to be sure not all MSF studies follow this route – to build on successful (progressive) "problem shifts", that is, to continuously reflect, assess, and re-examine the existing protective belt. For example, consider the concept of integration of policy community (Novotný et al. 2021). It is crucial to identify the structure of a policy community because it affects the gestation trajectory of policy ideas (proposals) in the policy stream. Thus, the concept helps to answer the question of how and why some policy ideas become viable policy alternatives (Herweg et al. 2018, 23). Based on his empirical observations, Kingdon (2011) argues that policy communities vary in their degree of fragmentation because some are extremely closed and tightly knit, and others are more diverse and fragmented. The degree of fragmentation determines the diffusion of ideas within a policy community and underlines the incremental dynamics of the gestation process. Zahariadis (2003) shifts focus from fragmentation to integration of policy networks (more fluid than communities) and specifies size, mode, capacity and access as important dimensions of integration. He further hypothesizes and provides empirical evidence to corroborate the point that integration affects the policy's tempo and content in the network. In a progressive problem shift, Herweg et al. (2018) move back to Kingdon's concept of policy community but retain the notion of integration developed by Zahariadis. They also reduce the concept's dimensions to two: size and mode. Consequently, Herweg et al. (2018) developed a new hypothesis: "as the integration of policy communities decreases, it becomes more likely that entirely new ideas can become viable policy alternatives" (Herweg et al. 2018, 30). Novotný et al. (2021) use policy network methodology to add empirical support to the latter hypothesis. What we have witnessed is progressive reflection, assessment, and re-specification to add empirical validity, nuance, and greater scope to hypotheses regarding integration of policy communities.

Comparative Conceptual Adaptation

Policy process research has increasingly become comparative (Dodds 2013; Tosun and Workman 2018), which implies applying the theories outside their typical scopes (Weible 2018, 365). This comparative turn also holds for MSF research. In their meta-literature review of MSF applications, Jones et al. (2016) document that researchers applied the MSF to different political systems literally around the world and to different levels of governance. Roughly one-third of these applications also compared policy processes at two or more levels of governance.

This finding is good news in principle. Following Sartori (1970, 57–8), embarking on world-wide comparisons has a methodological reason: If we conceive comparative research "as a method of control, then its generalizations have to be checked against 'all cases', and therefore the enterprise must be – in principle – a global enterprise" consisting of "systematic testing, against as many cases as possible, of sets of hypotheses, generalizations and laws of the 'if ... then' type".

While MSF research increasingly engages in word-wide comparisons, there is much room to improve systematic testing. Much of the MSF research so far applied Kingdon's (2011) inductively derived MSF one-to-one to: (i) other political systems than that of the United States; or (ii) other levels of governance. However, this unreflected application practice endangers analytical clarity.

Take applying the MSF to non-democracies as an example. Authoritarian election research demonstrates that elections (if they take place at all) have another role in the policy process than in democracies (see Gandhi et al. 2009 for an overview). Consequently, assuming that an election automatically opens an agenda window in non-democracies is at least questionable (cf. van den Dool 2022). Nevertheless, even within democracies, policy processes differ with the levels of governance analyzed. For instance, we know from research on partisan politics that elected officials' party membership is less likely to explain these officials' receptivity to specific ideas at the local level (cf. Thompson 2020, Schulze and Schoenefeld 2022) than they do at the national level (cf. Engler and Zohlnhöfer 2019, Schmidt 1993). Thus, the partisan affiliation of elected officials has less explanatory power at the local level compared to the national level. MSF research must take these differences into account to arrive at meaningful findings.

Sartori (1970, 57) highlights the danger of "conceptual stretching," defined as broadening a concept's meaning to the extent that it becomes too vague and amorphous to allow for world-wide comparisons. A significant proportion of MSF research has fallen into this trap. Literature reviews revealed that many MSF applications lack a shared understanding of the framework's concepts (e.g., Jones et al. 2016). Herweg and Zahariadis (2018), for instance, document that none of the MSF applications to European Union (EU) policy processes coincide with each other regarding how to define the EU's political stream. Unsurprisingly, critics question the MSF's explanatory potential (cf. Weible and Schlager 2016).

While we agree that MSF research has not yet fully exploited its explanatory potential, we see the MSF as a particularly promising lens for comparative policy process research. First, the often criticized figurative language (cf. Cairney and Jones 2016) can be turned into an advantage in comparative analyses. Following Przewroski and Teune (1970, 4), comparative research goes along with conceptual travelling. This means that depending on the system analyzed, researchers might have to find systemic-specific conceptualizations and operationalizations. Consequently, different indicators can –and must – be used to define the MSF's elements in comparative research. However, a prerequisite to turning the figurative language into an advantage is that researchers share a common understanding of what the framework's elements capture.

The initial MSF informs researchers about the operationalization of these elements in democracies. Take, for instance, the political stream. Its core elements are the national mood, interest groups, and government and legislature (Herweg, Zahariadis, and Zohlnhöfer 2018). These elements are seen as "an important promoter or inhibiter of high agenda status" at the federal level in democracies (Kingdon 2011, 163; Herweg, Huß, and Zohlnhöfer 2015). If researchers analyze non-democracies or different governance levels, conceptual travelling requires researchers to identify functional equivalents for these elements (Herweg 2017; Zohlnhöfer, Herweg, Zahariadis 2022).

Table 1.2　　　*Conceptual travelling of the elements of the political stream*

Conceptual travelling of the elements of the political stream in		
democracies (Herweg, Zahariadis & Zohlnhöfer 2018)	non-democracies (Herweg, Zahariadis & Zohlnhöfer 2022)	the European Union (Herweg 2017, Herweg & Zohlnhöfer 2022)
– National mood – Interest groups – Government and legislature	– National mood (if it touches on salient issues pivotal for regime stability) – Interest groups (if existent) – Autocratic leaders and actors close to them	– European mood (if existent) – European Commission, the Council of Ministers, and the European Council – European Parliament

Note:　　　To be applied if the policy issue falls into the ordinary legislative procedure.

Consequently, varying with the unit analyzed, the political stream looks different while still capturing the processes that determine the political climate (for an illustration, see Table 1.2).

If we look at comparative MSF research this way, researchers must decide where they locate their research on the "ladder of generality" (Collier and Mahon 1993, 846). They can either: (i) focus on a subset of cases defined by a large set of attributes (e.g., agenda-setting at the federal level of democracies, agenda-setting at the local level of non-democracies); or (ii) reduce the set of attributes the cases have to share to be considered in the analysis and thereby increasing their number (e.g., agenda-setting at all levels in democracies or agenda-setting at the federal level in political systems) (cf. Collier and Mahon 1993; Sartori 1970; in a similar vein, see Tosun and Workman 2018). Based on the focus chosen, this allows for thoroughly testing the MSF's explanatory potential. For instance, the MSF differentiates between different equifinal paths to open an agenda window (Herweg 2017). Is one of these paths more relevant in democracies than in non-democracies? Or is one of these paths more likely to open an agenda window at a specific policy making level?

While designing comparative MSF analyses this way is highly desirable, it puts a high barrier for comparative research, in particular for quantitative analyses given the immense amount of (fine-grained) data required to operationalize the MSF key elements (cf. Engler and Herweg 2019). Regardless of the case number, we encourage researchers to define clearly where on the ladder of generality their research is located, how the framework's concepts travelled to fit the units of analysis, and which of the MSF hypotheses were confirmed in the analysis. This approach has two advantages in terms of accumulating knowledge: First, it becomes evident at first sight how well the MSF explained the case(s) analyzed. Second, and we would say more importantly, it paves the way for coding their findings and conducting (medium- or even large-N quantitative) meta-analyses. Once again, the only prerequisite is that these analyses share the same understanding of the framework's basic ideas and define clearly where on the ladder of generality the case(s) considered are located.

THE MSF AND THEORIES OF POLICY CHOICE

The MSF does not explain everything all the time; rather, it is a systemic level framework (Zahariadis 2016b) that explains the policy process based on a set of assumptions. There exist a number of approaches developed for the purpose of understanding the policy process and in the quest for the most appropriate theory, it is fruitful to consider the degree of complementarity or competition among different explanatory theories. Zahariadis (2005) demonstrated that clearly articulating different perspectives and their explanatory limitations as well as identifying the conditions under which one perspective may achieve its explanatory potential is preferable to integrating perspectives in an attempt to synthesize models. Having said this, case studies often tend to offer a perfunctory treatment of different perspectives (Cairney, 2013), at times arriving at a foregone conclusion. Drawing from Allison's seminal analysis of the Cuban missile crisis, Zahariadis (2003) argues for the specification of assumptions and the conditions under which a theory provides a robust explanation.

As Allison (1971) showed, explanations may serve two distinct purposes. One explanation may be suited to a phenomenon better than others. By better, he meant more accurately and more aspects of it but with fewer required variables. Competing explanations personify the old saying of doing more with less. At the same time, when it comes to frameworks and theories of the policy process, because of the different emphasis theoretical frameworks place on different elements of the policy process, frameworks may be understood to provide different explanations for the same phenomenon. Upon parsing these explanations it may actually be that these explanations refer to different phenomena. We exemplify this by briefly pointing out a salient difference between MSF and punctuated equilibrium theory (PET). According to MSF, agenda setting refers to the occasion when "open windows present opportunities for the complete linkage of problems, proposals, and politics, and hence opportunities to move packages of the three joined elements up on decision agendas" (Kingdon 2011, 204). In PET, agenda setting is conceptualized as "the study of public, media and government attention to policy issues" (Cairney, 2011, p. X). What is more, while MSF focuses on problem framing rather than the rationality of actors, PET leans on the latter. Finally, the evolutionary focus on PET makes it unsuitable to studying change over truncated periods of time with qualitatively analyzed data, which are more suited to MSF applications and methods. In other words, the nuances in conceptual delineations and divergence of assumptions results in one policy framework providing a better explanation of a given policy puzzle than another.

An additional but less theorized aspect influencing the fit of a given framework to data analysis is the issue itself. Zahariadis (2016b) specified first- and second-order scope conditions under which MSF has more robust explanatory power. First-order scope conditions refer to the institutional environments (referred to by Zahariadis (2013, 811) as "institutional complexity"), whereas second-order scope conditions refer to situational environments, that is, the issue (the policy problem) itself (which Zahariadis (2013, 811) labelled "issue complexity"). Some institutional environments tend to be characterized by more clarity and rationality than others, and concomitantly, some issues lend themselves to a garbage can/MSF approach because of their high levels of ambiguity and low clarity.

We draw from Peters (2015), who differentiates between political and programmatic complexity. The former reflects the number of interests and actors involved in the process – the larger that number, the higher the complexity of an issue. The argument is that the more actors and interests involved in an issue, the more arduous the landscape becomes, and the more difficult it becomes to agree to a solution able to satisfy all competing interests. Ambiguous issues tend to be more politically complex, lending themselves to competing frames and conflicting solutions. Conversely, programmatic complexity refers to intrinsic aspects of the policy problem, including its technical context and a diffuse causality chain. Generally, programmatic complexity in technical terms is inversely correlated to political complexity. We posit that more politically complex problems are more suited to an MSF approach than technically complex issues. Notably, we are not arguing that politically complex issues characterized by high levels of ambiguity and a pronounced lack of preference clarity are suited to an MSF approach to the exclusion of other policy process theories; rather, we contend that generally, politically complex issues are better explained by an approach that conceptualizes the policy process to be fraught with political manipulation and symbols, a space where many solutions precede the problems that they are assigned to solve. As Zahariadis (2016b) asserts, such issues, including policy reform and administrative reorganization, themselves approximate garbage cans.

PLAN OF THE BOOK

This book examines how policymakers decide what issues to address and which options to adopt or implement under conditions of ambiguity. It is important to note that the MSF is a framework that does not explain every policy choice well; only those that fit the assumptions that the framework makes. Change the assumptions, and Pythia, to return back to the Greeks, will likely say something different. The ensuing chapters build on the basic assumptions outlined in this introduction and productively move the MSF in different directions.

The first part of the book deals with questions of theory. It seeks to elaborate on various aspects of the MSF. In this chapter, we introduced the assumptions, structure and logic of the MSF. Some of the ensuing chapters discuss in more detail concepts of the original framework that so far have received little attention in the scholarly literature. That is true for coupling as the "beating heart" of the framework, as Dana Dolan and Sonja Blum call it, but also for the role of the policy entrepreneur. At the same time, other chapters of this first part look at aspects that have not been theorized explicitly in the extant literature, including the scope of reforms, the termination of policies and the case of multi-level policy making.

In Chapter 2, Reimut Zohlnhöfer explores if the MSF is able to explain the scope of agenda and policy changes. Hitherto, MSF was mainly applied to analyze if change occurred at all and when it occurred. In contrast to other policy process frameworks like the Advocacy Coalition Framework or the PET, in each of which the scope or size of change plays an important analytical role, the MSF has been surprisingly silent on this issue. In his conceptual chapter, Zohlnhöfer argues that it should indeed be possible to explain the scope of change with the MSF. More concretely, if problems appear almost imperceptible, if no worked-out alternative exists, elements in the political stream hinder change, agenda space is lacking or concessions are necessary to secure the policy's adoption, change is likely to be small. In contrast, if the streams are all ready for coupling and a policy window opens that provides ample opportunities for policy and political entrepreneurs, significant change can occur. Such "big" policy windows can be long-neglected issues that eventually become pressing and huge focusing events in the problem stream, or landslide election victories and a strong movement of the national mood in the political stream.

Next, Georg Wenzelburger and Stefanie Thurm discuss if and how policy termination can be analysed using the MSF. Indeed, while the framework's scope of application has been widened from agenda setting to policy making and policy implementation, only a handful of studies have looked at policy termination from an MSF perspective. Wenzelburger and Thurm start out by summarizing the findings of studies of policy termination and then seek to transfer these results to the MSF. The authors suggest that the MSF should be well-placed to also explain policy termination. They argue that the problem and political streams in the case of termination should be no different from studies of agenda setting and policy making: If a policy is to be terminated, there needs to be a problem that the termination is argued to solve and the politics for termination must be right. Moreover, "termination windows" can open in either of these streams – and in the familiar way of either worsening indicators, feedback or a focusing event in the problem stream or a change of government or the national mood in the political stream. The policy stream, in contrast, is a bit different. Here the core question is what the situation looks like, once the policy is terminated. Will the situation be viable? So the fallback position without the policy needs to meet the criteria for survival. Moreover, but not too dissimilar from policy making, the policy might have to include some compensation for those citizens who used to benefit from the policy that is being terminated. Finally, the role of the policy terminator mirrors the traditional policy entrepreneur. At the same time, Wenzelburger and Thurm also introduce a role called "outside terminator", who becomes relevant during implementation of the policy termination and hence resembles "implementers" from MSF studies of policy implementation (see Fowler 2019).

Åsa Knaggård and Roger Hildingsson's Chapter 4 deals with multi-level policy making from an MSF perspective. While the fact that policies are made at different levels, from local to intergovernmental, is an undisputed part of modern policy making, MSF scholars only very recently have begun to theorize what this means for the framework and how these developments can be integrated into the MSF. Instead of presenting another case study on the issue, Knaggård and Hildingsson present a conceptual map of how agenda setting and policy making can be affected by multi-level dynamics from an MSF perspective. This conceptual map focuses on four relevant aspects that can be impacted by other policy making levels, namely actors, ideas, events and the institutional context. For example, actors can use policy making opportunities at different levels strategically and can exchange resources across levels. Similarly, ideas can travel from one level to the next. If, for example, a policy is successful at one level that will help convince the policy community at another level that the criteria for survival are fulfilled. Events can also impact various levels. Think of a focusing event at one level that affects the agenda at a different one or the effect regional elections can have on the political stream at the federal level. Finally, the institutional context is extremely relevant. Evidently, multi-level dynamics are more relevant for federal countries or members of strong International Organizations like the EU. But the type of government – democratic or autocratic – is also likely to be important.

Dana A. Dolan and Sonja Blum argue in Chapter 5 that coupling lies at the heart of the MSF. To capture the coupling process's importance, they introduce a revised MSF that consists of four processes: the problem stream, the political stream, the policy stream, and the coupling process. While the streams correspond with established MSF thinking, the authors structure the coupling process along three subcomponents: stream ripeness, the policy window, and coupling strategies. Dolan and Blum explicitly differentiate these subcomponents from actors who play a role in the process, most importantly, policy entrepreneurs. Nonetheless, policy entrepreneurs keep on playing an essential role in this revised MSF since their actions contribute to making the streams ripe and to couple them. Following the authors, the focus on the coupling process allows for analyzing (more) systematically successful and unsuccessful coupling strategies and accumulating knowledge across case studies.

Evangelia Petridou explores the motives of policy entrepreneurs in Chapter 6: what makes these political actors decide to invest resources and energy on the promotion of a policy? Traditionally, MSF and the policy entrepreneurship literature beyond Kingdon has understood these actors to have a specific policy in mind while they lay in wait for an opportunity to arise. Petridou, through a focus on policy implementation, offers a competing explanation based on market theorizations of entrepreneurship. She posits that there are conditions of necessity (external pressures) to which actors may respond to in promoting a policy that did not constitute an a priori policy preference for them. This argument challenges the mainstream thinking on policy entrepreneurship and nuances the concept of the policy entrepreneur and policy entrepreneurship more broadly.

The second part of the book explores applications of the MSF in different settings. We have divided them into two sections: the national and the local/international levels. Two applications in the Greek national setting go about leveraging MSF from different angles in two different policy sectors. In Chapter 7, Vassilis Karokis Mavrikos and Maria Mavrikou tackle health care policy. They seek to understand why some structural reforms successfully establish new policy paradigms while others fail. To this end, they focus on public health policymaking in Greece bookended by two focusing events: the 2003 SARS outbreak and the 2019 Covid-19 pandemic. The first event signalled the institutionalization of public health policy making in Greece, a paradigm tested by the 2019 pandemic. Collecting data from 62 elite interviews and a survey of 261 Greek public health policy stakeholders, the authors find that the policy paradigm of 2003 did not "survive" the implementation phase of the Covid-19 pandemic because of structural pathologies in the Greek system (including politicization and implementation gaps) resulting in the decoupling of streams. The study contributes to the theoretical development of MSF in a context of institutional instability, supporting earlier findings that marginalization of policy feedback and the monitoring of indicators are salient problem stream mechanisms and that venue creation is an important strategy of policy entrepreneurs.

Nikolaos Zahariadis and Evangelia Petridou stay with the Greek context in Chapter 8 by investigating the explanatory value of MSF in policy implementation of migration policy in Greece between 2012 and 2021. Based on Boswell and Rodrigues (2016), who argued that lack of administrative capacity and oscillating political support considerably hinder effective policy implementation, they hypothesize that: (i) inadequate administrative capacity likely decreases implementation effectiveness; and (ii) oscillating political support likely generates movement across modes of implementation. They find that implementation in Greece went from non-implementation to bottom-up implementation to coercion and finally to consensus, a dynamic trajectory with broader implications for MSF research.

Diego Sanjurjo applies the MSF in Chapter 9 to a Latin American case, namely gun control and gun liberalization policies in Brazil. Theoretically, the chapter uses an adaptation of the framework to the Latin American context the author himself introduced earlier (see Sanjurjo 2020). He argues that the political stream in particular needs some adaptation to make the MSF applicable in Latin America where political parties are weak and the national mood is polarized and in many instances easy to ignore for policy-makers, while interest groups can exert enormous influence on policy processes and the executive dominates Parliament. This slight but important adaptation is empirically tested for the case of Brazilian gun liberalization policies from the mid-2000s onwards. Indeed, despite a national mood that was not at all in favour of liberalization, several attempts at gun liberalization have made it onto the agenda due to the enormous influence of the gun lobby and individual members of Congress – but have failed to get the regulation of firearms removed entirely, partly due to the role of the Supreme Court.

In Chapter 10, Lacin Idil Oztig analyzes Turkish agenda-setting processes in the Covid-19 pandemic between 2020 and 2022. To do so, she builds on recent research according to which the MSF can travel to non-democratic settings (e.g., Zohlnhöfer, Herweg, Zahariadis 2022). Oztig moves this line of research further by incorporating Turkey's top-down approach to policy-making in MSF reasoning. Her analysis shows that this top-down approach affects, in particular, the political stream dynamic, the policy community's set-up, and the comparatively little importance of health associations regarding problem framing and working-out policies. One of Oztig's core findings is that President Erdogan used the Covid-19 crisis to increase citizens' trust in his political leadership by putting the Scientific Advisory Board (SAB) in charge of deciding how to react to the pandemic. Given citizen's high trust in medical professionals, Erdogan's commitment to comply with the SAB's recommendations was, among others, a means to increase his legitimacy.

While the MSF in its traditional form discusses agenda setting and policy making in democracies, Annemieke van den Dool reminds us in Chapter 11 that the majority of people in the world live under autocratic regimes. Hence, it is highly important to understand policy making in these settings better and, more specifically, find out if the MSF is also applicable in these contexts. One of the most interesting cases of autocratic policy making certainly is China. Annemieke van den Dool uses her earlier adaptation of the MSF to the

Chinese context and a set of hypotheses derived from Herweg, Zahariadis and Zohlnhöfer (2018) (see van den Dool 2022) to explain why the country's Soil Pollution Law took so long to be adopted. The adapted MSF can explain many aspects of the agenda setting and policy making processes the author observes. At the same time, she shows that the ability of the Chinese political leaders to block the release of information about conditions that could be turned into problems is key to understanding why the Soil Pollution Law took so long, hence underlining the importance of the type of regime.

Shifting focus to the subnational level, Taylor et al. examine in Chapter 12 how subnational focusing events lead to policy change in nested governing arrangements. To do so, this chapter qualitatively examines the 2014 drinking water crisis in Toledo, Ohio. A toxic algae bloom contaminated the drinking water supply, functioning as a focusing event that changed the agenda in the City of Toledo and the State of Ohio. The findings suggest that subnational contexts function similarly to national contexts in certain aspects. The politics and policy streams may not necessarily be independent. Focusing events may signal recurrent problems over a long duration. Finally, the authors find that policy change is (unsurprisingly) often superficial and focuses on advancing existing ideas that marginally address issues and are remedial as opposed to innovative ones that fundamentally reconfigure power dynamics within a particular policy domain.

In Chapter 13, Eriksson et al. arrive at a somewhat similar conclusion but use the case of the 2014 and 2018 forest fires in Sweden. They explain differences between the focal power of events at the local and national levels as well as the effects the events had on subsequent policy changes at the different levels. The findings suggest that the focal power of a rare event, such as the forest fires under examination, likely becomes less concentrated and policy alternatives in the policy stream tend to widen in scope when it moves from local to the national level. Moreover, events with limited local impact areas likely need to be aggregated with other similar events at the national level to have the same policy change impact. The implication for the MSF is that not all policy windows are created equal even if they are opened by the same focusing event. Moreover, policy entrepreneurial activity, access and strategies intensify in use and widen in scope as ideas move across different levels of government.

In Chapter 14, Stephen Ceccoli and Xinran Andy Chen advance the exploratory power of MSF by applying it to the subnational level of an autocratic regime, that of China. Through the empirical context of Covid-19 contagion mitigation policies in Shanghai, Ceccoli and Chen examine policy window openings and the implementation of a "bespoke" grid screening policy in March 2022. The empirical specificities of this study shed light on the timing and conditions favorable for policy window openings and they concur with prior subnational MSF scholarship suggesting that "policy windows need to be 'wedged' open at national and local levels" (Exworthy, et al. 2002, 93). What is more, this chapter somewhat challenges the critique that MSF "struggles to account for policy change resulting from governance processes across multiple governance levels" (Rietig 2021, 57). Finally, Ceccoli and Chen demonstrate that MSF is well-positioned to conceptualize subnational policymaking, even in China's autocratic system.

The final set of chapters in this volume turns to the international perspective. In Chapter 15, Rietig advances MSF's explanatory power in multi-level governance structures with the concept of multilevel reinforcing dynamics (MRD). Rietig's departure point is that cross-boundary and international policy problems necessarily involve more than one nation state as well as international institutions. MRD is a way to widen the scope of MSF by arguing that increasingly, MRDs across international, national, regional and local levels of governance influence the coupling of the policy, politics and problem streams as well as the actions of policy entrepreneurs who take advantage of policy windows. Rietig uses rich data from 30 years of European climate change policy and multilevel process with the United Nations Framework Convention on Climate Change to demonstrate how MSF may be adapted and expanded to account for vertical and horizontal multi-level interactions, taking the framework one step further in explaining global policy outcomes.

A significant share of MSF applications aims at explaining why "an idea's time come[s] when it does" (Kingdon 2011, xvii). In Chapter 16, Annette Elisabeth Töller reminds us that this is only half the story since Kingdon (2011, 69) highlights that the "blocking of an issue is at least as important an agenda-setting effect as positively promoting an issue". Consequently, her chapter focuses on non-decisions, i.e., decisions that have not been reached, and negative decisions, i.e., decisions that consciously do not contain a relevant issue that could well have been included in the decision. Töller argues that analyzing non-decisions requires a different methodological approach than analyzing negative decisions. Since the MSF offers hypotheses formulating conditions for (policy and/or agenda) change, they can easily be turned into the opposite to explain non-decisions. However, the MSF does not offer hypotheses dealing with or being transferable to negative decisions. Consequently, explaining negative decisions is explorative research focusing on the different coupling variants. Töller demonstrates how such explorative research can look like by applying her considerations to EU policy making, more specifically to the European Single-Use Plastics Directive. Her analysis of the coupling process reveals why bioplastics are not included in the European Single-Use Plastics Directive. Deriving insights from the analysis of this negative decision, the chapter concludes with expectations when negative decisions are more likely to be expected for environmental policy.

Exadaktylos, in Chapter 17 of this volume, stays in the context of EU policy making. First, he reviews the scholarship on EU-related public policy events and processes through the lens of MSF. He then tackles epistemological challenges involved in the study of EU policies using MSF and he offers solutions such as incorporating the temporal element in MSF studies and introducing process tracing as a means of capturing changes over time. The empirical innovation in Exadaktylos' chapter is to examine crises at the EU level using MSF. He does this by analyzing the Eurozone crisis of 2009, the Covid-19 pandemic during 2020, and the war in Ukraine in 2022. Exadaktylos highlights the versatility of MSF as a theory able to accommodate the complexity of the EU level; discussing crisis as a focusing event at the international level makes the concept an intervening variable able to change the trajectory of public policy making at the international as well as national level.

NOTES

1. The contribution by Vilém Novotný to this chapter was supported by the Czech Science Foundation under Grant 19-23794S.
2. Conversely, a related concept, that of uncertainty, is a state where there exists lack of information about a policy problem. The literature has traditionally sharply differentiated between ambiguity and uncertainty in the sense that more information has the potential to ameliorate uncertainty (Cairney, 2019; Zahariadis, 2003; 2007), but more information would not clarify ambiguity.

REFERENCES

Cairney, Paul. 2013. "Standing on the Shoulders of Giants: How Do We Combine the Insights of Multiple Theories in Public Policy Studies?" *Policy Studies Journal* 41 (1): 1–21

Cairney, Paul. 2011. *Understanding Public Policy: Theories and Issues.* London: Palgrave Macmillan.

Cairney, Paul, and Michael D. Jones. 2016. "Kingdon's Multiple Streams Approach: What Is the Empirical Impact of This Universal Theory?" *Policy Studies Journal* 44 (1): 37–58.

Cohen, Michael D., James G. March, and Johan P. Olsen. 1972. "A Garbage Can Model of Organizational Choice." *Administrative Science Quarterly* 17: 1–25.

Collier, David and James E. Mahon Jr. 1993. "Conceptual 'Stretching' Revisited: Adapting Categories in Comparative Analysis." *American Political Science Review* 87 (4): 845–55.

Dodds, Anneliese. 2013. *Comparative Public Policy.* New York: Palgrave Macmillan.

Edelman, Murray. 1988. *Constructing the Political Spectacle.* Chicago: University of Chicago Press.

Engler, Fabian, and Nicole Herweg. 2019. "Of Barriers to Entry for Medium- and Large-n Multiple Streams Applications: Methodologic and Conceptual Considerations." *Policy Studies Journal* 47 (4): 905–26.

Engler, Fabian, and Reimut Zohlnhöfer. 2019. "Left Parties, Voter Preferences, and Economic Policy-making in Europe." *Journal of European Public Policy* 26 (11): 1620–38.

Exworthy, Mark, Lee Berney, and Martin Powell. 2002. "'How Great Expectations in Westminster May Be Dashed Locally: The Local Implementation of National Policy on Health Inequalities." *Policy & Politics* 30 (1): 79–96.

Fowler, Luke. 2019. "Problems, Politics, and Policy Streams in Policy Implementation." *Governance* 32 (3): 403–20.

Gandhi, Jennifer, and Ellen Lust-Okar. 2009. "Elections under authoritarianism." *Annual Review of Political Science* 12 (1): 403–22.

Hajer, Maarten A. 2005. "Setting the Stage: A Dramatourgy of Policy Deliberation." *Administration and Society* 36 (6): 624–647.

Herweg, Nicole. 2013. "Der Multiple-Streams-Ansatz – ein Ansatz, dessen Zeit gekommen ist?" *Zeitschrift für Vergleichende Politikwissenschaft* 7 (4): 312–345.

Herweg, Nicole. 2016. "Clarifying the Concept of Policy-Communities in the Multiple-Streams Framework." In *Decision-Making under Ambiguity and Time Constraints: Assessing the Multiple-Streams Framework*, eds. Reimut Zohlnhöfer and Friedbert W. Rüb, 125–45. Colchester, UK: ECPR Press.

Herweg, Nicole. 2017. *European Union Policy making. The Regulatory Shift in Natural Gas Market Policy*. Basingstoke: Palgrave Macmillan.

Herweg, Nicole, Christian Huß, and Reimut Zohlnhöfer. 2015. "Straightening the Three Streams: Theorizing Extensions of the Multiple Streams Framework." *European Journal of Political Research* 54 (3): 435–49.

Herweg, Nicole, and Nikolaos Zahariadis. 2018. "The Multiple Streams Approach." In *The Routledge Handbook of European Public Policy,* eds. Laurie Buonanno and Nikolaos Zahariadis, 32–41. London: Routledge.

Herweg, Nicole, Nikolaos Zahariadis, and Reimut Zohlnhöfer. 2018. "The Multiple Streams Framework: Foundations, Refinements, and Empirical applications." In *Theories of the Policy Process*, 4th edition, eds. Christopher M. Weible and Paul A. Sabatier, 17–53. Boulder, CO: Westview Press.

Herweg, Nicole, Nikolaos Zahariadis, and Reimut Zohlnhöfer. 2022. "Travelling Far and Wide? Applying the Multiple Streams Framework to Autocracies." *German Political Science Quarterly* 63 (2): 203–23.

Herweg, Nicole, and Reimut Zohlnhöfer. 2022. "Analyzing EU Policy Processes Applying the Multiple Streams Framework." In *Elgar Encyclopedia of EU Public Policy*, eds. Paolo R. Graziano and Jale Tosun, 485–494. Cheltenham: Edward Elgar.

Jones, Michael D., Holly L. Peterson, Jonathan J. Pierce, Nicole Herweg, Amiel Bernal, Holly Lamberta, and Nikolaos Zahariadis. 2016. "A River Runs Through It: A Multiple Streams Meta-Review." *Policy Studies Journal* 44 (1): 13–36.

Kingdon, John. W. 2011 [1984]. *Agendas, Alternatives, and Public Policies*, 3rd edition. Boston: Longman.

Knaggård, Åsa. 2015. "The Multiple Streams Framework and the Problem Broker." *European Journal of Political Research* 54: 450–65.

Lakatos, Imre. 1970. "Falsification and the Methodology of Scientific Research Programmes." In *Criticism and the Growth of Knowledge*, eds. Imre Lakatos and Alan Musgrave, 91–196. Cambridge: Cambridge University Press.

March, James G., and Johan P. Olsen. 1984. "The New Institutionalism: Organizational Factors in Political Life." *American Political Science Review* 78 (3): 734–49.

Novotný, Vilém, Keiichi Satoh, and Melanie Nagel. 2021. "Refining the Multiple Streams Framework's Integration Concept: Renewable Energy Policy and Ecological

Modernization in Germany and Japan in Comparative Perspective." *Journal of Comparative Policy Analysis* 23 (3): 291–309.

Peters, B. Guy. 2015. *Advanced Introduction to Public Policy*. Cheltenham, UK: Edward Elgar.

Przeworski, Adam, and Henry Teune. 1970. *The Logic of Comparative Social Inquiry*. New York: Wiley & Sons.

Rietig, Katharina. 2021. "Multilevel Reinforcing Dynamics: Global Climate Governance and European Renewable Energy Policy." *Public Administration* 99(1): 55–71.

Roberts, Nancy C., and Paula J. King. 1991. "Policy Entrepreneurs: Their Activity Structure and Function in the Policy Process." *Journal of Public Administration Research and Theory* 1: 147–75.

Sabatier, Paul A. 2007. "Fostering the Development of Policy Theory." In *Theories of the Policy Proccess*, 2nd edition, ed. Paul A. Sabatier, 321–36. Boulder, CO: Westview Press.

Sanjurjo, Diego. 2020. "Taking the Multiple Streams Framework for a Walk in Latin America." *Policy Sciences* 53(1): 1–17.

Sartori, Giovanni. 1970. "Concept Misformation in Comparative Politics". *American Political Science Review* 64 (4): 1033–53.

Schmidt, Manfred G. 1993. "When Parties Matter: A Review of the Possibilities and Limits of Partisan Influence on Public Policy." *European Journal of Political Research* 30 (2): 155–83.

Schulze, Kai, and Jonas J. Schoenefeld. 2022. "Parteiendifferenz in der lokalen Klimapolitik? Eine empirische Analyse der hessischen Klima-Kommunen." *Zeitschrift für Vergleichende Politikwissenschaft* 15 (4): 525–50.

Taylor, Kristin, Stephanie Zarb, and Nathan Jeschke. 2021. "Ambiguity, Uncertainty and Implementation". *International Review of Public Policy* 3 (1). https://doi.org/10.4000/irpp.1638

Thompson, Daniel M. 2020. "How Partisan Is Local Law Enforcement? Evidence from Sheriff Cooperation with Immigration Authorities." *American Political Science Review* 114 (1): 222–36.

Tosun, Jale, and Samuel Workman. 2018. "Struggle and Triumph in Fusing Policy Process and Comparative Research." In *Theories of the Policy Process*, 4th edition, eds. Christopher M. Weible and Paul A. Sabatier, 329–362. Boulder, CO: Westview Press.

Turner, Victor 1995. *The Ritual Process: Structure and Anti-Structure* (Reprint Edition). New York: Aldine De Gruyter.

Van den Dool, Annemieke. 2022. "The Multiple Streams Framework in a Nondemocracy: the Infeasibility of a National Ban on Live Poultry Sales in China". *Policy Studies Journal* https://doi.org/10.1111/psj.12456.

Weible, Christopher M. 2018. "Moving Forward and Climbing Upward: Advancing Policy Process Research." In *Theories of the Policy Process*, 4th edition, eds. Christopher M. Weible and Paul A. Sabatier, 363–378. Boulder, CO: Westview Press.

Weible, Christopher M., and Edella Schlager. 2016. "The Multiple Streams Approach at the Theoretical and Empirical Crossroads: An Introduction to a Special Issue." *Policy Studies Journal* 44 (1): 5–12.

Zahariadis, Nikolaos. 2003. *Ambiguity and Choice in Public Policy: Political Manipulation in Modern Democracies*. Washington, DC: Georgetown University Press.

Zahariadis, Nikolaos. 2005. *Essence of Political Manipulation: Emotions, Institutions, and Greek Foreign Policy.* New York: Peter Lang.

Zahariadis, Nikolaos. 2007. "The Multiple Streams Framework: Structure, Limitations, Prospects." In Theories of the Policy Process, ed. Paul A. Sabatier, 65–92. Boulder, CO: Westview Press.

Zahariadis, Nikolaos. 2013. "Building Better Theoretical Frameworks of the European Union's Policy Process." *Journal of European Public Policy* 20 (6): 807–16.

Zahariadis, Nikolaos. 2016a. "Delphic Oracles: Ambiguity, Institutions and Multiple Streams." *Policy Sciences* 49: 3–12.

Zahariadis, Nikolaos. 2016b. "Setting the Agenda on Agenda Setting: Definitions, Concepts and Controversies." In *Handbook of Public Policy Angenda Setting*, ed. Nikolaos Zahariadis, 1–22. Cheltenham, UK and Northampton, MA: Edward Elgar.

Zohlnhöfer, Reimut. 2016. "Putting Together the Pieces of the Puzzle: Explaining German Labor Market Reforms with a Modified Multiple-Streams Approach." *Policy Studies Journal* 44: 83–107.

Zohlnhöfer, Reimut, Nicole Herweg, and Christian Huß. 2016. "Bringing Formal Political Institutions into the Multiple Streams Framework: An Analytical Proposal for Comparative Policy Analysis." *Journal of Comparative Policy Analysis* 18: 243–256.

Zohlnhöfer, Reimut, Nicole Herweg, and Nikolaos Zahariadis. 2022. "How to Conduct a Multiple Streams Study." In *Methods of the Policy Process*, eds. Christopher M. Weible, Samuel Workman, 23–50. New York/Abingdon: Routledge.

Zohlnhöfer, Reimut, and Friedbert W. Rüb (eds.). 2016. *Decision-Making under Ambiguity and Time Constraints: Assessing the Multiple-Streams Framework.* Colchester, UK: ECPR Press.

PART I

Theoretical contributions

2. How far does a policy change go? Explaining the scope of reforms with the Multiple Streams Framework

Reimut Zohlnhöfer

INTRODUCTION

In many instances, policy-makers, the public, but also academics are interested in the scope of reforms.[1] Policy-makers sometimes claim that they have adopted far-reaching reforms. For example, US President Joe Biden, when introducing his infrastructure plan in March 2021, argued: "It is not a plan that tinkers around the edges. It is a once-in-a-generation investment in America" (*New York Times* 2021). Similarly, former German Finance Minister Olaf Scholz called his multi-billion-euro-package to mitigate the economic effects of the Corona pandemic a "bazooka", hence trying to signify the immense size of the package (Haffert and Seelkopf 2022). Many other examples could be mentioned. In most cases, policy-makers thus seek to convince voters that they are assertive and doing what needs to be done.

The scope of reforms is also of interest for scholars of public policy. Many theories and frameworks try to explain the size of reforms. Think of Veto Player Theory (Tsebelis 2002): Here the veto player constellation determines the winset, which can be understood as the maximum scope of a reform under the given circumstances. Somewhat similarly, the Advocacy Coalition Framework (ACF) distinguishes between "minor" and "major policy change". While this distinction is related to where change occurs, in relation to secondary aspects of a program or to its policy core, we can also argue that minor policy change is less far-reaching than major policy change (Jenkins-Smith et al. 2018, 145). Finally, Punctuated Equilibrium Theory (PET) is all about the size of policy changes, as it seeks to explain why very often policy stability prevails or only incremental reforms are adopted while rarely – but more often than one would expect – "large-scale departures from the past" (Baumgartner, Jones and Mortensen 2018, 55), i.e., quite far-reaching policy changes occur. Related to PET, scholars have even discussed policy bubbles (Jones 2014;

see also Maor 2013), understood as overinvestment in a policy relative to the problems it is supposed to deal with.

In contrast, the Multiple Streams Framework (MSF) has paid little attention to these phenomena so far. The MSF has mostly focused on the occurrence and the timing of agenda (and policy) change and has rarely ever dealt with how far-reaching policy proposals (let alone: policy changes) are (Herweg 2013, 332–334). These are clearly important issues, however, and the above examples suggest that policy-makers, the public and scholars also deem the scope of reforms important. Hence, this chapter discusses whether the MSF is able to explain the scope of changes, too. While we know the framework is very good at explaining if and when agenda and policy change occurs, can it also explain the size of policy change?

I argue that there are indeed good reasons to believe that the MSF can, in principle, explain the scope of reforms. Developments in the streams, competition between issues during agenda coupling and the need to find majorities during decision coupling can help explain why only minor changes are adopted. For example, if no viable policy alternative is available in the policy stream, policy-makers fear strong opposition from interest groups or they are confronted with "big, slow-moving, and [almost] invisible" problems (Pierson 2003), agenda and policy changes are likely to be small. The same is true if the decision agenda is crowded and policy-makers lack the political resources to get a far-reaching change adopted or if veto actors block more far-reaching changes during decision coupling. In contrast, particularly large policy windows can trigger far-reaching reforms (Keeler 1993). For example, regarding political windows, if all streams are ready for coupling and a government wins a landslide election victory or the national mood is predominantly in favor of a reform, the ensuing agenda and policy change is likely to be large-scale. Similarly, if a severe crisis occurs or policy problems have been neglected for a long time, more far-reaching reforms are also likely.

The argument will be essentially conceptual in nature, but I will provide empirical examples to illustrate my points, mostly from German policy-making. While full-blown case studies would be desirable, it is not possible to provide a study for each of the various paths for far-reaching or incremental change. Hopefully, future research will assess whether the hypotheses deduced in this chapter prove helpful empirically. At this point, however, I think it is most important to draw the MSF community's attention to the issue of how to explain the scope of reforms and start a conversation about the factors that are relevant in this regard. This chapter is, to the best of my knowledge, the first one to discuss in a systematic way how the extent of reforms can be accounted for from an MSF perspective. While it is essentially an explorative exercise, I hope that it will spark a debate about this important issue.

I assume that readers are acquainted with the basic arguments of the MSF in its most recent iteration, hence also including, among other things, decision-making (if not, see Herweg, Zahariadis and Zohlnhöfer 2018 and the introduction to this volume). Therefore, in the following, I will focus on the factors that are likely to explain the occurrence of incremental and far-reaching change.[2] I start with potential explanations of incremental changes and discuss the three streams and agenda as well as decision coupling. Next, I will move on to large-scale reforms. As MSF essentially argues that all three streams need to be ready for coupling and a policy window open for any (significant) policy change, I do not discuss the streams here but focus on the policy windows to explain large-scale agenda (and policy) change. The final section concludes and discusses the issue of how to measure the scope of policy change empirically. This is an issue that will become increasingly relevant once scholars start testing the empirical implications of the theoretical considerations presented here.

HOW CAN THE MSF EXPLAIN THE SCOPE OF AGENDA AND POLICY CHANGE?

In the following, I discuss under which conditions the MSF would lead us to expect incremental or far-reaching agenda and policy changes. I start out with a discussion about how incremental change can come about before moving to factors, which make a significant change more likely.

When is Incremental Policy Change Likely?

Many routine decisions are likely to be of small scale. They adapt existing regulations to minor changes in the policy environment. For example, one could think of tax rates and welfare benefits being routinely (but not automatically) adapted as wages or prices rise. In these cases, the issue mostly goes unnoticed by the public and there might not be any relevant actor in or around government who advocates more far-reaching changes. These policy changes get adopted precisely because they are minor adaptations. In a way, they bypass the decision agenda in that they are part of routine decision-making, often prepared by the bureaucracy and mostly lacking controversy.

This may be one way insignificant change comes about. In many other – and more interesting – cases at least some policy entrepreneurs would want more far-reaching change but are unable to get their proposals on the agenda or get it adopted, at least in the way originally envisioned. There are several factors, which may lead to only minor policy change in these cases. Essentially, developments in each stream can prevent more significant change from occurring. For example, there might not be a worked-out alternative available; the adoption of a significant reform may be electorally too risky for policy-makers; problems may be big but slow-moving and thus essentially invisible for policy-makers; the agenda may be too crowded, or veto actors may dilute or even block a reform attempt during decision-making. Thus, essentially, every core element of the MSF can provide an explanation for the scope of policy change. In the following, I discuss these factors in more detail.

The policy stream

A classical MSF explanation for why a policy window closes unused is the lack of an available policy alternative (Kingdon 2003, 170). As Kingdon (2003, 142) explains: "Normally, before a subject can attain a solid position on a decision agenda, a viable alternative is available for decision makers to consider." If policy-makers do not have a worked-out policy proposal that enjoys sufficient backing in the policy community at their disposal, they do not have a clear understanding of how to respond to a problem – particularly given problematic policy preferences. Working out a new alternative while a policy window is open is usually impossible because the policy window very likely will have closed again before a worked-out alternative becomes available.

Nonetheless, there are probably some policy ideas around for any issue at any given point in time. The problem, however, is that none of them enjoys sufficient support among experts. Under these conditions, it is quite risky for policy-makers to embrace an option because they could easily be criticized not only on political grounds but also from large parts of the policy community. This criticism in turn could harm them electorally – particularly if the policy fails. As policy-makers are assumed not to have clear policy preferences, they will usually not advocate a policy as a matter of their own opinion (unless they themselves become policy entrepreneurs), so the potential electoral costs should provide them with disincentives to adopt a significant policy change. Hence, policy-makers will probably not respond at all or they will only respond in a merely symbolic way. That would result in a minor policy change at best.

One very telling example for such a situation is German policy concerning nuclear energy after the Chernobyl nuclear disaster in 1986 (for the following, see von Falkenhausen 2021). By the mid-1980s, the German public had started considering nuclear energy as problematic and at least the opposition parties had opted for an end of nuclear energy. Thus, the problem and political streams were ready for coupling.[3] Nonetheless, there was no credible policy alternative available. It was mostly unclear if a nuclear phase-out was technically feasible without power blackouts, whether it would be legal to end nuclear energy (nuclear power plants were owned by private companies) and how high the costs would be. Due to this lack of a worked-out alternative for a nuclear power phase out, the government could content itself with a much less far-reaching change, namely the establishment of a ministry for the environment and nuclear safety. Compare this with the response to the Fukushima disaster in 2011. While the government in 2011 was just as nuclear energy friendly as its predecessor in 1986, the opposition was able to demand an exit from nuclear energy with an entirely worked-out alternative – which indeed led the government to end the use of nuclear energy within slightly more than ten years.

Hence, I hypothesize:

H1: If no worked-out alternative is available in the policy stream, it is likely that no or only minor agenda or policy change occurs.

This scenario is based on one important condition (which is signified by the word "normally" in the above Kingdon quote). The problem to which policy-makers hardly respond (or not at all) is not particularly relevant politically, i.e., the government does not deem the existence of the problem to endanger its re-election. Only if that is the case, not doing much (or anything at all) actually becomes an option for a government.

The political stream
While in the previous case, I traced minor agenda and policy change back to developments in the policy stream, the constellation in the political stream can lead to insignificant change, too. Even if a government is willing to tackle a specific problem, it may face opposition against the policy in question from powerful interest groups, for example. That is of course rather the rule than the exception in pluralistic democracies. Nonetheless, MSF expects policy-makers to strike a balance between supporters and opponents of a specific proposal and the resources these groups control (Kingdon 2003, 150). If policy-makers (or policy-entrepreneurs) arrive at the conclusion that the balance of organized interests is tilted against a proposal, they will hesitate to pursue the issue further and if they do, they will only dare to take small steps, i.e., only incremental agenda or policy change is likely. For example, the pharmaceutical industry in Germany was often successful in keeping governments from including cost-cutting measures in the drug sector in their health reforms, hence reducing the scope of reforms (see, e.g., Bandelow and Hartmann 2007).

Similarly, the parliamentary opposition could mobilize its supporters or policy-makers may feel that the national mood is not supportive of the proposal. Given that the strong and vocal political opposition against the project could put a policy-maker's re-election in question, he or she could shy away from a reform or only adopt it in a much stripped-down and diluted form. An example would be the modest attempts at welfare state retrenchment since the 1980s, which have been explained with governments being alert to the electoral dangers of dismantling social programs. Even governments ideologically committed to substantial welfare state retrenchment, like the Thatcher Government in the UK or the Reagan administration in the US, did not dare to dismantle the welfare state and in a number of areas only produced minor changes (see Pierson 1994; Jensen, Wenzelburger, and Zohlnhöfer 2019). While policy entrepreneurs and governments may have expected that only adopting minor reforms may minimize political opposition, they might also have hoped that the insignificant reforms today may help get further reform steps adopted tomorrow, something Zahariadis (2003, 15) calls "salami tactics".

Hence, we can expect the following:

H2a: The stronger the resistance of interest groups against a proposal, the more likely it becomes that no or only minor agenda or policy change occurs.

H2b: The less supportive the national mood for a proposal and/or the more the opposition campaigns against a proposal, the more likely it becomes that no or only minor agenda or policy change occurs.

The problem stream

Minor agenda or policy change may also originate in the problem stream. MSF expects that problems come to policy-makers' attention via focusing events like severe accidents or crises, via indicators that show a substantial change for the worse or feedback that evidences that policy programs do not work as intended. In the process of problem definition, much depends on documenting the severity of the problem at hand, which is often done with the help of quantitative data (Kingdon 2003, 93) that prove a rapid deterioration of the situation. Some challenges do not pop up in this way, however, and thus are likely to escape policy-makers' attention – at least for extended periods of time. This is true in particular for "big, slow-moving and invisible" processes (Pierson 2003) – i.e., processes that do pose substantial policy challenges down the road but only produce minimal changes at any one point in time. Given the small size of the changes and the minimal immediate relevance, policy-makers are likely to underestimate these challenges at early stages when adjustments would be particularly effective. An example for this scenario could be the often rather insignificant response of many advanced democracies to demographic change or climate change. While "problem brokers" (Knaggård 2015) have warned the public about the extremely damaging long-term consequences of these developments for a long time, policy responses have mostly been moderate as these processes rarely culminate in a spectacular focusing event that underlines the urgency of far-reaching change. Hence, relevant reforms have mostly been minor.

Moreover, the causal processes behind "big and slow-moving" problems are likely to be contentious among problem brokers at least initially (think of climate change policy in the US). Given the long-time horizons the processes are likely to need to unfold, it is very hard to establish irrefutable evidence for any causal mechanism early on, on which policy change could be based. This fact can even by exploited by opponents of this policy change as they could try to mobilize "counter-evidence" that puts the originally assumed causal path into question. If the problem definition is controversial, however, even those policy-makers who learn about the problem are likely to refrain from investing a lot of political capital in an adequate solution. The consequence is, again, minor agenda and policy change at best. We can conclude that:

H3a: If conditions that could become problems build up very slowly, they are likely to spark only minor or no agenda or policy change.

H3b: If causal mechanisms between a condition and potential future harm are controversial, that condition is likely to spark only minor or no agenda or policy change.

Policy windows
A fourth mechanism that can lead to only incremental agenda or policy change in the MSF is competition between issues during agenda coupling. That is to say that although "a real perceived problem has a solution available, and there is no political barrier to action" (Kingdon 2003, 184), the issue may still not make it onto the agenda. The reason is that there exist other problems or issues that have to be dealt with and that accordingly there is simply no agenda space left for the issue at hand. Given policy-makers' limited time and cognitive resources, but also the scarcity of the political capital they can invest in the adoption of their proposals, policy-makers will only attend to the most relevant problems and issues (Kingdon 2003, 184–186; Baumgartner, Jones and Mortensen 2018). Probably the most important criterion for the relevance policy-makers attach to an issue is whether or not the issue is relevant for policy-makers' re-election (Herweg, Huß and Zohlnhöfer 2015, 437). If the persistence of a problem endangers a government's re-election, the government will deal with the issue while all other problems will have to take a back seat. For example, the German Government of Christian democrats and liberals under Angela Merkel (2009–2013) postponed or dropped the adoption of many of its economic policy projects, which originally had been the raison d'être for the coalition, or adopted them in a much watered-down version because the government had to deal with the Euro crisis (Zohlnhöfer 2015). Most importantly, the tax reform, which the liberals were advocating, was heavily diluted because neither political resources nor funding of a more significant reform was considered to be available, given the burdens and risks of the Euro crisis. So the crowdedness of the agenda with competing issues led to only incremental reforms in economic policy.

Similarly, other issues may be more politically rewarding than the issue at hand. For example, when tax revenues are high and the government's budget balance turns into the black, policy-makers are likely to prefer an increase of the generosity of welfare entitlements or tax cuts over a reduction of government debt. While the former policies are highly visible for voters (who might reward policy-makers for these policies at the ballot box in return), the latter are less likely to incite voters to vote for the government. As a consequence, the reduction of government debt will be minor. In this case, the moderate scale of the agenda or policy change with regard to public finances is the result of the popularity of alternative options. Hence, I hypothesize:

H4: If a policy proposal competes with other issues for policy-makers' attention and the competing issues are either relevant for policy-makers' re-election or are highly popular, only minor or no agenda or policy change regarding the proposal is likely.

Decision coupling
A failure to adopt large-scale change may not only be related to developments during agenda setting. Rather, a far-reaching proposal that made it onto the agenda may still be stalled or diluted at the decision-making stage. Put differently, the scope of policy change may also be decreased later during the policy-cycle. Depending on the institutional setting, the agreement of other actors than the political entrepreneur may be required and these veto actors may deem the proposal too far-reaching, too costly, unnecessary etc. Consequently, the political entrepreneur may be willing to accept concessions concerning her original proposal in order to get the policy adopted (Zohlnhöfer, Herweg and Huß 2016, 250–1). If the actor possessing veto power in the decision-making phase deems the concessions offered by the political entrepreneur insufficient, she might also block the proposal altogether, which, of course, would lead to no policy being adopted.

Policy processes in veto-ridden polities like Germany offer many examples of more far-reaching reforms being attenuated due to other veto actors like coalition partners and second chambers. For example, the Social democrats were not able to get a national minimum wage adopted in the first coalition with the Christian democrats under Angela Merkel (2005–09) but had to contend themselves with sectoral minimum wages (Dümig 2010, 288–90). Hence, the coalition partner demanded concessions that reduced the scope of the policy change – but only for a while because in the next iteration of the same coalition the Social democrats were finally successful in introducing a general minimum wage, thus providing evidence for the strategy of salami tactics. Germany's powerful second chamber (Bundesrat) has also helped reduce the scope of reforms. Examples include several tax reforms advocated by bourgeois governments that leftist majorities in the second chamber diluted or even blocked, while some of the tax hikes the social democratic led government of chancellor Gerhard Schröder had suggested were watered down by majorities of Christian democrats and liberals in the Bundesrat (e.g., Egle 2009; Zohlnhöfer 2003).

H5: If veto actors other than the political entrepreneur's party exist, for example coalition partners or second chambers with differing majorities, it becomes more likely that no or only minor policy change occurs.

What Causes Major Agenda and Policy Changes?

Political processes leading to major agenda or policy changes are not the mirror image of the processes that lead to minor changes according to MSF thinking. Rather, while it is certainly necessary for major change to occur that the three streams are ready for coupling, the issue is not stalled due to a crowded agenda and the proposal is not blocked during decision-making, these are simply necessary conditions for the occurrence of significant agenda or policy change. The actual processes leading to significant agenda or policy change are somewhat more complex, however. What seems to matter most for far-reaching change is the policy window. Some policy windows lend themselves to major change and even allow political entrepreneurs to get far-reaching reforms adopted (also see Keeler 1993).

Problem windows
A major policy change can be a response to a severe focusing event. Some focusing events "simply bowl over everything standing in the way of promi-nence on the agenda. … Such events demand some sort of action so clearly that even inaction is a decision" (Kingdon 2003, 96). Therefore, for policy-makers who want to be re-elected, not doing anything is often not an option anymore in such a situation, i.e., if a situation is considered a crisis by the relevant people in and around government. Rather, the government may well try to take advantage of the crisis – particularly if it is exogenous and the government can portray itself as a competent and prudent crisis manager.[4] Thus, given that something has to be done anyways and that political opposition is highly unlikely given the perceived urgency of the situation, the government will be careful not to be seen as doing too little – and will therefore likely be doing a lot. Time constraints are a critical element of all crisis responses – policies have to take immediate effect in order to mitigate the situation – and it is important to hit the target at the first attempt. These considerations also incite governments to adopt far-reaching changes in the face of a crisis. The (poten-tial) lack of a worked-out alternative is likely not to impede the adoption of a policy response due to the high urgency. Rather, the agreement of the policy community may be less relevant as governments have to act and will therefore look out for anything that appears to be workable. Again, the necessity of immediate success in combination with the adoption of a (potentially) less than worked-out policy alternative (or at least a policy alternative that is not specifically fitted to the situation at hand) is likely to trigger major change.

Take the German Government's response to the financial crisis of 2007–08 as an example (for the following see Enderlein 2010; Zohlnhöfer 2011). When it became clear that Germany's banking system and economy would be hit hard by the crisis in the fall of 2008, the government took unprecedented action. It guaranteed all private deposits (a policy hardly feasible if push had come to shove) and adopted a rescue package for banks worth up to €480 billion (slightly less than 20 percent of the country's GDP in that year). Moreover, stimulus packages of around 3.4 percent of GDP sought to mitigate the crisis' impact on the real economy. Scholars agree that the scope of these measures were unheard of for decades in Germany, i.e., extremely far-reaching changes, and that they were triggered by a severe crisis with potentially highly harmful outcomes. Given the crisis situation, potential concerns of members of the policy community (for example, about the feasibility of the deposits guarantee) could be ignore and veto actors circumvented.[5]

While in the case of the financial crisis it was clear what the problem was, in other cases, it is very difficult for voters but also for policy-makers, to make sense of a situation. Under these circumstances, experts can come to play an enormously important role as "problem brokers" (Knaggård 2015) because policy-makers have to rely on these experts to a considerable degree. Hence, if problem brokers paint a particularly bleak picture of the situation, the population will deem far-reaching measures necessary to fight the crisis.[6] Consequently, the government has little choice – and little incentive – but to adopt significant change. On the one hand, a decisive and competent response to the crisis based on scientific advice is likely to be a vote winner. On the other hand, the government has little to win by a minor change, even if it is success-ful, because the saved costs are not directly visible for the voters. Should the response that is less far-reaching than what the experts have deemed necessary not solve the problem, however, the government would have to preside over a veritable policy disaster that is likely to minimize its chances for re-election. Hence, for a policy-maker with problematic policy preferences under high uncertainty, a far-reaching change is the safest bet under these circumstances.

Take the SARS-CoV-2 ('Corona') virus crisis starting in 2020 as an example. At least initially, neither the general public nor policy-makers were able to assess how dangerous the new disease (Covid-19) would be and for whom, which transmission paths were possible and ultimately how to protect the populations. In Germany, a number of virologists became involved in explaining the situation to the public and policy-makers, most prominently Christian Drosten, a professor of virology at Charité university hospital in Berlin. His warnings about the dangers of the pandemic became pervasive in the public and seem to have affected the comparatively strict course of Germany's fight against the pandemic quite substantially (Alexander 2021, 32; 223–27). The relevant policies encompassed the severest restrictions of civil rights in German post-war history, including some measures, like dusk-to-dawn curfews, the effectiveness of which is at least controversial. Hence, the specific problem perception of a problem broker triggered far-reaching changes under conditions of exceptionally high uncertainty and ambiguity.[7]

The above arguments can be condensed in the following two hypotheses.

H6a: Severe focusing events make far-reaching agenda and policy change more likely.

H6b: If problem brokers with a perception of a condition as a very severe problem become prominent in the problem stream, far-reaching agenda and policy change becomes more likely.

Political windows
Policy windows opening in the political stream may also be conducive to far-reaching agenda and policy change under certain conditions. These can take two forms. On the one hand, an ideologically committed party may win an election and form a new government. Eager to fulfill its election promises and to meet the expectations of its followers and rank-and-file who may have fought for large-scale policy change during the election campaign, the new government may seek to prove its willingness and ability to deliver major policy change. As is customary in cases of "doctrinal coupling" (Zahariadis 2003, 72), the main task for the new government is to find a problem that fits the policy the party wishes to adopt. Because numerous conditions can be framed as a problem, the new government is extremely likely to find one for which the proposal in question can be regarded a solution. Moreover, given its recent election victory the new governing party will perceive the national mood to be on its side, so the political stream is also likely to be ready for coupling – even for major change (Keeler 1993).

What could speak against such significant changes under these conditions is the policy stream, which is expected to filter out ineffective, infeasible and too costly proposals. There is nothing in the policy stream, however, that renders far-reaching change impossible per se. It may even be that the policy experts prefer quite far-reaching responses to the problems, on which they work. Moreover, new governments, particularly ideologically committed ones, may well try to manipulate the policy stream by introducing new forums and listening to new think tanks. The newly elected Thatcher Government in the UK is a case in point (see Walters (1986) as an insider's view). Consequently, new governments may well adopt substantial deviations from the status quo, in particular during their 'honeymoon periods'.

The most relevant examples from the German context are some of the reforms, the newly elected government consisting of Social democrats and Greens adopted in 1998–99 – the only change of government in the country's post-war history in which all previous governing parties were replaced. The new government started with quite substantial reforms, including a reform of citizenship law that replaced regulations from 1913(!)(Busch 2003) and the phasing out of nuclear power that was not an option for the previous government (Mez 2003). Both changes can certainly be considered substantial (although the Greens in particular would have preferred even more far-reaching reforms) and in both cases they were driven by a new government that wanted to implement its ideas quickly.

On the other hand, the national mood can trigger far-reaching change. Policy-makers who are interested in their re-election will follow closely how public opinion assesses policies that are up for a decision. When policy-makers sense that the national mood is enthusiastic about a policy proposal, they are likely to be willing to put this issue on the agenda and get it adopted. It is also unlikely that this proposal is going to get blocked during decision coupling because other potential actors (even with veto power) will not want to be perceived as blocking a hugely popular proposal. Rather, other political actors – with or without veto power – (and the opposition in particular) will want to take advantage of the national mood, too. Therefore, as long as the proposal is broadly in line with the general ideological stance of the mainstream opposition parties, these parties will counter the government's proposal with more far-reaching suggestions. Given the high popularity of the original proposal, the governing party might take these additional suggestions on board and might even top them up further to make sure that itself and not the opposition will reap the electoral benefits of the popular proposal. This kind of outbidding between government and opposition is also likely to lead to major agenda or policy change.[8] Similarly, outbidding can also take place between two (or more) parties forming a coalition together. Examples abound during the expansion of the West European welfare states between the 1950s and the 1970s. For example, Christian democrats and Social democrats in Germany tried to outdo each other with regard to the highly popular increase of the generosity of old age pensions in 1957 and 1972. It was probably not by accident that these were two election years which brought the respective governing parties who were seen as responsible for the generous reforms their best-ever election results (Schmidt 1998, 81–86 and 96–98). Even quantitative studies have found this kind of outbidding for social spending (Hicks and Swank 1992).

From these considerations, we can deduce the following hypotheses:

H7a: Major agenda and policy change becomes more likely after a change of government.

H7b: The more different the ideological positions of the old and new governments are and the larger the election victory, the more likely far-reaching change occurs.

H8: The stronger the national mood favors a change, the more far-reaching that change is likely to be.

Post-issue-competition window

As discussed above, competition between issues can keep individual issues off the agenda or veto actors may block certain reforms. But the agenda may not remain blocked forever. Veto actors may change positions or lose their veto power and the agenda may become less crowded. At the same time, the problem that did not make it onto the agenda due to issue competition has not been dealt with or a potential solution may have been stalled. Consequently, the situation may have deteriorated (this argument builds on insights from Punctuated Equilibrium Theory (PET); see Baumgartner, Jones and Mortensen 2018). Policy-makers who face the worsening problem may now need to respond more drastically for two reasons. First, indicators, focusing events or feedback may indicate that the situation has changed for the worse, so the argument that more needs to be done may be convincing. Second, policy entre-preneurs are well aware of the rare window of opportunity that opens for their pet proposal – particularly as they may have experienced that 'their' issue has failed to make it onto the agenda previously. Knowing that the chance to get their policy proposal on the agenda will not return anytime soon and 'salami tactics' (Zahariadis 2003, 14) of many small changes is unlikely to materialize, they are likely to mobilize for a change that is as large as possible. As policy makers are (or can be made) aware of the previous failure to adopt change, they could be willing to accept a large-scale change.

The far-reaching German labor market reforms known as Hartz IV may provide an illustration at least for some parts of this argument (for the follow-ing see Hassel and Schiller 2010; Zohlnhöfer 2016). After unification, unem-ployment skyrocketed, and non-wage labor costs exploded. For a number of reasons, neither the bourgeois Kohl Government nor the Social democratic-led Schröder |Government were able to deal with the problem. The Schröder Government initially even hoped that the problem would go away on its own due to demographic change. The neglect of the issue indeed led to a worsen-ing labor market situation (which finally even threatened the government's re-election). When eventually a policy window opened, policy entrepreneurs were able to get many, quite far-reaching changes adopted as the government was willing to support almost any project that promised to reduce unemploy-ment (and help the coalition partners win the next election).

Hence, we can conclude:

H9: The longer issues have been kept off the agenda or were blocked by veto actor, the more likely significant change becomes.

CONCLUSION

This chapter has argued that the Multiple Streams Framework is not only able to explain if and when agenda and policy change occurs but also how far-reaching that change will be. I argue that minor change or the absence of reforms can be explained by developments in each individual element of the framework: problems may be big, but slow-moving, alternatives not available, the politics may incite less far-reaching change, the agenda may be too crowded or veto actors may demand concessions. Future research will need to distinguish further which factors lead to no policy change at all and which constellations allow at least for minor change. In contrast, for major agenda and policy change to take place, all streams need to be ready for coupling and policy windows offer particular opportunities, for example, when major focusing events occur, long-neglected issues finally become pressing, or as a response to a landslide election victory or a strong movement of the national mood.

The hypotheses deduced and empirically illustrated here need to be tested in more systematic empirical studies in the future. One of the thorny methodological issues, which I avoided in this chapter and which future empirical studies need to deal with, is the question of how to measure the scope of agenda and policy change. Clearly, MSF scholarship cannot resort to ACF's categories of 'minor' and 'major' policy change since this distinction relies on ACF's concept of belief system that is not applicable to the MSF. Similarly, although the analysis of the scope of changes could be considered a further incentive to turn to quantitative applications of the MSF (see Engler and Herweg 2019), MSF scholars are unlikely to employ quantitative data as a measure of scope of policy change as much of the PET literature does (e.g., Baumgartner et al. 2009). This is because most MSF studies consist of qualitative case studies (Jones et al. 2016, 27; Rawat and Morris 2016, 616), a method which is perfectly well suited to the research question in many cases. Moreover, Knill and Tosun's (2020, 215–18) suggestion to map the extent of change by the dimensions of policy density and policy intensity is quite elegant but essentially also a quantitative indicator. It remains to be seen how feasible this indicator of change can be for MSF studies. To the extent these measures are not applicable, scholars will have to make do with comparative assessments (how far has the reform departed from the past? how far-reaching was a change compared to other countries? etc.) or resort to Hall's (1993) classification of first-, second- or third-order change. Whatever the measurement used, it will be exciting to assess if the MSF is really able to explain the scope of reforms as good as it is capable explaining the occurrence and timing of change.

NOTES

1.   I would like to thank Moshe Maor for fruitful discussions and his insistence on the usefulness of concepts like "policy bubbles" and "policy over- and underreactions". Moshe made me realize how important it is that a framework

is able to explain the scope of a reform; at the same time, he convinced me that the Multiple Streams Framework is able to do just that. Moreover, I thank my co-editors for very helpful comments.

2. In the following, I will use the terms "incremental", "minor", "moderate" and "insignificant" agenda and policy change interchangeably. Similarly, the words "far-reaching", "large-scale", "major" and "significant" agenda and policy change are used synonymously. Finally, also the terms policy change and reform are used synonymously.

3. The political stream is considered ready for agenda coupling because in principle political entrepreneurs existed who were willing to seek a majority for phasing out nuclear energy. The fact that these political entrepreneurs came from the opposition might have made their task more difficult but certainly not impossible.

4. There may be situations, in which crises are unwelcome for the government, for example because the government itself might be blamed for the crisis or the unwanted consequences of it, and sometimes it is disputed whether a situation constitutes a crisis (cf. Boin et al. 2009). Under these circumstances, the above argument might not hold.

5. The responses to later economic crises, like to the economic repercussions of the Corona crisis of 2020–21 or the energy crisis following the Russian attack on Ukraine in 2022, followed very similar patterns.

6. It is probable that not all experts will paint the same bleak picture. Given the well-known negativity bias on the part of voters and probably policy makers, it is likely that those problem brokers with a more skeptical view will prevail. Another relevant factor in this regard could be the media: Who do they present as experts and how much controversy do they allow? These questions are beyond the scope of this chapter, however.

7. Certainly, an extensive analysis of the politics of the fight against the Corona pandemic in Germany is still lacking, so the empirical argument might need more nuance. Nonetheless, it is quite remarkable that Drosten dominated the Corona debate in Germany for substantial periods of time while other views seem to have been presented less prominently in public debate.

8. Note that it is not necessarily the government that puts forth a popular proposal, to which the opposition responds. It might just as well be the other way around, i.e., the opposition proposes something popular and the government tries to "steal" the project.

REFERENCES

Alexander, Robin. 2021. Machtverfall. Merkels Ende und das Drama der deutschen Politik. München: Siedler.

Bandelow, Nils and Anja Hartmann. 2007. "Weder Rot noch grün. Machterosion und Interessenfragmentierung bei Staat und Verbänden in der Gesundheitspolitik." In Christoph Egle and Reimut Zohlnhöfer (eds.): Ende des rot-grünen Projektes. Eine Bilanz der Regierung Schröder 2002–2005. Wiesbaden: Verlag für Sozialwissenschaften, 334–54.

Baumgartner, Frank R., Christian Breunig, Christoffer Green-Pedersen, Bryan D. Jones, Peter B. Mortensen, Michiel Nuytemanns, and Stefaan Walgrave. 2009. "Punctuated

Equilibrium in Comparative Perspective." American Journal of Political Science 53 (3): 603–20.

Baumgartner, Frank R., Bryan D. Jones and Peter B. Mortensen. 2018. "Punctuated Equilibrium Theory: Explaining Stability and Change in Public Policymaking." In Christopher M. Weible and Paul A. Sabatier (eds.): Theories of the Policy Process. 4th edition, Boulder, CO: Westview, 55–101.

Boin, Arjen, Paul 't Hart and Allan McConnell. 2009. "Crisis Exploitation: Political and Policy Impacts of Framing Contests." Journal of European Public Policy 16 (1): 81–106.

Busch, Andreas. 2003. "Extensive Politik in den Klippen der Semisouveränität: die Innen- und Rechtspolitik der rot-grünen Koalition." In Christoph Egle, Tobias Ostheim and Reimut Zohlnhöfer (eds.): Das rot-grüne Projekt. Eine Bilanz der Regierung Schröder 1998–2002. Wiesbaden: Westdeutscher Verlag, 305–27.

Dümig, Kathrin. 2010. "Ruhe nach und vor dem Sturm: Die Arbeitsmarkt- und Beschäftigungspolitik der Großen Koalition." In Christoph Egle and Reimut Zohlnhöfer (eds.): Die zweite Große Koalition. Eine Bilanz der Regierung Merkel 2005–2009. Wiesbaden: VS, 279–301.

Egle, Christoph. 2009. Reformpolitik in Deutschland und Frankreich. Wirtschafts- und Sozialpolitik bürgerlicher und sozialdemokratischer Regierungen. Wiesbaden: VS.

Enderlein, Henrik. 2010. "Finanzkrise und große Koalition: Eine Bewertung des Krisenmanagements der Bundesregierung. " In Christoph Egle and Reimut Zohlnhöfer (eds.): Die zweite Große Koalition. Eine Bilanz der Regierung Merkel 2005–2009. Wiesbaden: VS, 234–53.

Engler, Fabian and Nicole Herweg. 2019. "Of Barriers to Entry for Quantitative Multiple Streams Applications: Methodologic and Conceptual Considerations." Policy Studies Journal 47: 905–26.

Haffert, Lukas and Laura Seelkopf. 2022. "Corona und das Ende der deutschen Fiskalorthodoxie?" In Reimut Zohlnhöfer and Fabian Engler (eds.): Das Ende der Merkel-Jahre. Eine Bilanz der Regierung Merkel, 2018–2021. Wiesbaden: Springer, 193–16.

Hall, Peter A. 1993. "Policy Paradigms, Social Learning, and the State. The Case of Economic Policymaking in Britain." Comparative Politics 25: 275–296.

Hassel, Anke and Christof Schiller. 2010. Der Fall Hartz IV. Wie es zur Agenda 2010 kam und wie es weitergeht. Frankfurt/New York: Campus.

Herweg, Nicole. 2013. "Der Multiple-Streams-Ansatz – ein Ansatz, dessen Zeit gekommen ist?" Zeitschrift für Vergleichende Politikwissenschaft 7: 321–345.

Herweg, Nicole, Christian Huß, and Reimut Zohlnhöfer. 2015. "Straightening the Three Streams: Theorizing Extensions of the Multiple Streams Framework." European Journal of Political Research 54: 435–49.

Herweg, Nicole, Nikolaos Zahariadis and Reimut Zohlnhöfer. 2018. "The Multiple Streams Framework: Foundations, Refinements and Empirical Applications." In Christopher M. Weible and Paul A. Sabatier (eds.): Theories of the Policy Process. 4th edition, Boulder, CO: Westview, 17–53.

Hicks, Alexander M., and Duane H. Swank. 1992. "Politics, Institutions, and Welfare Spending in Industrialized Democracies, 1960–82." American Political Science Review 86 (3): 658–74.

Jenkins-Smith, Hank C., Daniel Nohrstedt, Christopher M. Weible, and Karin Ingold. 2018. "The Advocacy Coalition Framework: An Overview of the Research Program." In Christopher M. Weible and Paul A. Sabatier (eds.): Theories of the Policy Process. 4th edition, Boulder, CO: Westview, 135–71.

Jensen, Carsten, Georg Wenzelburger and Reimut Zohlnhöfer. 2019. "'Dismantling the Welfare State?' After Twenty-five years: What have we learned and what should we learn?" Journal of European Social Policy 29 (5): 681–91.

Jones, Bryan D., Herschel F. Thomas III, and Michelle Wolfe. 2014. "Policy Bubbles". Policy Studies Journal 42(1): 146–71.

Jones, Michael D., Holly L. Peterson, Jonathan J. Pierce, Nicole Herweg, Amiel Bernal, Holly Lamberta, and Nikolaos Zahariadis. 2016. "A river runs through it: a multiple streams meta-review." Policy Studies Journal 44 (1): 13–36.

Keeler, John T. S. 1993. "Opening the Window for Reform. Mandates, Crises, and Extraordinary Policymaking." Comparative Political Studies 25 (4): 433–86.

Kingdon, John W. 2003 [1984]. Agendas, Alternatives, and Public Policy. New York: Longman.

Knaggård, Åsa. 2015. "The Multiple Streams Framework and the Problem Broker." European Journal of Political Research 54: 450–65.

Knill, Christoph, and Jale Tosun. 2020. Public Policy: A New Introduction, 2nd edition. London, UK: Red Globe Press.

Maor, Moshe. 2013. "Policy Bubbles: Policy Overreaction and Positive Feedback." Governance 27 (3): 469–87.

Mez, Lutz. 2003. "Ökologische Modernisierung und Vorreiterrolle in der Energie- und Umweltpolitik? Eine vorläufige Bilanz." In Christoph Egle, Tobias Ostheim and Reimut Zohlnhöfer (eds.): Das rot-grüne Projekt. Eine Bilanz der Regierung Schröder 1998–2002. Wiesbaden: Westdeutscher Verlag, 329–50.

New York Times. 2021. "Biden Details $2 Trillion Plan to Rebuild Infrastructure and Reshape the Economy", available at https://www.nytimes.com/2021/03/31/business/economy/biden-infrastructure-plan.html (last accessed 13/04/2022).

Pierson, Paul. 1994. Dismantling the Welfare State? Reagan, Thatcher and the Politics of Retrenchment. Cambridge: Cambridge University Press.

Pierson, Paul. 2003. "Big, slow-moving, and … Invisible. Macrosocial processes in the study of comparative politics." In James Mahoney and Dietrich Rueschemeyer (eds.): Comparative Historical Analysis in the Social Sciences, Cambridge: CUP, 177–207.

Rawat, Pragati, and John Charles Morris. 2016. "Kingdon's 'Streams' Model at Thirty: Still Relevant in the 21st Century?" Politics & Policy 44: 608–38.

Schmidt, Manfred G. 1998. Sozialpolitik in Deutschland. Historische Entwicklung und internationaler Vergleich (2nd edition), Opladen: Leske+Budrich.

Tsebelis, George, 2002: Veto Players: How Political Institutions Work. Princeton/Oxford: Princeton UP/Russell Sage Foundation.

Von Falkenhausen, Christian. 2021. Politischer Wandel in der bundesdeutschen Kernenergiepolitik von 1975 bis 1997. Eine Multiple Streams Analyse mit einem Schwerpunkt zu den politischen Prozessen nach Tschernobyl und den Energiekonsensgesprächen. Heidelberg (unpublished PhD dissertation).

Walters, Alan. 1986. Britain's Economic Renaissance. Margaret Thatcher's Reforms 1979–1984. New York and Oxford: OUP.

Zahariadis, Nikolaos. 2003. Ambiguity and Choice in Public Policy: Political Manipulation in Democratic Societies. Washington, DC: Georgetown University Press.

Zohlnhöfer, Reimut. 2003. "Partisan Politics, Party Competition and Veto Players: German Economic Policy in the Kohl Era." Journal of Public Policy 23: 123–56.

Zohlnhöfer, Reimut. 2011. "Between a Rock and a Hard Place: The German Response to the Economic Crisis." German Politics 20 (2): 227–42.

Zohlnhöfer, Reimut. 2015. "A Coalition Whose Time Had Already Passed ... The Economic and Social Policies of the Second Merkel Government." In Gabriele D'Ottavio and Thomas Saalfeld (eds.): Germany After the 2013 Elections. Breaking the Mould of Post-Unification Politics? Farnham: Ashgate, 13–29.

Zohlnhöfer, Reimut. 2016. "Putting Together the Pieces of the Puzzle: Explaining German Labor Market Reforms with a Modified Multiple-Streams Approach." Policy Studies Journal 44 (1): 83–107.

Zohlnhöfer, Reimut, Nicole Herweg, and Christian Huß. 2016. "Bringing Formal Political Institutions into the Multiple Streams Framework: An Analytical Proposal for Comparative Policy Analysis." Journal of Comparative Policy Analysis 18: 243–56.

3. Policy termination meets Multiple Streams

Georg Wenzelburger and Stefanie Thurm

INTRODUCTION

Policy research using the Multiple Streams Framework (MSF) has flourished in recent decades and theoretical refinements as well as numerous empirical applications have advanced our knowledge considerably about how, when and why policies change (Herweg, Huß and Zohlnhöfer 2015; Howlett, McConnell and Perl 2015; Jones et al. 2016; Shephard et al. 2021; Zohlnhöfer, Herweg and Huß 2016). However, the rich empirical and conceptual literature has mainly focused on two stages of the policy process, namely agenda setting – the initial focus of Kingdon's work (Kingdon 2001) – and decision-making (Herweg, Huß and Zohlnhöfer 2015; Zahariadis 2003). Much more scarcely have researchers aimed at applying the core ideas of MSF to other stages of the policy process, such as implementation (Fowler 2019; 2022) or termination (Geva-May 2004). In this article, we contribute to filling this gap by systematically discussing how the MSF could be used to explain policy termination – a field of research that, while having a long tradition (Bardach 1976), has somewhat been left aside by policy research. To do so, we first review the literature on policy termination and adjacent strands (e.g., policy dismantling) and discuss the major findings of these studies. In a second step, we theorize to what extent the theoretical lens of the MSF can help us to study policy termination. Finally, we give some empirical illustrations from existing studies that try to relate MSF concepts to policy termination in order to give a fuller account of the applicability of MSF to the study of public policies.

POLICY TERMINATION: A STATE OF THE ART REVIEW

Policy termination represents an important step in classical models of the policy process. It can be understood as the "deliberate conclusion or cessation of specific government functions, organizations, policies, or programs"

(Brewer and deLeon, 1983). However, compared to publications on other stages of the policy process, such as agenda-setting and decision-making, the literature on policy termination has remained relatively sparse. After a few publications starting in the 1970s (Bardach 1976, Behn 1978; Brewer and deLeon 1983; Kaufman 1976), the pursuit of this issue has seemed to fade. Only in recent years have researchers shown a renewed interest in the subject (Adam and Bauer 2018; O'Neill et al. 2019; Thom 2021; Wenzelburger and Hartmann 2021).

While the fact that policy termination has never really established itself as a proper research strand might simply be due to researchers' preference for "beginnings, not endings" (Frantz 1997), it also proves to be a rather infrequent phenomenon empirically. Upon closer examination, many cases that seem to qualify as policy termination at first, can be understood much better through the classical lens of policy formation. This is the case whenever a new policy replaces or helps fade out an old policy. In other instances, policies might be dismantled, for example when social benefits are cut back, or restrictive laws are loosened (Bauer and Knill 2012). Still, this is not the same as a policy being abolished without immediate replacement.[1] The famous concepts of displacement, layering or conversion, discussed by Streeck and Thelen (2005) as mechanisms to institutional change, are illustrative examples of how policy change comes about and often involves partial termination of a policy (or an institution) overlapping with policy formation.

Cases which qualify as policy termination in the strict sense are relatively rare as the act of abolishing a policy is typically associated with high barriers.[2] First, policy termination can be financially costly. Even if the intention behind a termination might be saving costs, in the short run, the process might have contradictory effects. The expenses that arise include for example compensation payments for constituents and staff affected by the termination and, in some cases, payments for the termination of the policy itself (Frantz 1997). For example, Lowry (2005) reports that dam removals are less likely in US states with poor fiscal health, as removal is costly in the short run. Second, other forces, such as anti-termination coalitions and legal aspects, can lead to high institutional stability and prevent politicians from engaging in policy termination altogether (Bardach 1976; Frantz 1992; Geva-May 2004). Finally, electoral costs can be high and prevent policy-makers from abolishing a policy. This is especially true for policies that are popular with the electorates – such as the social policies (Svallfors 2012). The resilience of the welfare state during the neo-liberal governments of Thatcher and Reagan, which were ideologically strongly opposed to it, is a widely researched example to illustrate this mechanism (Pierson 1994). This is why politicians engage in blame avoidance strategies if such policies are dismantled (König and Wenzelburger 2014; Vis 2016). Beyond the general insight according to which policy termination is actually a rare event, policy scholars have nevertheless pondered the question which drivers actually raise the likelihood of policy termination – against all odds. The literature identifies several factors, which by and large can be divided into *external* factors, *internal* characteristics of the policy itself and *processual* factors[3].

External Drivers of Policy Termination

Among the external factors, *ideological and political drivers,* such as administrative change, are quoted regularly as drivers of policy termination (Bardach 1976; Berry et al. 2010, deLeon and Hernández-Quezada 2001, Lewis 2002). A new government can set itself apart from the previous administration by throwing old policies overboard. At the same time, a government is much less likely to terminate a policy which they have designed themselves, as that would mean admitting its own failure. For example, according to Lewis (2002), a turnover in Congress or the White House is the most influential factor for termination of government agencies. Additionally, ideological closeness can influence the diffusion of policy termination across states. Volden (2016) finds that unsuccessful policies in one state are more likely to lead to the termination of this policy in another state if the states are ideologically similar. Aside from the ruling government party, larger ideological movements in society are also said to affect termination. For example, according to Bardach (1976), a general aversion of the idea of "total institutions" arising among intellectual and political elites in the 1960s led to the closure of state hospitals and juvenile training schools. In a similar vein, Kirkpatrick, Lester and Peterson (1999) argue that the termination of federal revenue-sharing programs in the US in 1986 was largely influenced by a general ideological trend towards reducing the role and scope of government. Thus, the policy was terminated under the Reagan administration, although it was originally set up by the equally Republican Nixon government. However, the question if ideology presents itself as an important driver depends on the specific policy content as well. For example, while Krause, Hongtao and Feiock (2016) find that ideology has a significant influence on the termination of local greenhouse gas reduction initiatives, Graddy and Ye (2008) do not find ideology to be significant in the case of termination of local public hospitals.

More closely related to the policy itself are *public support, termination coalitions* and the existence of *policy terminators* (Bardach 1976; Behn 1976; Kirkpatrick, Lester and Peterson 1999; Lowry 2005). According to Bardach (1976), *policy opponents* fall into three categories: Oppositionists, who dislike the policy because it goes directly against their interests or values; Economizers, who would prefer reallocating financial resources to other areas or cutting costs altogether; and lastly Reformers, who see the policy termination as a necessary precondition for the installment of their preferred policy alternative. Bardach argues that in termination coalitions an oppositionist is most likely taking on a leading position as this group is expected to have the strongest personal interest in abolishing the policy. Closely related to those coalitions are *policy terminators* (Behn 1976; Geva-May 2004; O'Neill 2019). They are akin to Kingdon's policy entrepreneurs in so far as they are able to influence policy outcomes by actively investing their resources to reach the desired outcome (Kingdon 2001; Geva-May 2004). For example, Behn describes how department of youth services commissioner Jerome Miller succeeded in closing the Massachusetts training schools in the form of a 'one man show' (Behn 1976, 152). Such policy terminators are often able to promote certain issue frames and thus shift the political climate in the direction of policy termination. O'Neill et al. (2019) illustrate that Alderman Druh Farrell was the driving force behind ending water fluoridation in Calgary in 2011. By committing to bringing the issue back on the agenda while reframing it as not only a financial but also an ethical problem, Druh Farrell managed to win a sufficient coalition to terminate the policy. In other cases, policy terminators rather resemble mere administrators of the winding-down process. This is the case whenever someone is appointed specifically to dismantle a policy or an organization after the decision was already taken. However, these actors are not necessarily as vital for the success of a termination (Geva-May 2004). Additionally, extra-governmental interest groups can play an important role in terminating a policy which is shown for example by Graddy and Ye (2008) who find that the proportion of unionized sector workers is negatively associated with the termination of local public hospitals. Similarly, Lowry (2005) reports a significant correlation between the number of river restoration groups and the number of dam removals in the American states. O'Neill et al. (2019) stress the role of activist groups in the case of ending community water fluoridation in Calgary. Those activist groups were putting forward a number of arguments for the discontinuation of water enrichment. However, the argument that prevailed was referring to ethical reservations with respect to personal freedoms. It was argued that the policy of 'mass medication' needed to end regardless of any existing benefits. These observations correspond with Bardach's argument that oppositionists should be leading in any termination coalition as they have the greatest incentive and personal interest to pursue their agenda (Bardach 1976).

Rather directly related to the activity of interest groups is the perceived public support towards a policy. Returning to the case of water fluoridation in Calgary (O'Neill et al. 2019), perceived public support was decisive for policy termination. While public opinion on fluoridation had been split from the start, a slight majority actually supported the policy. However, around 2011, pro-termination activists were extremely successful in making themselves heard which led to a perceived shift in public opinion. O'Neill et al. quote one council alderman with the words "My job, as I understand it, is to follow (…) the direction from my constituents. Thus far (…) it is about 400 to 1 to say get this out of our water" (O'Neill et al. 2019, 110). Similarly, public mood contributed to the termination of APB, a former French university admission system. The algorithm behind the system was seen as unfair and opaque in large parts of society, which can be attributed to negative media coverage and several lawsuits against the policy (Wenzelburger and Hartmann 2021).

A final factor that has been regularly discussed in the literature refers to financial circumstances (Kirkpatrick, Lester and Peterson 1999; Krause, Hongtao and Feiock 2016; Graddy and Ye 2008; Lowry 2005; Ferry and Bachtler 2013). In general, financial pressures make spending cuts and austerity policies more likely and lead to what Bardach (1976) calls *periods of turbulence*. In such periods, for example when unemployment is extremely high, program terminations are accepted more readily by voters. If circumstances are understood to be precarious, relevant interest groups are more likely to accept the necessity of cutbacks and offer less resistance to them (Bardach 1976). However, whether a specific policy is affected by financial pressures depends largely on the policy specifics. Plausibly, the evidence suggests that budgetary constraints make policy termination more probable whenever an upkeeping of the policy is associated with high costs, whereas a policy remains in place when the cost of termination exceeds the cost of continuation in the short run. On the first mechanism, Graddy and Ye (2008) find for example that larger health budgets are associated with keeping local hospitals while lower state and local revenue growth rates make termination of those public hospitals more likely. In contrast, Lowry (2005) reports an example of the second mechanism: In fact, the removal of dams (policy termination) is more likely when states are in *better* fiscal health, because of the high costs associated with the removal in the short run. While research has not tackled this question explicitly so far, it is to be expected that policies with a predominantly regulatory character, which require neither high spending for their upkeeping nor for their termination, should be less affected by fiscal constraints.

INTERNAL DRIVERS OF POLICY TERMINATION

Besides external forces, *internal characteristics* of the policy itself affect if it is likely to be terminated or not. Features of a policy that are regularly reported to matter for termination include sunset provisions, longevity of the policy and (perceived) efficiency of the policy. The first factor that plausibly raises the likelihood of policy termination is the existence of sunset provisions and other automatic termination mechanisms (Bardach 1976; Kirkpatrick, Lester and Peterson 1999; Geva-May 2004). Policies can be directly designed to have a termination date or have other provisions that smooth the abolishment, for example success thresholds that need to be met in order for the policy to be kept up (Geva-May 2004). A case in point are the security measures implemented after 9/11 as anti-terrorist policies in Germany. As a reaction to civil rights criticism, the initial anti-terror law (from January 2002) was limited to 2007 and should be evaluated and, eventually, terminated or continued. After a first positive evaluation, the law was continued to 2012 and, again, to January 2021 before the measures were made unconditional on further evaluations (Wenzelburger 2022). As these prolongations necessitated to find new majorities in Parliament under different governments, the example shows the in-built risk of termination in the case of sunset legislation. As the status quo is termination, political actors have to actively find a majority each time that the "time is up".

Regarding longevity of a policy, conventional wisdom is that the risk of termination decreases, the older a policy gets. It can be expected that a longer lifespan goes hand in hand with supporting clientele and vested interests, leading to path dependent dynamics and high institutional stability (Kaufmann 1976; Lowi 1979). However, Carpenter and Lewis (2004) add important insight to our understanding of policy longevity with an analysis of U.S. federal government agencies. Their research shows that the risk of termination does not continuously decline over time. Instead, they report a strongly nonmonotonic hazard rate of termination, with the likelihood rising in the first years, reaching a maximum at about 12 years, and declining again, afterwards. This can be attributed to a learning experience for politicians and practitioners. If the policy does not reach the desired outcome in the first few years, it is at high risk of termination. Once this stage is overcome however, institutional stability rises, and abolishment becomes less likely over the years.

A number of studies come to the conclusion that policies which are (or which are perceived to be) *ineffective or inefficient* are more likely to be terminated (Krause, Hongtao and Feiock 2016; Turnhout 2009). For example, comparing climate protection initiatives by U.S. local governments, Krause, Hongtao and Feiock (2016) conclude that termination gets less likely the more milestones a community has already reached in their climate protection efforts. Additionally, government can learn from experienced inefficiencies in other jurisdictions: Volden (2016) reports that failure of welfare policies in U.S. states even leads to the termination of similar policies in other states. However, this learning effect is dependent upon the ideological closeness of those states which points to the highly political nature of policy termination (see above). Other cases demonstrate that it is rather the *perceived* efficiency or effectiveness of a policy that determines its chances of survival. In the case of water fluoridation in Calgary, O'Neill et al. (2019) discuss how public opinion towards the practice of fluoridation changed mainly due to greater efforts of

Table 3.1   *Drivers of policy termination*

External factors	Ideological and political factors
	– Administrative change
	– Changes in larger ideological orientation
	– Influence of other administrations
	– Termination coalitions
	– Policy terminators
	Financial pressure
	Periods of turbulence
Internal factors	(Perceived) efficiency or effectiveness of the policy
	Longevity of the policy
	Sunset provisions & other built-in termination mechanisms
Processual factors	Cushioning the blow
	Speed of the termination process

the termination coalition. In the beginning, those experts who spoke out in favor of the safety and efficiency of fluoridation succeeded in shaping public opinion. However, in 2011, the termination coalition grew louder. As a result, the impression arose that fluoridation was at best ineffective if not harmful.

Processual Factors and Policy Termination

Finally, *processual factors* play a role in the success of termination. First, one strategy to win over opponents of termination lies in *cushioning the blow* (Bardach 1976). This can be reached by compensating those affected by termination or by phasing out the policy slowly. In Behn's (1975) study of the closing of Massachusetts training school, it is reported that Jerome Miller kept employees on the payroll even though schools were already being shut down.

Second, while phasing out the policy slowly can help to reduce opposition formation, the decision to terminate itself benefits from *swiftness* (Behn 1978; Shulsky 1976; Kirkpatrick, Lester and Peterson 1999). For example, O'Neill et al. (2019) report that the termination of water fluoridation in Calgary was tabled relatively shortly after elections. While this process points to the influence of administrative change (see above), swiftness of the new administration was also decisive. The new council tabled the notice of motion so soon that opposition was taken by surprise and simply lacked the time to coordinate a concentrated effort to stop termination. Additionally, the council rejected a plebiscite and thus prevented another possibility to mobilize policy support.

THEORIZING POLICY TERMINATION THROUGH THE LENS OF THE MSF

Drawing on the discussion of the literature on policy termination presented in the last section, this section theorizes how the insights from the state of the art could be integrated in the MSF in order to derive specific hypotheses about how policy termination may come about. Indeed, policy termination has found renewed interest in recent years and some researchers have already tried to connect the findings of policy termination research with classic theories of the policy process – and the MSF (Geva-May 2004; O'Neill et al. 2019). Yet, a more systematic theorizing about how the different factors discussed in the termination studies could be related to the MSF is still missing and therefore the main aim of this section. We will structure our theorizing along the main building blocks of the MSF – such as the three streams, the policy entrepreneur and the policy window – and link it to the perspective of policy termination.

Termination and the Problem Stream

The first main element of the MSF which affects the probability of agenda change concerns the question whether a certain situation is considered to be problematic by political actors. Following Kingdon, a situation is interpreted as problematic when one observes a "mismatch between the observed conditions and one's conception of an ideal state" (Kingdon 2001, 110). The MSF situates the factors that contribute to the perception of such a problematic mismatch in the problem stream and mentions several possible mechanisms: Deteriorating indicators, focusing events or negative feedback from existing policies (Kingdon 2001, 90–102). To matter for problem definition, however, these conditions have to be interpreted as politically relevant problems, which is why different actors (such as "problem brokers", Knaggård (2015)) may compete about how to define a problem – for instance by comparing indicators (which, by comparison, show the necessity to act on a problem) or by linking them to fundamental values that are considered to be in danger (Kingdon 2001, 109–13). Hence, the way in which a focusing event, e.g., a crisis, can be exploited by political actors, for example, depends heavily on how it is interpreted and which problems are linked to it (Wenzelburger, König and Wolf 2019) – which is why "framing contests" (Boin, t'Hart and McConnell 2008) have been shown to start in such cases between actors aiming at pushing forward a certain problem definition.

In any case, when a condition is interpreted as problematic, the stream can be considered as ready for coupling, which greatly increases the chances for agenda change. A policy window opens in the problem stream and policy entrepreneurs may seize the opportunity to present their pet policy as solution to the problem. Kingdon (2001, 165) describes a policy window as "an opportunity for advocates of proposals to push their pet solutions, or to push attention to their special problems". If the initial impetus comes from the problem stream, such "consequential coupling" (Zahariadis 2003, 72) increases the probability of an agenda and, relatedly, a policy change.[4]

Interestingly, many of the termination drivers discussed above are closely linked to the problem stream as they may be starting points for the definition of a policy as being a candidate to be terminated. Clearly, from the "external factors" of termination, financial considerations (Kirkpatrick, Lester and Peterson 1999) can be directly related to the aspect of "deteriorating indicators" from the MSF which greatly matter for problem definition. Focusing events have also been discussed in the literature on policy termination – Bardach (1976, 130) speaks of "periods of turbulence, in which many people's optimistic expectations about their own life chances are shaken". He links these periods to termination via a special mechanism of problem definition, namely the fact that crises can be used to attack policies that are protected by special interest groups. In his reasoning, such a period of turbulence "weakens the moral aversion to disrupting the life patterns of persons who have come to presume upon, and rely upon, the continuance of particular government activities" (Bardach 1976, 130). Case studies on how welfare state retrenchment policies have been decided provide first-hand evidence on how actors communicate the termination of popular policies by linking crises to the narrative that everybody has to participate at a common effort (even well-organized groups) (König 2016; Kuipers 2006; Wenzelburger 2011).

"Internal factors" for termination can also be linked to the problem stream. The inefficiency of existing policies (e.g., Graddy and Ye 2008; Krause, Hongtao and Feiock 2016) can be subsumed under the umbrella of negative feedback from existing policies in MSF-terms – and has been widely discussed as a major driver of policy termination. In fact, the insight that it might actually be mainly the perception of inefficiency that affects the likelihood of termination shows that researchers of policy termination are well aware of the fact that it is the interpretation of the status quo that matters – a perception that may well be strategically pushed by certain actors, such as termination coalitions (O'Neill et al. 2019).

Termination and the Political Stream

However, consequential coupling starting in the problem stream is only one possibility for a policy window to open. A second mechanism, "doctrinal coupling" (Zahariadis 2003), can also initiate agenda change. In contrast to consequential coupling, it is not a perceived problem which opens the window, but political dynamics which Kingdon describes as follows:

> [Q]uite apart from bringing problems to the attention of people in and around government, such events as a new majority in Congress or a new administration occur. These developments in the political stream have a powerful effect on agendas, as new agenda items become prominent and others are shelved until a more propitious time. (Kingdon 2001, 145)

Key components of the political stream that may affect agenda-setting are changes to "public mood, pressure group campaigns, election results, partisan or ideological distributions in Congress and changes of administration" (Kingdon 2001, 145). Hence, it is mainly the general political context including party competition and public opinion that matter here as they can generate occasions in which new issues may enter the agenda. Interestingly, Kingdon himself does not give a clear-cut answer how these different factors relate to each other, although he seems to attach a somewhat more important role to the national mood (Kingdon 2001, 164). On the other hand, it has been shown that the dynamics within the political arena are key, too, which is why Herweg et al. (2018, 25) claim that changes of government will strongly increase the chances for new policy ideas to reach the decision agenda even if the national mood or interest groups may not be in favor.

How do these insights relate to the termination literature? In fact, several expectations about the dynamics in the political stream formulated by the MSF have been discussed in studies of policy termination. From the "external factors", change in government and administration have been identified already by Bardach (1976) as one of the facilitating conditions for policy termination – and they reflect neatly the criteria for the ripeness of the political stream, namely election results and partisan and ideological distributions in Congress as well as changes of administration. Several empirical studies have corroborated this relationship (Kirkpatrick, Lester and Peterson 1999). While pressure group campaigns are often mentioned as possible constraints that need to be overcome (Graddy and Ye 2008), pressure groups can also take on an active role in advancing policy termination. For example, Lowry (2005) discusses the major influence of environmental groups that lobby for river restoration measures when it comes to removal of dams in American states. Finally, the public mood – interpreted by Kingdon (2001) as the perception of public opinion by politicians – has also been named as a facilitating condition – not only in the contexts of Bardach's discussion of periods of turbulence which affect the expectations of the citizens but also more concretely in terms of the extent and the homogeneity of popular support for specific policies (Graddy and Ye 2008). Perceived public support has been shown to play a large role for example in the cases of the French university admission system APB (Wenzelburger and Hartmann 2021) and the termination of water fluoridation in Calgary (O'Neill et al. 2019) (see above).

Termination and the Policy Stream

According to the MSF, policy formation is deeply linked to the *policy stream*. In this stream, policy communities of specialists in issue-specific subsystems consisting of "researchers, congressional staffers, people in planning and evaluation offices and in budget offices, academics, interest group analysts" (Kingdon 2001, 116) discuss different policy proposals (on subsystems, see also Baumgartner and Jones 1993; Sabatier and Weible 2007). Oftentimes, several proposals are discussed at the same time, compete with others and are reformulated over and again in a softening-up process, which also involves checking the receptiveness of key actors for a certain proposal. For a proposal to survive in this process, it has to fulfil several criteria – such as technical and budgetary feasibility of the policy, normative acceptance within the policy community and in the public (Kingdon 2001, 151). Moreover, completely new policy alternatives are more likely to surface in fragmented communities, as the "lack of structure leaves the agenda free to shift from one time to another in a more volatile fashion" (Kingdon 2001, 121).

In contrast to the problem stream and the political stream, where many of the findings from the termination literature could easily be integrated, it is less clear how the policy-stream and the "policy primeval soup" (Kingdon 2001, 116) of proposals that float around in this stream could actually be related to termination: In a sense, proposals should not matter if we are to explain termination. Drawing on Wenzelburger and Hartmann (2021), one can nevertheless argue that the policy stream could matter for termination to be successful – at least in two ways: The first case is a situation in which policy termination is rather a re-branding of an existing policy for symbolic reasons – by adopting a functional equivalent to an existing policy with another name. Politicians can use such actions for electoral purposes, for instance. Bauer and Knill describe this "dismantling by symbolic action" as follows:

> This strategy seeks to ensure that any dismantling intention is clearly and directly attributed to political decision makers. In other words, political actors very deliberately declare their intentions to dismantle existing policies. (...) At the same time, however, political declarations do not lead to respective outputs, hence remain symbolic. (Bauer and Knill 2012, 44)

When such a re-branding of policies is used, the policy stream is important because decision-makers need to have a policy alternative up and working which can easily replace the existing policy.

The second case describes a situation of actual policy termination, that is a decision to abolish a policy without having an alternative solution at hand. Why would we, in such a case, consider the policy stream? Following Wenzelburger and Hartmann (2021), one can argue that decision-makers need, at least, to make sure that the fallback position – that is the situation after the termination of the policy – is viable. If the consequences of terminating an existing policy are disastrous and would lead to chaos, this clearly is a problematic situation for decision-makers and would impede dismantling of the existing policy. Hence, the main aspects that the MSF identifies as criteria of survival of policy ideas in the softening up process may also be important when it comes to evaluating whether the fallback position is viable. If, for instance, the fallback solution is financially too costly or normatively unacceptable, this should make policy termination less likely. Therefore, Wenzelburger and Hartmann (2021, 5) argue that, the fallback position "is, in the case of termination, the alternative policy" and competes with the policy to be dismantled.[5] Consequently, and similar to the dynamics in the policy stream, we could therefore also expect that experts of the policy area that are interested in terminating the existing policy, e.g. the termination coalitions discussed above, would advocate for the viability of the fallback position in order to make the abolishment of the existing policy more probable. The softening-up process would therefore involve presenting the fallback position as a viable alternative to the policy in place thereby paving the way to its termination.

Finally, beyond the question of the viability of the fallback position, policy termination involves a "policy" itself – namely the decision of how to organize the dismantling process. Again, different ways of dismantling an existing policy may be discussed and mainly relate to technical aspects. However, as the termination literature shows us, the process of dismantling is not apolitical. Instead, several "processual factors" have been shown to affect the likelihood of policy termination, such as the speed of the termination process and the strategy to "cushion the blow", that is to compensate those who are negatively affected by the dismantling of an existing policy (see Table 3.1). Clearly, these processual factors are intertwined with the question of how (un)popular the policy actually is – an aspect that can therefore be related to the political stream (see Figure 3.1). Depending on the popularity, processual factors may therefore be more or less relevant. Nevertheless, it is important to emphasize that the design of the termination policy itself can be a crucial element influencing whether the decision to abolish a policy will actually be taken. The literature on blame avoidance (Vis 2016; Weaver 1986) and the strategic timing of unpopular reforms (Wenzelburger et al. 2020; Zohlnhöfer 2007) tells a lot about how important such processual factors are.

Policy Entrepreneurs and the Policy Window

In the MSF, the coupling process is intimately related to the concept of the policy entrepreneur who seizes the opportunity of an open policy window to present her pet policy as the solution to a perceived problem. For policy termination, policy terminators (or termination coalitions) have been discussed as fulfilling an equivalent function, pushing for the abolishment of an existing policy (Behn 1976; Geva-May 2004; O'Neill 2019) by actively investing time and resources. From the literature, two main types of terminators can be distilled: First, some studies have found terminators to engage in issue framing, pushing a certain interpretation of the status quo as being problematic and the fallback position as the better alternative (O'Neill et al. 2019). This has been shown, for instance, for the water fluoridation example, where the non-fluoridation was presented as viable fallback position. The activities of this first kind of "policy terminators" resemble quite closely the description of a policy entrepreneur with the only difference that there is no new policy to be promoted but the termination of an existing policy together with the fallback position.

The second type of policy terminator is much more at odds with the MSF's understanding of a policy entrepreneur. In fact, some termination studies find what Geva-May (2004, 329) calls "outside terminators", that is persons appointed to implement the termination decision. According to Behn (1978), the reason to leave the implementation of dismantling decisions to outsiders has to do with the electoral consequences of policy termination. He argues that "clearly, as terminator, an outsider will be much more willing to make the unpopular statements and issue the discomforting directives that may be necessary to ensure termination" (Behn 1978, 403). Hence, terminators of this second type are not genuinely interested in policies as such but resemble more managers that simply have the job of dismantling the existing policy and are appointed for political reasons to shield elected officials from opposition. In a way, they are much more linked to the implementation process, which is why the concept of the "outside terminator" instead of the "policy terminator" may be more appropriate in this case.

The differentiation between an "outside terminator" and the "policy terminator" is also useful to distinguish between the capacities needed for their respective actions. Whereas termination studies indicate that "policy terminators" do need similar skills than policy entrepreneurs – such as a good network and a good intuition of how to frame the fallback position as a viable alternative to the existing policy – outside terminators need the political intuition of how to overcome resistance in the implementation of a termination decision and the management skills to execute the dismantling.

Figure 3.1 draws together the different parts of our theorizing and presents a stylized framework of how the MSF could be used to inform studies of policy termination. It shows that both the problem stream and the political stream can easily accommodate the internal and external drivers of policy termination as identified by the empirical studies on policy termination (see Table 3.1). For the policy stream, we have argued that the viability of the fallback position is crucial for the coupling of the streams, because if the fallback position after abolishment of a policy was untenable and led to chaos, policy termination most probably would not occur. Moreover, the policy stream also takes up aspects of the design of the policy termination itself, such as the question of how the termination is strategically timed (speed) or whether losers from the abolishment are compensated ("cushioning the blow"). Finally, the graph also includes the policy terminator as described above, who invests time and energy to convince decision-makers of the need to terminate existing policies and of the viability of the fallback position.

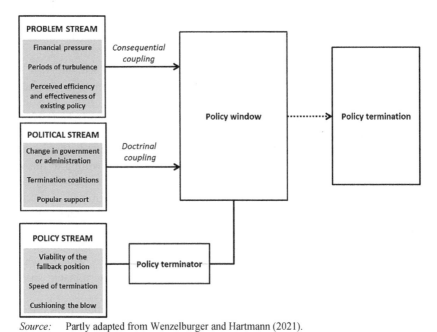

Source: Partly adapted from Wenzelburger and Hartmann (2021).

Figure 3.1   Policy termination through the lens of the MSF

CONCLUSION

The literature on the MSF is quickly expanding and leads both to theoretical refinements and more and more empirical applications. Whereas these developments have greatly enhanced our understanding of the policy process in Western democracies and elsewhere (Herweg, Zahariadis and Zohlnhöfer 2022), most of the literature is concerned with policy formation – the classic field of application – and, more recently, with implementation. In contrast, only a handful of studies have theorized how the MSF could also be fruitfully used to analyze policy termination and empirically investigated whether the core concepts of the MSF help us to explain when, why and how policies are abolished. In this chapter, we have aimed at providing conceptual guidance for such applications.

Drawing on a review of the studies of policy termination and a systematization of the drivers of policy termination identified in this literature, we have discussed how these insights can be combined with core concepts of the MSF. Our theorizing shows that the problem stream and the political stream can be very easily used to incorporate drivers of policy termination. Financial pressures or periods of turbulence – external drivers of policy termination according to the literature – fit well into the general argument of the problem stream according to which such drivers may be used to direct political actors' attention to problems. Similarly, the fact that a change in government or administration has been shown to facilitate policy termination fits squarely with the political dynamics the MSF theorizes to occur in the political stream. In the policy stream, we have argued that two components are key for policy termination to be more likely: First, the fallback position, i.e., the state of affairs after the abolishment of a policy, has to be viable; and second, the design of the termination policy itself, e.g., the speed of the process, has to be seen as appropriate. If this is the case, the policy stream may also be ripe for coupling. Finally, we also discuss the concept of "policy terminators" and emphasize the need to differentiate between pure "outside terminators" who are appointed to implement a termination decision and "policy terminators" who, similarly to policy entrepreneurs, engage in activities aimed at promoting the termination policy as well as the viability of the fallback position.

While our theorizing brings together main insights from the literature on policy termination and the theoretical concepts of the MSF, our discussion can only be seen as a starting point and is open to further refinements. These can come via empirical applications or re-analyses of existing case studies through the lens of the MSF; but they can also be grounded in further theorizing. In particular, recent refinements and extensions of the MSF (Herweg, Huß and Zohlnhöfer 2015; Howlett, McConnell and Perl 2015; Knaggård 2015;

Shephard et al. 2021; Zohlnhöfer, Herweg and Huß 2016) that have nuanced our understanding of some key concepts could be included in a more extensive model of policy termination seen from a MSF perspective. For instance, the conceptualization of a second "decision coupling" (Herweg, Huß and Zohlnhöfer 2015) could be a starting point for bridging the literatures between policy termination, MSF and the insights on the political dynamics of adopting an unpopular policy – which policy termination often is.

NOTES

1. For discussions of more fine-grained and nuanced definitions of the policy termination concept, see Adam & Bauer (2018).
2. Admittedly, different policy areas could be more or less easy to terminate with regulatory policies being probably more open to termination than distributive policies. We thank the editors for pointing out this.
3. For an overview see also O'Neill et al. 2019.
4. However, as Kingdon (2001, 171–72) points out, whether a policy window is actually open is also a matter of perceptions: Actors can also perceive an open policy window when this is not the case or be too late with their proposal.
5. While our single case study does not allow us to present a systematic analysis of necessary conditions, the theoretical considerations point to the obvious fit between the MSF as theoretical lens and theoretical reasoning based on relationships of necessity and sufficiency (Sager and Thomann 2016, Shephard et al. 2021).

REFERENCES

Adam, Christian, and Michael W. Bauer, 2018. "Policy and Organizational Termination." In *Oxford Research Encyclopedia of Politics*. Oxford Research Encyclopedias, ed. William R. Thompson, Oxford: Oxford University Press.

Bardach, Eugene. 1976. "Policy Termination as a Political Process." *Policy Sciences* 7 (2): 123–31.

Bauer, Michael W., and Christoph Knill. 2012. "Understanding Policy Dismantling: An Analytical Framework." In *Dismantling Public Policy: Preferences, Strategies, and Effects*, eds. Michael W. Bauer, Andrew Jordan, Christoffer Green-Pedersen, and Adrienne Héritier. Oxford: Oxford University Press.

Baumgartner, Frank, and Bryan D. Jones. 1993. *Agendas and Instability in American Politics*. Chicago: University of Chicago Press.

Behn, Robert D. 1975. Termination: How the Massachusetts Department of Youth Services Closed the Public Training Schools. Duke University, Institute of Policy Sciences and Public Affairs, Ch. 1.

Behn, Robert D. 1976. "Closing the Massachusetts Public Training Schools." *Policy Sciences* 7 (2): 151–71.

Behn, Robert D. 1978. "How to Terminate a Public Policy: A Dozen Hints for the Would-be Terminator." *Policy Analysis.* 4 (3): 393–413.

Berry, Christopher R., Barry C. Burden, and William G. Howell. 2010. "After Enactment: The Lives and Deaths of Federal Programs." *American Journal of Political Science* 54: 1–17.

Boin, Arjen, Paul t'Hart, and Allan McConnell. 2008. "Crisis Exploitation: Political and Policy Impacts of Framing Contests." *Journal of European Public Policy* 16 (1): 81–106.

Brewer, G. D., and P. deLeon. 1983. *The Foundations of Policy Analysis*. Ridgewood, IL: Dorsey Press.

Carpenter, Daniel and David E. Lewis. 2004. "Political Learning from Rare Events: Poisson Inference, Fiscal Constraints, and the Lifetime of Bureaus." *Political Analysis* 12 (3): 201–32.

deLeon, Peter, and José Mario Hernández-Quezada. 2001. "The case of the National Solidarity Program in Mexico: A Study in Comparative Policy Termination." *International Journal of Public Administration* 24 (3): 289–309.

Ferry, Martin and John Bachtler. 2013. "Reassessing the concept of policy termination: The case of regional policy in England." *Policy Studies* 34 (3): 255–73.

Fowler, Luke. 2019. "Problems, Politics, and Policy Streams in Policy Implementation." *Governance* 32 (3): 403–20.

Fowler, Luke. 2022. "Using the Multiple Streams Framework to Connect Policy Adoption to Implementation." *Policy Studies Journal* 50 (3): 615–39.

Frantz, Janet E. 1992. "Reviving and revisiting a termination model." *Policy Sciences* 25 (1): 175–86.

Frantz, Janet E. 1997. "The high cost of policy termination." *International Journal of Public Administration* 20 (12): 1097–2119.

Geva-May, Iris. 2004. "Riding the Wave of Opportunity: Termination in Public Policy." *Journal of Public Administration Research and Theory* 14 (3): 309–33.

Graddy, Elizabeth A., and Ke Ye. 2008. "When Do We "Just Say No"? Policy Termination Decisions in Local Hospital Services." *Policy Studies Journal* 36 (2): 219–42.

Herweg, Nicole, Christian Huß, and Reimut Zohlnhöfer. 2015. "Straightening the Three Streams: Theorising Extensions of the Multiple Streams Framework." *European Journal of Political Research* 54 (3): 435–49.

Herweg, Nicole, Nikolaos Zahariadis, and Reimut Zohlnhöfer. 2018. "The Multiple Streams Framework: Foundations, Refinements and Empirical Applications." In *Theories of the Policy Process*, 4th edition, eds. Weible, Christopher M. and Sabatier, Paul A., 17–54. Boulder: Westview.

Herweg, Nicole, Nikolaos Zahariadis, and Reimut Zohlnhöfer. 2022. "Travelling Far and Wide? Applying the Multiple Streams Framework to Policy-Making in Autocracies." *Politische Vierteljahresschrift* 63 (2): 203–23.

Howlett, Michael, Allan McConnell, and Anthony Perl. 2015. "Streams and Stages: Reconciling Kingdon and Policy Process Theory." *European Journal of Political Research* 54 (3): 419–34.

Jones, Michael D., Holly L. Peterson, Jonathan J. Pierce, Nicole Herweg, Amiel Bernal, Holly Lamberta Raney, and Nikolaos Zahariadis. 2016. "A River Runs through It: A Multiple Streams Meta-Review." *Policy Studies Journal* 44 (1): 13–36.

Kaufman, Herbert. 1976. *Are government organizations immortal?* Washington, DC: Brookings.

Kingdon, J. 2001. *Agendas, Alternatives, and Public Policies*. New York: Longman.

Kirkpatrick, Susan E., James P. Lester, and Mark R. Peterson. 1999. "The Policy Termination Process." *Review of Policy Research* 16 (1): 209–38.

Knaggård, Åsa. 2015. "The Multiple Streams Framework and the Problem Broker." *European Journal of Political Research* 54 (3): 450–65.

König, Pascal, and Georg Wenzelburger. 2014. "Towards a Theory of Political Strategy in Policy Analysis." *Politics & Policy* 42 (3): 397–427.

König, Pascal. 2016. "Communicating Austerity Measures During Times of Crisis: A Comparative Empirical Analysis of Four Heads of Government." *British Journal of Industrial Relations* 18 (3): 538–58.

Krause, Rachel M., Hongtao Yi, and Richard C. Feiock. 2016. "Applying policy termination theory to the abandonment of climate protection initiatives by U.S. local governments." *The Policy Studies Journal* 44 (2): 176–95.

Kuipers, Sanneke. 2006. *The Crisis Imperative : Crisis Rhetoric and Welfare State Reform in Belgium and the Netherlands in the Early 1990s.* Amsterdam: Amsterdam University Press.

Lewis, David E. 2002. "The Politics of Agency Termination: Confronting the Myth of Agency Immortality." *Journal of Politics* 64: 89–107.

Lowi, Theodore J. 1979. *The End of Liberalism: The Second Republic of the United States.* New York: Norton.

Lowry, William R. 2005. "Policy Reversal and Changing Politics: State Governments and Dam Removals." *State Politics and Policy Quarterly* 5 (4): 394–419.

O'Neill, Brenda, Taruneek Kapoor, and Lindsay McLaren. 2019. "Politics, Science, and Termination: A Case Study of Water Fluoridation Policy in Calgary in 2011." *Review of Policy Research,* 36 (1): 99–120.

Pierson, Paul. 1994. *Dismantling the Welfare State? Reagan, Thatcher, and the Politics of Retrenchment.* Cambrigde: Cambridge University Press.

Sabatier, Paul, and Christopher Weible. 2007. "The Advocacy Coalition Framework: Innovations and Clarifications." In *Theories of the Policy Process,* ed. Paul Sabatier, 189–220. Boulder: Westview.

Sager, Fritz, and Eva Thomann. 2016. "Multiple streams in member state implementation: politics, problem construction and policy paths in Swiss asylum policy." *Journal of Public Policy,* 37 (3): 287–314.

Shephard, Daniel D., Anne Ellersiek, Johannes Meuer, Christian Rupietta, Ruth Mayne, and Paul Cairney. 2021. "Kingdon's Multiple Streams Approach in New Political Contexts: Consolidation, Configuration, and New Findings." *Governance* 34 (2): 523–43.

Shulsky, Abram N. 1976. "Abolishing the District of Columbia Motorcycle Squad." *Policy Sciences* 7 (2): 183–97.

Streeck, Wolfgang, and Kathleen Thelen. 2005. "Introduction: Institutional Change in Advanced Political Economies." In *Beyond Continuity: Institutionl Change in Advanced Political Economies,* eds. Wolfgang Streeck and Kathleen Thelen, 3–19. Oxford: Oxford University Press.

Svallfors, Stefan. 2012. "Welfare States and Welfare Attitudes." In *Contested Welfare States,* ed. Stefan Svallfors, 1–24. Stanford: Stanford University Press.

Thom, Michael. 2021. "Does Program Evaluation Affect Program Termination? Insights from the Repeal of Corporate Tax Incentives for the Motion Picture Industry." *Policy Studies Journal* 49 (4): 1135–59.

Turnhout, Esther. 2009. "The rise and fall of a policy: Policy succession and the attempted termination of ecological corridors policy." *Policy Sciences* 42 (1): 57–72.

Vis, Barbara. 2016. "Taking Stock of the Comparative Literature on the Role of Blame Avoidance Strategies in Social Policy Reform." *Journal of Comparative Policy Analysis* 18 (2): 122–37.

Volden, Craig. 2016. "Failures: Diffusion, Learning, and Policy Abandonment." *State Politics & Policy Quarterly* 16 (1): 44–77.

Weaver, Kent R. 1986. "The Politics of Blame Avoidance." *Journal of Public Policy* 6 (4): 371–91.

Wenzelburger, Georg. 2011. "Political Strategies and Fiscal Retrenchment: Evidence from Four Countries." *West European Politics* 34 (6): 1151–84.

Wenzelburger, Georg. 2022: "Kontinuität statt Überbietungswettlauf. Die Law and Order Politik der Regierung Merkel IV." In Das Ende der Merkel-Jahre. Eine Bilanz der Regierung Merkel 2018–2021, eds. Reimut Zohlnhöfer and Fabian Engler. Wiesbaden: Springer, 387–414.

Wenzelburger, Georg, Carsten Jensen, Seonghui Lee, and Christoph Arndt. 2020. "How Governments Strategically Time Welfare State Reform Legislation: Empirical Evidence from Five European Countries." *West European Politics* 43 (6): 1285–314.

Wenzelburger, Georg, and Kathrin Hartmann. 2021. "Policy formation, termination and the multiple streams framework: the case of introducing and abolishing automated university admission in France." *Policy Studies.* Online first.

Wenzelburger, Georg, Pascal König, and Frieder Wolf. 2019. "Policy Theories in Hard Times? Assessing the Explanatory Power of Policy Theories in the Context of Crisis." *Public Organization Review* 19 (1): 97–118.

Wenzelburger, Georg. 2011. "Political Strategies and Fiscal Retrenchment: Evidence from Four Countries." *West European Politics* 34 (6): 1151–84.

Zahariadis, Nikolaos. 2003. *Ambiguity and Choice in Public Policy*. Washington, DC: Georgetown University Press.

Zohlnhöfer, Reimut, Nicole Herweg, and Christian Huß. 2016. "Bringing Formal Political Institutions into the Multiple Streams Framework: An Analytical Proposal for Comparative Policy Analysis." *Journal of Comparative Policy Analysis.* 18 (3): 243–56.

Zohlnhöfer, Reimut. 2007. "The Politics of Budget Consolidation in Britain and Germany: The Impact of Blame Avoidance Opportunities." *West European Politics* 30 (5): 1120–38.

4. Multilevel influence and interaction in the Multiple Streams Framework: A conceptual map

Åsa Knaggård and Roger Hildingsson

INTRODUCTION

Many policy issues are connected to multiple political levels – through their structure or the way they are included in and acted upon in the policy process. Examples include issues ranging from climate and energy governance (e.g., Jordan et al. 2012; Lovell 2016; Rietig 2021), health (e.g., Bache and Reardon 2013; Oborn, Barett, and Exworthy 2011) and drug policy (Alimi 2015; Cairney 2009; Hoe et al. 2016) to economic and trade governance (e.g., Ackrill and Kay 2011; Lips 2020). Policy issues characterized by multilevel dynamics seem to increase in a globalized world, leading public policy scholars to study policy processes not easily confined to one political level. Although many Multiple Streams Framework (MSF) studies involve such dynamics, so far, few grapple explicitly with the multilevel nature of policy processes (e.g., Ackrill and Kay 2011; Bache and Reardon 2013; Goyal 2021; Hoe et al. 2016; Lovell 2016, 2017; Rietig 2021). A review study by Jones et al. (2016) concluded that 20 percent of the reviewed MSF studies focused on two political levels, six percent on three levels, and one percent on four or more. This indicates a need for a theoretical elaboration within the MSF on how influences and interactions across political levels take place and shape agenda setting and policy making, including their impact on the three streams, actors and policy windows. In this chapter, we conceptually map how multilevel influences and interactions can be understood and accounted for within the MSF.

Although most MSF studies are focused on national policy processes, there is nothing in the set-up of the framework that confines it to a particular political level, as evident from the many applications at international and subnational levels, like state, region and local level (Jones et al. 2016). Cairney and Jones (2016) argue that the MSF can be applied to any place, time and issue area. We argue this universality also includes multilevel influences and interactions. By focusing on the reception of ideas by policy actors, not on the origin of those ideas, Kingdon (2003) enabled MSF studies to account for multilevel influences and interactions as well. As a consequence, the MSF does not operate with clear system demarcations of what is endogenous and exogenous in terms of political level. Even if it places focus squarely on agenda setting and decision making within a particular governmental system, which, by necessity, is confined to one political level, the streams are not necessarily contained to that level. Due to this, we argue that the MSF is well-suited to study the multilevel aspects of policy processes. At the same time, the MSF is not developed to consider the possible importance of where ideas come from for agenda-setting and decision-making processes. We argue that it is central to consider the origin of ideas, as it can influence how ideas are received and, thus, affect the possibilities to successfully couple the streams.

There have been attempts to develop the theoretical ability of the MSF to capture multilevel influences and interactions. In order to do so, several studies have drawn on other theories, including policy diffusion and transfer (e.g., Goyal 2021; Cairney 2009), policy mobility (Lovell 2016; 2017), transnational advocacy (Hoe et al. 2016), and multilevel governance (Rietig 2021). Such studies have made a first step toward clarifying the influence and interaction across political levels in the MSF. Building on these and other MSF studies (e.g., Ackrill and Kay 2011; Bache and Reardon 2013; Baek 2021; Brunner 2008; Santos and Kauko 2022; Shephard et al. 2021; Zahariadis 2008), as well as other public policy frameworks (e.g., Baumgartner, Jones, and Mortensen 2018; Jenkins-Smith et al. 2018) and research on multilevel governance and policy transfer and diffusion (e.g., Dolowitz and Marsh 2012; Haas 1992; Hooghe and Marks 2003; Stone 2012), we conceptually map influences and interactions across political levels and their effects on agenda setting and policy making within the MSF.

There are two main ways to study multilevel influences and interactions within the MSF. The first is to track the streams wherever they flow, also across political levels (see e.g., Bache and Reardon 2013; Goyal 2021; Lovell 2016; Shephard et al. 2021). Actors, ideas and events can, in different ways, relate to developments at several political levels. These connections can be understood as a natural part of the problem, policy and politics streams. Such an approach can capture how actors acting at different levels interact, how ideas flow between political levels, and how events taking place elsewhere can influence policy processes. It can also make sense of how institutional contexts with built-in multilevel characteristics influence agenda setting and decision making (see Figure 4.1). The second way to study multilevel influences and interactions is to focus on parallel processes playing out at different political levels and how they influence each other (see Rietig 2021). We need to account for both these ways of understanding multilevel influences and interactions within the MSF.

First, we will give a sense of how some MSF studies have approached influences and interactions across levels, presenting some of the more elaborate attempts in more detail. Thereafter, we will conceptually map how multilevel influences and interactions can be understood within the MSF.

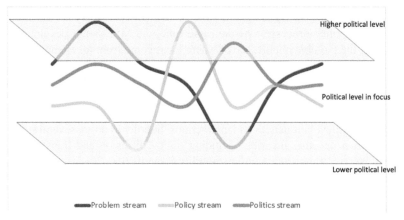

Source: Own illustration.

Figure 4.1   Streams flowing across political levels

MSF STUDIES OF MULTILEVEL INFLUENCES AND INTERACTIONS

Many MSF studies have focused on policy processes that in different ways transcend or cross political levels. Such studies often highlight the interaction across levels by focusing on actors in the policy stream. They draw attention to policy communities that span levels (e.g., Oborn et al. 2011; Hoe et al. 2016; Fisher 2012), transnational policy entrepreneurs trying to influence national policy makers (e.g., Alimi 2015; Shephard et al. 2021), policy entrepreneurs utilizing windows and venue shopping at multiple levels (e.g., Rietig 2021), and international funding agencies changing the influence of policy entrepreneurs working within countries (e.g., Hoe et al. 2016). Similarly, in the problem stream, studies highlight the work of international problem brokers to influence national agendas (e.g., Brunner 2008). Other studies show how internationally developed knowledge and indicators are drawn on in national policy processes to frame problems (Santos and Kauko 2022), legitimize policies (Baek 2021; Hoe et al. 2016; Lovell 2017), and build coalitions in both the policy and politics streams (Baek 2021). Further, studies have shown that international or global focusing events can be important for national policy processes (Hoe et al. 2016; Santos and Kauko 2022). Even in the politics stream, which earlier research has pointed out as mostly confined to one political level (e.g., Bache and Reardon 2013), studies have located influence across levels, pointing to the interconnectedness of decision-making arenas and to how action on one arena can affect policy processes on others (Brunner 2008; Rietig 2021). Examples are how decisions at G8 meetings can influence national policy processes (Brunner 2008), and how even failures of the international community to come to agreement can spark action at the national level (Rietig 2021).

MSF scholars have taken influence and interaction across political levels into account in various ways. However, few studies systematically engage with the issue, in terms of the levels covered, the direction of influence, and the different elements of the MSF. As apparent above, most studies focus on how developments at the international or global level influence national policy processes, especially through the policy stream. Fewer studies look for influences from lower to higher levels or for interaction across other levels than the international and national.

Two studies need a more detailed presentation as they, in different ways, contribute to the challenge of including all levels, directions, and elements of the MSF. The first one by Rietig (2021), while empirically focusing on the EU and the international level in climate governance, strives to cover all levels and directions of influence by using insights from multilevel governance scholarship (see e.g., Hooghe and Marks 2003; Benz, Broschek, and Lederer 2021). She focuses on "multilevel reinforcing dynamics" to analyze how issues move up and down between interdependent political levels. She argues that agenda coupling on a higher political level can enable decision coupling on a lower level and vice versa. Rietig (2021) argues that multilevel reinforcing dynamics are long-term and iterative processes, enabling policy entrepreneurs to venue shop. In many ways, the multilevel reinforcing dynamics resembles the spillover effect included in the MSF. According to Kingdon (2003), spillover occurs when action in one policy area sets a precedent for action in another policy area. Rietig (2021) shows how such spillover dynamics also work across political levels as well as sequentially over time.

The second study in need of a more detailed presentation is Goyal (2021), also focusing on spillover processes or, as he puts it, "prior policy activity in a sender and/or a trans-jurisdictional actor can systematically influence each policy-making stream of the receiver" (p. 645). Connecting the MSF with policy transfer and diffusion theory, he suggests an account that captures all three streams. He includes not only spillover between levels but also across jurisdictions at the corresponding political level, for instance between subnational units or states in a federation. His focus is on how policy activity 'elsewhere' (Goyal 2021, 641) changes the dynamics of the three streams, for example regarding underlying societal problems, problem framing and issue awareness, policy alternatives and learning, and changes to the national mood and power dynamics. Goyal's attempt is ambitious when it comes to including all three streams, but does neither consider different directions of influence nor other directions of influence than the global to the national.

In the following, we outline a conceptual map able to capture influences and interactions that cut across political levels and go in different directions, which covers all parts of the MSF.

A CONCEPTUAL MAP OF MULTILEVEL INFLUENCES AND INTERACTIONS

The conceptual map is based on how multilevel influences and interactions can be manifested through *actors*, *ideas*, *events* and *institutional contexts*. The first three of these – actors, ideas and events – are well-established aspects of the MSF and can be understood as vital elements of the three streams. The fourth element – institutional contexts – has been given less attention in MSF work, although increasingly so in recent years (see Herweg, Zahariadis, and Zohlnhöfer 2018). It is also different in character to the other three, capturing the institutional structure in which actors, ideas and events come to have multilevel influence or interact across levels. In this section, we structure the discussion around these four, rather than around each of the three streams. The reason is that multilevel influence and interaction pertaining to each of the four elements plays out in similar ways in the three streams. This should not be seen as providing a modus operandi for MSF studies but rather allows us to outline a conceptual map of the important features to look out for in striving to understand how multilevel influence and interaction might affect policy processes. These features, further discussed below, are summarized in Figure 4.2.

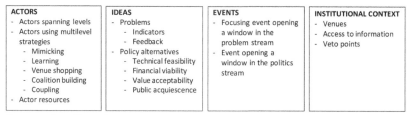

ACTORS	IDEAS	EVENTS	INSTITUTIONAL CONTEXT

- Actors spanning levels
- Actors using multilevel strategies
  - Mimicking
  - Learning
  - Venue shopping
  - Coalition building
  - Coupling
- Actor resources
	- Problems
	  - Indicators
	  - Feedback
	- Policy alternatives
	  - Technical feasibility
	  - Financial viability
	  - Value acceptability
	  - Public acquiescence
		- Focusing event opening a window in the problem stream
		- Event opening a window in the politics stream
			- Venues
			- Access to information
			- Veto points

Source: Own illustration.

Figure 4.2 *Features of the conceptual map*

Actors

Actors are a central element in the MSF. Following recent developments of the MSF (Herweg, Zahariadis, and Zohlnhöfer 2018), we consider four types of actors – problem brokers, policy entrepreneurs, political entrepreneurs and policy communities. Interaction across political levels is principally possible for all of these, although there might be large differences between them in terms of how common such interactions are. For three of them – problem brokers, policy entrepreneurs and policy communities – many studies have shown how they act across levels (e.g., Lovell 2016, 2017; Rietig 2021; Shephard et al. 2021). The empirical evidence for political entrepreneurs working over political levels is much weaker. The reason is that the political entrepreneur generally operates within a given institutional context, striving to build support for policy adoption from within a particular governmental system (see Herweg, Huß, and Zohlnhöfer 2015). Another difference between the four types of actors is that problem brokers, policy entrepreneurs and polit-ical entrepreneurs all act to either get an issue onto the political agenda or to get a policy adopted. Policy communities work more narrowly on developing policy alternatives. Despite these differences, much of the dynamic is similar across actor types.

In principle, there are two ways in which the MSF actors can be understood to engage in multilevel interactions. The first is that actors through their organization can span levels. The second is that actors use multilevel strategies that make them interact across levels. There is considerable overlap between the two, as actors that are confined to one level can make use of multilevel strategies to interact across political levels, whereas actors spanning levels can utilize their organizational capacities as well as multilevel strategies. The reason to highlight the difference is that actors spanning levels might have access to more resources needed for influencing or interacting across levels, discussed below. We will first present the two kinds of interactions, followed by a discussion on actors' resources.

Actors spanning political levels

Actors spanning levels can be organizations or networks acting as brokers, entrepreneurs or policy communities. The clearest example might be civil society organizations with tiers at different levels. Typical examples are confederations of interest groups such as labor unions (ILO), environmental movements (e.g., Friends of the Earth, European Environmental Bureau) and business associations (e.g., Business Europe) with nested representation stretching from local to national and international levels. Political parties can also be nested in this way, as is often present in the relationship between national and local branches of a party or, within the EU context, between EU parliamentarians and their parties at the Member State level. Such organizations are "porous", as Herweg, Zahariadis and Zohlnhöfer (2018, 23) call them, as they let ideas and people travel across levels, although to differing degrees. They can also be understood as porous in the way they might enable knowledge, access to policy makers and credibility to be used on multiple levels.

Another type of level-spanning actor is networks with members active at different levels. These are usually not nested. Instead, they consist of overlapping networks with individuals active on multiple levels (e.g., Bache and Reardon 2013; Rietig 2021). One example is transnational coalitions, like the Climate Action Network, formed by national and international civil society organizations. Another example is epistemic communities (Haas 1992), which can be characterized as consisting of overlapping transnational and national networks. Such networks might be important as problem brokers and policy communities. An example of such a problem broker is the research network that predated the Intergovernmental Panel on Climate Change (IPCC) and called out for political action on climate change (Agrawala 1998). Several MSF studies have highlighted the role of transnational policy communities (Bache and Reardon 2013; Goyal 2021; Rietig 2021), which are more likely to be found in some issue areas, for example technically dominated ones, such as in energy or climate policy (Goyal 2021; Knaggård and Hildingsson forthcoming; Lovell 2016). Furthermore, individuals can under some circumstances be understood to span political levels, for example, in terms of how individual ministers in national governments are also part of the European Council of Ministers. Here, it is the multilevel character of the EU governance system that mandates politicians to be active on several political levels.

Actors using multilevel strategies

The second way in which MSF actors can interact across levels is the use of strategies that implies collaborating with other actors or drawing on ideas and events at other levels. We will here elaborate on five types of strategies – mimicking, learning, venue shopping, coalition building and coupling. Although not an exhaustive list of multilevel strategies, they represent the most important ones discussed in the literature (see e.g., Aviram, Cohen, and Beeri 2020; Baumgartner, Jones, and Mortensen 2018; Cairney and Yamazaki 2018; Jenkins-Smith et al. 2018; Zohlnhöfer, Herweg, and Huß 2016). We have not included framing here, although it might be considered a multilevel strategy. The reason is that framing can be seen as an integral part of several of the other strategies, and we discuss it further in relation to problems and policy alternatives under the section on ideas.

The first strategy, mimicking, has been developed in the transfer and diffusion literature, (e.g., Dolowitz and Marsh 2012; Stone 2012). In that literature, mimicking often refers to transferring policy from one jurisdiction to another, but mimicking is also possible between political levels (e.g., Lovell 2016; 2017). Mimicking becomes especially salient in situations with high time pressure (Lovell 2016). Actors can mimic problem frames and policy alternatives as presented by actors at other levels, thereby transferring ideas from one level to another (Goyal 2021). Importantly, by mimicking, MSF actors not only utilize the ideas of others but are also able to piggyback on their credibility and reputation or on the success of implemented policies. To draw on higher-level actors' credibility and reputation could be especially important, whereas policies implemented at lower levels – proving their feasibility – could lead to adoption becoming more likely on higher levels. An illustrative example of how mimicking might work is captured by the well-known "California effects" – i.e., when higher regulatory standards in one jurisdiction inspire actors in other jurisdictions to lobby for similar standards – also conceptualized as "the Brussels effect" (Bradford 2020) to account for how higher-level regulatory standards (such as in EU law) inspire actors to push for similar policies in lower-level jurisdictions. Several legal principles, such as the precautionary principle and the polluter pays principle, have been mimicked across levels, often first from national to international level and then in the reversed direction.

The second strategy, learning, implies a change in how actors understand the functioning of the world (not present in mimicking) and, following from that, a shift in their position or activities (e.g., Dolowitz and Marsh 2012; Gerlak and Heikkila 2011; Moyson 2017). In real world cases, the line between learning and mimicking might be hard to draw, as it can be difficult to establish if such a shift has taken place or not. Regardless of such epistemological difficulties, learning can be important in several ways for understanding multilevel influences and interactions in the MSF (Baek 2022; Goyal 2021). Problem brokers can learn from the activities of brokers at other levels about how to frame issues to reach particular audiences. Policy communities and policy entrepreneurs can learn about the design and feasibility of policy alternatives, while the latter also about how those alternatives can be successfully coupled to problems. Political entrepreneurs can learn about how to build political support and convince the public.

The third strategy, venue shopping, might be chosen by problem brokers and policy entrepreneurs to target one or more political levels, possibly more benign to the problem or policy alternative than the level at which the actor is usually active (Rietig 2021; Shephard et al. 2021; Zahariadis 2008). In political systems with several strong government levels, like federal systems or the EU, venue shopping is more likely than in political systems with only one strong government level. For neither policy communities nor political entrepreneurs venue shopping is a core strategy. The former does not seek out arenas to try to convince audiences, and the latter are focused on gathering political support for policy adoption in a particular governmental system. However, over longer periods of time, policy adoption at other levels can influence the possibilities for adoption (Rietig 2021). It is, therefore, possible for political entrepreneurs to act to form political support for a decision at another level to increase later possibilities for adoption in the governmental system where they are normally active. The EU context provides ample opportunities for this, like in the case of how the German Government in the 1980s pushed for a deregulation of the European telecom market to avoid domestic blame (Zohlnhöfer 2007).

The fourth strategy is coalition building. There are several examples in the MSF literature of how actors build coalitions across political levels (e.g., Hoe et al. 2016; Shephard et al. 2021). Two main types of such coalition building can be important within the MSF (see Hoe et al. 2016). The first type is higher-level actors supporting lower-level ones to influence the lower-level agenda or the possibilities to make a decision (e.g., Shephard et al. 2021). Such coalition building can provide funding for organizations or networks to develop and promote policy alternatives, ideas and policy expertise. They can also provide credibility and legitimacy to particular problem frames, policy alternatives and political deals. An example of this is how policy experts at the OECD support domestic actors, for instance a leading think-tank pushing for carbon pricing in the case of Mexico (Skovgaard and Sachs Ferrari 2022). The second type of coalition building is lower-level actors supporting higher-level ones. Such coalition building can provide knowledge of real-world problems, know-how about running policies and, through those, credibility and legitimacy, which can strengthen the higher-level actor's position. This dynamic can be seen for instance in the international climate negotiations, where local and indigenous communities have sometimes been included in national delegations to strengthen the country's negotiation position. That the direction of influence in these cases goes mostly in one direction does not mean that coalition partners are not mutually benefiting (see Shephard et al. 2021).

The fifth strategy is coupling, which is the most developed strategy of the five in the MSF literature. To what extent the other multilevel strategies contribute to agenda change and policy adoption is contingent on how well policy entrepreneurs, in particular, are able to couple the three streams. To what extent coupling can utilize ideas and events from other levels or connect problem frames and policy alternatives that resonate with the politics stream at another political level is an open question. Policy entrepreneurs need to have a good sense of both political and public sentiments concerning actors and ideas at other political levels. In some instances, negative sentiments can be connected with international or global actors and ideas (see e.g., Shephard et al. 2021), especially in cases where the political ideology dominating at lower levels is nationalistic in focus and narrowly focused on domestic issues. There might also be distrust and negative sentiments between a national government and state, regional or local level governments. Such negative sentiments might depend on the governments at different levels being governed by parties with different ideologies. Such differences might be based in different positions on the left-to-right political scale, but also in different positions concerning organizational matters like the extent of subsidiarity and decentralization. Such negative sentiments will influence the use of all strategies discussed above, although the influence from other levels can be more easily masked for mimicking and learning.

Influence on actors' resources

When it comes to the success of problem brokers, policy entrepreneurs and political entrepreneurs to influence the ripeness of the three streams, it is contingent on circumstances, but also related to their resources (Herweg, Zahariadis, and Zohlnhöfer 2018; Kingdon 1995; Knaggård 2015; Zahariadis 2005). According to Kingdon (2003, 122), the resources of policy entrepreneurs include "time, energy, reputation, and sometimes money". Herweg, Zahariadis, and Zohlnhöfer (2018) add access to policymakers. Although not as developed as in the Advocacy Coalition Framework (Jenkins-Smith et al. 2018), the role of actor's resources needs to be considered, as they can be affected by interaction across levels. One of the resources that all three actors share is their connections and access to people on the inside of governmental systems (see Herweg, Zahariadis and Zohlnhöfer 2018; Knaggård 2015). Interaction across levels, especially in terms of venue shopping at both higher and lower levels might prove difficult, as actors might be less well-connected at other levels. Venue shopping does not affect the resources of actors spanning levels, like civil society organizations and political parties, in the same way. It will be easier for such actors to get access to policy-making fora at multiple levels. Even if this does not pertain to all individuals, they still might be able to influence other levels by pitching in problem framings and policy alternatives.

A second type of resource that can be affected by interaction across levels is credibility and reputation. Instead of weakening MSF-actors' resources, interaction can lead to gains in credibility or reputation. By drawing on the credibility or reputation of a higher-level actor, problem brokers, policy entrepreneurs and political entrepreneurs alike can boost their own credentials by being viewed in the light of more credible or authoritative actors. Such credibility and reputation can be based on superior knowledge of problems or policy alternatives (like the IPCC or similar assessment bodies), a claim to moral authority (like the church or the UN) or to ideological authority (like political leaders). In the same sense, the credibility of lower-level actors can be drawn on higher up in the system, as they might have personal experience of and knowledge about problems and policy alternatives that higher-level actors lack (like communities witnessing on local effects of global processes). A third type of resource that can be drawn on is financial support, usually from higher-level to lower-level actors (see e.g., Shephard et al. 2020).

Ideas

Ideas cannot be understood as divorced from actors – it is actors that frame and promote them. However, focusing on problems and policy alternatives and where they come from provides an additional layer to the conceptual map we are outlining. We wish to point out that the repertoire of ideas about problems and policy alternatives that actors can utilize expands, if ideas present at other political levels are considered (see also Cairney and Zahariadis 2016). Further, the fact that actors at other levels have tested problem and policy ideas by framing, promoting and coupling them, can change the dynamic among ideas in important ways, making some seem more relevant, legitimate and viable.

The expansion of available ideas generates possibilities to mimic and learn, but it can also influence the salience of problems and policy alternatives. One example of this is the presence of indicators for benchmarking public performance of similar government systems, like OECD rankings, the PISA rankings, or statistical comparisons of unemployment rates or public health. Such indicators are usually constructed by governmental agencies or civil society organizations at a higher level to influence policies at lower levels (see e.g., Baek 2021; Goyal 2021; Hoe et al. 2016; Santos and Kauko 2022). Kingdon (2003, 111) pointed out that such comparisons can be important for understanding conditions as problems and research has shown that they can also be used to motivate action (Lovell 2017; Santos and Kauko 2022). The direction of influence for indicator comparisons will mostly be from higher to lower levels, depending on the nested character of political systems.

Feedback, which is another carrier of ideas that can have multilevel characteristics, instead, is more likely to travel from lower to higher levels. The reason for this is that feedback comes from enacted policies and programs, which often are implemented at lower levels, but rarely on higher ones. According to Kingdon (2003, 100ff), it can, beyond knowledge about policies and programs, also provide knowledge about problems. Indicators and feedback developed at one level to influence another, can have important implications for policy processes. Benchmarking among a group of similar governmental systems might be more effective in pointing out a problem, than domestic indicators could be, as the comparison, if negative for a government, showcases that it is possible to do better. Thus, it highlights the difference between the present situation and what is possible. This is in line with Kingdon's (2003, 19) way of understanding how indicators influence our perception of a problem only when set in relation to an imagined better situation. Feedback from policies or programs enacted at lower levels could instead be more easily ignored, as different governmental actors at the lower level might fare very differently. This could be the case in terms of how much and how rapid countries have decreased their greenhouse gas emissions (which varies quite a lot), or in terms of how successful subnational governments are in providing sufficient housing for their residents.

The second aspect to consider in terms of how problem and policy ideas are influenced across levels pertains to their salience. Problem and policy alternatives sometimes seem to be en vogue and spread around the world (e.g., Pi Ferrer and Alasuutari 2019). When it comes to policy alternatives, the MSF contains explanations for how this can be understood. The criteria for survival of policy alternatives in the "policy primeval soup" (Kingdon 2003) – technical feasibility, financial viability, value acceptability and public acquiescence (Herweg, Zahariadis, and Zohlnhöfer 2018; Kingdon 2003, 131ff) – provide a way to understand the salience of policy alternatives and how they are influenced by ideas being voiced, coupled and adopted at other political levels. The more policy communities investigate policy alternatives, regardless of at which level, the more will be known about their technical feasibility and financial viability. Policy adoption can have an additional effect on the survival criteria by developing the technical feasibility and changing the financial viability (Goyal 2021). A case in point is how the increased deployment of wind power and solar photovoltaics has generated technological learning, which has reduced costs and, in turn, led to a rapid market expansion of new renewable energy technologies (see e.g., Samadi 2018). It is less clear if debates about a policy alternative or its adoption at another political level has the same influence on value acceptability and public acquiescence, although it is possible. One example is when policy alternatives are experimented with at lower political levels, making the public and policy-makers more familiar with those policy alternatives, which over time can shift their value positions and lead to policy adoption at a higher political level.

Finally, we wish to point out that the salience of ideas cannot be understood without considering how problems and policy alternatives are framed by problem brokers and policy entrepreneurs. How ideas originating from other political levels are framed is crucial for their reception among both politicians and the general public. Here, the "national mood," or possibly the "European mood" (Zahariadis 2008) or "subnational moods", comes into play. The national mood, as well as the perception of it among policy makers, can be pro or against ideas or actors at another level, affecting the value of and potential for multilevel strategies, like mimicking, learning and coalition building. For example, several studies have shown a difference in how likely countries are to use knowledge held by transnational actors (Baek 2022; Hoe et al. 2016). National mood could be involved in explaining this. However, the salience of ideas can be manipulated (Zohlnhöfer, Herweg, and Huß 2016) by skillful framing, either hiding or highlighting the inspiration or support from other levels, depending on dominating sentiments (as discussed earlier).

Events

The third element of the conceptual map is events of different kinds. The MSF highlights a number of such events as crucial for agenda-setting and decision-making processes. These events can either take place in the problem stream or the politics stream, opening windows for agenda setting or decision making. Such events can take place at other political levels and influence policy processes in two ways. The first is when an event occurs at one political level and leads to the opening of a window at another political level. The second relates to when policy entrepreneurs make use of windows at other levels. Whereas the first illustrates how the streams can transcend political levels, the second points out how parallel processes at different levels can be used strategically by actors.

When it comes to events that open windows at other political levels, they can occur either in the problem or the politics stream. An example of the first could be the publication of global or regional assessments, such as PISA or the IPCC, which opens agenda windows at lower political levels (see e.g., Santos and Kauko 2022). In a similar vein, focusing events like global economic recessions (Skovgaard 2014) or a WTO-ruling (Ackrill and Kay 2011) can open agenda windows at lower political levels. The Covid-19 pandemic is a recent case in point of how a health crisis with global reach opened windows for rapid and fundamental national policy measures, which were largely unthinkable before the pandemic, including vast financial recovery programs. Even more recently, the 2022 US Supreme Court decision to overturn the previous *Roe v Wade* ruling sparked referendums on abortion rights in a number of states. More localized crises, like natural disasters or school shootings, can open agenda windows at higher political levels. These types of events are in line with the predominating understanding of focusing events within the MSF.

Less considered in MSF studies are events in the politics stream that open windows at other levels. Such events can, for example, be shifts in government or political leadership and budget decisions. The extent to which events actually will open such windows is not clear and must be seen as contingent on how well-connected a governmental system is to other political levels. In countries with partly autonomous or devolved subnational regions or local municipalities, higher-level events can open lower-level windows. A case in point is how a shift in government in London could open a window in Edinburgh for more Scottish self-determination. The opposite could also be the case, where a referendum of independence in Scotland could open a decision window in London. In nested governance systems, where a decision on a higher level automatically generates the need for decision making on a lower level, a much wider range of events might open lower-level windows. This is the case in the EU, where the adoption of directives opens decision windows in Member States. International negotiations portray a similar kind of dynamic, where an agreement negotiated at the international level needs to be ratified at the national level. In both cases, decisions made at the first level creates a decision window at another level. Another example is when losses in lower-level elections opens a window for the losing party to reprioritize political positions at the national or federal level. However, the opening of a window is no guarantee of successful agenda setting or decision making, but provides opportunities for policy and political entrepreneurs.

Using windows that open at other levels is intimately connected to the strategy of venue shopping. By utilizing such windows, policy and political entrepreneurs having limited success can push an issue onto the agenda or contribute to getting a political deal for adoption at another level. Actors can utilize windows at lower levels, which is seen when national policy makers take active part in election campaigns on lower levels. This behavior can change the salience of issues on higher levels and has much in common with the dynamics captured in the social-technical transitions literature, which is focused on how policy alternatives are developed in niches and from there upscaled to challenge established regimes (e.g., Derwort, Jager, and Newig 2021). The opposite, when entrepreneurs use windows at higher political levels, can affect the likelihood of agenda or policy changes at lower levels (see Rietig 2021). Such strategic behavior can be motivated by calculations of decisions at higher levels forcing lower-level governments to follow, for instance in the implementation of EU decisions. It can also be motivated by blocking issues from the agenda, as in the case of national leaders using international conflicts to gain domestic popularity and support.

Institutional Context

Finally, the fourth element of our conceptual map is the formal institutional context in which agendas change and decisions are made. We have already touched upon quite a number of such formal institutional aspects, as well as informal ones. As the formal institutional context seldom receives much consideration in MSF studies (Zohlnhöfer, Herweg, and Huß 2016; but see Bolukbasi and Yildirim 2022), we wish to point out its importance for understanding the role of multilevel influence and interaction for agenda setting and decision making. The key insight is that the institutional set-up of governmental systems is critical for the space for such influences and their potential impact.

One of the crucial aspects for the potential of multilevel influence and interaction is to what extent governmental systems are multilevel and in what way. Research has pointed out how the centralization of a system affects, for example, the availability of arenas (Bolukbasi and Yildirim 2022; Cairney and Zahariadis 2016). Federal government systems offer more venue choice than unitary ones. On the other hand, unitary government systems might be strongly devolved, resulting in a similar range of venues as in federal ones. This makes it possible to venue-shop and couple problems and policy alternatives at different levels and possibly also increasing possibilities for mimicking and learning. However, these differences can be manipulated by entrepreneurs claiming that an issue belongs to a particular level.

The EU is a special case when it comes to its institutional context. Several studies have applied and adapted the MSF to the EU context (e.g., Ackrill and Kay 2011; Becker 2019; Herweg 2017; Zahariadis 2008). The set-up of EU institutions provides ample space for multilevel influence and interaction. The mandated interaction between the executive and legislative bodies of the EU – the Commission, the Council and the Parliament – in itself contains interaction across levels as the Council consists of national governmental representatives, while the Commission represents the Union and the Parliament is selected directly by the EU citizens. In the same way as in international negotiations, two-level games (Putnam 1988) become important in the case of Council decisions. Such games point to the need to find common ground among negotiators, while also retaining support at home (Zahariadis 2005). In such cases, package deals and concessions are crucial instruments (see Zohlnhöfer, Herweg, and Huß 2016), opening up for multilevel influence. A further aspect of the EU, which is important when considering multilevel influence and interaction, is the role of interest groups. Although important in most government systems, they are especially important in channeling ideas to the EU institutions (Rozbicka and Spohr 2016). These circumstances increase the multilevel influences and interactions also for business associations and civil society organizations acting as problem brokers or policy entrepreneurs.

When it comes to the institutional context, differences between strong and weak democracies as well as different forms of autocracies have to be considered. Initially, all MSF applications were on western-style democracies, whereas the applications to other types of democracies as well as to more autocratic states have increased over the years (see Herweg, Zahariadis, and Zohlnhöfer 2018). More research is needed, especially on autocratic systems, to sort out the differences in terms of multilevel influence and interaction, to which some of the chapters in this volume will contribute. Still, some preliminary conclusions can be drawn. Some differences between systems are related to the extent to which actors outside of government can influence the agenda and to the presence of veto points. Such opportunities should be larger in liberal democracies, but might also vary among democracies as Bolukbasi and Yildirim (2022) point out. In systems where access to information is restricted and the agenda and decision making are controlled by a smaller group of actors, more attention needs to be focused on processes internal to the government. However, such systems do not rule out multilevel influences and interactions completely. For example, mimicking and learning might be important strategies, although venue shopping and coalition building might not (e.g., Du and Baark 2021; see also Shephard et al. 2020). We also expect that indicators and feedback from other levels are less influential. Due to the restriction of information spreading, events at other levels would probably open fewer windows for agenda setting and decision making.

In order to better understand multilevel influences and interactions, scholars need to devote more attention to the institutional context in which agenda and policy change take place. To what extent is the system allowing for such influences and interactions and in what way? Without answering these questions, it will be difficult to assess their impact.

CONCLUDING REMARKS

The conceptual map presented in this chapter provides a wide range of ways in which multilevel influence and interaction can play a role for agenda setting and decision making in the MSF. The range of ways in which such influences and interactions can take place – mapped in this chapter – should be understood as possibilities for multilevel influence and interaction, which will be present to different degrees in specific cases. Instead of theoretically developing the MSF, this chapter has endeavored to bring out the theoretical possibilities already inherent in the framework and its later developments, to capture how influences and interactions across political levels, from the global to the local, and in different directions influences different parts of the MSF. The map outlined here is not intended as a methodological description of how multilevel dynamics can be studied. Instead, by focusing on four elements – actors, ideas, events, and institutional contexts – through which such influences and interactions can take place, the chapter provides a conceptual map to analytically orient MSF scholars grappling with multilevel dynamics in their cases. The map also opens up a comparative research agenda exploring the circumstances under which multilevel influence and interaction plays a role for agenda setting and decision making and its most likely pathways through the multiple streams. The chapter provides some initial ideas on possible hypotheses that such a research agenda could focus on, but much more analytical and empirical work is needed. This chapter lays the foundation for a more systematic and consistent treatment of multilevel dynamics in MSF studies. However, while providing a conceptual map is a first step, testing its usefulness for MSF scholars to navigate multiple levels and streams is a necessary next step.

REFERENCES

Ackrill, Robert, and Adrian Kay. 2011. "Multiple Streams in EU Policy-Making: The Case of the 2005 Sugar Reform." *Journal of European Public Policy* 18 (1): 72–89.

Agrawala, Shardul. 1998. "Context and Early Origins of the Intergovernmental Panel on Climate Change." *Climatic Change* 39 (4): 605–20.

Alimi, Deborah. 2015. "'Going Global': Policy Entrepreneurship of the Global Commission on Drug Policy." *Public Administration* 93 (4): 874–89.

Aviram, Neomi Frisch, Nissim Cohen, and Itai Beeri. 2020. "Wind(ow) of Change: A Systematic Review of Policy Entrepreneurship Characteristics and Strategies." *Policy Studies Journal* 48 (3): 612.

Bache, Ian, and Louise Reardon. 2013. "An Idea whose Time Has Come? Explaining the Rise of Well-Being in British Politics." *Political Studies* 61 (4): 898–914.

Baek, Chanwoong. 2021. "Understanding Windows for Global Policy: An Examination of the Free-Semester Program in Korea." *Compare: A Journal of Comparative & International Education* 51 (3): 398–415.

Baumgartner, Frank R., Bryan D. Jones, and Peter B. Mortensen. 2018. "Punctuated-Equilibrium Theory: Explaining Stability and Change in Public Policymaking." In *Theories of the Policy Process*, 4th edition, eds. Christopher M. Weible and Paul A. Sabatier, 55–101. New York: Routledge.

Becker, Peter. 2019. "The reform of European cohesion policy or how to couple the streams successfully." *Journal of European Integration* 41(2): 147–68.

Benz, Arthur, Jörg Broschek, and Markus Lederer, eds. 2021. *A Research Agenda for Multilevel Governance.* Cheltenham: Edward Elgar.

Bradford, Anu. 2020. *The Brussels Effect: How the European Union Rules the World.* Oxford: Oxford University Press.

Brunner Steffen. 2008. "Understanding Policy Change: Multiple Streams and Emissions Trading in Germany." *Global Environmental Change Part A: Human & Policy Dimensions* 18 (3): 501–07.

Bolukbasi, H. Tolga, and Deniz Yildirim. 2022. "Institutions in the Politics of Policy Change: Who Can Play, How They Play in Multiple Streams." *Journal of Public Policy*, doi:10.1017/S0143814X2100026X.

Cairney, Paul 2009. "The Role of Ideas in Policy Transfer: The case of UK Smoking Bans since Devolution." *Journal of European Public Policy* 16(3), 471–88.

Cairney, Paul, and Michael D. Jones. 2016. "Kingdon's Multiple Streams Approach: What Is the Empirical Impact of This Universal Theory?" *Policy Studies Journal* 44 (1): 37–58.

Cairney, Paul, and Mikine Yamazaki. 2018. "A Comparison of Tobacco Policy in the UK and Japan: If the Scientific Evidence is Identical, Why Is There a Major Difference in Policy?" *Journal of Comparative Policy Analysis: Research and Practice* 20 (3): 253–68.

Cairney, Paul and Nikolaos Zahariadis. 2016. "Multiple Streams Approach: A Flexible Metaphor Presents An Opportunity to Operationalize Agenda Setting Processes." In Nikolaos Zahariadis, ed., *Handbook of Public Policy Agenda Setting*. Cheltenham: Edward Elgar, 87–105.

Derwort, Pim, Nicolas Jager, and Jens Newig. 2021. "How to Explain Major Policy Change Towards Sustainability? Bringing Together the Multiple Streams Framework and the Multilevel Perspective on Socio-Technical Transitions to Explore the German 'Energiewende'." *Policy Studies Journal*, 50 (3): 671–99.

Dolowitz, David P., and David Marsh. 2012. "The Future of Policy Transfer Research." *Political Studies Review* 10: 339–45.

Du, Coco Dijia, and Erik Baark. 2021. "The Emergence of Environmental Policy in China: Multiple Streams and the Shaping of a Technocratic Bias." *China: An International Journal* 19 (4): 32–51.

Fisher, Susannah. 2012. "Policy Storylines in Indian Climate Politics: Opening New Political Spaces?" *Environment & Planning C: Government & Policy* 30 (1): 109–27.

Gerlak, Andrea. K. and Tania Heikkila. 2011. "Building a Theory of Learning in Collaboratives: Evidence from the Everglades Restoration Program." *Journal of Public Administration Research and Theory* 21 (4): 619–44.

Goyal, Nihit. 2021. "Policy Diffusion through Multiple Streams: The (Non-)Adoption of Energy Conservation Building Code in India." *Policy Studies Journal* 50 (3): 641–69.

Haas, Peter M. 1992. "Introduction: Epistemic Communities and International Policy Coordination." *International Organization* 46 (1): 1–35.

Herweg, Nicole. 2017. *European Union Policy-Making: The Regulatory Shift in Natural Gas Market Policy*. Basingstoke, UK: Palgrave Macmillan.

Herweg, Nicole, Christian Huß, and Reimut Zohlnhöfer. 2015. "Straightening the Three Streams: Theorising Extensions of the Multiple Streams Framework." *European Journal of Political Research* 54 (3): 435–49.

Herweg, Nicole, Nikolaos Zahariadis, and Reimut Zohlnhöfer. 2018. "The Multiple Streams Framework: Foundations, Refinements, and Empirical Applications." In *Theories of the Policy Process*, 4th edition, eds. Christopher M. Weible and Paul A. Sabatier, 17–53. New York: Routledge.

Hoe, Connie, Daniela C. Rodriguez, Yeşim Üzümcüoğlu, and Adnan A. Hyder. 2016. "Quitting like a Turk: How Political Priority Developed for Tobacco Control in Turkey." *Social Science & Medicine* 165: 36–45.

Jenkins-Smith, Hank C., Daniel Nohrstedt, Christopher M. Weible, and Karin Ingold. 2018. "The Advocacy Coalition Framework: An Overview of the Research Program." In *Theories of the Policy Process*, 4th edition, eds. Christopher M. Weible and Paul A. Sabatier, 135–71. New York: Routledge.

Jones, Michael D., Holly L. Peterson, Jonathan J. Pierce, J. J., Nicole Herweg, Amiel Bernal, Holly Lamberta Raney, and Nikolaos Zahariadis. 2016. "A River Runs through It: A Multiple Streams Meta-Review." *Policy Studies Journal* 44 (1): 13–36.

Jordan, Andrew, Harro van Asselt, Frans Berkhout, David Huitema, and Tim Rayner. 2012. "Understanding the Paradoxes of Multilevel Governing: Climate Change Policy in the European Union." *Global Environmental Politics* 12 (2): 43–66.

Kingdon, John W. 2003. *Agendas, Alternatives, and Public Policies*. 2nd edition. HarperCollins College.

Knaggård, Åsa. 2015. "The Multiple Streams Framework and the Problem Broker." *European Journal of Political Research* 54 (3): 450–65.

Knaggård, Åsa and Roger Hildingsson. Forthcoming. "The Swedish Carbon Tax Revisited: Multiple Streams Cutting across Policy Areas and Political Levels." Policy Studies Journal, in review.

Lips, Wouter. 2020. "The EU Commission's Digital Tax Proposals and Its Cross-Platform Impact in the EU and the OECD." *Journal of European Integration* 42 (7): 975–90.

Lovell, Heather. 2016. "The Role of International Policy Transfer within the Multiple Streams Approach: The Case of Smart Electricity in Australia." *Public Administration* 94 (3): 754–68.

Lovell, Heather. 2017. "Mobile Policies and Policy Streams: The Case of Smart Metering Policy in Australia." *Geoforum* 81: 100–08.

Moyson, Stéphane. 2017. "Cognition and Policy Change: The Consistency of Policy Learning in the Advocacy Coalition Framework." *Policy and Society* 36 (2): 320–44.

Oborn, Eivor, Michael Barrett, and Mark Exworthy. 2011. "Policy Entrepreneurship in the Development of Public Sector Strategy: The Case of London Health Reform." *Public Administration* 89 (2): 325–44.

Pi Ferrer, Laia and Pertti Alasuutari, 2019. "The Spread and Domestication of the Term 'Austerity:' Evidence from the Portuguese and Spanish Parliaments." *Politics & Policy*, 47 (6): 1039–65.

Rietig, Katharina. 2021. "Multilevel Reinforcing Dynamics: Global Climate Governance and European Renewable Energy Policy." *Public Administration* 99 (1): 55–71.

Rozbicka, Patrycja, and Florian Spohr. 2016. "Interest Groups in Multiple Streams: Specifying Their Involvement in the Framework." *Policy Sciences* 49 (1): 55–69.

Samadi, Sascha. 2018. "The Experience Curve Theory and its Application in the Field of Electricity Generation Technologies – A Literature Review." *Renewable and Sustainable Energy Reviews* 82: 2346–64.

Santos, Íris, and Jaakko Kauko. 2022. "Externalisations in the Portuguese Parliament: Analysing Power Struggles and (De-)Legitimation with Multiple Streams Approach." *Journal of Education Policy* 37 (3): 399–418.

Shephard, Daniel D., Anne Ellersiek, Johannes Meuer, Christian Rupietta, Ruth Mayne, and Paul Cairney. 2021. "Kingdon's Multiple Streams Approach in New Political Contexts: Consolidation, Configuration, and New Findings." *Governance* 34 (2): 523.

Skovgaard, Jakob. 2014. "EU Climate Policy after the Crisis." *Environmental Politics* 23 (1): 1–17.

Skovgaard, Jakob, and Sofía Sachs Ferrari. 2022. "The Unlikely Mexican Carbon Tax – A Question of Economic-Environmental Synergies?" *Journal of Environmental Planning & Management.* https://doi.org/10.1080/09640568.2022.2081136.

Stone, Diane. 2012. "Transfer and Translation of Policy." *Policy Studies* 33 (6): 483–99.

Zahariadis, Nikolaos. 2005. *Essence of Political Manipulation: Emotion, Institutions, and Greek Foreign Policy.* New York: Peter Lang.

Zahariadis, Nikolaos. 2008. "Ambiguity and Choice in European Public Policy." *Journal of European Public Policy* 15 (4): 514–30.

Zohlnhöfer, Reimut. 2007. "Entstaatlichungspolitik: Die Liberalisierung und Privatisierung des Telekommunikationssektors in Deutschland und Großbritannien." In *Der Wohlfahrtsstaat: Eine Einführung in den Historischen und Internationalen,* eds. Manfred G. Schmidt, Tobias Ostheim, Nico A. Siegel, and Reimut Zohlnhöfer, 389–406. Vergleich, Wiesbaden: Verlag für Sozialwissenschaften.

Zohlnhöfer, Reimut, Nicole Herweg, and Christian Huß. 2016. "Bringing Formal Political Institutions into the Multiple Streams Framework: An Analytical Proposal for Comparative Policy Analysis." *Journal of Comparative Policy Analysis* 18 (3): 243–56.

5. The beating heart of the Multiple Streams Framework: Coupling as a process

Dana A. Dolan and Sonja Blum

THE BEATING HEART OF THE MSF: COUPLING AS A PROCESS

Coupling lies at the heart of Kingdon's argument about "what makes an idea's time come" (1995, 1), in other words, why an issue gains or loses status on the policy agenda.[1] Using the analogy of a space launch, Kingdon (1995, 166) described the moment of time when the "all systems go" command arrives. After a lengthy period of preparation for launch, hearts race as all hopes and fears about the mission's goals, the rocket's structural integrity, and the favorability of launch conditions converge. Another apt metaphor for the coupling process in the Multiple Streams Framework (MSF) is the beating heart. It both alludes to the range of feelings that policy process participants may hold and is a symbol of the dynamic center of a system that brings a set of interrelated processes to life. Without coupling as the central heart of the policy process, the three evolving streams of problems, policies, and politics serve no larger purpose. Indeed, the answer to the question, "what makes an idea's time come?" is not found in any one stream, but in the convergence of activities that take place during the metaphorical launch window that enables a policy decision.

Yet discussions about the MSF typically highlight the visual metaphor of evolving streams rather than the more abstract notion of their confluence. Using the space launch metaphor, this would be analogous to prioritizing attention to launch preparations while ignoring the countdown and liftoff. Recent theoretical reviews have lamented the MSF's underdeveloped conceptual status (Cairney and Jones 2016, 49; Cairney and Zahariadis 2016, 100–01), specifically highlighting coupling as one of its most theoretically challenging aspects (Greer 2015, 417, 422–23). When coupling is addressed, authors tend to repeat Kingdon's metaphorical language (i.e., changes in problem or political streams opened windows of opportunity for policy entrepreneurs to couple the streams). This language, while memorable and convenient for veteran MSF researchers, can be impenetrable to those new to the MSF. Thus, advancing a more reflective use and understanding of this concept can advance the MSF's theoretical development and further efforts to accumulate knowledge across case studies (Cairney and Zahariadis 2016; Jones et al. 2016). Empirically, it can enrich analyses of specific cases by illuminating how issues rise on the policy agenda or are blocked from consideration, how policies are designed and packaged, and how they fare once they are up for consideration.

In light of these goals, we focus on *conceptualizing* the notion of coupling as the critical research task that precedes operationalization. Following Adcock and Collier (2001), we recognize the iterative nature of research by treating Kingdon's initial formulations of concepts as the basis for transforming (less precise) *background concepts* into *systematized concepts* while also modifying systematized concepts through *friendly amendments*. Essentially, systematized concepts are analytically useful definitions that aim to capture the full meaning of a concept. In contrast, operationalization produces indicators that tend to reduce a concept's full range of meaning(s) to assist scholars in efficiently measuring concepts. For example, recent scholarship suggests operationalizing coupling activities through evidence identified in a variety of sources, including interviews with policy participants (Zohlnhöfer, Herweg, and Zahariadis 2022, 38–39). Our choice to focus on conceptualization recognizes both the challenge of identifying context-specific indicators that are equivalent across diverse contexts, and the diverse ontological and epistemological commitments of MSF scholars (for a discussion, see Ritter and Lancaster 2018).

We begin by reinterpreting Kingdon's metaphorical description of coupling in analytic terms, then build on the foundational MSF literature to propose a systematic conceptualization of *coupling as a process* that is equal in importance to the three streams of problems, policies, and politics. Along the way, we suggest fruitful areas for future research. Next, we present recent theoretical advances that deserve more widespread attention, including testing in other contexts and further conceptual refinement. These selected works do not represent a full literature review; however, we recommend this as future research. We conclude by summarizing our main points and highlighting the value of methodological diversity in furthering the MSF's conceptual development.

THE FOUNDATIONS OF COUPLING

The concept of coupling in policy processes was originally developed in 1984, in the first edition of Kingdon's *Agendas, Alternatives, and Public Policies*. Below, we embrace its descriptive metaphors of flowing streams (processes) and windows that open and close (opportunities for change) to establish an intuitive understanding of the process. Next, we clarify these ideas by drawing on Dolan's (2021) analytic interpretation of Kingdon's ideas. Together, these perspectives lay the foundation for a Kingdonian understanding of coupling that we build on in later sections.

The Process Behind the Metaphor

Kingdon describes three streams or processes (problems, policies, and politics). Each evolves according to its own logic and timing, sometimes oblivious to developments in other streams and other times interacting in important ways. The most dramatic interaction occurs during an opportune period called a *policy window*, when an advocate called a *policy entrepreneur* successfully presents their favored policy alternative as a solution to a salient problem at a time when policymakers' attention to an issue is high. This linking activity is the *coupling process*. As a process, coupling is analytically distinct from the activity's outcome and the actors involved. If the policy entrepreneur is successful, the linked issue package will rise from the governmental agenda to the decision agenda where busy policymakers will devote some part of their limited attention to making an authoritative decision. The decision itself may vary, e.g., a legislative bill may be adopted or fail; a regulation may be blocked or put into effect. The decision may be delayed, or may never arrive, leaving the issue to recede from the agenda. Alternatively, if an attempted coupling fails, the issue package of connected problems, solutions, and political considerations can be reconfigured to try again. Kingdon emphasized this "loosely coupled" nature of the system (Kingdon 1995, 229, 173), using metaphorical verbs that suggest coupled streams could be easily uncoupled and reconfigured: "streams are *coupled* as if they were boxcars on a train track; *linked* to each other as if making a chain; and *hooked* like fish on an angler's pole" (Dolan 2021, 170).

Coupling as Stream Interactions: Complete and Partial Couplings

Kingdon described at least two types of interactions between streams. The *complete coupling* of all three streams is the core dynamic in the MSF, while *partial couplings* occur when two of the three streams interact (Dolan, 2021). Figure 5.1 uses the streams metaphor to depict three kinds of partial couplings, and one complete coupling. Figure 5.2 reinterprets the process analytically, employing a Venn diagram to illustrate a partial coupling of the policy and problem streams, that is then linked to the political stream for a complete coupling.

While the streams metaphor suggests that partial couplings appear and disappear over time until a complete coupling occurs, an analytic perspective

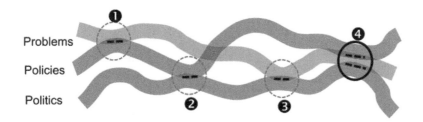

"At points along the way, there are partial couplings: solutions to problems, but without a receptive political climate ❶; politics to proposals, but without a sense that a compelling problem is being solved ❷; politics and problems both calling for action, but without an available alternative to advocate ❸. But the complete joining of all three streams ❹ dramatically enhances the odds that a subject will become firmly fixed on a decision agenda." (Kingdon 1995:202)

Source: Dolan (2021).

Figure 5.1   Complete and partial couplings of MSF Streams

clarifies that all three types of partial couplings can coexist, mirroring the complex web of connections among real-world problems, potential solutions, and political opportunities. This notion of partial couplings helps clarify the extent to which Kingdon's problem, policy, and political streams are independent.

The Not-So-Independent Streams

Empirical scholars continue to (re)discover that the streams are not always independent, despite Zahariadis' (2007, 2014) explanation of *stream independence* being a conceptual device and a heuristic assumption. In fact, this debate has a long history that began with the first edition of Kingdon's Agendas book. In this book's second edition, Kingdon attempted to address this confusion: "Even on reflection, I still think these streams flow along largely on their own, each according to dynamics not much related to the others" (Kingdon 1995, 228). In other words, stream dynamics are "largely", but not fully independent. He subsequently illustrated their interdependence with two examples. Streams interact when participants attempt to couple the streams by constructing solutions (in the policy stream) that aim to solve issues (in the problem stream). They also interact when participants develop policies (in the policy stream) to protect bureaucratic turf or pursue organized groups'

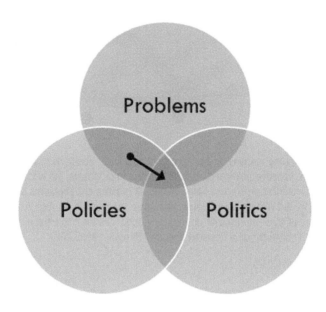

Source: Dolan (2021).

Figure 5.2   Transforming a partial coupling into a complete coupling

economic interests (in the political stream). These are prime examples of Kingdon's partial couplings.

Thus, the key to understanding stream independence – the times that streams do not interact – is understanding when they do interact via complete couplings or partial couplings. Although participants may be active in more than one stream without prompting stream interactions, it is only when they success-fully couple two or more streams that streams interact. Furthermore, partial couplings may be quite common, as Kingdon noted: "Couplings are attempted often, and not just close to the time of final enactment" (1995, 229). The fre-quency and impact of these partial couplings is an empirical question that can refocus scholars' attention away from debates about stream (in)dependence and toward analyzing stream interactivity.

Coupling as a Core MFS Process

Three recent meta-reviews of studies suggest that many MFS concepts are unclear to empirical scholars. Indeed, a comprehensive analysis of 311 peer-reviewed MSF applications (Jones et al. 2016), found that only about a third mentioned all five structural elements: the three streams of problems, policies, and politics; plus the policy window and policy entrepreneurs (see Zahariadis 2014). Moreover, very few applications engaged with the subcomponents of these structural elements. This led the study authors to conclude that the overall MSF research program was "disturbingly incoherent" and in need of "more systematic theory development" (Jones et al. 2016, 31). Among the suggestions for improving this situation, Cairney and Jones (2016, 52) called for more conceptual development, noting that "what qualifies as an MS[F] major component is likely contestable." We take this comment to heart.

To help close the gap between MSF theory and empirical practice, this chapter attends to the dynamics of coupling as a process by reexamining the MSF's conceptual specification, including its core concepts and selected subcomponents. Specifically, although the process of coupling is partially captured in the policy windows concept, windows merely represent opportunities for coupling. And while window subcomponents (like *coupling logic*, as explained below) allude to the process, they do not fully explain it. Furthermore, while the policy entrepreneur concept illuminates the actor engaged in coupling activities, characterstics that make these actors successful at coupling, like persistence and access, also fall short for describing the coupling process itself. In sum, the concepts of policy windows and policy entrepreneurs do not fully capture the dynamic process of coupling.

Against that backdrop, our revised conceptual model characterizes coupling as a core MSF process. Our proposal aligns with Kingdon's presentation of the MSF as a complex process model that is divided into several subprocesses. Most visible are the three processes in which problems, policies, and politics evolve over time, semi-independently, while at times coming together through a fourth process called coupling. We follow Kingdon in making a clear distinction between processes and participants. This is because policy entrepreneurs can be active in many and perhaps all of the four core MSF processes, regardless of their position "in or out of government, in elected or appointed positions, in interest groups or research organizations" (Kingdon 1995, 122). Indeed, Kingdon complements his lengthy discussions of policy entrepreneurs' activities in the policy stream and the coupling process (in chapters 6 and 8, respectively) with more succinct descriptions of their roles in the problem stream (e.g., Kingdon 1995, 115) and political stream (e.g., Kingdon 1995, 149, 151). Figure 5.3 follows Kingdon's lead and builds on Zahariadis' (2014) overview. It emphasizes the coupling process while incorporating its signature feature, the policy window, as one of its subcomponents. Although the policy entrepreneur is not represented visually in this processual view of the MSF, the activities of this central actor are captured within the subcomponents of coupling. Finally, we retain the remaining structural elements of the problem, policy, and political streams (along with their existing subcomponents, not shown here).

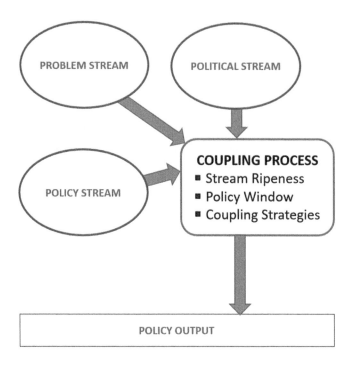

Source: Authors.

Figure 5.3   Revised MSF conceptual diagram incorporating coupling as a process

By realigning the MSF's conceptual diagram with Kingdon's original speci-fication, this refined conceptualization clarifies the coupling process as a core component and responds to the critiques of recent meta-reviews mentioned earlier. The next section examines the subcomponents of the coupling process shown in Figure 5.3.

CORE SUBCOMPONENTS OF COUPLING

Whereas the preceding section laid the foundation for understanding coupling, particularly for those new to the MSF, this section raises the structure of the conceptual house by examining its three subcomponents: *stream ripeness*, *policy windows*, and *coupling strategies*. In doing so, we incorporate as friendly amendments those well-established theoretical advancements that fit easily with the foundations, that help fill important gaps, and that have proven useful in diverse empirical MSF applications.

Stream Ripeness

Coupling is more likely to occur when the three streams are *ripe*, meaning each is primed for coupling to other streams. Determining when a stream is ripe, however, is no simple matter because stream ripeness, like the notion of coupling itself, is a metaphor. Visible indicators often exist, yet ripeness itself is a subjective interpretation of a situation, making it a perception that policy entrepreneurs can attempt to influence as part of the coupling process. Below, we discuss what constitutes stream ripeness for each stream.

Problem stream ripeness
The life of an issue begins as a condition out in the world, with no causal force in the policy process. The condition is interpreted as a problem only when it compares unfavorably with a preferred condition. Second, for it to become a public problem, its resolution must entail government (versus private) intervention. In addition, a third aspect of problem stream ripeness elevates a subset of concerns above the universe of "all" public problems the government could potentially address.

As a socially constructed concept, analysts must understand whose perspective matters in assessing problem stream ripeness. Zohlnhöfer and colleagues (2022, 31) highlight policymakers' perceptions when they operationalize problem stream ripeness. They advise researchers to identify which indicators, focusing events, and/or feedback offer evidence that problem brokers framed conditions as problematic and subsequently attracted policymakers' attention. Another possibility is that ripeness emerges earlier, when a problem broker's framing of a problematic issue successfully dominates the policy sphere (Knaggård 2015). Kingdon's perspective on whose perspective matters is expansive, referring most often to "[important] people in and around government" (p. 90, 91, 114), while occasionally mentioning "government officials" (p. 113), "decision makers and those close to them" (p. 91), and even "public and governmental attention" (p. 115). Indeed, the relevant actors may differ depending on the issue, because some issues are highly visible and important to the mass public, others only relevant to attentive publics, and some merely attracting a few specialists as "policies without publics" (May 1991).

We adopt an expansive view by conceptualizing problem stream ripeness as a perception held by important people in and around government that a condition qualifies as a problem requiring government intervention, based on their subjective assessment of several problem stream factors, including indicators, focusing events, and policy feedback. Future research could assess the empirical literature to understand how scholars have conceptualized and operationalized problem stream ripeness in practice, including evidence regarding which actors appear most influential.

Policy stream ripeness

The policy stream is ripe when at least one proposal has been refined in enough detail to draw support from policy community experts as a viable alternative. Here, *viability* means the proposal meets all three criteria for survival: (1) it is technically possible to implement the proposal (*technical feasibility*); (2) it aligns with the prevailing values of policy community members (*value acceptability*); and (3) it is likely to withstand anticipated threats against its adoption (*future constraints*, i.e., *budget constraints* meaning whether the financial cost of the proposal falls within an acceptable range, *public acquiescence* meaning whether the public is unlikely to object to the proposal, and *politicians' receptivity* meaning whether elected officials are likely to support the proposal) (Kingdon 1995, 131–39). To be sure, policy entrepreneurs may advocate for nonviable proposals as part of an effort to acclimate or *soften up* policy experts to a new idea, perhaps with the intent to spark further proposal development (Kingdon 1995, 127–31). Similarly, politicians may advance nonviable proposals for political reasons, such as gaining publicity and building their reputation (Kingdon 1995, 38–40) or signaling commitment to uphold campaign promises (Kingdon 1995, 62–63). Thus, it bears repeating that proposal viability is evaluated by policy community experts.

Because the policy community is a collective entity, multiple viable proposals may compete for experts' support. Analysts must consider this competition as well as the degree of *community fragmentation* when assessing policy stream ripeness (Kingdon 1995, 118–20). Zohlnhöfer and colleagues (2022, 33) take this into account in operationalizing policy stream ripeness as occurring when most policy experts are no longer undecided but have made up their minds to support one or another proposal (though not necessarily the *same* proposal). We add that if subsets of experts support several viable policy options – regardless of whether they compete with or complement each other – the policy stream is still considered ripe. However, an abundance of viable options may influence the coupling process by contributing to *window overload*, as discussed below.

Political stream ripeness

In the political stream, aspects of the political environment influence policymakers' receptivity to pursuing policy change. Specifically, policymakers attend to shifts in the *national mood*, *organized interests*, and *events within the government* (Kingdon 1995; Zahariadis 2014). Sometimes all three of these elements favor change, indicating the political stream is ripe and ready for coupling. At other times, all three elements are opposed, and the stream is clearly not ripe. And when these three elements pull in different directions, "participants somehow total them up and arrive at a balance, or a notion of the preponderance of pressure in the political stream" (Kingdon 1995, 163–64). Exactly how policymakers total up the three elements of political pressure is unclear with one exception: as Kingdon repeatedly emphasized (1995, 20, 164, 199), when an election (an event in the government) coincides with a national mood favoring increased government intervention, their combined force can have an extremely powerful impact on the policy agenda, overcoming even strong opposition from organized interests. Future research may aim to understanding the preponderance of pressure in the political stream beyond the election-mood combination.

Political stream ripeness can be conceptualized as policymakers' receptivity to attending to an issue based on their interpretation of the preponderance of political pressures stemming from shifts in the national mood, organized interests, and governmental events. Zohlnhöfer and colleagues (2022, 36) have operationalized political stream ripeness (during agenda-setting) as the willingness of a political entrepreneur to sponsor or support a proposal through the decision-making stage.

Future research might consider the extent to which stream ripeness may influence the strength of coupling and reduce the likelihood of later decoupling (as we discuss below).

Policy Windows

The *policy window* metaphor represents a fleeting opportunity for policy entrepreneurs to attempt to couple the streams and elevate their issue or problem on the policy agenda (Kingdon 1995, 166). As such, policy windows do not possess agency: they open and close with little effect unless coupling is successful. Notably, Jones et al.'s (2016) metareview found that policy windows were more popular than any other MSF concept, however studies rarely employed the subcomponents of *coupling logic*, *decision style*, and *institutional context*. In light of their findings and our close reading of the foundational MSF literature, we propose three alternative subcomponents that capture the key subprocesses: *window openings*, *window overload*, and *window closures*. We incorporate coupling logic in our discussion of window openings (below), then consider the role of decision style and institutional context in a later section on coupling strategies.

Window openings

According to the foundational literature, policy windows "open infrequently, and do not stay open long" (Kingdon 1995, 166); they are "scarce, ephemeral, and sometimes predictable" (Zahariadis 2003, 70). Of course, these terms are relative. Indeed, Kingdon described windows that remained open for two years, while predictable windows like program renewals seem to be frequent occurrences. Yet, it is widely agreed that when a policy window opens, it can have a dramatic effect on the policy agenda by prioritizing attention to certain issues over others, depending on their fit with the circumstances that opened the window (Kingdon 1995, 173–75).

Two types of policy windows are commonly recognized. Developments in the problem stream open *problem windows*. These *political windows* encourage *consequential coupling logic*, where problems incentivize participants to seek viable solutions (Zahariadis 2003, 72).Thus, ideas that can be reasonably seen as solutions to the problem that opened that window move ahead in the decision queue. Alternatively, a window may open due to developments in the political stream. These *political windows* encourage *doctrinal coupling logic*, where solutions prompt a search for problems that can be used to justify their selection (Zahariadis 2003, 72). Thus, ideas that appear responsive to the political pressures that opened the window will be prioritized.

In addition to problem and political windows, we coin the term *spillover windows* to identify occasions when a successful coupling in one policy arena opens a window for a related subject (Kingdon 1995, 190–94). Furthermore, we suggest that these precedent-setting windows spark *opportunistic coupling logic* when entrepreneurial policymakers seek the credit-claiming and publicity benefits that can be gained from transferring successful policies to new arenas. Notable research that engages with spillover notions include Ackrill and Kay's (2011) distinction between exogenous and endogenous spillover effects, and Copeland and James (2014) notion of the reverse of a spillover, or *spillback*. Further analysis is needed to understand spillover windows, both conceptually and in empirical practice.

Window overload

Regardless of how the window opens, coupling is more likely to be successful during open policy windows. Sensing this opportunity, policy entrepreneurs rush to take advantage of it. *Window overload* occurs when the capacity of the policy system is overwhelmed by the number of problems and solutions clamoring for attention, restricting participants' attention to a subset of ideas despite many others having fully ripened streams (Kingdon 1995, 184–86). Overload is a *natural* consequence of entrepreneurial competition during open windows. Additionally, it can be pursued *strategically* in an effort to thwart policy action (Kingdon 1995, 176; see also Winkel and Leipold 2016, 123).

So, problems and solutions are abundant, yet "people in and around govern-ment also find themselves coming up against a series of constraints. If the costs of paying attention are too high, otherwise worthy items are prevented from becoming prominent" (Kingdon 1995, 88).

Of note, Zahariadis introduced a related system capacity notion of *problem load*, referring to the number of difficult problems occupying the attention of policy makers (2003, 154). Like Kingdon, he was inspired by Cohen, March, and Olsen's (1972) garbage can theory, suggesting that future work to clarify the relationship between these concepts would be a valuable addition to MSF theory.

Window closures
When windows close, the issues they prioritized in the decision-making queue may lose their status. Windows can close for at least four reasons (Kingdon 1995, 169–70). First, when an issue is addressed, participants naturally shift their attention to other issues. Second, when efforts fail to bear fruit, partic-ipants may reserve their political capital and resources for less challenging opportunities. Third, the circumstances that opened a window may change again (e.g., the urgency of a crisis fades, once-abundant resources are depleted, or additional turnover displaces newly arrived personnel who were receptive to an issue). Finally, without a viable policy option, windows will likely close even in the presence of strong political pressures to address pressing problems. Future research to enrich the MSF's conceptual framework could explore how empirical scholars understand and detect window closures.

Coupling Strategies

The first two subcomponents of the coupling process – whether or not streams are ripe, and a policy window is open – set the stage for action, although there are no guarantees. Metaphorically, this is the launch window, when the stars are aligned, and all systems are "go". Policy entrepreneurs compete to push their problems and proposals into prominence on the agenda. Will they argue that their concern is a pressing problem, advocate that their proposal is at least a partial solution, or broker support for their priorities in response to a changed political situation? How will they handle competition from other policy entre-preneurs pushing their own alternatives? How these questions are answered determines the nature of the coupling process and influences its outcomes. The approaches available to policy entrepreneurs comprise the coupling process's final component, coupling strategies.

Coupling strategies as a distinct type of entrepreneurial strategy

Coupling strategies are patterns of action intentionally employed by policy entrepreneurs to create partial and complete couplings. Like all strategies, they represent actions aimed at shifting future developments toward a preferred goal and are distinct from the actors who select and deploy them. In the MSF, that actor is the policy entrepreneur, whose goal is to couple the streams in such a way that their preferred problem definition or policy alternative is part of the final package that policymakers prioritize for attention and (ideally) adopt as official policy. From this perspective, the proximate goal of coupling the streams is a necessary condition for the ultimate goal of proposal acceptance. Yet they need not wait until a window is open to begin the process of coupling; partial couplings can help ripen the streams in advance.

Policy entrepreneurs are crucial for coupling the streams (Zahariadis 2014, 35–36, 38–40), yet not all entrepreneurial strategies they employ qualify as coupling strategies. For example, some strategies seek to ripen the problem stream e.g., those used by problem brokers to frame conditions as public problems (Knaggård 2015). Others attempt to ripen the policy stream, such as "floating trial balloons" (Kingdon 1995, 129–30) to gauge potential resistance to a new idea. Still others aim to ripen the political stream, e.g., building coalitions of support for a proposal (Herweg, Huß, and Zohlnhöfer 2015). Beyond these *stream-ripening strategies*, policy entrepreneurs may employ *capacity-building strategies* for networking and developing expertise. While obviously important, stream-ripening and capacity-building strategies support processes beyond this chapter's scope.

Coupling strategies in MSF scholarship

Kingdon sprinkled examples of coupling strategies throughout his text, and many have been elaborated on in recent scholarship. For example, risk-averse policymakers may be persuaded to support a dramatic or costly policy solution by breaking it up into incremental steps (Kingdon 1995, 80). This strategy relates to *salami tactics* (Zahariadis 2003) and *concessions* (Herweg, Huß, and Zohlnhöfer 2015) in that they build political support by shrinking the size and scope of a proposal, at least temporarily. A second example builds political support for a weak proposal aimed at blocking a more burdensome solution (Kingdon 1995, 103–04). This strategy is a variation of *policy commissioning* (Ackrill and Kay 2011), where policymakers act entrepreneurially by selecting an available policy in response to a political need. A third example involves coalition-building to raise political receptivity by "giving people their pet provisions in return for support" (Kingdon 1995, 160). This strategy is related to *package deals* (Herweg, Huß, and Zohlnhöfer 2015) and *issue linking* (e.g., Brouwer and Biermann 2011; Zahariadis and Exadaktylos 2016; Dolan 2021), because it obtains support by expanding the size and scope of a proposal. Each of these examples suggests a partial coupling – for example, building receptivity in the political stream by modifying a proposal in the policy stream, and only later tying in the problem stream as justification for policy actions.

The list above includes strategies employed in a variety of policy process stages (suggesting additional research, beyond the scope of this chapter), yet it is far from a comprehensive survey. Zahariadis (2003, 2005) expanded the list by proposing that policy selection could be manipulated through *framing* (representing policy images as gains or losses from the status quo), *symbols* (arousing emotional responses), and *affect priming* (leveraging preexisting moods). More recently, Zahariadis and Exadaktylos (2016) added *institutional rule manipulation* (including network management and venue shopping) and *side payments* (coalition building through policy designs that incorporate payments and sanctions) to the list.

The coupling strategies mentioned above only scratch the surface of opportunities to enhance our understanding of coupling. Building on Petridou and Mintrom's (2021) suggestion for future research regarding the contexts in which strategies are deployed, one valuable direction would explore whether and how *decision styles* and *institutional contexts* influence the selection and use of coupling strategies. Another fruitful path forward would integrate the broader literature, beyond MSF, on policy entrepreneurs' strategies,. Examples include Brouwer and Huitma's (2018) differentiation among attention- and support-seeking strategies (rhetorical persuasion, exploiting focusing events); linking strategies (coalition building, issue linking); relational management strategies (networking, trust building); and arena strategies (venue shopping, timing). Such an endeavor could disentangle which strategies are useful beyond the agenda-setting stage (e.g., decision-making, implementation) and for purposes other than coupling (e.g., stream-ripening, capacity-building).

Future research on the coupling process could consider the necessity and sufficiency of the these subcomponents for the prospects of coupling success. Several research questions immediately come to mind: Must all three streams be ripe for an issue before coupling can take place? Dolan (2021), for example, suggests that this expectation can be relaxed for specific sets of linked issues. Must an appropriate coupling strategy be employed by policy entrepreneurs? Alternatively, particular circumstances or luck could favor success despite the use of inappropriate strategies. Must a policy window be open (and not overloaded) before coupling can occur? This last question is particularly challenging since open policy windows are difficult to identify prospectively. Interrogating the subcomponents in this way would illuminate how they act together to facilitate coupling.

RECENT THEORETICAL ADVANCES ON COUPLING

Recent scholarship holds promise for developing sophisticated analyses of coupling. Rather than being fully established MSF extensions, these theoretical advancements comprise various levels of maturity, offering fruitful opportunities for researchers to refine concepts, identify scope conditions, and examine implications.

Widening the Applicability of Coupling Across the Policy Cycle

The MSF has been extended beyond agenda-setting, with implications for the coupling process. One approach extends the MSF to explain decision-making without requiring any modifications to the framework (Zahariadis 2003). At the agenda-setting stage, successfully coupling the streams means that the issue currently on the governmental agenda moves to the decision agenda where it will get serious attention from policymakers. Successful coupling at the decision-making stage means that the issue currently on the decision agenda moves into the implementation stage, for example, as adopted legislation or enacted executive order. With this approach to extending the MSF beyond agenda-setting, the only implication for the coupling process is a change in the outcome of successfully coupling the streams. In cases where policy agendas and decisions evolve rapidly or are highly intertwined, this approach is straightforward to apply and interpret.

Other scholars recommend changes with more substantial implications for coupling. Herweg, Huß, and Zohlnhöfer (2015) improve the analytic distinction between agenda-setting and decision-making by conceptualizing two windows and, subsequently, two coupling processes. In this two-window MSF model, the first stage is *agenda coupling*, and the policy entrepreneur's goal is to join the streams during an open *agenda window*. If successful, agenda coupling results in a worked-out proposal that becomes an input to the policy stream for the second window, where decision coupling takes place. Here, political entrepreneurs attempt to join the streams during an open decision window using strategies such as package deals, concessions, and manipulation that may revise a policy package to appeal to more decision makers (Zohlnhöfer, Herweg, and Huß 2016). By analytically separating agenda-setting from decision-making, the two-window coupling model can capture when an issue advances to the decision agenda yet fails to be adopted. It can also help explain the variation between a viable policy proposal developed by experts in the policy community and the version of that proposal that is ultimately adopted (Herweg, Zahariadis, and Zohlnhöfer 2018, 33).

This adaptation represents a widened approach to coupling that has been applied in a variety of democratic political contexts. This includes the supranational context of the EU (Becker 2019), the parliamentary system of Germany (Zohlnhöfer, 2016), and the presidential systems of Brazil and Uruguay (Sanjurjo 2019). Other studies offer rationales for not using the two-window MSF model, e.g., in the UK (Heaphy 2022, 229), and in advice following a transnational (US/Mexico) governance study (Koebele 2021, 613). Future research could investigate the conditions under which the two-window model is preferable over a simpler one-window MSF model. Relatedly, the two-window model's applicability to diverse political systems may benefit from efforts to identify the underlying institutional features that influence coupling processes.

Another approach widens the MSF even further, to account for complex interactions across the entire policy cycle. Howlett, McConnell and Perl (2016) refined a five-part framework that employs a cloth-weaving metaphor that reconceives the three familiar MSF streams as threads. During policy formulation, a *process thread* of official rules, norms, and procedures joins the mix, while a fifth *programme thread* of specific policy instruments joins during implementation. The complexity this framework embraces illuminates nuanced aspects of policymaking (e.g., the role of decision styles and institutional context) and underscores the challenge of maintaining connections between coupled elements across policy stages.

Similarly, Zahariadis and Exadaktylos (2016) associated multiple streams in the implementation stage with the notion of decoupling. The idea of elements being linked together through a coupling process already implies that these elements can be disentangled again because, over time, solutions can be seen as less-and-less fitting for a problem at hand, or because political priorities shift towards an alternate course of action. Zahariadis and Exadaktylos (2016, 77) argue that during the implementation stage, the main "aim is to prevent decoupling", and they empirically find respective decoupling strategies being employed.

These wider perspectives conceptualize coupling not as a singular moment, but rather an ongoing process that involves both joining the streams and maintaining their interconnection. To better understand coupling dynamics across all policy stages, future research will benefit from investigating the complimentary processes of decoupling and recoupling.

Deepening the Conceptual Understanding of Coupling

Another literature stream deepens our conceptual understanding of the coupling process. Following Béland (2015), Winkel and Leipold (2016) conceptualized the MSF's streams as discursive patterns: repeated logical arrangements of ideas in spoken or written language. From this perspective, policy entrepreneurs couple the streams by developing storylines that logically connect problems, policies, and politics. Highlighting the discursive nature of policy dynamics makes the coupling process visible as the "skillful strategic manipulation of perceptions" (Winkel and Leipold 2016, 122) using, e.g., emotionalization or rationalization.

Subsequently, Blum (2018, 2021) proposed the notion of *argumentative coupling*, that links problem, policy, and/or politics issues through arguments. She notes that discursive analyses of coupling often remained focused on *problem-policy* linkages with coupling logics – consequential or doctrinal coupling – taking off from the problem or policy vantage point (Zahariadis 2003). The concept of argumentative coupling proposes the existence of a third logic that complements consequential and doctrinal coupling, namely *political coupling*. If, for instance, a policy adviser proposes to address a problem (e.g., the climate crisis) because of its electoral value in swaying voters, then the politics and problem streams are argumentatively coupled (see Töller, in this volume, for an illustration of political coupling). Alternatively, a policy entrepreneur may propose a policy option (e.g., lowering taxes) to satisfy the demands of organized interests. Here the politics and policy streams are argumentatively coupled (Blum 2018). Argumentative coupling thus can illuminate the coupling process by identifying discursive evidence of linkages among all three streams – not only during open policy windows, but also as part of the softening-up process that paves the way for a successful coupling.

Separately, Dolan (2021) developed the concept of *multiple partial couplings*. Grounded in a close reading of Kingdon's partial couplings (see above), she showed that because policy issues are not processed serially, partial couplings involving separate issues may exist simultaneously, connecting various pairs of problems, policies, or political opportunities to each other. Under certain circumstances, policy entrepreneurs may employ issue-linking strategies to connect a set of partially coupled issues in a configuration that connects all three streams. Consequently, multiple partial couplings of linked issues can facilitate coupling for issues facing three adverse conditions: (1) salient problems with viable solutions that lack political receptivity; (2) politically urgent demands to address salient problems that lack viable solutions; and (3) viable solutions with high political receptivity, despite lacking salient problems. Examples of such issues abound in today's complex and ambiguous world, often involving long-term governance problems like global climate change, future pandemics, democratic erosion, and nuclear threats from aggressive states. Multiple partial couplings suggest that coupling is possible even without all streams being ripe for a particular issue. These conceptual advances were subsequently employed by Goyal (2021) to investigate program, process, and political outcomes involving solar energy policy in India.

Recognizing the compatibility of Blum's and Dolan's ideas, Möck, Vogeler, Bandelow, and Hornung (2022) combined the two. The authors see argumentative coupling as explaining the "how" of coupling (i.e., the language and logics entrepreneurs employ to link specific elements between streams), and partial coupling as illuminating the "what" of coupling (i.e., the arguments that relate streams to one another). The authors combined approach, *relational coupling*, is operationalized as discourse networks and investigated using discourse network analysis. The relational couplings notion thus offers an innovative way to operationalize coupling.

All these advancements share two common understandings of coupling. First, coupling is an interpretive act, highlighting some elements from within the streams (while ignoring others) and linking them in a specific way. These activities may be driven by political reasoning. Second, that a processual understanding of coupling is apt, highlighting the notion that coupling occurs throughout the policy process by establishing and maintaining connections between streams. These works deepen our conceptual understanding of coupling as a process while suggesting alternatives for operationalizing the concept in MSF applications.

CONCLUSION: RECONCEPTUALIZING COUPLING AS A PROCESS

This chapter has argued that coupling activities crystallize as one of four core processes in the MSF, at equal status with the three streams of problems, policies, and politics. This modification to the MSF's conceptual specification can help resolve long-standing concerns that policy windows and policy entrepreneurs are conceptually vague, making operationalization challenging (e.g., Cairney and Zahariadis 2016, 100–02). Specifically, the policy window metaphor represents the context in which participants acting in the role of policy entrepreneurs operate. Although policy windows and policy entrepreneurs are core to the MSF, they do not fully capture the dynamic process of coupling.

Our systematic (re)conceptualization of coupling highlights three subcomponents, while differentiating them from actors who play a role in the process (e.g., policy entrepreneurs). Windows constitute part of the larger coupling process that explains how interactions among (semi-independent) streams generate the context for coupling and mediate the effect of entrepreneurial activities. Beyond policy windows, we identify two additional subcomponents: stream ripeness and coupling strategies. These three subcomponents parallel the parts of the main MSF hypothesis proposed by Herweg, Zahariadis, and Zohlnhöfer (2018, 30): "Agenda change becomes more likely if (a) a policy window opens [i.e., the *policy window* subcomponent], (b) the streams are ready for coupling [i.e., the *stream ripeness* subcomponent], and (c) a policy entrepreneur promotes the agenda change [i.e., the *coupling strategy* subcomponent]." These three subcomponents elaborate the conditions under which coupling is more likely to be successful. Our clarification can assist empirical MSF scholars in identifying evidence that can be used to trace developments in the policy process, whether or not attempts to couple the streams are ultimately successful.

In sum, our reconceptualization of coupling as a core MSF process takes a step forward in refining the framework and enhancing its ability to accumulate knowledge across case studies. Future studies could build on our reconceptualization in several ways, as suggested in the sections above. In support of these, a valuable contribution could mirror Jones et al.'s (2016) meta-analysis of empirical MSF applications to understand how scholars engage with the coupling process as conceptualized in this chapter. Coupling, reconceived as a core process of the MSF, represents a fertile area for future theoretical and empirical research.

More practically and immediately, scholars can draw on these theoretically rich *Level 2 Systematized Concepts* to either refine or operationalize them as *Level 3: Indicators* in ways that are relevant to their case contexts and methodological commitments. As Adcock and Collier (2001, 534–36) discuss at length, contextual differences can threaten measurement validity, defined as "whether operationalization and the scoring of cases adequately reflect the concept the researcher seeks to measure" (p. 529). One approach to addressing this fundamental concern of contextual specificity is to develop equivalent indicators that measure systematized concepts in ways relevant for their diverse case contexts. Scholars can develop their own contextually specific indicators or employ indicators borrowed or adapted from existing studies such as those discussed above. In this chapter, we indicated several suggestions for operationalizing these concepts offered by Zohlnhöfer et al. (2022), as perhaps the first paper offering practical guidance for developing empirical MSF studies. Future research, beyond the scope of this study, could usefully expand on these suggestions.

Notably, this chapter highlighted unique insights from methodologically diverse studies. One way to build knowledge is by formulating falsifiable hypotheses, operationalizing them for a given context, and testing the resulting expectations against the evidence in an empirical case (e.g., Herweg, Huß, and Zohlnhöfer 2015). Alternative approaches employ process tracing to identify causal mechanisms to develop causal explanations of cases or to refine theory (Copeland and James 2014; Dolan 2021; Heaphy 2022). Still others employ discourse analysis of policy statements to derive insights that highlight interpretation as a strategic act in an ambiguous world (Winkel and Leipold 2016; Blum 2021; Möck et al. 2022). Indeed, methodological pluralism may hold the key to further conceptual development, and for developing richer empirical case studies using the MSF.

NOTE

1.   Our thanks go to the Editors of this book for very helpful comments on earlier versions of this chapter. We would also like to thank participants of the COPPR 2023 for valuable feedback, with particular thanks to the MSF panel discussant Rob DeLeo.

REFERENCES

Ackrill, Robert, and Adrian Kay. 2011. "Multiple Streams in EU Policy-Making: The Case of the 2005 Sugar Reform." *Journal of European Public Policy* 18 (1): 72–89.

Adcock, Robert, and David Collier. 2001. "Measurement Validity: A Shared Standard for Qualitative and Quantitative Research." *American Political Science Review* 95 (03): 529–46.

Becker, Peter. 2019. "The Reform of European Cohesion Policy or How to Couple the Streams Successfully." *Journal of European Integration* 41 (2): 147–68.

Béland, Daniel. 2015. "Kingdon Reconsidered: Ideas, Interests and Institutions in Comparative Policy Analysis." *Journal of Comparative Policy Analysis: Research and Practice* 0 (0): 1–15.

Blum, Sonja. 2018. "The Multiple-Streams Framework and Knowledge Utilization: Argumentative Couplings of Problem, Policy, and Politics Issues." *European Policy Analysis* 4(1): 94–117.

Blum, Sonja. 2021. "2. Upcycling a Trashed Policy Solution? Argumentative Couplings for Solution Definition and Deconstruction in German Pension Policy." In *The Political Formulation of Policy Solutions: Arguments, Arenas, and Coalitions*, eds. Zittoun Philippe, Fischer Frank, and Nikolaos Zahariadis. Bristol, UK: Bristol University Press, 21–44.

Brouwer, Stijn, and Frank Biermann. 2011. "Towards Adaptive Management: Examining the Strategies of Policy Entrepreneurs in Dutch Water Management." *Ecology and Society* 16 (4): 5.

Brouwer, Stijn, and Dave Huitema. 2018. "Policy Entrepreneurs and Strategies for Change." *Regional Environmental Change* 18 (5): 1259–72.

Cairney, Paul, and Michael D. Jones. 2016. "Kingdon's Multiple Streams Approach: What Is the Empirical Impact of This Universal Theory?" *Policy Studies Journal* 44 (1): 37–58.

Cairney, Paul, and Nikolaos Zahariadis. 2016. "6. Multiple Streams Approach: A Flexible Metaphor Presents an Opportunity to Operationalize Agenda Setting Processes." In *Handbook of Public Policy Agenda Setting*, Cheltenham, UK and Northampton, MA, US: Edward Elgar Publishing, 90–105.

Cohen, Michael D., James G. March, and Johan P. Olsen. 1972. "A Garbage Can Model of Organizational Choice." *Administrative Science Quarterly* 17 (1): 1–25.

Copeland, Paul, and Scott James. 2014. "Policy Windows, Ambiguity and Commission Entrepreneurship: Explaining the Relaunch of the European Union's Economic Reform Agenda." *Journal of European Public Policy* 21 (1): 1–19.

Dolan, Dana A. 2021. "Multiple Partial Couplings in the Multiple Streams Framework: The Case of Extreme Weather and Climate Change Adaptation." *Policy Studies Journal* 49 (1): 164–89.

Goyal, Nihit. 2021. "Explaining Policy Success Using the Multiple Streams Framework: Political Success Despite Programmatic Failure of the Solar Energy Policy in Gujarat, India." *Politics & Policy* 49 (5): 1021–60.

Greer, Scott L. 2015. "John W. Kingdon, Agendas, Alternatives, and Public Policies." In *The Oxford Handbook of Classics in Public Policy and Administration*, eds. Steven J. Balla, Martin Lodge, and Edward C. Page. Oxford, UK: Oxford University Press, 417–30.

Heaphy, Janina. 2022. "British Counterterrorism, the International Prohibition of Torture, and the Multiple Streams Framework." *Policy & Politics* 50 (2): 225–241.

Herweg, Nicole, Christian Huß, and Reimut Zohlnhöfer. 2015. "Straightening the Three Streams: Theorising Extensions of the Multiple Streams Framework." *European Journal of Political Research* 54 (3): 435–49.

Herweg, Nicole, Nikolaos Zahariadis, and Reimut Zohlnhöfer. 2018. "The Multiple Streams Framework: Foundations, Refinements, and Empirical Application." In *Theories of the Policy Process*, eds. Christopher M. Weible and Paul A. Sabatier. Boulder, CO: Westview Press, 17–54.

Howlett, Michael, Allan McConnell, and Anthony Perl. 2016. "Weaving the Fabric of Public Policies: Comparing and Integrating Contemporary Frameworks for the Study of Policy Processes." *Journal of Comparative Policy Analysis: Research and Practice* 18 (3): 273–89.

Jones, Michael D. et al. 2016. "A River Runs Through It: A Multiple Streams Meta-Review." *Policy Studies Journal* 44 (1): 13–36.

Kingdon, John W. 1995. *Agendas, Alternatives, and Public Policies, Second Edition.* 2nd edition. New York, NY: HarperCollins College Publishers.

Knaggård, Åsa. 2015. "The Multiple Streams Framework and the Problem Broker." *European Journal of Political Research* 54 (3): 450–65.

Koebele, Elizabeth A. 2021. "When Multiple Streams Make a River: Analyzing Collaborative Policymaking Institutions Using the Multiple Streams Framework." *Policy Sciences* 54 (3): 609–28.

May, Peter J. 1991. "Reconsidering Policy Design: Policies and Publics." *Journal of Public Policy* 11 (2): 187–206.

Möck, Malte, Colette S. Vogeler, Nils C. Bandelow, and Johanna Hornung. 2023. "Relational Coupling of Multiple Streams: The Case of COVID-19 Infections in German Abattoirs." *Policy Studies Journal.* http://onlinelibrary.wiley.com/doi/abs/10.1111/psj.12459 (February 4, 2022).

Petridou, Evangelia, and Michael Mintrom. 2021. "A Research Agenda for the Study of Policy Entrepreneurs." *Policy Studies Journal* 51 (2): 351–374.

Ritter, Alison, and Kari Lancaster. 2018. "Multiple Streams." In *Handbook on Policy, Process and Governing*, eds. H. K. Colebatch and Robert Hoppe. Cheltenham, UK, Edward Elgar Publishing.

Sanjurjo, Diego. 2019. *Gun Control Policies in Latin America.* Cham, Switzerland, Springer.

Winkel, Georg, and Sina Leipold. 2016. "Demolishing Dikes: Multiple Streams and Policy Discourse Analysis." *Policy Studies Journal* 44 (1): 108–29.

Zahariadis, Nikolaos. 2003. *Ambiguity and Choice in Public Policy: Political Decision Making in Modern Democracies.* Washington, US, Georgetown University Press.

Zahariadis, Nikolaos. 2005. *Essence of Political Manipulation: Emotion, Institutions, & Greek Foreign Policy*. New York, US, Peter Lang.

Zahariadis, Nikolaos. 2007. "The Multiple Streams Framework: Structure, Limitations, Prospects." In *Theories of the Policy Process* (2nd edition), ed. Paul A. Sabatier. Boulder, Westview Press, 65–92.

Zahariadis, Nikolaos. 2014. "Ambiguity and Multiple Streams." In *Theories of the Policy Process*, eds. Paul Sabatier and Christopher M. Weible. Boulder, CO: Westview Press, 25–58.

Zahariadis, Nikolaos, and Theofanis Exadaktylos. 2016. "Policies That Succeed and Programs That Fail: Ambiguity, Conflict, and Crisis in Greek Higher Education." *Policy Studies Journal* 44 (1): 59–82.

Zohlnhöfer, Reimut, Nicole Herweg, and Christian Huß. 2016. "Bringing Formal Political Institutions into the Multiple Streams Framework: An Analytical Proposal for Comparative Policy Analysis." *Journal of Comparative Policy Analysis: Research and Practice* 18(3): 243–56.

Zohlnhöfer, Reimut, Nicole Herweg, and Nikolaos Zahariadis. 2022. "How to Conduct a Multiple Streams Study." In *Methods of the Policy Process*, New York, US, Routledge.

6. From policy entrepreneur to policy entrepreneurship: Examining the role of context in policy entrepreneurial action

Evangelia Petridou[1]

INTRODUCTION

Theories of the policy process are tools that help us untangle the complexity of the process of public policy making. This process is defined as "the interactions that occur over time between public policies and surrounding actors, events, contexts, and outcomes" (Weible, 2018, 2), where public policies constitute the decisions (encompassing actions and non-actions) that governments – in every level of governance – make in their jurisdiction (Mintrom, 2012; Weible 2018). It follows that any theory seeking to make knowledge claims about the policy process must account for mechanisms linking actors (agency) and structure, albeit to different degrees of emphasis. Indeed, the problem of agency and structure, a long-standing research conundrum in political science, refers to the difficulties developing a theory that adequately accounts for both the agentic power of actors and the structural factors that enable or constrain the actions of these actors. Agents are embedded in institutional contexts which qualify their actions, whereas structures are constantly reproducing themselves (Bogason 2000; Giddens 1984; for an extended discussion, see Petridou 2017).

The Multiple Streams Framework (MSF) is a theory of the policy process that foregrounds ambiguity and the ability of actors (individual or small groups) to use political manipulation to achieve their policy goals (Zahariadis 2003). In contrast to other theories explaining the policy process, MSF stresses the importance of agency in the framing of problems and policy solutions and developing persuasive arguments. The framing of problems and delivery of persuasive arguments are often carried out by a distinct kind of political actor, the policy entrepreneur. These "advocates for proposals or for the prominence of ideas" (Kingdon 2011, 122) are crucial for the theoretical architecture of MSF: the coupling of streams does not happen automatically; an entrepreneur must actively couple them during an agenda or a decision window in order for an issue to be elevated to the agenda or for it to be decided upon (Herweg, Huß, and Zohlnhöfer 2015; Herweg, Zahariadis, and Zohlnhöfer 2018).

Policy entrepreneurs have provided an attractive alternative to the purely rational political actor and have long been credited with being agents of public policy change (Frisch Aviram, Cohen and Beeri 2021; Mintrom and Norman 2009; Mintrom and Vergari 1996; Petridou and Mintrom 2021; Schneider and Teske with Mintrom, 1995). The entrepreneur is one of MSF's moving parts with the purpose of contributing to the explanation of something – be it elevation of an issue to the agenda or enactment of a policy, or less frequently, policy implementation. It therefore functions as the independent variable. However, even as the scholarship on policy entrepreneurship has exploded in the past three decades, some aspects remain poorly understood, including factors affecting entrepreneurial action in the first place (Petridou and Mintrom 2021). In Kingdon's conceptualization of MSF (2011) policy entrepreneurs emerge fully formed and clearly identified, incentivized by opportunities to promote their personal interests, a desire to promote their values, or out of fanciful motives, such as "the love of the game" or being "policy groupies" (Kingdon 2011, 123). MSF studies focusing on elements other than policy entrepreneurs are even less circumspect when it comes to these actors. They exist as a category, often they are unnamed, the process of identifying them is less than rigorous, and the conditions that facilitate their emergence remain decidedly opaque.

Traditionally and in the decades after Kingdon (2011), the scholarship has predicated entrepreneurial action in the policy process on focused intentionality, tenacity, and a keen sense of opportunistic behavior to achieve success in the form of effecting or, at times, obstructing change (see Arnold 2022; Petridou and Mintrom 2021), even at the stage of policy implementation (see Arnold 2015; Lavee and Cohen 2019) The pluralistic, antagonistic, and contentious original context in Kingdon's work, the American federal Government, is a breeding ground for dynamic individuals seeking opportunities to promote their pet policy. What is more, the policy sectors under examination in Kingdon's original work, health care and transportation, are highly contentious in the American national context – the former perennially so, the latter especially during the 1970s, when Kingdon's study took place. Though he finds that in most case studies comprising his work policy entrepreneurs are present, factors that enable or constrain their emergence are not examined. To Kingdon's credit, such an analysis would have been beyond the scope of his study, where policy entrepreneurs were an independent, rather than the dependent, variable.

In summary, I argue that whereas we understand fairly well how entrepreneurial strategies contribute to elevating an idea to the agenda or affecting policy change, the underlying contextual factors that affect the emergence of entrepreneurs remain less researched. For this reason, the study on the process of policy entrepreneurship remains incomplete. I therefore move away from the entrepreneur as an actor and take a step towards entrepreneurship as a process. I specifically focus on structuring the understanding of the incentives of the entrepreneur. Any actor may decide to take it upon themselves to act entrepreneurially. Furthermore, they can act entrepreneurially in one instance, but perhaps not in another, which begs the question: what makes a person decide to invest resources for the promotion of a policy solution?

Factors underpinning the emergence of policy entrepreneurs have received less attention with few exceptions, including the classic study in local economic development by Schneider and Teske with Mintrom (1995) and Schneider and Teske (1992) and a later study in environmental policy by Kalafatis and Lemos (2017) providing explanations for the emergence of entrepreneurs as rational actors in local urban economies based on public choice literature. Understanding the influence of the institutional context in which policy entrepreneurs are embedded, including how it affects their emergence and what incentives they result in, would go some way towards understanding the process of policy entrepreneurship in policy making. It would also be a way to insert the role of institutions in MSF, an area Herweg, Zahariadis, and Zohlnhöfer (2018) identified as a potential point of development.

More specifically, in this chapter, I offer a nuanced understanding of the policy entrepreneur, based on contextual conditions that drive them towards entrepreneurial action. Based on Petridou et al. (2023), I lean on the market theory of entrepreneurship (Kirzner 1973; 1997; van der Zwan, Thurik, Verheul, and Hessels 2016), differentiating between entrepreneurship by opportunity and entrepreneurship by necessity based on the reasons underpinning the choices of those who decide to take on entrepreneurial action. In the policy sphere, I label these *proactive* and *reactive* policy entrepreneurship, respectively. My purpose is not to add a new actor in the mix; rather, I wish to shed light on how institutional contexts incentivize the policy entrepreneur and inform their role in the policy process within the MSF. Context in public policy is a very broad concept, and it is beyond the scope of this chapter to examine it in its entirety. Instead, I focus on reactive and proactive entrepreneurship as a means of providing an alternative to the theorization of the policy entrepreneur as an actor motivated by the emergence of opportunity – the actor reacting to external (political/administrative) pressure in the implementation stage of the policy process. I am not arguing that entrepreneurial strategies are necessarily different based on whether the entrepreneur is reactive or proactive. Even so, it is of theoretical and practical value to understand what drives entrepreneurs (Arnold 2022).

In the remainder of this chapter, I first briefly outline my research design; I then provide an overview of the policy entrepreneur as developed by Kingdon, followed by a brief review of the literature that ensued. I then discuss institutional factors and policy implementation as context, before I outline conditions of opportunity vs. conditions of necessity. I conclude with the the-oretical and practical contributions of nuancing policy entrepreneurial action as proactive and reactive, and I offer some implications for further research.

RESEARCH DESIGN

This chapter is theoretical, a conceptual piece building an argument as opposed to building on data, with a focus on the implementation stage of the policy process – the stage where it has been traditionally less likely to observe policy entrepreneurs (though see Arnold 2015). The focus of this chapter on implementation serves as a kind of illustrative case (Levy 2008). Though tra-ditionally we find fewer entrepreneurs in the implementation stage, it is during this stage that I can more readily illustrate external (political) pressure applied to a potential entrepreneur figuring in their decision calculus. An actor imple-menting public policy, an implementer, has potentially career considerations at stake when deciding whether to act entrepreneurially or not. Having said all this, motivations for reactive entrepreneurship – predicated on conditions of necessity – exist in the entire policy process.

THE POLICY ENTREPRENEUR'S CONTRIBUTION TO THE POLICY PROCESS: KINGDON'S IDEAS

MSF explains well *what* it is that policy entrepreneurs do in the policy process while also touching briefly upon *why* and *who* they are. The Kingdonian (2011) policy entrepreneur is a tenacious, well-networked, consequential actor, who, when a window of opportunity opens, couples previously uncon-nected streams. As a result, an idea (or policy proposal) gains prominence. This is not to say that entrepreneurs are superhuman. The concept of the entre-preneur is a device contributing to the most pronounced strength of the MSF: the systematization of propitiousness. For it is due to propitiousness that the time of an idea has come, and an actor must elevate it to prominence. Policy entrepreneurs constitute an indispensable component of the policy process and regardless of whether they operate inside or outside government, hold elected or appointed positions, the one characteristic they have in common is the fact that they are willing to hedge their resources for future returns – much like market entrepreneurs. These returns may constitute material, purposive or sol-idary benefits. Policy entrepreneurs promote their personal interest, which may take different forms depending on their other identities. Personal interest for an entrepreneur who holds an appointed position may translate in the "protection of bureaucratic turf" (Kingdon 2011, 23), which in turn translates in protecting or advancing one's job, or maximizing the budget or the political relevance of the organization for which the entrepreneur works. Conversely, if the entrepreneur is a politician, future returns concern electoral gain – political survival and power. Finally, if the policy entrepreneur is a member of an interest group, personal interest may concern remaining relevant in the policymaking process and maintaining a seat at the policy making table.

Personal gain is not the only driver of policy entrepreneurial behavior, according to Kingdon. Pet policy solutions may also be the result of ideological adherence akin to activism. Policy entrepreneurs are found to believe in the public good engendered by their preferred policy solution and they act in order to promote it. Finally, policy entrepreneurs may be motivated by the enjoyment of "being part of the action" (Kingdon 2011: 123). Kingdon (2011) notes that one finds at least one person, often more, who drive the promotion of a policy almost always in case studies. These are not heroic figures; rather, they are tenacious actors waiting for an opportunity to arise so that at the appropriate time their idea might be more easily accepted. They push continuously for a proposal. Sometimes they miss the mark, other times they find it. Policy entrepreneurs, be it politicians or public servants, educate the public, their colleagues, or specialized audiences with speeches, reports, studies, and other means. Erstwhile perceived or real failures may be seen as part of the softening up process of the policy community.

Policy entrepreneurs are instrumental in laying down the groundwork for the advancement of an idea; they soften institutional rigidities and are alert to "opportunities for action on given initiatives" (Kingdon 2011, 166), constituting policy windows, which occur and stay open for a limited time. Entrepreneurs must be ready to act and couple the separate streams in order to elevate the issue and its attendant solution to the government agenda or to the decision agenda, and thus bring the policy solution closer to enactment. Zahariadis (2003) summarizes policy entrepreneurs by pointing out that central to MSF is the "concept of manipulation that is, the systematic distortion, misrepresentation, or selective presentation of information by skilled policy entrepreneurs who exploit opportunities in a world of unclear goals, opaque technology, and fluid participation" (p. 18). He goes on to say that (political) manipulation is a means of controlling ambiguity. To this end, entrepreneurs manipulate, in the sense that they construct focused narratives often based on a selective choice and synthesis of information in order to delineate a policy problem so that they may propose a solution they already have (Zahariadis 2003). More specifically, "a problem definition is a statement of a goal and the discrepancy between it and the status quo" (Stone 2002, 133). However, under conditions of ambiguity which are present in most wicked problems of our times, neither the definition of the goal nor the means to achieve it are objective and universally accepted. Any facts (bits of information) on which they are based come with words and numbers and thus, they are a portrayal of one of many points of view. Creativity in a decision-making system has less to do with the capacity to amass information, and much more with controlling how this information is cast. Indeed, "innovation is a matter of combining already available bits of information in a new way of or orienting them towards new ends" (Price 1971, 318). In summary, entrepreneurs reduce ambiguity by constructing a plausible policy reality through the use of political manipulation. As Zahariadis (2003) notes, however, manipulation is part of politics and need not entail dark motives or deceit; "entrepreneurs who manipulate [...] misrepresent but not necessarily deceive" (p. 20). Manipulation serves to give meaning, it aims to clarify and provide identity (Zahariadis 2003), thus reducing ambiguity surrounding a policy problem.

THE POLICY ENTREPRENEUR BEYOND MSF

The undeniable appeal of the concept of the policy entrepreneur rests with the concept's offering an alternative to the thin explanatory value of rational choice and the self-maximizing actor. It offers a versatile and powerful concept to theorize agency in public policy making. The entrepreneur in politics offers an attractive heuristic capturing the broader concept of agency in the policy process. It is unsurprising, then, that the literature on policy entrepreneurs has exploded in the past three decades. Scholars have theorized policy entrepreneurs, and to a more limited extent policy entrepreneurship, beyond their function as the coupler of streams in the MSF. This scholarship has focused on understanding *who* the entrepreneur is in terms of the attributes and skills they have, and *how* they go about promoting dynamic change. Some scholars have examined the *where* (see Kalafatis and Lemos 2017), but the *why* that is, what drives entrepreneurs, has not received much scholarly attention (though see Arnold 2022).

More specifically, scholarly attention has been paid to the catalytic role policy entrepreneurs play in bringing about dynamic policy change (Carter and Scott 2010; Mintrom 2000; Mintrom and Norman 2009; Schneider and Teske 1992; Schneider, Teske and Mintrom 1995; Mintrom and Thomas 2018; Sheingate 2003), including environmental policy (Huitema, Lebel, and Meijerink 2011; Ingold and Christopoulos 2015; Mintrom 2019; Kalafatis and Lemos 2017; Verduijn 2015), economic development (Olausson and Svensson 2019; Petridou 2017; Schneider and Teske 1992; Schneider, Teske, and Mintrom 1995), crisis management (Petridou and Sparf 2017), education (Mintrom 2000), foreign policy (Blavoukos and Bourantonis 2012; David 2015), and social policy (Hammond 2013), though this is by far not an exhaustive list (see also Frisch-Aviram, Cohen, and Beeri 2019, for an overview). A segment of policy entrepreneurship literature suggests that entrepreneurs belong to the political elite; they are reported to be exceptional actors or high-level decision makers (Christopoulos 2006; Christopoulos and Ingold 2015; Frish-Aviram, Cohen, and Beeri 2019), whereas to a lesser extent, scholars have examined policy entrepreneurship among bureaucrats (see, however, Frish-Aviram, Cohen, and Beeri 2018; Hysing and Olsson 2012; Petridou 2018) thus spanning the gamut of political actors. Indeed, policy entrepreneurs matter.

Michael Mintrom pioneered the scholarship on policy entrepreneurs and has contributed immensely to the ontological and epistemological advancement of the concept. He outlined a set of six assumptions underpinning the concept of policy entrepreneur (Mintrom 2000). First, policy entrepreneurs must be creative and insightful and be able to calculate how their proposals will affect the policy debate in the long run. Second, policy entrepreneurs are socially sensitive, and perceptive enough to be able to view problems from many different angles. These two assumptions relate to previously articulated theories of policy entrepreneurs and the tenet that they must be alert and in tune with the community so that they are able to discern emergent problems. Third, policy entrepreneurs must be able to move in and out of a variety of social and political settings – they must be well networked. Fourth, policy entrepreneurs must be able to argue persuasively, to use effective rhetoric for the purpose of transforming existing perceptions. By reframing an issue "the entrepreneur generates 'needs' and then meets those needs with specific responses" (Scheider, Teske, and Mintrom, 1995, 43). Fifth, policy entrepreneurs must be able to build teams able to pursue their goal successfully. Sixth, they must be able to "lead by example" that is, inspire their team with their vision for the future, which must appear realistic.

Finally, the entrepreneur is not an individual working in isolation; rather the milieu in which they operate is very important; the social nature of entrepreneurship is widely accepted in the scholarship (Mintrom 2000). Contacts are commonly the main source of ideas that public entrepreneurs come across and take advantage of. They are social actors embedded in local networks, which in turn can alleviate some of the risks and costs of entrepreneurship.

Later research has reshuffled these assumptions, differentiating among the attributes (that may be nurtured), skills (that may be acquired by actors possessing the attributes) and strategies that policy entrepreneurs deploy based on attributes and skills (Mintrom 2019). Policy entrepreneurial skills include ambition; social acuity (understanding the political environment); credibility (being considered to have what it takes to do the job); sociability (the ability to understand how one's suggestions will be accepted by others), and tenacity. Skills include strategic thinking; building teams; collecting evidence (to use in successful arguments); making arguments; engaging multiple audiences; negotiating, and networking. Finally, policy entrepreneurial strategies include problem framing; using and expanding networks; working with advocacy coalitions; leading by example and scaling up change processes.

INSTITUTIONS AND POLICY IMPLEMENTATION AS CONTEXT

As mentioned elsewhere in this chapter, policy entrepreneurs may come from inside or outside government. This implies that they hold different identities, which are part of the broader context influencing their emergence, the scope of the strategies they may use, and the possibility of their success in effecting change. A limitation of MSF is that traditionally, it has not explicitly provided for political institutions and path dependency. However, as Herweg, Zahariadis, and Zohlnhöfer (2018) note, nothing in the structure and assumptions of MSF precludes the insertion of institutions in the framework. Bolukbasi and Yildirim (2022) did just that, offering ways that formal and informal institutions affect entrepreneurial behavior, including who "is allowed" to act entrepreneurially, what venue they may use, the level of success they may have, and the strategies they may use. Conversely, Petridou and Mintrom (2021) discuss four ways which would further the examination of contextual factors in conjunction with the different identities of policy entrepreneurs in terms of their emergence and the strategies they employ in their efforts towards affecting change. These include the substantive policy sector in which they wish to effect change; the broader system or level of governance in which they are active, how they relate to others within their operating context, and the stage of the policymaking process in which they are active.

I propose that an appropriate context to illustrate formal and informal institutional power differentials as comprising conditions of necessity incentivizing policy entrepreneurship is the implementation stage of the policy process. Even though implementation was not the focus of MSF in Kingdon's work, later work has explored the analytical power of MSF in that stage of the policy process (Boswell and Rodrigues 2016; Zahariadis and Exadaktylos 2016). Fowler states: "[w]hile implementers may be able to withstand challenges to the status quo from any single stream (i.e., shift in public opinion, focusing events), when coupled, implementers have no choice but to respond. Otherwise, they risk a breakdown of political coalitions, challenges to their legitimacy, implementation failures, or issues returning to the policy agendas as policy entrepreneurs shift pressure back to policymakers" (Fowler quoted in Fowler 2022, 619). Fowler (2022) goes on to say that if policy implementers (public servants) do not respond, actors who supported the adoption of the policy will in turn question the legitimacy and competence of implementers, placing them under the spotlight (see also Fowler 2019; Reed 2014).

I pick up the argument at the point where the implementers must respond after the adoption of a policy solution. In Fowler's theorization, there exist policy entrepreneurs among the implementers in the implementation stage, just as they exist in the agenda setting and policy adoption stage. I circle back to Kingdon (2011), who lists career benefits as an incentive for policy entrepreneurial action. I argue that the political pressure exercised to implementers/public servants can constitute conditions of necessity, forcing the implementer to act entrepreneurially as a reaction to pressure, rather than a focused intentionality cultivated over time waiting for an opportunity to implement a favorite policy. If this is the case, we must account for the power differentials that result in political pressure and revise our theorization of policy entrepreneurs acting solely out of the alertness to opportunities. In the implementation stage, they may just as well act as a response to political pressure and implement an idea that they had not supported prior to being put in the position to implement it. Such a response and lack of prior intentionality would constitute reactive policy entrepreneurial action, as opposed to the mainstream, proactive policy entrepreneurial action, which, based on the market model, has dominated the literature thus far. In the next section, I turn to market entrepreneurship literature.

CONDITIONS OF OPPORTUNITY, CONDITIONS OF NECESSITY

The importance of market entrepreneurs as crucial societal actors who develop and introduce new products and services to the market has been examined extensively. The actions of market entrepreneurs often catalyse new forms of economic and social activity (Casson 1982; Kirzner 1997; Schumpeter 1934). In the market, entrepreneurs face competition. Indeed, Kirzner (1973) posits that competition is analytically inseparable to entrepreneurship. The market consists of a series of interacting decisions made by consumers, entrepreneur-producers, and the owners of resources. Existing producers, perceiving threats to the share of the market they control, often resist the actions of new entrepreneurs trying to break into a new market. Entrepreneurs distinguish themselves from mainstream business owners because they demonstrate creativity and innovation in their intentional efforts and ability to "[perceive] opportunities for entrepreneurial profits" (Kirzner 1973, 16). Entrepreneurs lie in wait and are able to recognize an opportunity – and in that act perceive the possibility of gaining profit – to sell something at a higher price than that they can buy it for and for this reason, anyone may become an entrepreneur

(Kirzner 1973). This is also the rationale underpinning Kingdon's (2011) theorization of the policy entrepreneur.

This classic theorization of market entrepreneurship capturing the intentionality that underpins the alertness to new profit opportunities is reflected in the concept of *entrepreneurship by opportunity*. However, not all market entrepreneurs are motivated by the prospect of taking advantage of an opportunity structure; not all market entrepreneurs patiently wait for an opportunity to introduce a new product or a novel means of production to the market. People choose self-employment (and self-employment is used as a proxy for entrepreneurship by the Global Entrepreneurship Monitor, GEM) because they "cannot find any other suitable work" (Angulo-Guerrero, Pérez-Moreno, and Abad-Guerrero 2017; Reynolds, Bygrave, Autio, Cox, and Hay 2002, 6). People who choose self-employment because they feel they have no other viable employment choice engage in *entrepreneurship by necessity.*

More specifically, in the market, entrepreneurs by necessity choose to act entrepreneurially for two reasons: first, they do not have another choice when it comes to employment, second, in their national context there is no safety net in terms of unemployment insurance or re-training programs (Fairlie and Fossen 2018; Serviere 2010). Actors driven to entrepreneurship by necessity "perceive entrepreneurship as the only option for their survival" (Serviere 2010, 42, see also Acs, Arenius, Hay, and Minniti 2004). In other words, the distinction between entrepreneurship by opportunity and entrepreneurship by necessity is a question of motive. What drives people to invest energy, time, and other resources and take the risks associated with being an entrepreneur in the first place? Motives of entrepreneurs by opportunity include intrinsic factors, such as recognizing and taking advantage of opportunities for social advancement and independence and the need to achieve. In contrast, entrepreneurship by necessity is motivated by extrinsic pressures: family and economic pressures (for example due to unemployment) often leading to an unsatisfactory economic status. The implication is that entrepreneurship by opportunity is predicated on human agency whereas entrepreneurship by necessity is imposed on actors by exogenous pressures (Shane, Locke, and Collins 2003). In summary, opportunity entrepreneurs recognize and actively pursue an opportunity, often while they are already employed elsewhere and out of personal interest. The implication of this is that the potential entrepreneur has a choice. Conversely, entrepreneurship by necessity is often the best "but not necessarily the preferred" option (Reynolds et al., quoted in van der Zwan et al. 2016, 274).

Indeed, given the origins of the policy entrepreneur in the market literature, it is not unreasonable to explore nuances of the term based on contextual factors that further specify the motivations of entrepreneurs and have the potential to inform their entrepreneurial actions. I propose that in the politics sphere, actors may be driven to entrepreneurship because of a perceived necessity, including professional survival. I argue that this nuanced conceptualization of the market entrepreneur, based on the perceived necessity (rather than volition) to act entrepreneurially, which in turn depends on the wider political context, is fruitful in policy entrepreneurship as well. Proactive policy entrepreneurs (policy entrepreneurs by opportunity) decide to assume risks and invest the necessary resources to advocate for the design and/or implementation of a public policy based on intentionality. This implies an *a priori* preferred policy solution and the focused seeking of political opportunity. Conversely, reactive policy entrepreneurs (policy entrepreneurs by necessity) decide to assume risks and invest the necessary resources to advocate for the design and/or implementation of a public policy solution as a result of external pressures and often as the best, but not always the preferred choice.

Susceptibility to exogenous pressures implies power differentials – the ability of one actor to impose their will (or sanctions) to another. In the implementation stage of the policy process, a public servant may be subject to top-down pressure by either a higher governance level (national or state, depending on the political system) or their political masters (if at the national level) to seek and promote a satisfying solution that was not their preferred choice. The point I wish to make is that the nuance between proactive and reactive entrepreneurship is a question of the factors that push an actor to invest resources in entrepreneurial action. Empirical research is needed to specify the conditions under which reactive policy entrepreneurs emerge, based on the stage of the policymaking process in which they are active; the substantive policy sector in which they wish to effect change; the broader system or level of government in which they operate, and how they relate to others within their operating context.

CONCLUSIONS AND DISCUSSION

In this chapter, I offered a nuanced understanding of the policy entrepreneur based on market entrepreneurship theory. More specifically, I outline an actor who decides to take on entrepreneurial action based on conditions of necessity as opposed to the focused intentionality and tenacious seeking of opportunity. This means that policy entrepreneurs may promote a policy solution not because it was their *a priori* preferred choice, but because they felt they had no other choice. The theoretical contributions of this chapter are threefold. Indeed, conceptualizing conditions of necessity that render policy entrepreneurial action a response to exogenous pressures has a number of implications of the scholarship on policy entrepreneurs and their role in the policy making process. First, it adds analytical rigor to the identification of the policy entrepreneur – what motivates them? Must they be opportunity seekers or is policy entrepreneurial action also a means of surviving the political game? Exploring the *why* of policy entrepreneurship contributes to the broader understanding of political agency. Second, conceptualizing necessity takes a step towards understanding entrepreneurship as a process, by inserting, from a different angle, power differentials embedded in political institutions as an incentive for policy entrepreneurial action. Third, it enriches the explanatory value of MSF in the implementation stage of the policy process by bringing in the dimension of bureaucratic politics and the interplay between policy adoption and policy implementation.

Concomitantly, a number of questions emerge. First, do reactive entrepreneurs use a different set of strategies? In the market, entrepreneurship by necessity is deemed to not lead to innovation – is this the case in politics as well? Second, if innovation is not part of policy entrepreneurial action, are reactive entrepreneurs ontologically different from proactive entrepreneurs? There are additional epistemological questions. In the market, entrepreneurs are asked why they chose to start a company. In the field of policy entrepreneurship, this would entail a two-step process: first, the policy entrepreneur must be identified and then asked about their motives for being entrepreneurial, which entails a rigorous operationalization of necessity vs opportunity. What is more, the temporal dimension must be taken into account. Policy implementation might initially result in reactive entrepreneurship for one entrepreneur, but with the passage of time opportunities may be created and seized by another. Finally, such research into the nuances of policy entrepreneurs has practical in addition to the theoretical value, in that it may provide guidelines for practitioners wishing to make a difference in public policy.

NOTE

1.   I would like to acknowledge funding from FORMAS, Sweden, FR-2019/0002 (Putting out Fires: A Multiple Streams Analysis).

REFERENCES

Ackrill, Robert, and Adrian Kay. 2011. "Multiple streams in EU policy making: the case of the 2005 sugar reform." *Journal of European Public Policy* 18 (1): 72–89. doi:10.1080/13501763.2011.520879.
Acs, Zoltan J, Pia Arenius, Michael Hay, and Maria Minniti. 2005. "Global Entrepreneurship Monitor: 2004 Executive Report." In *Secondary Global Entrepreneurship Monitor: 2004 Executive Report*, ed Secondary Acs, Zoltan J, Pia Arenius, Michael Hay, and Maria Minniti. Reprint, Reprint.
Anderson, S. E., DeLeo, R. A., & Taylor, K. 2019. "Policy Entrepreneurs, Legislators, and Agenda Setting: Information and Influence." *Policy Studies Journal* 0 (0). doi:10.1111/psj.12331.

Angulo-Guerrero, María J., Salvador Pérez-Moreno, and Isabel M. Abad-Guerrero. "How Economic Freedom Affects Opportunity and Necessity Entrepreneurship in the OECD Countries." *Journal of Business Research* 73 (2017/04/01/ 2017): 30–37. https://doi.org/https://doi.org/10.1016/j.jbusres.2016.11.017. https://www.sciencedirect.com/science/article/pii/S0148296316306543.

Arnold, Gwen. 2015. "Street-Level Policy Entrepreneurship." *Public Management Review* 17: 307–27.

Arnold, Gwen. 2022. "A Threat-Centered Theory of Policy Entrepreneurship." *Policy Sciences* 55: 23–45.

Blavoukos Spyros and Dimitris Bourantonis. 2012. "Policy Entrepreneurs and Foreign Policy Change: The Greek–Turkish Rapprochement in the 1990s." *Government and Opposition* 47 (04): 597–617. doi:doi:10.1111/j.1477–7053.2012.01376.x.

Bogason, Peter. 2000. *Public Policy and Local Governance: Institutions in Postmodern Society*. Cheltenham, Edward Elgar.

Bolukbasi, H. Tolga, and Deniz Yıldırım. 2022. "Institutions in the Politics of Policy Change: Who Can Play, How They Play in Multiple Streams." *Journal of Public Policy* 42: 509–28.

Callaghan, Timothy, and Steven Sylvester. 2019. "Private citizens as policy entrepreneurs: Evidence from autism mandates and parental political mobilization." *Policy Studies Journal*.

Carter, Ralph G., and James M. Scott. 2009. *Choosing to Lead: Understanding Congressional Foreign Policy Entrepreneurs*. Durham, NC: Duke University Press.

Casson, Mark. 1982. *The Entrepreneur: An Economic Theory*. Totowa, NJ: Barnes and Noble.

Christopoulos, Dimitrios C. (2006) "Relational attributes of political entrepreneurs: a network perspective." *Journal of European Public Policy* 13.5: 757–78.

Christopoulos, Dimitrios C., and Karin Ingold (2015). "Exceptional or just well connected? Political entrepreneurs and brokers in policy making." *European Political Science Review* 7.3: 475–98.

Cohen, Michael D., March, James G. & Olsen, Johan P. 1972. "A Garbage Can Model of Organizational Choice." *Administrative Science Quarterly* 17 (1): 1–25.

Dawson, Christopher, and Andrew Henley. "'Push' Versus 'Pull' Entrepreneurship: An Ambiguous Distinction?". *International Journal of Entrepreneurial Behavior & Research* (2012).

David, Charles-Philippe. 2015. "How Do Entrepreneurs Make National Security Policy? A Case Study of the G.W. Bush Administration." In *Entrepreneurship in the Polis: Understanding Political Entrepreneurship*, eds. Inga Narbutaité Aflaki, Evangelia Petridou and Lee Miles. Burlington, VT: Ashgate. 151–70.

Fairlie, Robert W., and Frank M. Fossen. 2019. "Defining Opportunity Versus Necessity Entrepreneurship: Two Components of Business Creation." NBER Working Paper No. w26377 https://papers.ssrn.com/sol3/papers.cfm?abstract_id=3472812#.

Faling, M., Biesbroek, R., Karlsson-Vinkhuyzen, S., & Termeer, K. (2018). "Policy entrepreneurship across boundaries: a systematic literature review." *Journal of Public Policy* 1–30. doi:10.1017/S0143814X18000053

Fowler, Luke. 2022. "Using the Multiple Streams Framework to Connect Policy Adoption to Implementation." *Policy Studies Journal* 50: 615–39.

Frisch Aviram, Neomi, Nissim Cohen, and Itai Beeri. 2020. "Wind(Ow) of Change: A Systematic Review of Policy Entrepreneurship Characteristics and Strategies." *Policy Studies Journal* 48: 612–44.

Giddens, Anthony. 1984. *The Constitution of Society: Outline of the Theory of Structuration.* University of California Press.

Hammond, Daniel. R. 2013. "Policy Entrepreneurship in China's Response to Urban Poverty." *Policy Studies Journal* 41 (1): 119–146. doi:10.1111/psj.12005.

Henderson, D. (2019). "Policy entrepreneurship in context: Understanding the emergence of novel policy solutions for services innovation in Finland and Ireland." *Science and Public Policy.* doi:10.1093/scipol/scz020.

Herweg, Nicole, Nikolaos Zahariadis, and Reimut Zohlnhöfer. 2018. "The multiple streams framework: Foundations, refinements, and empirical applications." In *Theories of the Policy Process*, 4th edition, eds. Christopher M. Weible and Paul A. Sabatier, 17–53. Boulder, CO: Westview Press.

Herweg, Nicole, Christian Huß, and Reimut Zohlnhöfer. 2015. "Straightening the Three Streams: Theorising Extensions of the Multiple Streams Framework." *European Journal of Political Research* 54: 435–49.

Huitema, Dave, Louis Lebel, and Sander Meijerink. 2011. "The Strategies of Policy Entrepreneurs in Water Transitions Around the World." *Water Policy* 13: 717–33. https://doi.org/10.2166/wp.2011.107.

Hysing, Erik, and Jan Olsson. 2011. "Who Greens the Northern Light? Green inside Activists in Local Environmental Governing in Sweden." *Environment and Planning C: Government and Policy* 29 (4): 693–708. doi:10.1068/c10114.

Jones, Michael D., and Mark K. McBeth. 2010. "A narrative policy framework: Clear enough to be wrong?" *Policy Studies Journal* 38 (2): 329–53.

Jordan, Andrew, and Dave Huitema. 2014. "Policy Innovation in a Changing Climate: Sources, Patterns and Effects." *Global Environmental Change* 29: 387–94. https://doi.org/10.1016/j.gloenvcha.2014.09.005.

Kalafatis, Scott E., and Maria Carmen Lemos. 2017. "The Emergence of Climate Change Policy Entrepreneurs in Urban Regions." *Regional Environmental Change* 17: 1791–99.

Kingdon, John. W. 2011. *Agendas, Alternatives, and Public Policies* (3rd edition). Boston: Longman.

Kirzner, Israel M. 1973. Method, Process, and Austrian Economics. Washington, DC: Lexington Books.

Kirzner, Israel M. 1997. "Entrepreneurial Discovery and the Competitive Market Process: An Austrian Approach." *Journal of economic Literature* 35: 60–85.

Lavee, Einat and Nissim Cohen. 2019. "How street-level bureaucrats become policy entrepreneurs: The case of urban renewal." *Governance* 32 (3): 475–492. doi:10.1111/gove.12387.

Levy, Jack S. 2008. "Case Studies: Types, Designs, and Logics of Inference." *Conflict Management and Peace Science* 25: 1–18.

March, James G. and Johan P. Olsen. 1989. *Rediscovering Institutions: The Organizational Basis of Politics.* New York: Free Press.

Meijerink, Sander, and Dave Huitema. 2010 "Policy entrepreneurs and change strategies: lessons from sixteen case studies of water transitions around the globe." *Ecology and Society* 15 (2).

Meydani, Assaf. 2015. "Political Entrepreneurs and Institutional Change: Governability, Liberal Political Culture, and the 1992 Electoral Reform in Israel." In *Entrepreneurship in the Polis: Understanding Political Entrepreneurship*, eds. Inga Narbutaité Aflaki, Evangelia Petridou and Lee Miles 87–102. Burligton, VT: Ashgate.

Mintrom, Michael. 2000. *Policy Entrepreneurs and School Choice.* Washington: Georgetown University Press.

Mintrom, Michael. 2012. *Contemporary Policy Analysis.* Oxford: OUP.

Mintrom, Michael. 2013. "Policy entrepreneurs and controversial science: governing human embryonic stem cell research." *Journal of European Public Policy* 20 (3), 442–57. doi:10.1080/13501763.2012.761514.

Mintrom, Michael. 2019. "So You Want to Be a Policy Entrepreneur?" *Policy Design and Practice* 2: 307–23.

Mintrom, Michael. and Joannah Luetjens. 2017. "Policy Entrepreneurs and Problem Framing: The Case of Climate Change." *Environment and Planning C: Politics and Space* 35 (8): 1362–77.

Mintrom, Michael, and Joannah Luetjens. 2019. "International Policy Entrepreneurship." In *The Oxford Handbook of Global Policy and Transnational Administration,* 111. Oxford: OUP.

Mintrom, Michael, and Philippa Norman. 2009. "Policy Entrepreneurship and Policy Change." *Policy Studies Journal* 37 (4): 649–67. doi:10.111 1/j.1541–0072.2009.00329.

Mintrom, Michael, Christopher Salisbury, and Joannah Luetjens. 2014. "Policy entrepreneurs and promotion of Australian state knowledge economies." *Australian Journal of Political Science,* 49 (3): 423–38. doi:10.1080/10361146.2014.934657.

Mintrom, Michael, and Sandra Vergari. 1998. "Policy Networks and Innovation Diffusion: The Case of State Education Reforms." *Journal of Politics* 60: 126–48.

Olausson, Albin, and Petra Svensson. 2019. "Nya Förvaltningsideal – Byråkrater Och Entreprenörer I Samhällsbyggnadsprocessen." In *Ett Nytt Kontrakt För Samhällsbyggnande,* ed. Josefina Syssner, 37–57. Boxholm, Sweden: Linnefors Förlag.

Ostrom, Elinor. 1965. "Public Entrepreneurship: A Case Study in Ground Water Basin Management." University of California-Los Angeles, Department of Political Science. Retrieved http://hdl.handle.net/10535/3581.

Petridou, Evangelia. 2014. "Theories of the Policy Process: Contemporary Scholarship and Future Directions." *Policy Studies Journal* 42: S12-S32.

Petridou, Evangelia. 2017 "Political Entrepreneurship in Swedish: Towards a (Re) Theorization of Entrepreneurial Agency." Doctoral Dissertation, Mid Sweden University.

Petridou, Evangelia. 2018. Entrepreneurship in the Swedish municipal polis: the case of Mer [*] Östersund. *Policy Studies* 1–20. doi:10.1080/01442872.2018.1434872.

Petridou, Evangelia, Roine Johannsson, Kerstin Eriksson, Gertrud Alirani, and Nikolaos Zahariadis. (2023) "Theorizing Reactive Policy Entrepreneurship: A Case Study of Swedish Local Emergency Management. *Policy Studies Journal* 00 (0): 1–17.

Petridou, Evangelia, and Michael Mintrom. 2021. "A Research Agenda for the Study of Policy Entrepreneurs." *Policy Studies Journal* 49: 943–67.

Petridou, Evangelia, and Jörgen Sparf. 2017. "For Safety's Sake: The Strategies of Institutional Entrepreneurs and Bureaucratic Reforms in Swedish Crisis Management 2001–2009." *Policy and Society* 36: 556–74.

Price, David E. 1971. "Professionals and 'Entrepreneurs': Staff Orientations and Policy Making on Three Senate Committees." *The Journal of Politics* 33 (2): 316–36. doi:doi:10.2307/2128728.

Reynolds, Paul D., William D. Bygrave, Erkko Autio, Larry W. Cox, and Michael Hay. 2002. "Global Entrepreneurship Monitor: 2002 Executive Report." Kauffman Foundation. https://papers.ssrn.com/sol3/papers.cfm?abstract_id=1509260.

Roberts, Nancy C. and King, Paula J. 1991. "Policy Entrepreneurs: Their Activity Structure and Function in the Policy Process." *Journal of Public Administration Research and Theory: J-PART* 1 (2): 147–75.

Serviere, Laura 2010. "Forced to Entrepreneurship: Modeling the Factors Behind Necessity Entrepreneurship." *Journal of Business and Entrepreneurship* 22 (1): 37–53.

Shanahan, Elizabeth A., Michael D. Jones, Mark K. McBeth, and Claudio M. Radaelli. 2018. "The narrative policy framework." In *Theories of the Policy Process*, eds. Christopher M. Weible and Paul A. Sabatier, 173–213. New York: Routledge.

Shane, Scott, Edwin A. Locke, and Christopher J. Collins. 2003. "Entrepreneurial Motivation." *Human Resource Management Review* 13: 257–79.

Schneider, Mark, and Paul Teske. 1992. "Toward a Theory of the Political Entrepreneur: Evidence from Local Government." *The American Political Science Review* 86: 737–47. doi:10.2307/1964135.

Schneider, Mark, Teske, Paul, and Mintrom, Michael. 1995. *Public Entrepreneurs: Agents for Change in American Government*. Princeton: Princeton University Press.

Schumpeter, Joseph A. 1934. *The Theory of Economic Development*, trans Redvers Opie. Cambridge, Mass: Harvard University Press.

Sheingate, Adam D. 2003. "Political Entrepreneurship, Institutional Change, and American Political Development." *Studies in American Political Development* 17 (2): 185–203.

Shockley, Gordon E., Roger R. Stough, Kingsley E. Haynes, and Peter M. Frank. 2006. "Toward a theory of public sector entrepreneurship." *International Journal of Entrepreneurship and Innovation Management* 6 (3): 205–23.

Svensson, Petra. 2019. "Formalized Policy Entrepreneurship as a Governance Tool for Policy Integration." *International Journal of Public Administration* 42 (14): 1212–21. doi:10.1080/01900692.2019.1590401.

Stone, Deborah A. 2002. *Policy Paradox: The Art of Political Decision Making*. New York: WW Norton.

Verduijn, Simon. 2015. "Setting the Political Agenda: A Policy Entrepreneurial Perspective on Urban Development in the Netherlands." In *Entrepreneurship in the Polis: Understanding Political Entrepreneurship*, eds. Inga Narbutaité Aflaki, Evangelia Petridou and Lee Miles. Burlington, 55–72. VT: Ashgate.

Weible, Christopher M. 2018. "Moving forward and climbing upward.: Advancing policy process research." In *Theories of the Policy Process* (4th edition), eds. Christopher M. Weible and Paul A. Sabatier, 363–78. New York: Routledge.

Zahariadis, Nikolaos. 2003. *Ambiguity and Choice in Public Policy: Political Decision Making in Modern Democracies*. Washington, DC: Georgetown Press.

Zahariadis, Nikolaos, and Theofanis Exadaktylos. 2016. "Policies That Succeed and Programs That Fail: Ambiguity, Conflict, and Crisis in Greek Higher Education." *Policy Studies Journal* 44: 59–82.

van der Zwan, Peter, Roy Thurik, Ingrid Verheul, and Jolanda Hessels. "Factors Influencing the Entrepreneurial Engagement of Opportunity and Necessity Entrepreneurs." *Eurasian Business Review* 6 (3): 273–95. https://doi.org/10.1007/s40821–016–0065–1. https://doi.org/10.1007/s40821–016–0065–1.

PART II

Applications: National level

7. Shifting ideational paradigms in public health: Connecting design and implementation in Greek health policy

Vassilis Karokis-Mavrikos and Maria Mavrikou

INTRODUCTION

The Multiple Streams Framework (MSF) has long enjoyed prominence as an analytical tool for the study of policy change (Kingdon 1984). Scholarly applications have spanned contexts and policy fields (Jones et al. 2015) and have been highly successful in uncovering the mechanisms underpinning policy shifts, especially in the decision agenda (Herweg, Zahariadis and Zohlnhöfer 2018). As change is dynamic, recent accounts have extended the MSF's focus to the implementation stage (Fowler 2019; Sager and Thomann 2017). An emerging challenge in the literature concerns connecting policy design and implementation (Fowler 2022; Zahariadis and Exadaktylos 2016) to understand why some bills provisioning radical change succeed in shifting policy trajectories but others do not. We intend to contribute to this research agenda through a longitudinal account of public health policy in Greece. We apply the MSF toolkit to the study of public health policy change, centering our analysis on two focusing events: the 2003 SARS outbreak and the Covid-19 pandemic. The first triggered the institutionalization of public health policymaking for the first time in Greece's modern history (Bill 3172/2003) and the second tested the degree of entrenchment of the new paradigm nearly two decades later. In doing so, we evaluate the interrelation of policy design and implementation and uncover contextually-driven insights for the potential theoretical advancement of the framework.

RESEARCH DESIGN

Our approach builds on the insights of Blum (2021) and Zahariadis and Exadaktylos (2016) (also see chapter 5, this volume) as we view streams couplings during agenda-setting and decision making as fragile and potential decouplings during implementation as detrimental to structural change. We decide to zoom in on the mechanisms which maintain or disrupt couplings and determine whether and how they are connected to the process of policy adoption. As a result, we first explore how the first dedicated public health Bill in Greece's modern history was introduced in 2003 after two decades of neglect and then evaluate how the drivers and resisting forces behind the reform have influenced its implementation trajectory. Guiding our analysis are two hypotheses:

H1: The rise of public health to the decision agenda was the outcome of successful policy entrepreneurship, which extended the focus of policy change beyond the health services sector.

H2: Resisting forces in the policy and politics stream, which persistently impeded the establishment of a public health system, have developed into drivers of decoupling during implementation.

Our hypotheses are inspired by the relevant literature (Mavrikou 2021; Zilidis 2005), echo the MSF logic and capture the interrelation between policy design and implementation which underpins the study. Furthermore, they support a hypothesis-generating design (Levy 2008), allowing the identification of mechanisms which could inform further MSF theorizing and be tested in future applications of the framework.

To guide the analysis, we employ a qualitative, process-tracing approach grounded on primary sources. In studying the mechanisms of policy change for public health in 2003, we rely on legal documents – Bills, parliamentary deliberation transcripts and policy evaluation reports – and 42 semi-structured elite interviews with relevant policymakers and experts between 1983 and 2003. Interviews were conducted in two waves (January 2018–January 2019 and February 2019–February 2020). Criteria for participant selection included occupation, involvement in the drafting of legislative proposals and the timing of policymaking participation. The processing of data from the first wave further informed the selection of respondents for the second. Interviewees were guaranteed anonymity and are referenced with their occupation. Questions were drafted in alignment with the five MSF structural elements – the problem, policy and politics streams, policy entrepreneurs and windows of opportunity – and were adjusted across interviews depending on the role and experience of each respondent.

We complement our data with further document analysis, 20 additional interviews and a survey of 261 stakeholders in Greek public health policymaking today to evaluate the reform's implementation trajectory and capture the degree of entrenchment of the holistic paradigm to health.[1] The MSF-guided structure was maintained for both data collection and processing. Respondents were selected through purposive and quota sampling to maximize response rates and ensure representative participation from an intrinsically small-N sampling frame (Etikan et al., 2016; Acharya et al., 2013). Occupation and age were selected as the two core criteria and the intended sampling distribution was determined after the institutional mapping of stakeholders. Our sampling process aimed for the equal and analogous representation of 85 percent of our sample from stakeholders in the Public Sector, the Private Sector and Research Centers/Universities and the equal and analogous representation of the remaining 15 percent of our sample from participants in NGOs/Patients Associations and the Media. Moreover, to include both veteran and novice stakeholders, we aimed for the equal and analogous representation of participants in the over 60, under 30 and 31–40 age groups for 30 percent of the sample and the equal and analogous representation of participants in the 41–50 and 51–60 age groups for the remaining 70 percent of the sample. Our survey produced a response rate of 52 percent (261/503) and our participants fitted the intended profile (Figures 7.1, 7.2).

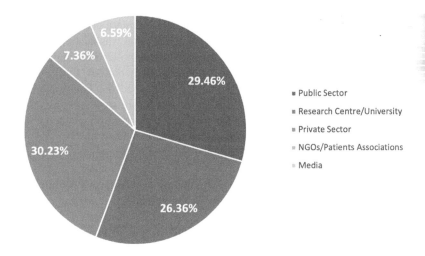

Figure 7.1   Sample occupation

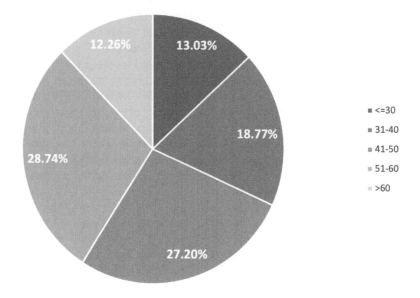

Figure 7.2   Sample age

1983–2003: FROM HEALTHCARE TO PUBLIC HEALTH

Following the fall of military dictatorship in 1974, Greece entered a modern era of parliamentary democracy. Democratic transition was accompanied by a frenzy of reforms as institutional configurations and policymaking processes had to be built from scratch. In health, the modern outlook of the sector was introduced by Bill 1397/1983, which established the Greek National Health System (GNHS), a public system of healthcare services. Over time, a medicine-centric perspective came to define sector's policymaking with pressing public health problems remaining unaddressed and ideas advocating the establishment of a public health policy framework struggling to emerge.

The Problem Stream: Public Health Problems Accumulate Without Established Feedback and Monitoring Mechanism

Driving the establishment of the GNHS in 1983 was a willingness to institute universal healthcare coverage by the socialist PASOK Government. "At the core of the system's vision lied equality: in access and in the level of care received" (interview with former health policy advisor). However, during the following decades, health inequalities emerged as one of the dominant problems facing the sector. "Truly universal healthcare coverage was fundamentally incompatible with the financing model underpinning the GNHS, which included multiple public insurance funds with separate budgets reimbursing different subgroups of the Greek working population" (interview with Ministry of Health (MoH) staffer). As the financing regime remained unmodified, inequalities kept growing exponentially. By 2002, findings of the World Health Organization (WHO) and the Greek National School of Public Health showed that income, education, and occupation could predict services usage at the panhellenic level, while those most in need appeared insufficiently treated by the public system (National School of Public Health 2002).

Extending health inequalities, a continuous rise in chronic and infectious diseases signified an unhealthy Greek population on the aggregate and pointed to structural deficiencies beyond secondary care. During the 1990s, Greece experienced frequent resurgence in the spread of measles and exhibited the highest death rate from tuberculosis among all Member States of the European Union (WHO 2021; Maltezou, Spyridis and Kafetzis 2000; Abel-Smith et al 1994). Meanwhile, avoidable mortality rates and unhealthy population habits showed consistent increase between 1980 and 2003, with Greece topping the EU in percentage of smokers (National School of Public Health 2007; Tountas et al. 2009). In the turn of the twenty-first century, "child obesity rates reached epidemic proportions" (interview with specialist doctor and former health policy advisor) with over 40 percent of boys and over 30 percent of girls being considered overweight or obese by 2003 (Georgiadis and Nassis 2007; Jackson-Leach and Lobstein 2006).

Nevertheless, these developments repeatedly failed to instigate debate around public health deficiencies as Greek health policy between 1983 and 2003 was devoid of formal attention-mobilizing mechanisms. "Instruments dedicated to consistent monitoring, evidence-based advisory and policy evaluation were massively underdeveloped" (interview with health economics expert and former health organization director). Despite legal provisions, evaluative and advisory bodies at the central and regional level – such as the Central Council for Health and Regional Health Authorities – faced long delays in their establishment, understaffing, and marginalization. As a result, the impact of indicator monitoring and policy feedback – two recognized driving forces of issue recognition in the MSF's problem stream – was neutralized.

Ultimately, it was focusing events bringing problems to light, such as the AIDS outbreak in the 1980s "illuminating state gaps in prevention and communication" (interview with community care expert). As issues built up cumulatively, they were brought to light with increased momentum during subsequent public health crises. In 2003, the looming threat of SARS-Cov-1, amidst Greece's preparation for the hosting of the 2004 Olympic Games, "brought simultaneous attention to systemic failures, institutional deficiencies and lack of management and coordination planning for public health" (interview with public health policy advisor to the Minister of Health). As renowned epidemiologist Dimitris Trichopoulos categorically stressed "emergency adjustments could never cover for the years and years of undermining public health policymaking" (Foura 2003). Together with developments in the politics stream, as outlined in the following sections, the SARS-Cov-1 epidemic triggered the opening of a window of opportunity for public health reform.

The Policy Stream: Politicization and Implementation Gaps Limit Venues for Public Health Policy Entrepreneurship

Regardless of the magnitude of issues, achieving policy change demands innovative ideas as "solutions chase problems" in the MSF logic (Kingdon 1984). In Greek health policy, the development and dissemination of ideas for public health had to overcome institutional fluidity and intense politicization which limited the availability of policy venues and reinforced the sector's dominant medicine-centric paradigm.

With public health remaining outside the realm of consideration in the founding law of the GNHS in 1983, "secondary care received the bulk of infrastructure investment during the first half of the 1980s" (interview with former director of Regional Health Authorities). Ideas promoting a shift of focus to public health were first generated by primary care specialists, who "advocated for higher investment in prevention, primary care and community care and higher interconnectedness between these domains and hospital services under the dogma of integrated care" (interview with primary and community care specialist and former MoH health policy advisor). During the late 1980s and early 1990s, these prevention and primary care experts exercised policy entrepreneurship through the health sector's formal policymaking channels, but their strategy proved ineffective.

Overtime, the de facto policymaking process for health significantly diverged from the *de jure* institutional design. Senior advisory instruments such as the Central Council for Health became weak and marginalized. Frequent changes in personnel through political appointments and the limited uptake of ideas by the MoH led to the Council's reports and proposals "rotting in the ministry's drawers" (interview with former Minister of Health). Beyond the Central Level, attempts by this first wave of policy entrepreneurs to advance a public health agenda from within – through Local Health Centers, the first point of contact with the system of services – were impeded by jurisdictional conflict and implementation gaps. The involvement of segmented insurance funds in primary care had introduced a second supervising ministry to the field – the Ministry of the Employment – increasing institutional friction. Moreover, the non-establishment of Regional Health Authorities, provisioned to oversee hospitals and Local Health Centers and transfer needs-based guidance to the MoH, "had left the street and the top levels of policymaking disconnected" (interview with former Local Health Centers coordinator). As a result, the efforts of policy entrepreneurs proved unsuccessful both in achieving influence over policymakers and in instigating dialogue within the policy community to refine and soften up policy alternatives for public health.

The failed policy advocacy brought to light the fact that meaningful policymaking venues in Greek health policy were few and heavily controlled. As politicization and non-implementation perpetuated, agenda-setting and decision-making turned increasingly centralized. For example, the abolishment of the Central Council for Health was followed by the establishment of two Special Secretariats within the MoH to undertake its duties (Bill 2071/1992), further narrowing the scope of instruments involved in policymaking. Meanwhile, the frequent institutional turnover highlighted that in Greek health policy, venues could be created at will, serve temporary functions, and be easily abolished after. As a result, policy formulation between 1983 and 2003 took place exclusively in dedicated reform design committees. They were set-up to deliver reforms, worked under the direct supervision of the Minister of Health, and were disbanded following the submission of a draft Bill. For policy entrepreneurs, no matter the content of their proposals, this regime offered uncontested levels of access and influence on policymakers. For governments, it allowed direct control over discussed and accepted alternatives and it enabled the evidence-based legitimation of decisions through the involvement of selected experts.

Throughout the 1980s and the 1990s, experts and advisors involved in the drafting of Bill 1397/1983 proved most successful in populating the reform design venues. Taking advantage of non-implementation and public administration undermining, these stakeholders "capitalized on their previous experience in policy formulation and forged strong connections with policymakers" (interview with former Minister of Health). Over time, they engaged in repeated role switching, occupying political, administrative, and scientific positions and extending their presence and influence in the policy subsystem. Between them, this group of policy entrepreneurs shared common preferences for maintaining the status quo and "addressing emerging challenges through minor adjustments to the established paradigm" (interview with specialist doctor and former health policy advisor). "Actors with a medicine-oriented outlook and the willingness to prolong their involvement in policymaking would persistently promote different implementation tracks for the same set of legislated policies" (interview with public health expert and former health organization director). As a result, ideas extending the focus of policymaking from hospital services to public health would struggle both to emerge and to be communicated to policymakers.

Driven by the experience of failure, the prevention and primary care specialists who had first introduced public health alternatives to the Greek health policy sector during the late 1980s, re-evaluated their strategy during the late 1990s. First, inspired by international developments and external policy feedback, they reformulated the content of their pet proposals. New international trends, epitomized by a strong emphasis on the social determinants of health in WHO's guidelines and evaluation reports (Ashton and Seymour 1988), coincided with an independent evaluation of the Greek health policy sector by a Committee of Foreign Experts in preparation for the country's entry to the European Single Market. "Although the Committee's findings and recommendations, highlighting the narrow focus and subpar administrative capacity of the Greek health policy paradigm, did not find short-term policy responsiveness, they proved crucial in shifting the perspective of public health policy entrepreneurs" (interview with health economics expert and former member of advisory committees in health). More specifically, the stressing of the need to acknowledge and manage the intrinsically multisectoral nature of public health policymaking incited a new wave of policy advocacy, promoting the institutionalization of the holistic perspective to health and the establishment of an independent system of public health services. Seeking to achieve value acceptability, policy entrepreneurs disassociated the proposed new system from the GNHS, as it would further include services in prevention, primary care, hygiene, the environment, social policy etc. (interview with public health expert and former reform design committee member). Moreover, championing technical feasibility and resource adequacy, they argued that "many of the system's components were already in place but lacked coordination and a common orientation towards fostering better population health" (interview with public health expert and former health authorities' director).

Second, with an added decade of systemic presence, public health policy entrepreneurs realized the need to pursue the establishment of a dedicated reform venue in order to successfully reach and influence policymakers; a strategy of venue creation (Mavrikou 2021). As such, they followed a fundamentally different advocacy approach, steering away from formal policymaking channels and administrative instruments and instead pursuing the establishment of a distinct policy entrepreneurial identity within the policy community. Although they functioned less as an organized collective and more as tacitly like-minded agents, they exhibited common tendencies in "highlighting the distinction of public health and hospital care in the public and the policy dialogue and reiterating the idea of an unrecognized system of public health services, extending the health sector" (interview with public health specialist and member of reform design committees). When a suitable window of opportunity would arise, policy entrepreneurs for public health aimed to be in a position credibly claim the creation of a dedicated venue for public health reform.

The Politics Stream: Powerful Organized Interests, Turnover in the Ministry of Health and Governance Modernization

In Greek health policy, the establishment of the GNHS in 1983 generated short-term ideological polarization, but its consolidation drove long-term ideological convergence. Viewed as a flagship initiative of the PASOK Government, the system of public hospital services was contested by the right-wing leading opposition party of New Democracy, "with prominent party members promising its abolishment if a change in government was to occur" (interview with health economics expert and former medicines organization director). However, fearing the political cost of doing away with free healthcare, New Democracy withdrew its reactionary agenda once in power and consolidated the GNHS with Bill 2071/1992. Ever since, both major parties exhibited commonality in preferences vis á vis health policy, opting to accept the structural blocks of the established policy paradigm and to diverge only in organizational and administrative matters. As such, "reforms would usually re-legislate previously unimplemented provisions with marginal differences in their proposed implementation trajectories" (interview with MoH staffer). Bills would mostly serve political and re-election considerations as "Greece is a country where reforms are named after ministers; a minister who does not deliver a reform, even if change is minimal, is politically stigmatized" (interview with former Minister of Health).

While the impact of government turnovers was decreasing, as ideological variance faded away, interest group influence persistently grew. Overtime, among organized interests, hospital doctors and insurance funds turned out to be most successful in enabling and blocking the adoption of reforms. Hospital doctors served as a powerful ally to the PASOK government in the 1983 GNHS founding bill and capitalized on their special status as exclusively subordinate to the MoH. Being the cornerstone of the GNHS, "they developed the ability to veto unfavourable proposals from the agenda-setting stage and were highly supportive of policy entrepreneurship promoting the preservation of the status quo" (interview with health policy advisor and doctors' association representative). Insurance funds, having maintained their independent status "despite provisions for unification in early drafts of bill 1397/1983", used their interconnectedness with business and workers interests beyond the health sector to block their organizational or institutional reformation (interview with management expert and former MoH policy advisor). In the year 2000, intentions to establish a universal health payer by Minister of Health Alekos

Papadopoulos caused his resignation, as he lost backing by the party leadership which was unwilling to clash with the segmented insurance funds.

In the rigid politics stream, it was the appointment of Papadopoulos's successor, Minister Konstantinos Stefanis, in 2002 that re-instigated momentum for reform. The incumbent PASOK Government, led by Prime Minister Kostas Simitis, had been re-elected two years earlier with a pre-electoral agenda of governance modernization. More than half-way into the four-year government term, "the Prime Minister was feeling pressure to deliver on his ambitious promises with respective legislative output" (interview with former PASOK MP). Although the ideological approach to health policy had remained stable, revitalizing governance through a public health reform arose as a possibility. Meanwhile, in the context of crisis produced by the SARS-Cov-1 epidemic and the residual turmoil from Papadopoulos's resignation, Minister Stefanis felt added pressure to deliver a marquee legislation. Shortly after his appointment, the Minister declared in the EU Council of Health Ministers, during the Greek Presidency, that "the pandemic should not be the cause to exercise public health policymaking but be a reminder of the ever-present state responsibility for public health" (European Parliament, 2003).

Bill 3172/2003: Policy Change for Public Health

The developments in the politics stream and the multitude of public health problems in the problem stream produced a suitable window of opportunity for policy entrepreneurs to pursue streams coupling for public health. Nevertheless, the sector's idiosyncratic policymaking process – centralized, and dependent on temporary policy venues – and the well-consolidated policy paradigm continued posing formidable impediments. Ultimately, the shift in the strategy of public health policy entrepreneurs since the mid-1990s proved instrumental in navigating the previously insurmountable obstacles. Both the vision for public health as a field and a system of services extending the health sector and the decision to not meddle with the organization of insurance funds decreased potential conflicts with powerful organized interests. Meanwhile, the adoption of the holistic perspective and the emphasis on coordinating established but disconnected services – to satisfy technical feasibility and resource adequacy – rendered the proposed policy alternatives compatible with demands for governance modernization. Recognizing the prevailing political winds, policy entrepreneurs for public health explicitly promoted the establishment of a public health policymaking framework as a governance response to a multifaceted crisis – the SARS-Cov-1 epidemic – and a legacy reform for Greece's upcoming hosting in the Olympic Games in 2004. Therefore, we confirm H1.

In 2003, policy entrepreneurship for public health succeeded, as a dedicated committee for reform was set up under the supervision of Minister Stefanis and was populated exclusively by public health advocates. Urgency and the avoidance of friction with the established status quo allowed the uncontested drafting, submission and adoption of the reform. Bill 3172/2003, the first public health legislation in Greece's modern history, formally recognized that the exercise of all public policy can impact the population's quality of health, instituted an independent and intersectoral system of public health services with distinct aims and functions and provisioned the dynamic readjustment of intended outcomes based on new evidence inputs.

2003–2022: Re-evaluating the Policy Paradigm

Nearly two decades after disruptive policy change in agenda-setting and policy adoption, Greece came face to face with another major public health crisis, the Covid-19 pandemic. Extending our MSF analysis to the country's strategic response to the Covid-19 outbreak, we assess the implementation trajectory of Bill 3172/2003, evaluate whether couplings were maintained, and explain how pervasive but unaddressed contextual idiosyncrasies of the design stage prove instrumental for the entrenchment of the new policy paradigm. To do this, we focus on the following three components: participation, which includes elements of the policy and the politics stream, monitoring, which encapsulates the dynamics of the problem stream, and the interplay between holistic public health delivery and medicine-centric care, which illuminates the overarching policy outlook.

Participation

Faced "with a threat policymakers and experts alike knew very little about but which inherently called for evidence-informed responses" (interview with doctor and Rector of the National and Kapodistrian University of Athens), Greece was provisioned to manage the pandemic through a system of consistent inputs, scientific processing, and informed outputs. Between 2003 and 2005 (when Bill 3370/2005 complemented Bill 3172/2003), three instruments with dedicated expertise in public health were established: the National Council for Public Health (NCPH), provisioned to serve as the chief scientific advisory instrument, the General Secretariat for Public Health, provisioned to serve as a hub of administrative public health expertise within the MoH, and the Centre for Disease Control and Prevention (KEELPNO), provisioned to contribute to the management of infectious and non-infectious diseases. Nevertheless, shortly after the Covid-19 outbreak reached Europe in February 2020, an 11-member National Committee for the Protection of

Public Health against Covid-19 was succeeded by a 26-man Committee for the Response to Emergency Public Health Threats from Infectious Causes, which was in turn complemented by a 10-member Committee for the Coordination and Monitoring of Governmental Policymaking. Much like before, with the adoption of Bill 3172/2003, the Greek approach showed reliance on ad hoc instruments.

The chief public health authority, the National Public Health Organization (NPHO) – a rebranded version of KEELPNO – was attributed a mostly administrative role, focusing on the registering of cases and the dissemination of guidelines and recommendations. When asked to evaluate its contribution to the management of Covid-19, stakeholders in Greek public health policy ranked it below interventions of extraordinary nature (such as the social distancing measures) as well as hospital units' transformations, with a mean score of 7.21 out of 10 (Figure 7.3). "The NHPO performed beyond expectations but that was because of transparency and executive consistency; not because of showing leadership as equivalent authorities did in, for example, Scandinavian countries" (interview with epidemiologist and MoH advisor during the SARS-Cov-1 epidemic).

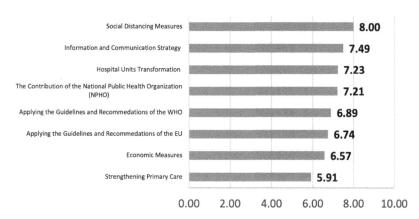

Figure 7.3   *Contribution of interventions to the management of Covid-19 (average evaluation)*

Moreover, the first pandemic-driven legislative revision, introduced in March 2020 (Bill 4675/2020), abolished the NCPH and replaced it with a Committee of Public Health Experts, which "is yet to report any work" (interview with former health authorities' director). Despite having been introduced as "an advisory instrument of the highest ranking in public health matters, reporting directly to the MoH, the Council never received serious political attention, becoming progressively more and more marginalized". "When I was appointed NCPH President, I asked for a team of staff to run a study on the determinants of health. I was presented with a couple of unqualified political appointees who had just graduated high school" (interviews with two former NCPH presidents).

Ultimately, the development of a decentralized system with meaningful specialized public health instruments was hindered by the same policymaking tendencies which marginalized public health considerations in the decades before the adoption of Bill 3172/2003. Politicization remained the norm. The staffing of all newly established public health bodies and authorities was subject to political appointments, "which were not always meritocratic" (interview with health economics expert and former hospital manager). As a result, long-term policy advocacy was rendered impossible. In the short-run, changes in government were accompanied by the drafting of various "Action Plans" for public health, often in cooperation with the WHO, but these were rarely acted upon. "There were pandemic response plans produced both between 2008–2010 (under a PASOK administration) and between 2014–2019 (under the left-wing SYRIZA administration). Nevertheless, facing the Covid-19 pandemic, the New Democracy administration did not rely on any of them because provisioned preparatory work had not been carried through and because they were drafted by opposition parties" (interview with communications expert and former coordinator of Public Health Action Plans).

Last, while permanent instruments were marginalized, temporary venues continued being favored to meet policy demands – as confirmed by the numerous Committees leading decision-making during the Covid-19 response. When asked about resources which most contribute to the exercise of public health policy, 64.37 percent of stakeholders selected scientific justification and research as essential while only 19.16 percent selected quantifiable aims (Figure 7.4). In a regime which inherently promotes the legitimation of politically-influenced decisions rather than the evidence-informed pursuit of public health outcomes, value acceptability is favored over technical feasibility for the survival of policy programs.

Monitoring and Managing the Quality of Health

In the Greek public health policy framework, complementing inclusive and scientifically-informed policymaking was to be the consistent monitoring of quality of health indicators to address emerging challenges and correct the trajectory of implementation if outcomes did not align with the intended goals. As such, at the start of the Covid-19 pandemic, the timely and accurate registering of cases was defined as a top priority for Greece. "The government intended to stay on top of the disease's development and contain clusters of infections

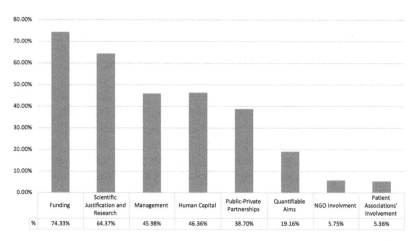

Figure 7.4   Resources contributing to better public health policymaking

before they mass-spread" (interview with member of the Covid-19 Specialists Committee). Faced with the pressures of a rapidly spreading disease, alarming deficiencies in monitoring infrastructure shortly came to light.

Despite the presence of dedicated instruments for epidemiological surveillance, Greece never established comprehensive disease registries. First, in the absence of primary care gatekeepers, "disease cases were only registered if patients were hospitalized" (interview with doctor and former hospital manager). Second, without self-reporting mechanisms and universal access to patient files, no aggregate data could be processed and comorbidities remained unassessed. Third, Regional Health Authorities – eventually set up in 2001 after two decades of re-legislation – were assigned to supervise and manage unreasonably large territories, with limited executive power. "The Sixth Regional Health Authority is managed only by a chief administrator and two deputies and covers [an area of] nearly one-fourth of the country" (interview with former Minister of Health). Facing a pandemic, Regional Health Authorities could not hire additional personnel to meet demands while "Regional Health Labs had been locked up for years due to lack of staffing and equipment" (interview with former Regional Health Council President). Last, KEELPNO's loss of credibility and eventual abolishment once again undermined institutional continuity. Ultimately, the same drivers that did not allow the mobilization of policymakers' attention to public health problems before the voting of Bill 3172/2003 – i.e., the lack of feedback and monitoring mechanisms – also prevented the new institutional framework from addressing emerging needs.

As a result, contact-tracing infrastructure for Covid-19 had to be built from scratch. Over time, a cases and vaccinations registry, connected to a digital prescription system and digitized patient records, was developed. However, emergency solutions during conditions of crisis rarely address widescale policy failures (Mahoney and Thelen 2010). Covid-19 monitoring was assigned to the Ministry of Civil Protection, with the government seeking to capitalize on administrative expertise. Ultimately, without decentralized monitoring instruments, it became a common sighting for "Deputy Minister of Civil Protection Kostas Hardalias and Infectious Diseases Specialist Sotiris Tsiodras to jump on helicopters so to assess rises in cases in rural areas" (interview with former health authorities' director).

"Expectedly, after the first lockdown was lifted in May 2020, Greece persistently struggled to contain local and regional outbreaks in their early stages" (interview with member of the Covid-19 Specialists Committee). By November 2020, a University of Athens initiative for the testing of water to monitor the concentration of infections had emerged as the most successful surveillance mechanism.

Submitting their evaluations to our survey in the midst of the first two waves of the Covid-19 pandemic, stakeholders in Greek public health policy ranked the monitoring and measuring of the population's quality of health with 4.54 out of 10, less than the middle evaluation value of 5. Moreover, all other systemic functions regarding threats and needs assessments were ranked among the least fulfilled in the current operation of the Greek public health system. The containment of health inequalities and the assessing of socio-economic determinants was ranked with 4.12, the measuring and improving of health services effectiveness with 4.14 and the setting of aims for the population's quality of health with 4.23 (Figure 7.5). The aggregate stakeholder insights show consensus admittance that long-standing problems which the 2003 public policy framework was designed to address remain prevalent – most prominently, health inequalities – and that the Greek public health system has failed in most aspects of health indicator surveillance.

Complementing these findings, a 2020 NPHO report further stressed that "in Greece, data, apart from being inadequate – and often outdated –, they are also difficult to process, compare with other inputs, and be used to inform interventions". Meanwhile, chronic diseases – especially ischemic heart disease, lung cancer and diabetes – largely linked to unhealthy lifestyles and delayed diagnoses, remain drivers of alarming rates of early mortality (Vollset et al. 2017). All in all, public health problems are now increasing, fact which the pandemic has helped to amplify.

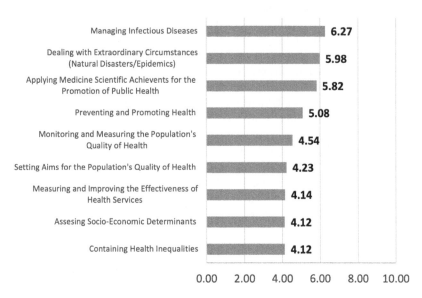

*Figure 7.5   Degree of fulfilment of public health policymaking aims
             (average evaluation)*

Holistic Approach to Health or Still a Medicine-Centric Paradigm?

Extending problem recognition and policy participation, the outbreak of the
Covid-19 pandemic further exposed the balance of priorities in Greek health
policy vis-á-vis public health. This last element is crucial in the study of coupling persistence, as it lies beyond the structural features of the policymaking
process. Rather, it captures whether the principles and ideas underpinning
change have successfully shifted the perspective of the policy community
and the goals of future policymaking. In a sector that was dominated for over
two decades by a strong medicine-centric orientation, the entrenchment of the
holistic approach to health when dealing with public health matters is essential
for policy change to be defined as successful.

At the start of the Covid-19 pandemic, "making sure the GNHS would
not collapse was our primary aim" (interview with Prime Minister Kyriakos
Mitsotakis). Immediately after the Committee for the Response to Emergency
Public Health Threats from Infectious Causes was set up as the chief policy
advisory instrument, "it was branded as a Committee of Infectious Disease
Specialists by many experts, politicians and the public" (interview with former
Minister of Health). Among the Committee's members, half specialized in
infectious diseases, most were professors of medicine, a few specialized in

epidemiology and none in public health. Especially in the early stages of the pandemic response, the priorities of Greek policymaking were predominantly oriented towards the sustainability of the hospital sector and relied on the guidance of medical experts (Zahariadis and Karokis-Mavrikos 2022). Governance reflexes pointed to the absence of a holistic perspective, in stark contrast with the policy paradigm which Bill 3172/2003 sought to introduce.

According to the WHO, and as quoted in all Greek Health Action Plans since 2016, "health in Greece is hospital-centric, as it prioritizes therapy over prevention. There is no referrals system, and, in practice, there is no network of public health services" (WHO 2016). Among Greek public health policy stakeholders, as shown in our survey responses, the nature of public health remains most closely associated with traditional, care-oriented fields, specifically prevention (selected by 73.18 percent), hospital care (selected by 56.70 percent) and primary care (selected by 42.53 percent). On the contrary, only 36.02 percent of participants in the Greek public health policy community consider the evaluation of health needs and only 34.48 percent consider the containment and elimination of health threats as crucial descriptors of the nature of public health (Figure 7.6). Importantly, these latter two are listed as the defining features of public health policymaking in the Greek legislative framework.

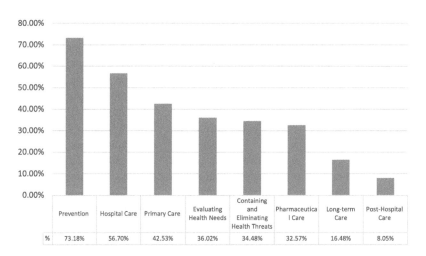

	Prevention	Hospital Care	Primary Care	Evaluating Health Needs	Containing and Eliminating Health Threats	Pharmaceutical Care	Long-term Care	Post-Hospital Care
%	73.18%	56.70%	42.53%	36.02%	34.48%	32.57%	16.48%	8.05%

Figure 7.6   Fields which best describe the nature of public health

Moreover, when asked to select essential scientific fields aiding public health policymaking, the majority of stakeholders pick medicine (85.06 percent), epidemiology (82.38 percent) and health economics (49.04 percent) as their top options. Statistics, linked to monitoring and the pursuit of measurable systemic outcomes are selected by only 37.16 percent of respondents while communications, social and political sciences, connected to the holistic perspective to health, are selected by 12.26, 9.58 and 7.65 percent of stakeholders respectively (Figure 7.7).

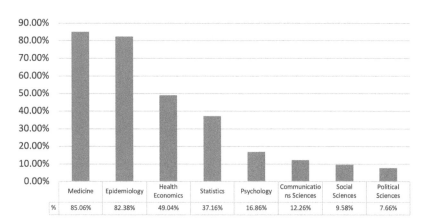

| % | 85.06% | 82.38% | 49.04% | 37.16% | 16.86% | 12.26% | 9.58% | 7.66% |

Figure 7.7   Scientific fields which can best support public health policymaking

On the aggregate, there is consensus admittance among Greek public health policy stakeholders that the current functioning of the Greek public health system does not serve the holistic approach to health. In a dedicated question, 68 percent of respondents evaluated the degree to which the holistic approach is promoted with scores from 0 to 5 out of 10 and only 2 out of the 261 participants gave perfect or near-perfect evaluations of 9 and 10 (Figure 7.8).

Following the passing of Bill 3172/2003, entrepreneurship for public health was not followed through with the development of organized public health lobbying or the institutionalization of public health expertise. The persistence of politicization, implementation gaps and public administration turnovers deprived public health policy entrepreneurs from venues to maintain momentum and continue steering policy outcomes in times of normalcy. Meanwhile, the governance outlook attributed to the 2003 reform impacted its legacy, disassociating it from the health sector's policy progression. As a result, within the Greek health policy community, the dominant perspective to the goals and means of the policy paradigm did not shift in accordance with the new public health principles. As shown by the aggregate insights of our survey, public health policy stakeholders still maintain a care-centric orientation and agree

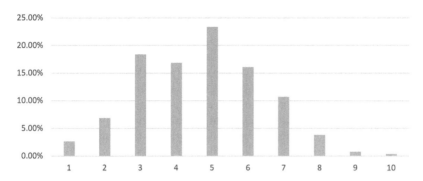

Figure 7.8   Degree to which the Greek public health system serves the holistic approach to health

that the current functioning of the Greek public health system is not in accordance with the holistic approach to health.

> The truth is that bill 3172/2003 passed through parliament without much deliberation but, unfortunately, it also did not have the greatest impact. It should be mentioned that the legislative content is impressive, but the provisions fail to develop an implementation map, which curtails their momentum. If you read the bill carefully, it describes epidemiological monitoring strategies, policy programs for the documentation of health needs, combatting inequalities etc. However, what was lacking was interventions to the public policymaking process which would allow such aims to be fulfilled by public policies" (interview with public health expert and MoH policy advisor).

CONCLUSIONS AND DISCUSSION

Innovative bills do not always renovate policymaking as the scope of change is contained during implementation. To understand why, we have concluded, focus may need to be shifted to structural features of the policymaking process, which manifest in the design stage and prove pervasive throughout. Our longitudinal process tracing application of the MSF to Greek public health policymaking uncovered the driving forces behind the passing of the first dedicated public health Bill in Greece's modern history in 2003 after two decades of resistance and the causes of streams decoupling since.

The agenda-setting phase of Greece's marquee public health reform – Bill 3172/2003 – was defined by repeated failures in policy advocacy as ideas struggled both to break through and to reach policymakers. In the policy stream, the legacy of the country's NHS-founding Bill proved pervasive. Intense politicization, implementation gaps and the absence of expertise beyond medicine produced a highly homogeneous policy community with a clear hospital-centric orientation. In the politics stream, ideological convergence between major parties and the high infiltration of policymaking outcomes by organized interests – most prominently specialist doctors and insurance funds – contributed to the preservation of the status quo. In the absence of a public health policy framework, public health problems, such as rises in infectious diseases and health services inequalities, faced a cumulative building up but struggled to mobilize attention. The undermining of administrative instruments neutralized the impact of policy feedback and indicator monitoring as mechanisms bringing issues to light. Ultimately, policy entrepreneurship to promote a public health outlook within the NHS fell victim to the absence of institutional venues as the true locus of policymaking lay beyond formal policymaking channels. Administrative turnovers – and more rarely crises – triggered the opening of windows, led to the establishment of ad hoc policy design instruments, and produced bills which would re-legislate previously unimplemented provisions.

Policy entrepreneurs for public health, driven by systemic experience and external influxes of ideas, revisited their strategy since the late 1990s. First, they identified the need to pursue advocacy through venue creation and second, they embraced the holistic perspective to public health, speaking of a system of services which would extend the health sector. In 2003, the SARS-Cov-1 epidemic coincided with a tumultuous resignation in the MoH leadership and pressures in the political stream for the PASOK Government to act on its modernization agenda. Having built a distinct identity as public health experts and strategically aligning their pet proposals with a governance reformation, policy entrepreneurs succeeded in populating a dedicated design committee for public health reform. The adoption of Bill 3172/2003 introduced the holistic perspective to public health in Greek policymaking, however, despite establishing a new system of services and new policy goals, it did not address the policy process pathogenies which had impeded change since the 1980s.

As a result, the new policy paradigm failed to be entrenched and stream decoupling ensued. The Covid-19 pandemic brought to light that Greek public health policymaking remains rudimentary in terms of institutions and resources, underdeveloped in terms of function and marginalized in terms of policy priorities. Our analysis of the implementation trajectory for Bill 3172/2003 confirmed H2, that "resisting forces in the policy and politics stream which persistently impeded the establishment of a public health system have developed into drivers of decoupling during implementation". More importantly, we were able to uncover the mechanisms driving this process and identify that all of them connect to contextual features which defined policy design.

First, politicization and implementation gaps re-emerged, only this time extending to the new public health instruments. Both plagued policy continuity, minimized recurring public health debate and stagnated the generation of new ideas in the primeval soup. Moreover, they had an indirect impact on the problem stream as they maintained the limited contribution of policy feedback and indicator monitoring in bringing problems to light. The Covid-19 pandemic, a focusing event, was the first time public health came to the epicenter of governmental attention since the 2003 reform. Second, the perpetuation of venue creation and interest group infiltration allowed the containment of the magnitude of policy change even after the reform had been introduced. The same set of stakeholders that had opposed public health policymaking in the past were allowed continued involvement in future policy decisions, while governments could once again operate with limited checks and balances. The resorting to multiple ad hoc committees, populated predominantly by medical specialists during the Covid-19 response epitomizes the institutionalization of this idiosyncratic practice. Last, propagated by the aforementioned developments, the non-emergence of consistent public health entrepreneurship did not allow the policy community to embrace the new outlook; the holistic perspective to health. As highlighted by our survey, Greek public health stakeholders still view public health through a care-centric lens. The governance angle attributed to the 2003 reform, although perhaps essential for its passing, was detrimental to its legacy. To this day, in the eyes of most, it has not been viewed as a structural disruption to the trajectory of Greek health policy.

The conclusions have the potential to instigate future research agendas for the MSF. First, applications of the framework in contexts of institutional instability – with fluidity, politicization and public administration undermining – can corroborate conclusions on the marginalization of policy feedback and indicator monitoring as problem stream mechanisms as well as on venue creation as an essential policy entrepreneurship strategy. Second, future research is also encouraged to explore further the linkages between design and implementation for the persistence of streams couplings. Across contexts, addressing institutionalized patterns of problem recognition, policy participation and interest accommodation which impede change are perhaps essential prerequisites for reforms to produce paradigmatic shifts, no matter how ambitious the new means and goals of policy programs are. If such mechanisms become systematically evaluated across case studies, the framework's capacity in better assessing the dynamic phenomenon of policy change could be enhanced greatly.

NOTE

1.   Both the interviews and the survey were conducted between 15.07.2020 and 13.12.2020.

REFERENCES

Abel-Smith, Brian et al. 1994. *Report on the Greek Health Services.* Athens: Pharmetrica.

Ashton, John and Howard Seymour. 1988. *The New Public Health.* Oxford: Oxford University Press

Blum, Sonja. 2021. "Upcycling a Trashed Policy Solution? Argumentative Couplings for Solution Definition and Deconstruction in German Pension Policy." In *The Political Formulation of Policy Solutions: Arguments, Arenas, and Coalitions*, eds. Zittoun Philippe, Fischer Frank, and Nikolaos Zahariadis, 21–44. Bristol, UK: Bristol University Press.

European Parliament. 2003. "6. Severe Acute Respiratory Syndrome (SARS)." *European Parliament Debates: Tuesday, 13 May 2003 – Strasbourg.*

Foura, Galini. 2003. "Greece is unprepared for Pneumonia." *Kathimerini.* May 11.

Fowler, Luke. 2019. "Problems, politics, and policy streams in policy implementation." *Governance* 32: 403–20.

Fowler, Luke. 2022. "Using the Multiple Streams Framework to Connect Policy Adoption to Implementation." *Policy Studies Journal.*

Georgiadis, Giorgos and George Nassis. 2007. "Prevalence of overweight and obesity in a national representative sample of Greek children and adolescents." *European Journal of Clinical Nutrition* 61 (9): 1072–74.

Herweg, Nicole, Nikolaos Zahariadis and Reimut Zohlnhöfer. 2018. "The Multiple Streams Framework: Foundations, Refinements and Empirical Applications." In *Theories of the Policy Process*, 4th edition, eds. Christopher M. Weible and Paul A. Sabatier, 17, 53 Boulder, CO: Westview.

Jackson – Leach, Rachel and Tim Lobstein. 2006. "Estimated burden of paediatric obesity and co-morbidities in Europe. Part 1. The increase in the prevalence of child obesity in Europe is itself increasing." *International Journal of Pediatric Obesity* 1 (1): 26–32.

Jones, Michael. D et al. 2015. "A River Runs Through It: A Multiple Streams Meta-Review." *Policy Studies Journal* 44: 13–36.

Kingdon, John W. 1984. *Agendas, Alternatives, and Public Policies.* Boston: Little Brown.

Levy, Jack S. "Case studies: Types, Designs, and Logics of Inference." *Conflict Management and Peace Science* 25 (1): 1–18.

Mahoney, James and Kathleen Thelen. 2010. *Explaining Institutional Change: Ambiguity, Agency, and Power.* Cambridge: Cambridge University Press.

Maltezou, Helena, Panagiotis Spyridis and Dimitrios Kafetzis. 2000. "Extra-Pulmonary Tuberculosis in Children." *Archives of Disease in Childhood* 83: 342–46.

Mavrikou, Maria. 2021. *Designing public health policies* (in Greek). Hellenic National Archive of Doctoral Theses.

National School of Public Health. 2002. *Report on the Self-Evaluation of Health Quality: Health and Health Services in the Greek Population* (in Greek). Athens: National School of Public Health.

National Public Health Organization. 2020. *Health Map* (in Greek).

National School of Public Health. 2007. *Report on Preventable Mortality 1980–2003* (in Greek). Athens: National School of Public Health.

Sager, Fritz and Eva Thomann. 2017. "Multiple streams in member state implementation: Politics, problem construction and policy paths in Swiss asylum policy." *Journal of Public Policy* 37 (3): 287–314.

Tountas, Giannis et al. 2009. *The Greek Population's Health* (in Greek). Athens: Papazisis.

Vollset, Stein Emil et al. 2017. "Fertility, mortality, migration, and population scenarios for 195 countries and territories from 2017 to 2100: a forecasting analysis for the Global Burden of Disease Study." *The Lancet* 396: 1285–1306.

World Health Organization (WHO). 2021. "Measles: Reported cases by country." *Global Health Observatory data repository.* Retrieved from https://apps.who.int/gho/data/view.main.1540_62.

World Health Organization (WHO). 2021. *Greece: Profile of Health and Well-being.* Retrieved from https://www.euro.who.int/__data/assets/pdf_file/0010/308836/Profile-Health-Well-being-Greece.pdf.

Zahariadis, Nikolaos, and Theofanis Exadaktylos. 2016. "Policies That Succeed and Programs That Fail: Ambiguity, Conflict, and Crisis in Greek Higher Education." *Policy Studies Journal* 44 (1): 59–82.

Zahariadis, Nikolaos, and Vassilis Karokis-Mavrikos. 2022. "Centralization and Lockdown: The Greek Response." In *Policy Styles and Trust in the Age of Pandemics*, eds. Nikolaos Zahariadis, Evangelia Petridou, Theofanis Exadaktylos and Jörgen Sparf, 79–100. Abingdon, Routledge.

Zilidis, Christos. 2005. *Reform in Health (2000–2004). The Principles and the Frame of Development for Health Policy (in Greek).* Athens: Mediforce.

8. Multiple Streams, policy implementation and the Greek refugee crisis

Nikolaos Zahariadis and Evangelia Petridou

The middle of the 2010s was characterized by increased mobility of populations from the Middle East and Africa towards Europe. The route of most prospective refugees took them through Greece, and specifically through a small number of Greek islands that are geographically proximate to Turkey. The Greek administration and society, battered for years by an economic crisis, proved unable to adequately provide the services necessary for the reception, processing, housing, and societal integration of migrants. In this chapter, we pose the question: why have efforts to address the Greek refugee crisis mostly failed to produce the desired results? Applying Boswell and Rodrigues' (2016) Multiple Streams Framework (MSF) on implementation, we argue that the lack of administrative capacity and oscillating political support pose nearly insurmountable problems to effective policy implementation. Effective implementation is defined as the distance between intended and actual outcomes and seeks to specify the reasons why the distance widens (or not) over time. Taking a dynamic view of the issue, we find that the same issue evolves over time. Depending on administrative capacity and political support, migration outcomes tend to go through phases from non-implementation to bottom-up implementation to coercion and finally to consensus. Our argument implies a dynamic cycle of implementation with significant social and political implications.

Our study is informed by two objectives. First, we explore the implementation aspects of MSF, something that has not received wide scholarly attention. We examine a highly salient issue that deals with the weak target population of irregular migrants. Given that implementation may take different forms depending on the implementing agent's preferences (Herweg and Zohlnhöfer, forthcoming), we keep the target population out of the equation to focus more squarely on the interaction between policy makers, street-level bureaucrats and NGOs. Second, the migration crisis is important not only because it has received inadequate scholarly attention so far but also because at its core, the Syrian crisis, represents what António Guterres, then United Nations (UN) High Commissioner for Refugees (UNHCR) and current UN Secretary General, claimed to be "the biggest humanitarian emergency of our era" (Edwards 2014). In 2016, an estimated record of between 4.1 and 5.3 million unauthorized immigrants crossed into Europe (Pew Research Center 2019). By 2022, that number shrank to 199,900 (European Commission 2022). We focus on Greece (2012–21) because it has been at the center of the migration crisis and because migration patterns have shifted dramatically from the central Mediterranean route (Italy) to the eastern Mediterranean route (Greece) and more recently back to the western (Spain) and central Mediterranean routes.

We first outline a theoretical framework of implementing migration policy and specify expectations. We then proceed to examine implementation outcomes in the Greek islands of Lesvos and Samos from 2015–22. The findings have implications for MSF and theories of implementation as well as migration policy.

A FRAMEWORK OF POLICY IMPLEMENTATION

We seek to understand the highly varied results in implementing migration policy. While there exist numerous definitions of implementation, many scholars adopt Mazmanian and Sabatier's (1983, 20) definition as "the carrying out of a basic policy decision, usually incorporated in a statute but which can also take the form of important executive orders or court decisions". Decisions are usually implanted in statutes that link objectives to desirable outcomes. Perspectives on implementation involve an assessment on whether the achieved outcomes match the intended outcomes at the time of policy formulation. Analyzing implementation may rely on top-down, bottom-up or hybrid models, with the latter attempting to bridge the gap between the first two approaches. Top-down models of implementation, exemplified by Pressman and Wildavsky's (1973) study, operationalize effective implementation as the degree of attaining intended goals decided at the policy formulation stage (Knill and Tosun 2020). In other words, implementation is about matching policy objectives and achieved outcomes. Conversely, bottom-up models take a more fluid, process-oriented view on public policy, assessing policy implementation against the preferences of the actors involved and whether the process itself allowed for learning and capacity building (see, e.g., Hjern and Porter 1981). Finally, hybrid models seek to bridge the gap between the policy makers who make the policy decisions at the macro level, and the street-level bureaucrats who implement policy at the micro-level (Knill and Tosun 2020).

Boswell and Rodrigues (2016) employ the MSF's concepts of problem, policy, and politics streams (Zahariadis 2003; Herweg, Zahariadis and Zohlnhöfer 2018) to offer a hybrid model by using organizational theory that informs the application of MSF on policy implementation. More specifically, they use organizational theory to operationalize the politics and problems streams as they relate to the bureaucratic organizations tasked with implementing policy. Outcomes are based on variations in the two streams. We chose their MSF model of implementation for two reasons. First, we aim to bridge the gap between policy makers and implementing agents. Second, they are the only ones, to our knowledge, who discuss the possibility of what we observe: a cycle of implementation modes. They articulate two expectations: first, because bureaucracies involved in policy implementation are dependent on political leaders for legitimacy and resources, strong support by the central authority for a policy tends to put pressure on these bureaucracies to adjust their service delivery structure so that they implement the policy as directed. At the same time, institutions (bureaucracies included) are notoriously slow to respond to external pressures. Boswell and Rodrigues' (2016) second expectation is that when organizational problems do not fit the policy decided at the central level, implementation will likely yield sub-optimal results, i.e., outcomes not envisioned by central authorities. In MSF terms, the authors conceptualize implementation as the coupling or joining together of political support (or not) with problem fit. Implementation will vary depending on whether the politicians at the center strongly (or weakly) support a course of action that is congruent with the dispositions of local agents (street bureaucrats) who are tasked with addressing an important problem.

Combining two scales of politics with problem fit results in a four-way typology of implementation modes. Consensual implementation involves strong political support and a good fit with problems at the organizational level, so the implementing organization is more likely to collaborate with the central authority in the implementation process, though this does not mean that the implementation will be successful. At the opposite end, when there is neither political support nor a good fit with problems, then the implementing organization finds it difficult to implement policy; neither resources nor political guidance is there to support the process. Weak political support but a good fit for the problem will translate into the organization driving the bottom-up implementation process, while implementation becomes a top-down coercive process when there exists political support but the fit for the problem is weak at the organizational level, thus rendering the implementing organization unwilling to make the necessary changes for implementation.

Following Boswell and Rodrigues (2016), we hypothesize that implementation will vary according to factors in the political and problem streams. They identify four types of implementation, but their view is somewhat static in the sense that they assume modes of implementation will stay the same throughout the life cycle of an issue. They briefly posit modes may shift (p. 520), but the authors do not elaborate on why and what direction they may follow.

We take a more dynamic view and theorize both the reason for their shift and the likely trajectory by arguing modes of implementation will likely shift over time driven by performance. The mechanism of improving (or not) implementation effectiveness involves adequacy of administrative capacity. Movement across modes of implementation is generated mainly by oscillating political support. Greater distance between intended and actual outcomes signifies greater ineffectiveness. When the distance in outcomes widens due to implementation, we first observe a clear movement by "street" bureaucracies to improve results. This effort puts local agencies at the forefront of policy. However, to counterbalance this prominence of bureaucrats, politicians re-frame the policy objectives to showcase their involvement in the hopes of attracting voters. Such counter-balancing creates rifts between agencies and their paymasters, generating political strife in the form of coercion or decoupling of policy objectives and bureaucratic action.

H1: Inadequate administrative capacity will likely decrease implementation effectiveness.

Administrative capacity refers to three elements: coordination, legal tools, and resources. Perhaps the most important task of implementation is coordination or steering: the ability of agencies to effectively perform tasks at the right time and in the right sequence. For example, providing meals to refugees involves a significant amount of coordination: a provider must be procured, which could be the military, and meals must be prepared and distributed without gaps in service delivery. The process is hampered if, for example, volunteers show up to distribute food that has not yet been delivered, or alternatively, not properly stored, and hence wasted. In addition, legal and administrative tools need to be developed and already operating for implementation to be effective (May, 2012). For example, legislation needs to be passed before the military can be brought in to manage migrant camps. Infrastructure, such as adequate facilities, must be in place before migrants are able to stay there. Adequate sanitation infrastructure must be available to ensure a relatively frictionless reception center. For example, Hille and Knill (2006) have found that capacity is more important than the nature of political system in explaining implementation of EU laws in countries prior to EU accession. It is possible that lack of capacity shapes perceptions of problems. One cannot address problems that one is not equipped to address. The same is true with the political stream. Support for a policy that does not produce desired results is politically ruinous.

Resources refer to material tools and human resources available to government to complete the proposed tasks. Falkner et al. (2004) found that resources explain non-compliance to EU law better than political opposition. Food has to be purchased and stored, agents have to be compensated for work performed. Transportation equipment must be secured in timely fashion before migrants can be moved from place to place, as needed. Sometimes, there is inadequacy of expertise. For example, registering and deciding on asylum-seekers are tasks that require legal competence. Security operations, such as patrolling territorial waters, have to be performed by appropriate personnel. If such personnel do not exist in adequate numbers, implementation will suffer. Paucity of resources clearly affects performance. Fewer resources when the economy shrinks hamper implementation effectiveness by causing registration delays or leading to overcrowding conditions in the migration case. In MSF terms, they likely lead to decoupling of problems from their political supporters, generating the need for blame avoidance and change (Hood 2011). While politicians will likely seek to blame local agents or others for lack of performance, agents will likely fire back with support from the local community. The argument will likely be "we are trying to address a real problem that the center does not comprehend". It is a powerful argument that resonates politically, especially when local communities are facing a catastrophe. Such confrontation sets the stage for a change of course.

H2: Oscillating political support will likely generate movement across modes of implementation.

As Boswell and Rodrigues mention, movement across implementation modes is driven mainly by political support. However, they do not elaborate on why this may be the case and in which direction. We begin by assuming problematic preferences and unclear technology. When there is weak political support in the political stream and inadequate administrative capacity, bureaucrats are faced with an impossible task. They are asked to implement a policy but are not given the tools, the political support or even the definition of what they should be doing. Under these conditions, administrative discretion increases substantially; "implementers are the primary decision makers" (Fowler 2019, 408). The end result is a chaotic implementation or lack thereof. It seems everyone is doing what they want without an overall purpose.

The main issue is lack of clear and consistent communication between policy makers and implementing agencies. Communication contains the problem, objectives, and the organizational process linking the two. Communication within organizations and policy systems fulfills five major functions: monitoring and compliance, motivation, problem solving, conflict management, and sense making (Neher 1997). The message needs to be consistent throughout every turn of the process to effectively perform these functions and create certainty among stakeholders, proponents, and opponents of the policy. Frequent shifts in problem definition or outcome indicators signal confusion to stakeholders and discourage compliance. Different messages encapsulate different cause and effect chains, which can be used as evidence of internal conflicting goals, high interdependence, and disagreement or ignorance about solutions. For example, proclaiming migrants are temporary and then claiming the need for them to be socially integrated sends mixed messages as to temporary status and creates confusion which undermines vital local support, increasing resistance to implementation. As Taylor et al. (2021, 104) hypothesize, unclear messages about the goals of policy decrease the likelihood of implementation. Because social integration is a highly complex and uncertain process, building more refugee centers sets in motion a politically volatile and long process with dubious results that agents may hesitate to implement.

If the problem persists, i.e., when agents are called upon to implement seemingly aimless policies, their dispositions become important. This is when perceptions of problem fit become essential. The likely result is bottom-up implementation and the possible appearance of non-governmental organizations seeking to fill the gap. Communication affects and is affected by the disposition of implementing agents. It is critical to build support for policy in order for agents to comply with policy maker demands. By implication, agents must be convinced they (their agencies or communities, however defined) will gain or at least not lose resources or prestige. For reasons well-articulated by Schattschneider (1960) issue conflict expands as new actors enter the political arena. New actors may raise new issues and point to unexplored deleterious implications if implementation proceeds as planned. Goal displacement makes issues more complex and agents likely more cautious, reducing accountability and compliance (Pressman and Wildavsky 1973).

The emergence of robust bottom-up implementation creates formidable political problems. The political stream may be ripe, but agents hold different views of problem fit; they may define problems in very different ways or not at all. Politicians appear out of step with events on the ground as agents possibly move in different directions depending on local conditions. To recover their sense of leadership, they will likely "put themselves in front" by launching initiatives, which may involve clarification of objectives, new programs, new definitions of the problem etc. These initiatives will likely clash with established action on the ground because they are designed not to solve the problem but showcase politics. Unclear or fluid organizational technology in the form of resources and capacity becomes a liability because, especially in centralized systems, the national government provides the tools to solve problems that may not exist, at least in the minds of street-level bureaucrats. Administrative capacity may increase in absolute terms but not in ways that may fit the problem as defined on the ground. Political support is likely to strengthen but the drift of the dispositions between politicians and agents will likely lead to coercive or decoupled implementation. At this point, it is difficult to ascertain which direction implementation will take; so, we will let the empirical case point to the direction.

METHODS AND DATA

We employ a single case study design aimed at examining, in detail, a historical episode (Greek migration policy) for the purpose of developing an explanation that may be transferable to other events (George and Bennett 2005). This in-depth examination of a single case aims to refine the typology brought forth by Boswell and Rodrigues (2016) so that it may be tested in other cases.

We use three sources of data to assess the empirical validity of expectations in line with case study research (Yin 2014). The first includes publicly archival material and data from international organizations. The second involves statements and interviews by policy makers and EU officials in the media. The third includes elite interviews and participant observations in meetings with national, regional, and local officials and NGO members, and academic experts in the field of migration policy in Greece.

The primary data collection took place in three instances. First, we conducted nine interviews on the island of Lesvos in June 2016 – where the majority of migrants have crossed into Greece – with local and regional officials, volunteers, and NGO members, two interviews in Thessaloniki with one university academic and one NGO member in May 2016, and two interviews in Athens with two university academics in June 2016. Second, in October 2018, a delegation from Sweden led by the Swedish Migration Board conducted interviews with the NGOs Metadrasi and Praxis, officials from the Hellenic Police, Frontex, the Greek Coastguard, the Asylum Service, the Greek Ministry for Migration, the United National High Commissioner for Refugees (UNHCR), the International Organization for Migration (IOM), the Hellenic Center for Disease Control and Prevention (KEELPNO) and the Reception and Identification Service (RIS). Following those interviews, we also visited the reception and identification camp in Samos. Finally, we collected further data during visits to Lesvos in June 2019, December 2021, and June 2022. We visited the new camp at Mavrovouni and conducted interviews with officials at UNHCR, leaders at the camp, and a local NGO. Our data consist of extensive notes taken during the interviews and meetings, which were thematically analyzed based on the Boswell and Rodrigues (2016) typology and our added concept of administrative capacity.

GREEK MIGRATION POLICY AND ITS IMPLEMENTATION, 2012–21

Greece has been an important first EU country of arrival for migrants and refugees mainly heading to northern Europe. Whereas the number of migrants crossing the Greek border fluctuated over the years, that number peaked in 2015 with 821,000 people crossing the border into Greece (IOM 2015).

The Policy Landscape in Greece Prior to 2015

Greek migration policy had historically been ad hoc and indifferent to EU conventions. This changed in 2012 for three important reasons. First, Greece tightened immigration procedures and brought about drastic changes in detention and repatriation policies. Forced by a European Court of Justice decision in 2011, which found that 90 percent of all irregular entry into Europe was through the Greek borders (IOM 2016b), the Greek Government began implementing more stringent detention policies and tightened security at the borders. Frontex, the EU's external border forces, supplemented Greek patrols of sea routes in the Aegean – many Greek islands are just a few miles off the Turkish coast. As a result, detention and repatriation policies became stricter to follow EU Directives and the Dublin II Regulation more closely, which deals with immigration in the EU (McDonough and Tsourdi 2012).

Second, the economic crisis and consequent austerity measures had a significant impact on implementing Greek migration policy. As the economy dove into a tailspin – Greek real income fell by more than one-fourth since 2009 and unemployment soared to more than 25 percent in 2012 (Zahariadis 2015) – social and political good will evaporated. The far-right political party Golden Dawn capitalized on social discontent and set up food banks for Greek citizens only. Moreover, government policy was heavily criticized for deficiencies in asylum processes, maintaining inappropriate conditions in migrant camps, and following often arbitrary and irregular repatriation policies (Human Rights Watch 2015).

Third, geopolitical developments in the region, especially the implosion of Qaddafi's regime in Libya and the civil war in Syria, reshuffled routes and sources of migrant origin. Italy witnessed the highest refugee waves in 2012–13 largely following the deteriorating situation in Libya. However, as Syria's war intensified and as the number of deaths increased among those crossing the Mediterranean, refugees began seeking alternative and safer routes through Greece.

In summary, even though it was aided a bit by EU funds, the administrative capacity of the Greek state when it came to migration policy was particularly low. Implementation was characterized by a lack of institutional structures and administrative know-how, compounded by a drawn-out financial crisis that further restricted meagre public sector resources and external crises. Concomitantly and until 2015, political support in that phase was rather anemic.

A Tidal Wave of Migrants Creates the Need for a New Approach, 2015–19

A new government in Greece and heavy bombardment by Russian planes in Syria precipitated a mass exodus of Syrians seeking asylum in neighboring lands and in Europe. After winning the national election in January 2015, the radical left-right coalition government in Greece between the Radical Left (SYRIZA) and the party of Independent Greeks (ANEL) signaled a change in policy. The minister in charge of migration policy, Tasia Christodoulopoulou, noted the government's intention to stop indiscriminate detentions, gradually releasing asylum-seekers and illegal migrants that have been detained for long periods. The aim was to follow a more humanitarian approach and offer alternatives to detention, such as open shelters and voluntary returns.

Implementation was non-existent because the political stream did not cope with the problem at hand. The Greek Government lost control of the situation as the number of migrants arriving from the Turkish coast surpassed every expectation. When asked about the waves of migrants washing on Greek shores, Prime Minister Alexis Tsipras stunningly quipped during a press conference in September 2015: "What borders? Does the sea have borders we didn't know about" (*Proto Thema* 2015)? Indicative of the magnitude of the problem is the simple fact that in July 2015 alone, Greece received more refugees than in the entire previous year. Moreover, the Greek executive had no structures in place to provide housing for refugees. Hundreds of thousands of refugees were left to fend for themselves in the streets of Athens and other big cities while many residents of Greek islands bitterly complained about the lack of suitable accommodations, planning, and funding (Tagaris 2015). By August 2015, the UNHCR described the situation in the Greek islands as "total chaos" with completely inadequate accommodation, water, medical, and sanitation infrastructure (BBC 2015). Implementation was episodic and idiosyncratic, reflecting the preferences of the groups involved. One could argue the situation resembled more non-implementation because there was no well-articulated Greek migration policy.

At the transnational level, on March 18, 2016, the EU and Turkey signed a joint statement governing the return of "irregular migrants" crossing from Turkey into Greek islands as from 20 March 2018 (European Commission 2016). The agreement stipulated that migrants arriving in Greek islands would be registered and their application would be processed by the Greek authorities. Moreover, migrants had the right to appeal the decision by the Greek asylum service, a process that could take months.

This agreement resulted in migrants bottlenecking in the Greek islands, delays in asylum processing and the returns to Turkey, substandard conditions in the camps, and what was de facto "the outsourcing of the responsibility and 'burden' to the front-line states" (Dimitriadi 2016, 3). In 2018, this last statement was echoed by Brigadier General Dimitris Mallios and Ilias Miltiadis Klapas, General Secretary for migration policy. Klapas stated in a meeting with stakeholders that the 'migration crisis' demanded European (and not just Greek or Italian or Spanish) solutions, necessarily involving some kind of EU-wide population redistribution and a concomitant responsibility reallocation.

We now turn to administrative capacity in the form of inter-agency coordination and collaboration at the front lines aimed at sufficiently managing the flows of people. Such cooperation would be even more salient in the exacerbated conditions in the Greek island migrant camps. Given the lack of political will to address the issue, several non-governmental organizations got involved in the process of receiving and housing migrants. The (bottom-up implementation) process began to reflect the preferences of street-level bureaucrats who had little guidance from the state and were called upon to solve a very complex crisis. In addition to a European Commission presence, officials from the United Nations High Commission for Refugees (UNHCR), Reception and Identification Service (RIS) (the Greek public sector entity running the migrant camps at that time), Asylum Service, the Greek Organization of Public Health (then named KEELPNO), the European Union Agency for Asylum (then European Asylum Support Office, EASO), Europol, the European Border and Coast Guard Agency (FRONTEX), the International Organization of Migration (IOM), Hellenic Police, the non-governmental organizations (NGOs) Metadrasi, and Praxis, and the Greek military were on the ground in the migrant camps by 2018.

Implementation was hampered by low administrative capacity including relative lack of coordination. As an interviewed official at a migrant camp said in June 2019, the pathologies of the Greek public sector undermined effectiveness. As an example of implementation ineffectiveness, a Greek coastguard liaison office had to always be present with Frontex personnel patrolling waters because the latter had no jurisdiction in individual Member States' territory. When a vessel with migrants was spotted, information was passed onto the Hellenic Coastguard, which could not always respond promptly as it was overwhelmed by the sheer numbers of arrivals. Migrants may have therefore been welcomed by NGOs, but that created serious complications. Locals and NGOs were advised not to help the new arrivals because they could be charged with human trafficking. In other words, an overwhelmed public sector could not respond effectively, and NGOs were afraid to help.

Once new arrivals walked, or were transported, to the camps, the Hellenic Police got involved. It searched the migrants and their belongings, removed passports, mobile phones, and sharp objects; until the initial interviews were carried out, the migrants were considered detainees. At that time, a KEELPNO physician asked them questions to determine disability or the presence of any communicable diseases. It is at this stage where migrants' vulnerability status was assessed. But there were not enough Greek physicians to handle all the cases, creating huge bottlenecks. For example, at one point in 2019, there was a sole Greek physician for the entire Moria camp in Lesvos (aided by doctors from NGOs), which served at that time 19,000 migrants.

The lack of institutional structures and political unwillingness (or perhaps incompetence) to address the magnitude of the problem were evidenced in the activities of international organizations and NGOs. The UNHCR did not have an operative role in the hot spots. They had administrative tasks, were responsible for informing migrants of their rights and assisted with vulnerability assessments. Together with EASO, they followed up cases of extremely vulnerable people acting as observers and financing housing where available. The IOM collected data and, in collaboration with NGOs, mainly provided legal advice. Four different NGOs were involved in providing critical services for the migrants mainly because Greek civil servants could not. Metadrasi was the only organization providing interpreters and guardians for unaccompanied minors. Indeed, the public sector in Greece did not employ any translators whatsoever; the government was completely reliant on the services of Metadrasi. The Greek Council for Refugees (GCR) provided legal aid, while the Association for Social Support of Youth (ARSIS) managed accommodation. NGOs also collaborated in age assessment and dealt with sexual and gender-based violence.

In terms of logistics, the Greek military handled the contracts for food provision and cleaning and maintenance of the hot spot area. There were no kitchen facilities in the camp in Samos, which was a disused military camp. Food was catered in, managed by a contract tendered through public procurement every 90 days. Tight procurement rules are a legacy of a historically corrupt public sector and years of austerity measures. The military was a competent actor when it came to procuring food; however, the overcrowding in the camp and the penuriousness of the facilities made the distribution of food a tedious and disruptive process. This stressed people out as they feared they would not get enough food or water for the day.

As an example, the Samos camp was set up for an occupancy of about 700 and as of October 11, 2018, it was housing upwards of 4,000 people rendering living conditions of the migrants supremely substandard. In Moria (Lesvos) as late as September 2019, 19,000 were crowded in and around a camp that was built to house 3,000 (later 3,500) people. Migrants were housed in containers with one larger room, one smaller room, and a kitchen area. The human bottleneck had resulted in two or three families living in one room and people having to sleep in shifts. Even at that, the containers were not enough so people spilled beyond the borders of the camp in makeshift tents.

In summary, in early 2015, implementation of migration policy was episodic and idiosyncratic. The situation began to change with the signing of the 2016 EU agreement with Turkey and the organization of camps in Greek islands to process the incoming migrants. Eventually, implementation of policy reflected the preferences of street-level bureaucrats, NGOs, and to a lesser extent international organizations. Confirming our hypothesis, political will, mainly in collaboration with EU officials, provided the requisite problem frame that gave implementation some direction: organized camps, regular food distribution, processing facilities, etc.

Consensus Following Coercion? 2019–22

National elections on 7 July 2019 brought to power a center-right government, which promised to address the problem of migration more effectively. Wishing to downplay the politically explosive consequences of migration, the new government downgraded the Ministry of Migration to its previous status as a Directorate in the Ministry of Interior and Administrative Reform. However, it quickly changed course and reconstituted the Ministry for Migration Policy and Asylum because the problem of migration exacerbated in the summer 2019. Political will changed direction and so did implementation.

As the flows of migrants increased in the summer of 2019, so did the political pressure on the new government to do something different from its predecessor. The decision was made to chart a new direction based on four points:

- Lower the numbers of migrants in camps on the islands by transferring many of them to less crowded camps on the mainland.
- Reduce the numbers staying in Greece by expediting the asylum process, limiting the number of appeals, and more robustly patrolling the borders.
- Limit the role of NGOs.
- Transform the reception and identification centers (so-called hot spots) from open into closed camps, i.e., limit access, while building new ones that could handle more people and also house those about to be repatriated.

The policy ran into significant problems, especially from local populations, who felt that building new camps amounted to housing more people. In other words, the government got more involved politically, but the problem frame was contested. Unlike our theory's prediction, it was not the street-level bureaucrats who protested or somehow led implementation astray, but it was local governments and the islanders. As an islander whom we interviewed in June 2022 said, the problem frame transitioned from "we will do better" to "by building more camps, we invite more migrants". Open riots in some islands hampered implementation plans. Government spokesperson, Stelios

Petsas, summed it all up at the time: "We understand that there is a problem of trust that was created over the previous years. But the closed facilities will be built, and we are calling on the public to support this" (*The Guardian* 2020). In short, we are witnessing coercive implementation where national political will clashed with local governments over the problem frame, and of course, the content of policy.

Eventually, the government got its wish mainly because it established its tough-on-migration credentials by the Turkish border in January 2020 and by the arrival of the Covid-19 pandemic. The Greek Government successfully defended its borders as thousands of irregular migrants, after having been bused in by Turkish authorities, demanded entry (Tzimas 2021). Moreover, as the Covid-19 pandemic brought lockdowns throughout the country, political pushback subsided following the dramatic decreases in migration flows. Camp overcrowding was reduced as the numbers fell to more manageable levels and administrative capacity increased. For example, the number of migrants housed in Mavrovouni (the successor camp to Moria in Lesvos which had since burned down) dropped in June 2022 to below 1,000, a number unthinkable two years prior. As a result, NGOs have begun to limit their presence in the islands and transform their operations from reception to integration of migrants. As an NGO interviewee mentioned in June 2022, NGOs have adapted their operations as the problem (and needs) have changed. Equally importantly, greater administrative capacity over time made a difference. Services provided by NGOs, such as translation, are now provided by camp staff. A member of the UNHCR aptly summarized the situation: "there may still not be enough resources, but we now have expertise and experience to address the next crisis". It appears that we have entered a period of consensual implementation.

CONCLUSION

We examined the implementation of Greek migration policy since 2012 to identify the reasons behind varying degrees of effectiveness. Applying Boswell and Rodrigues' (2016) adaptation of MSF on implementation, we hypothesized that the lack of administrative capacity and oscillating political support affect outcomes, which tend to go through various phases. We found that implementation went from non-implementation to bottom-up implementation to coercion and finally to consensus.

Our argument has two implications for MSF research. First, we have taken a dynamic view of the implementation process to showcase the effects of the problem and political streams onto implementation effectiveness. But the two streams are linked together by administrative capacity. When it is absent, we witness episodic or idiosyncratic implementation. Street-level bureaucrats and mostly NGOs and other organizations take charge of policy, but they naturally implement it in ad hoc ways. As the problem persists partly because policy is ineffective, political will steps in to ameliorate the situation and provide needed coordination and administrative capacity. Street-level bureaucrats begin to take over the process and address the situation as they see fit. As political resolve strengthens, policy implementation shifts partly in response to new preferences at the top but also because shifts in policy also imply shifts in problem definition. This is a contested process which may be accompanied by political conflict. Over time, the acquisition of expertise and political support for the new policy leads to what could be termed as consensus implementation.

Second, while we hypothesized the logic of administrative capacity and politics as the driving forces behind the cycle of implementation, we also uncovered that political support shifted because a new government came into power. Migration flows dwindled markedly because of the 2016 EU agreement with Turkey and because of the Covid-19 pandemic. It is tempting to add these factors to the explanation, but we must be careful not to overestimate our capabilities, especially when it comes to such unpredictable crises as the pandemic. All we can say is that the Greek case shows that administrative capacity tends to increase over time and that consequently increases implementation effectiveness. However, shifts in political support tend to move based on the ebb and flow of electoral politics, which, as MSF assumes, flows independently of any one policy issue. The implication is that had the elections not produced the result they did, the cycle we have described would have been less likely. More importantly, we confirm and extend the point made by MSF. Legislative turnover affects policy not only by bringing new ideas and people to the fore but also by deeply shaping their implementation.

REFERENCES

Boswell, C. & Rodrigues, E. 2016. "Policies, politics and organizational problems: Multiple streams and the implementation of targets in UK government*." Policy and Politics* 18: 507–24 at https://doi.org/10.1332/030557315X14477577990650.

British Broadcasting Corporation (BBC). 2015. "Migrant 'chaos' on Greek islands - UN refugee agency." Retrieved on July 10, 2016. Available from http://www.bbc.co.uk/news/world-europe-C33818193.

Dimitriadi, A. 2016. "The Impact of the EU-Turkey Statement on Protection and Reception: The Case of Greece." Working Paper 15, ELIAMEP. Retrieved November 10, 2018 from http://www.iai.it/sites/default/files/gte_wp_15.pdf.

Edwards, A. 2014. "Needs soar as number of Syrian refugees tops 3 million." United Nations High Commissioner for Refugees, August 29, at http://www.unhcr.org/53ff76c99.html.

European Commission. 2022. "Statistics on Migration to Europe." At https://ec.europa.eu/info/strategy/priorities-2019-2024/promoting-our-european-way-life/statistics-migration-europe_en#illegalbordercrossings.

Falkner, G., M. Hartlapp, S. Leiber, and O. Treib. 2004. "Non-compliance with EU directives in the member states: Opposition through the backdoor?" *West European Politics* 27 (3): 452–73.

Fowler, L. 2019. "Problems, politics, and policy streams in policy implementation." *Governance* 32: 403–20.

George, A. L., and A. Bennett. 2005. *Case Studies and Theory Development in the Social Sciences*. Cambridge, MA: MIT Press.

The Guardian. (2020). "Police and protesters clash on Greek islands over new migrant camps." February 25. At https://www.theguardian.com/world/2020/feb/25/police -and-protesters-clash-on-greek-islands-over-new-migrant-camps .

Herweg, N. and R. Zohlnhöfer. (forthcoming). "Multiple streams in policy implementation." In *Handbook of Public Policy Implementation*, eds. F. Sager, C. Mavrot, and L. R. Keiser. Cheltenham: Edward Elgar.

Herweg, N., N. Zahariadis, and R. Zohlnhöfer. 2018. "The Multiple Streams Framework: Foundations, Refinements and Empirical Applications." In *Theories of the Policy Process,* 4th edition, eds. C. M. Weible and P. A. Sabatier, 17–52. New York and London: Routledge.

Hille, P. and C. Knill. 2006. "'It's the bureaucracy, stupid:' The implementation of the *acquis communautaire* in the EU candidate countries, 1999–2003." *European Union Politics* 7 (4): 531–52.

Hjern, B. and D.O. Porter. 1981. "Implementation structures. A new unit of administrative analysis." *Organization Studies* 2 (3): 211–27.

Hood, C. 2011. *The Blame Game: Spin, Bureaucracy, and Self-Preservation in Government*. Princeton, NJ: Princeton University Press.

International Organization for Migration (IOM). 2015. "Irregular migrant, refugee arrivals in Europe top one million in 2015: IOM." Retrieved on September 24, 2016. Available from https://www.iom.int/news/irregular-migrant-refugee-arrivals-europe -top-one-million-2015-iom.

Knill, C., and J. Tosun. 2020. *Public Policy: A New Introduction*. 2nd edition. London: Bloomsbury Academic.

McDonough, P. and E. Tsourdi. 2012. "The 'other' Greek crisis; Asylum and EU solidarity." *Refugee Survey Quarterly* 31 (4): 61–100.

May, P. J. 2012. "Policy design and implementation." In *The SAGE Handbook of Public Administration,* 2nd edition, eds. B. G. Peters and J. Pierre, 279–91. London: Sage.

Mazmanian, D. A. and P. A. Sabatier. 1983. *Implementation and Public Policy*. Glenview, IL: Scott, Foresman.

Neher, W. W. 1997. *Organizational Communication – Challenges of Change, Diversity, and Continuity*. Boston: Allyn and Bacon.

Pew Research Center. 2019. "Europe's Unauthorized Immigrant Population Peaks in 2016, Then Levels Off." November 13. At https://www.pewresearch.org/global/ 2019/11/13/europes-unauthorized-immigrant-population-peaks-in-2016-then-levels -off/.

Pressman, J. L. and A. Wildavsky. 1973. *Implementation*. Berkeley, CA: University of California Press.

Proto Thema. 2015. "Latest Tsipras furor: 'What borders? Does sea have borders we didn't know about?'" ThemaNews.gr. Retrieved on October 16, 2016. Available from http://en.protothema.gr/latest-tsipras-furor-what-borders-does-sea-have-borders-we -didnt-know-about/.

Schattschneider, E. E. 1960. *The semi-sovereign people*. New York: Holt, Rinehart, and Winston.

Tagaris, K. 2015. "Migrant influx strains Greece as economy suffers. Reuters.com." Retrieved on July 10, 2016. Available from http://www.reuters.com/article/us -europe-migrants-greece-idUSKBN0NE2EM20150423.

Taylor, K., S. Zarb, and N. Jeschke. 2021. "Ambiguity, uncertainty and implementation." *International Review of Public Policy* 3 (1): 100–20.

Traynor, I. 2016. "Is the Schengen dream of Europe without borders becoming a thing of the past?" *The Guardian*, January 5, at https://www.theguardian.com/world/2016/ jan/05/is-the-schengen-dream-of-europe-without-borders-becoming-a-thing-of-the -past.

Tzimas, S. 2021) "'We fought man-to-man' to hold the Evros border." *Ekathimerini*, March 5, at https://www.ekathimerini.com/in-depth/special-report/1156395/we-fought-man-to -man-to-hold-the-evros-border/.

Zahariadis, N. 2003. *Ambiguity and Choice in Public Policy*. Washington, DC: Georgetown University Press.

9. More guns, less violence? Putting the Multiple Streams Framework to the test against Bolsonaro's gun liberalization agenda

Diego Sanjurjo

INTRODUCTION

Despite the extraordinary levels of violence plaguing many countries, gun control is largely absent from public and political debates in Latin America, where the specific issue is normally subsumed within general concerns over public security (Sanjurjo 2019). In some countries, it gains public and political attention intermittently, mostly after episodes of extreme violence or high-profile murder cases. When it happens, gun violence turns into a matter of polarized debate for a couple of weeks but can hardly adhere to the public and media attention for long.

Brazil is one of the very few exceptions in this regard, as gun control has turned into a salient topic of discussion more than once in the last two decades. In fact, it was at the center of Jair Bolsonaro's presidential campaign in 2018, as he pledged to abolish existing gun laws and liberalize their acquisition and use by civilians as part of a "law and order" message that resonated strongly with voters (Hunter and Power 2019). However, this is only the last chapter of a longstanding political battle that began in the 1990s and led to the approval of the 2003 Disarmament Statute,[1] which prohibited the carrying of firearms and strongly discouraged their possession and use among civilians. What is more, the Statute included the legislator's desire to implement a comprehensive ban on firearm sales to civilians, a controversial aspect that was finally rejected in 2005 through a national referendum.

The goal of this chapter is twofold. On the one hand, to explain why gun control has turned into a hot political issue once again in Brazil since the presidential campaign of 2018 and the arrival of Jair Bolsonaro to the Presidency. The second is the empirical test of a set of proposed modifications of the Multiple Streams Framework (MSF) that may allow a more appropriate application to the Latin American context, where legislatures and political parties are frequently weak, whereas powerful interest groups can exert a very strong influence over executives that usually dominate policymaking (Sanjurjo 2020b).

With these goals in mind, this chapter is structured in the following manner. The next section will introduce the proposed modifications of the MSF's political stream. A third section will then apply the analytical framework to explain several agenda-setting processes in Brazil. The fourth section discusses the empirical findings. The article ends with conclusions.

AGENDA-SETTING AND THE MULTIPLE STREAMS FRAMEWORK IN LATIN AMERICA

Latin America is by no means a single or homogeneous area, but its political culture and tradition present a series of shared characteristics that are emphasized when compared to the US. This is because the political values of the latter are mainly democratic, liberal and committed to representative government, whereas those of Latin America have historically been more elitist, authoritarian, hierarchical, corporatist, and patrimonial (Kline and Wade 2018; Wiarda 2001).

Structural differences of this magnitude also have a toll on policymaking. Context matters, and public policies are not independent variables that can be isolated from the political and social factors that shape and sustain them in the region (cf. Franceschet and Díez 2012; Scartascini et al. 2010). Weak and fragile states, inchoate party systems, limited pluralism, widespread corruption or chronic poverty, are all crucial factors that are not always present or decisive but are still indispensable for understanding and explaining agenda-setting and policy formation.

For that reason, in a study entitled *Taking the Multiple Streams Framework for a walk in Latin America* (Sanjurjo 2020b), we challenged the general portability of the framework by confronting it with a political reality that compromised some of its assumptions. And even though the MSF appeared to be capable of capturing the different dynamics at play, the study concluded that the political stream could be modified in order to acknowledge political contexts in which legislatures and political parties are frequently weak, structural inequalities polarize public opinion and undermine social cohesiveness, while powerful interest groups can exert a very strong influence over executives that usually dominate policymaking.

Within the dynamics of the MSF, this is of course the realm of the *political stream*, made up by actors and processes that act and develop at the level of macro-politics. Three elements were especially relevant in Kingdon's (1995) original work: swings in the national mood, interest group pressure campaigns and administrative or legislative turnovers. Among the three elements, national mood swings and administrative or legislative turnovers were supposed to exert the greatest influence on political agendas.

However, the operationalization of this stream was somewhat unclear and so was the role of political parties. Hence, it is the element of the MSF that has been modified most, as researchers have attempted to improve its efficacy in dissimilar contexts. For instance, when dealing with parliamentary systems, Zahariadis (1995, 33–36) suggested combining the three into the ideology and strategy of governing parties, which reflected the dominance that majority parties would have over the political stream. Herweg, Huß, and Zohlnhöfer (2015) agreed with this revision but suggested that public opinion and interest groups should not be dismissed but rather kept as secondary variables that have a strong effect over party behavior. Finally, for the German case, Zohlnhöfer and Huß (2016) found that the national mood and organized interests needed to be taken into account and suggested a return to Kingdon's original conception.

For Latin America, we suggested that a more appropriate political stream should acknowledge political contexts in which legislatures and political parties are weak, public opinion is polarized and indifferent, and influential interest groups can exert a very strong weight over executives that control policymaking. Consequently, and as portrayed in Figure 9.1, the political stream could have the presidential coalition and interest groups at the center stage, with the national mood as a secondary variable (Sanjurjo 2020b).

This proposal draws from three common premises of policymaking in the region. The first is the critical predominance of the executive in policymaking because of the powers granted by certain forms of presidential systems but also to the habitual weakness and subordination of courts, legislatures, and other mechanisms of horizontal accountability (Cheibub, Elkins, and Ginsburg 2011; O'Donnell 1994).

The second is the enhanced influence of certain interest groups in policy formation (Hochstetler and Friedman 2008; Klimovich and Thomas 2014), which is a consequence of the representation voids left by fragile parties and party systems (Mainwaring and Scully 1995; Roberts 2015), the prevailing influence of corporatist practices (Chen 2018; Schmitter 1974) and weak and dependent states (Franceschet and Díez 2012; Hellman, Jones, and Kaufmann 2003).

The third is the incidence of structural inequalities – in terms of income distribution, access to social services, and ability to participate in public life – that shape the national mood in ways that polarize public opinion and undermine social cohesiveness and cross-class solidarity (Blofield and Luna 2011; Oxhorn 2003).

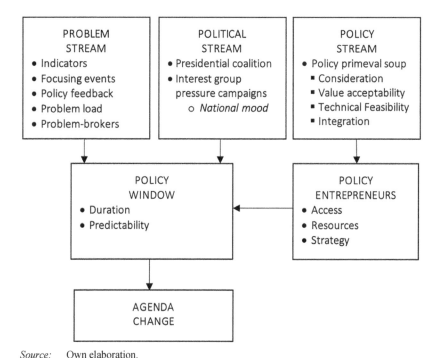

Source: Own elaboration.

Figure 9.1   The modified Multiple Stream Framework for Latin América²

GUN LIBERALIZATION: AN IDEA WHOSE TIME HAS COME AGAIN

Since the 2018 presidential elections, gun control has turned into a relatively salient issue for the first time in Brazil since the referendum campaign of 2005. For that matter, the MSF will be applied to a timeframe that begins in 2006 and ends with the most current developments in 2021. The empirical analysis will be organized in accordance with the structure and dynamics of the MSF. Therefore, each stream will have its own section and the agenda coupling process will be condensed in a particular section as well.

The Problem Stream: Homicides on the Rise and Distrust in Authorities

When it comes to *indicators*, the most relevant is the brutal epidemic of violence that Brazil has been suffering since the 1990s (Murray, Cerqueira, and Kahn 2013). Among the many visible dimensions of the problem, homicides draw the most attention. Brazil is an extreme case for that matter. With over

65,000 in 2017, the country has more murder cases per year than any other country in the world. Despite not having any widespread violent conflict in its recent history, the homicide rate almost tripled in the last four decades, going from 11.5 killings per 100,000 inhabitants in 1980 to 31.6 in 2017 (BRAZIL: MS/SVS/CGIAE n.d.; ipea and FBSP 2022). Since then, homicides appear to be receding, but this is challenged by the fact that violent deaths due to indetermined causes have grown considerably during the same period (ipea 2021). Moreover, the historic homicide growth is largely a consequence of the increase in gun homicides. Guns were namely the instrument of choice in only 43.9 percent of all homicides back in 1980, but that percentage has been close to 70 percent since 2003 (ipea and FBSP 2022; Waiselfisz 2015).

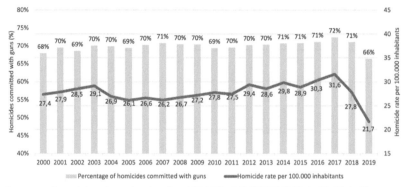

Source: Own elaboration using data from BRAZIL: MS/SVS/CGIAE (n.d.), Waiselfisz (2015b), and ipea (2021).

Figure 9.2   *Homicide rates and percentage of homicides committed with guns in Brazil, 2000–19. *Rates per every 100,000 population*

Regarding *policy feedback*, the Disarmament Statute of 2003 was criticized by many once it came into force. Gun users and gun rights advocates called it into question because it made gun acquisitions more difficult. In the case of self-defense, for instance, it allowed civilians to acquire a maximum of two guns and raised the requirements that they needed to satisfy to be granted licenses. This was of course the Statute's main goal: to filter out risky candidates, but also discourage less motivated individuals from acquiring firearms, at least through legal channels. This may have been accomplished, as legal gun sales plummeted by more than 60 percent after the Statute's implementation (Pekny et al. 2015).

In addition, the overall impact of the Statute is heavily contested. On the one hand, there is practically a consensus in the Brazilian scientific community regarding its positive effects. For instance, several studies argue that the law had a powerful impact on gun deaths and homicides on the years that followed its approval, as the national homicide rate per 100,000 inhabitants went from 29.1 in 2003 to 26.1 in 2005 (Figure 9.2) (de Souza et al. 2007; Waiselfisz 2015). But not everyone agrees with these findings. The reported improvement in the national homicide statistics hides the fact that only a minority of the federal states reduced their gun deaths after the Statute's implementation, while the rest stayed unchanged or continued the former positive trend. More importantly, the state of São Paulo was largely responsible for the overall improvement and its reduction in gun deaths began a year before the approval of the Statute (Ib.: 2015).

What seems more likely, therefore, is that the Statute emphasized a drop in homicides that occurred as a result of the modernization of São Paulo's police forces and the approval of several other security policies at the state level. In consequence, the most important factor does not seem to be the passing of national legislation, but the vigor with which the legislation was enforced on a state level and how it supplemented other security policies and programs (Goertzel and Kahn 2009). Ultimately, the positive impact that the Disarmament Statute had on gun deaths was no longer noticeable by 2010, when killings began to rise again at a fast pace until 2017 (Figure 9.2). This strengthened the widespread opinion that this was not an effective policy for controlling crime and violence.

When it comes to *focusing events*, it is not hard to find especially dreadful episodes that drew international attention to Brazil's armed violence in the last few decades. A good example was the assassination of the city councilwoman of the Municipal Chamber of Rio de Janeiro, Marrielle Franco, in 2018. However, most Brazilians are arguably accustomed to a widespread climate of everyday violence, which is why crimes and acts of violence must be especially striking to draw the media's attention for more than a couple of days. For this reason, it is unclear to what extent particularly violent episodes drew specific attention to gun control. As pointed out by Fonseca et al. (2006, 31) to explain the development of the Disarmament Statute, "it was not specific tragedies that mobilized society, but the acknowledgement that the country lives a permanent civil war".[3]

The fourth variable under consideration is the *problem load*, that we operationalize through election polls and the classical "most important problem" question (Figure 9.3) (Datafolha 2015, 2022). In this regard, preoccupations over violence and insecurity became the most pressing issue for the first time in 2007. After that, they remained among the top three concerns of Brazilians until the last years of Dilma Rousseff's presidencies (2011–16), when the country fell into a dramatic and multidimensional crisis that turned public opinion on its head. After that, violence and insecurity competed for attention with an economic emergency caused by a prolonged recession, a political crisis of rising polarization and falling trust in established parties, as well as a corruption crisis brought to the fore by the Lava Jato investigation (Hunter and Power 2019). The only other time when violence and insecurity were the most pressing issues was precisely in 2019, when Jair Bolsonaro came into office, but it did not last. In 2020 the Covid-19 pandemic quickly turned health and poverty/hunger into the most pressing issues and violence and security have been relegated to marginal positions ever since.

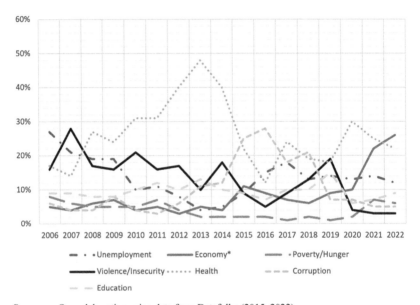

Source: Own elaboration using data from Datafolha (2015, 2022).

Figure 9.3   *Main problem facing the country, 2006–19. *Economy includes "economy", "inflation" and "salaries". **When there is more than one measure per year, yearly average is used.*

At last, *problem brokers* (Knaggård 2015) are important as well in the process, as several researchers became involved with gun violence in the second half of the 1990s. Specific research institutes were created within universities, while researchers and activists established NGOs that also worked on the ground (Ballestrin 2010). Prominent among those were the Centre for Violence

Studies at the University of Sao Paolo (NEV-USP), the Sou da Paz Institute, Viva Rio, and the Religion Studies Institute (ISER). These were the first to investigate gun-related issues in Brazil and in Latin America. By the end of the decade, they were producing a steady flow of reports about the impact of guns on urban violence (Cukier and Sidel 2006, 218–20; Lucas 2008).

It is worth noting that unlike in the US, where it is possible to find problem-brokers holding conflicting views, in Brazil the landscape seems to be rather homogeneous with academics and researchers only pulling towards disarmament or more stringent gun control. Those who interpret and frame conditions as problems on the other side of the aisle are politicians, opinion leaders related to the far right and practitioners closely related to police and military corporations. Particularly in their case, the line that separates problem-brokers and policy entrepreneurs becomes blurred, as many of these individual and collective actors are policymakers or are involved in the development of policy alternatives.

In this sense, and as the next sections will show, policymakers in favor of gun liberalization interpret the violence epidemic as the result of the state's inability or unwillingness to control crime, which in turn would make armed self-defense not only a fundamental right, but also an imperative (Macaulay 2019; Quadros and Madeira 2018). In consequence, indicators and focusing events associated with armed violence are interpreted as evidence of the Disarmament Statute's failure, proving them right and academics and human rights activists wrong (Sanjurjo 2020a). The problem load, on the other hand, can only change their priorities so much, as many of them are openly funded by the Brazilian weapons industry (Macaulay 2019).

The Policy Stream: More Guns, Less Violence

Oddly enough, it was the approval of the Disarmament Statute in 2003 that promoted ideas that challenged its theoretical principles and causal relations (Sanjurjo 2020a, 2021). Such a backlash became popular among security practitioners, gun enthusiasts and all those who consider guns their only real defense against crime. Their views and policy efforts are spearheaded by politicians and practitioners closely related to police and military corporations, whose ideas can be framed in what Faganello (2015) refers to as an authoritarian-securitarian ideology. Accordingly, society would be marked by the loss of authority and by the constant threat of violent crime, as well as by a marked divide between good and bad citizens. The latter should be subjected to hardline policies and not constantly defended through human rights discourses.

From this point of view, gun liberalization is a central element of a policy paradigm that also pushes for the legal protection of police agents, punitive sanctions and lowering the minimum age for criminal liability (Macaulay 2019; Quadros and Madeira 2018). Brazilians would have a right to self-defense and stringent gun control policies would take that possibility away from good citizens for the sole benefit of armed criminals. Furthermore, gun possession and use are seen as fundamental rights that make individual liberty possible (Lissovsky 2006). Hence, the Disarmament Statute would have greatly aggravated the security situation but also put inherent rights and liberties at risk. As a result, policy alternatives vary but share common goals: to modify or revoke the Disarmament Statute in order to allow gun carrying and liberalize gun sales (Sanjurjo 2021).

Pushing these ideas were mostly firearm enthusiasts, hunters, shooters, security practitioners and rightwing politicians, who since the approval of the Disarmament Statute set out to regain the gun control policy community from the dominance of academics, researchers and human rights activists. As of 2003, civil society groups became organized and founded several organizations that worked primarily online and through social media (Quintela and Barbosa 2015). The Brazilian weapons industry (Dreyfus, Lessing, and Purcena 2010) was also deeply engaged, with both state-owned and private companies pushing against those policies that hurt the industry's revenues and interests (Sanjurjo 2020a).

Their ideas were met with strong opposition since the beginning and had to compete within a growingly polarized policy community that was dominated by those who favor disarmament and reject the punitive practices that characterize the Brazilian police and armed forces (Sanjurjo 2020a). Such a polarized and fragmented community implied a policy primeval soup in which gun liberalization ideas were difficult to consider and accept, but their development and dissemination were facilitated by the fact that the Disarmament Statute eventually proved incapable of containing armed violence. Moreover, the causal relations between an armed citizenry and lower levels of violence were scientifically disputed but easily conceivable (Lott 1998; Quintela and Barbosa 2015), while all its components were technically feasible. After all, the main idea was none other than to find a way to revoke the Disarmament Statute.

The Political Stream: Bolsonaro and the Bullet Front

Public support for different gun regulations is influenced by various factors. In favor of more stringent policies is the persistent belief by most Brazilians that gun proliferation is an important risk factor for crime and violence. This belief clashes with partisan opposition from the left, with the notion of gun possession and use as individual rights and with the widespread lack of confidence in the state's capacity to control crime, which in turn would make armed self-defense a necessity (Faganello 2015; Hunter and Power 2019; Macaulay 2017).

Overall, these factors help explain the national mood swings that occurred at the beginning of the 2000s, when the Disarmament Statute was approved with great public support but then lost one of its main elements through a national referendum (Sanjurjo 2020a, 2021). Despite this outcome, however, and even though crime continued growing and so did the demand for public security, public support for loosening gun legislation remained a minority view among Brazilians. Bolsonaro's stance against gun control made views on the issue diverge along partisan lines during the 2018 presidential election (Russo 2020), but the belief that the government should not make gun possession easier for regular civilians has remained between 55 and 66 percent of the population since 2013 (Datafolha 2019; Oliva 2022). Even right after President Bolsonaro was elected, most Brazilians were still in favor of maintaining the Disarmament Statute in place and 70 percent even rejected his proposal to facilitate gun carrying among civilians (Datafolha 2019).

Public opinion polls did not discourage policymakers, however. As hypothesized above, public opinion is usually polarized and indifferent in Brazil and Latin America, which makes policymakers less sympathetic to popular moods and to the possibility of being penalized at the ballot box for specific policy choices (Sanjurjo 2020b). As the next section will show, *administrations and legislatures* were crucial in the agenda-setting process, since not only President Jair Bolsonaro (Bolsonaro, 2019) adopted gun liberalization as his political pet project, but also a series of legislators that had a crucial impact on the process: Federal Congressmen Alberto Fraga, Luis Antonio Fleury, Rogério Peninha Mendonça, and Laudivio Carvalho (Lourenço 2015; Pekny et al. 2015; Quadros and Madeira 2018).

Much more influential than the national mood were the nonpartisan parliamentary groups known as the *bancada da bala*, which gather policymakers who are strongly in favor of gun rights and sympathize with a tough-on-crime position (Faganello 2015; Macaulay 2019). Notable among these is the Public Security Parliamentary Front (PSPF) and the Committee on Public Security and Organized Crime, which gather many politicians funded by the Brazilian weapons industry. The latter had always tried to influence policymakers to oppose any additional regulations that could hurt the industry's revenues and interests, but their investment in political candidates that supported liberal gun laws received an impressive return over the years, helping to elect an unprecedented number of candidates to congress and to state legislatures around the country. The PSPF, for example, had 210 founding members in 2011, which expanded to 299 and then to 306 in the 2015 and 2019 legislatures (Hinz, Vinuto, and Coutinho 2020).

With the additional support of police and military corporations, the Bullet Front has grown into one of the largest caucuses in the National Congress and now amasses considerable agenda-setting power and influence. Its radical wing is made up of former security practitioners who become policymakers in order to work for the preservation of their common values and interests. President Jair Bolsonaro, himself a former Army Captain, was one of the most active and fervent members of the PSPF for many years. With the advent of his presidency, the heavy influence of the *bancada da bala* is no longer limited to the Legislative Power. So much so, that Bolsonaro's original cabinet included no less than seven military ministers (Hinz, Vinuto, and Coutinho 2020; Quadros and Madeira 2018).

At last, *pressure campaigns* in favor of gun rights and liberalization are led by what one might describe as a local gun lobby, mainly comprised by the Bullet Front and the national weapons industry, but also by several user associations of gun dealers and enthusiasts, hunters and shooters. Such groups were always against any policy that would obstruct their access to firearms, but their political counter-campaign only intensified as of 2003, when it became clear that disarmament ideas could find support in the country's capital. Thus, whereas disarmament and gun control advocates led an intense campaign between 1999 and 2005 (Lucas 2008), supporters of gun rights were practically idle until the subject entered the governmental agenda in 2003 (Sanjurjo 2020a, 150). It was at that point that they became organized and concentrated all their efforts to win the referendum and then modify or revoke the Disarmament Statute. With this purpose, gun rights advocates founded several organizations that worked primarily online and through social media, such as the Movement Viva Brazil, the Armaria and the Movement for Legitimate Defense (Quintela and Barbosa 2015).

Agenda Coupling

There were several efforts to revoke the Disarmament Statute and loosen gun regulations in the studied time frame, as policy entrepreneurs tried to use windows of opportunity to couple the streams together and push their pet projects into the political agenda. Most of them did not get congressional approval or were contested by judicial review processes, but others found a way through provisional decrees by Bolsonaro's Executive. This section will focus only on those that were particularly meaningful to the overall process.

In retrospect, the approval of the Disarmament Statute in 2003 initiated a strong and enduring mobilization of conservative forces that formed a powerful local gun lobby. Its efforts were spearheaded by the Bullet Front, which grew in numbers and influence with every legislative election (Hinz, Vinuto, and Coutinho 2020; Macaulay 2019). One of their first major offensives materialized in a Direct Unconstitutionality Action, to which the Federal Supreme Court responded in 2007 by upholding the general constitutionality of the Statute, albeit overruling specific sanctions for illegal gun carrying. The latter had been severely limited by the Disarmament Statute and there were several attempts to ease these restrictions in the following years (Pekny et al. 2015, 14). Despite these challenges, policy entrepreneurs had little chances of success, as stringent gun control enjoyed the support of both the public and the government, and it seemed to have a positive impact on security indicators.

The next relevant window of opportunity opened in the problem stream in 2011, when homicides began to rise again and put the efficacy of the Statute into question. The policy and political streams were loosely coupled since the referendum campaign (2003–05) and policy entrepreneurs seized the opportunity to couple the problem stream as well. Several Bills were put forward, but the most relevant agenda-coupling process took place in 2012 with the Bill 3,722 by Federal Congressman Rogério Peninha Mendonça, which proposed the complete revocation of the Statute and the modification of various related measures. Among others, increasing the number of guns and ammunitions that could be purchased per person, abolishing cyclical tests aimed at proving the technical aptitude for handling weapons, and reducing the minimum age required for gun purchases from 25 to 21 years Pekny et al. 2015, 15–16).

This so-called Firearm Control Statute was opposed by Rousseff's Executive and did not have enough support in Congress. Nevertheless, it circulated through several congressional commissions and gained momentum as the Bullet Front grew in numbers after the 2014 elections. In 2015, a substitute Bill by Federal Congressman Laudivio Carvalho was approved by a special appointed commission, but so far it has not been voted by the plenary. The time seemed right with Bolsonaro's accession to power in 2018 and the results of the legislative elections of 2019, which made gun rights promoters anxious for a swift approval (Costa 2019). Even more, as violence and insecurity were the most pressing issues in the country that year, but this did not last. The Covid-19 pandemic caused havoc in Brazil and brought health and poverty to the forefront in 2020. Since then, less than 4 percent of Brazilians consider violence and insecurity the most pressing issue and Bills seeking to ease gun regulations have not been able to find enough support in Congress.

So far, the Disarmament Statute remains in place and the question is whether policy entrepreneurs will be able to exploit such major political windows of opportunity before it is too late. Without enough support in Congress, Bolsonaro's Executive has issued several provisional decrees since 2019 that facilitate gun acquisition and use. Among other dispositions, they increase the types and number of guns that civilians can acquire, they enable the carrying of more guns for self-defense, and they facilitate gun acquisition and carrying by security agents and municipal guards. Gun control proponents have voiced their rejection and both the Public Ministry as well as opposition parties have challenged their constitutionality in the Federal Supreme Court. In some cases, unconstitutionality actions have led to the publication of new decrees that override the previous ones (Instituto Igarapé & Instituto Sou da Paz 2020; Instituto Igarapé 2021).

FINDINGS AND DISCUSSION

The application of the MSF proved that the framework is capable and well-suited to explain why agendas change or stay constant in Brazil. Moreover, it provided a comprehensive explanation for the last reentrance of gun control in the country's political agenda during Bolsonaro's Presidency.

Accordingly, it was the referendum of 2005 to decide over the ban on the sale of firearms to civilians that set a precedent for years to come, as contending entrepreneurs coupled antagonistic policy solutions to the same policy problem. In this way, both gun control and gun liberalization were pushed as solutions to the ever-growing problem of gun violence and crime (Sanjurjo 2021). Since then, and particularly after homicidal violence began to rise again in 2011, entrepreneurs that oppose the Statute have tried to liberalize gun laws, accomplishing their own agenda-coupling processes in 2012 and 2019.

The process presents some particularities worth discussing. The first is the role played by the courts – and specifically the Federal Supreme Court – in the agenda-coupling processes, which is not a particular feature of this case study. On the contrary, the Brazilian political system possesses several elements that favor the judicialization of politics and it is common for political minorities to invoke the Constitution against laws and normative acts issued by the legislative and executive powers (Arantes 2005).

Depending on the case, the MSF can acknowledge judicial review processes in different ways. Sometimes, their use is only a possibility that the opposition or electorate may or may not invoke. However, the mere possibility of challenging the constitutionality of a norm already imposes constraints on policy ideas, because the threat of a policy reversal makes changing the status quo more expensive in political terms. Hence, conformity to constitutional norms can be an important criterion for survival in the policy stream (Sanjurjo 2020a, 160; Zohlnhöfer and Huß 2016). Other times, judicial review processes can trigger new agenda-setting processes altogether, playing the role of focusing events, veto players or even policy entrepreneurs (Nowak 2010).

Furthermore, President Bolsonaro has issued several presidential decrees, but most agenda-coupling processes were led by political entrepreneurs in Parliament, which challenges the well accepted notion that Brazilian presidents define the legislative agenda (Alston et al. 2008; Ames 2001). This finding is consistent with recent investigations that identify the Brazilian criminal policy field as exceptional and one where legislators are particularly active as agenda-setters (Silveira Campos and Azevedo 2020). However, it is important to remember that the Bullet Front's modus operandi is that of an authentic pressure group (Quadros and Madeira 2018), which leads to processes of producer capture within the legislative arena that favor the interests of police and military corporations, as well as of the private security sector and the local weapons industry (Macaulay 2017).

Therefore, the process also stands out due to the decisive role of interest groups. Just as the gun control movement forced gun control into the public and political agendas and managed to keep it as a key political issue between the 1990s and 2005 (Sanjurjo 2020a, 2021), the approval of the Statute in 2003 triggered the awakening of interest groups and power groups on the other side of the divide. Thus, the political backlash against gun control that since then has maintained the issue on the agenda is spearheaded by politicians who often belong to police and military corporations and are funded by the national weapons industry. President Bolsonaro is perhaps the most prominent and openly defends these special interests (Macaulay 2019).

Despite being on opposing ends, these interest groups were able to fill representation voids and capture political demands that Brazilian political parties did not represent nor mediate. This is hardly exceptional. At times, party-oriented legislators seem to be becoming more common in Brazil and their party system appears to be advancing towards institutionalization (Hagopian, Gervasoni, and Moraes 2009). Nevertheless, in terms of organizational coherence and connections with voters, political parties remain weak and can hardly fulfill their roles as intermediary institutions. There are various reasons for this, but among the most important is a proportional electoral system that favors volatility and fragmentation, weakens party control over politicians and facilitates the election of legislators representing special interests (Mainwaring, Power, and Bizzarro 2018).

On the one hand, this makes the formation of fronts or factions – such as the *bancada da bala–* common in Congress, and their members often place loyalty to their organization or interest above the party. This makes certain interest groups particularly influential (Oliveira Gozetto and Thomas 2014). On the other hand, it favors the development of clientelist electoral markets, through which legislators negotiate with executives and trade legislative power for access to pork and resources (Desposato 2006; Rose-Ackerman and de Mattos Pimenta 2020). As a result, the legislative powers of the President are enhanced, even though the lack of discipline and responsiveness of their contingent is a recurring problem that forces them to constantly negotiate. This may explain why Bolsonaro resorts so frequently to provisional decrees, which allows him to enact new legislation promptly and without congressional approval (Alston et al. 2008; Ames 2001).

Conversely, public support did not seem to be so important for the agenda-setting processes that tried to revoke the Disarmament Statute. In fact, public support for loosening gun regulations remained a minority during the entire period (Datafolha 2019; Oliva 2022), but this did not prevent policy entrepreneurs from trying to couple the streams together many times. Likewise, the fact that President Bolsonaro has issued various provisional decrees liberalizing gun laws suggests that the Disarmament Statute does not remain in place because of the public support it enjoys, but due to the difficulties that the President is facing to form a legislative majority and prevent or surpass judicial review processes.

CONCLUSION

Whereas gun control is largely absent from public and political debates in most parts of Latin America, in Brazil it has remained a recurring political issue for over 20 years. The last attempts gained prominence worldwide, as Jair Bolsonaro's government had gun rights and liberalization at the center of its agenda. This chapter has tried to explain this phenomenon with the help of the Multiple Streams Framework, putting the pieces of the puzzle together and adding a synthetic and multidimensional perspective to the existing local literature on gun control and agenda-setting.

Accordingly, proponents of gun liberalization were able to exploit the rise in homicides and their close relations with the President and legislators to couple the streams together and systematically reintroduce the issue in the agenda. Overall, political parties and public opinion played a secondary role in a process that was marked by the strong influence of legislators representing special interests. In consequence, the agenda-setting process mirrored a political stream that acknowledges that political parties are frequently weak in Latin America, while interest groups and special interests can have a major influence over legislatures and executives in policymaking.

In this respect, the agenda-setting processes were partly consistent with our recommended political stream for Latin America, which acknowledges that legislatures and political parties are frequently weak, public opinion is polarized and indifferent, while certain interest groups can be highly influential over executives that largely control the agenda-setting process (Sanjurjo 2020b). This is also usually the case in the Brazilian political system, but the present case study supports the notion of a particular policy sector in which legislators representing special interests can also be quite relevant. Further research is needed to see if this dynamic is determined by the operations of particular pressure groups in Parliament – such as the Bullet Front – or if this is the legislative consequence of a party system that at times seems to be advancing towards institutionalization, albeit with a strong influence of special interests and frequently on the edge of the law.

NOTES

1. BRAZIL: Law n° 10.826/2003, and Regulatory Decree n° 5.123/2004.
2. Figure 9.1 suggests that a more appropriate political stream for Latin America should acknowledge political contexts in which legislatures and political parties are weak, public opinion is polarized and indifferent, and influential interest groups can exert a very strong weight over executives that control policymaking. Consequently, the political stream could have the presidential coalition and interest groups at the center stage, with the national mood as an influential secondary variable (Sanjurjo 2020b).
3. "*[...] não foram tragédias específicas que mobilizaram a sociedade e sim a constatação de que se vive no país uma guerra civil permanente*" (Fonseca et al., 2006, 31).

REFERENCES

Alston, Lee J., Marcus André Melo, Bernardo Mueller, and Carlos Pereira. 2008. "On the Road to Good Governance: Recovering from Economic and Political Shocks in Brazil." In *Policymaking in Latin America: How Politics Shapes Policies*, eds. Ernesto Stein, Mariano Tommasi, Pablo Spiller, and Carlos Scartascini, 111–53. Washington, D.C.: Inter-American Development Bank and David Rockefeller Center for Latin American Studies.

Ames, Barry. 2001. *The Deadlock of Democracy in Brazil*. Michigan: The University of Michigan Press.

Arantes, Rogério B. 2005. "Constitutionalism, the Expansion of Justice and the Judicialization of Politics in Brazil." In *The Judicialization of Politics in Latin America*, eds. Rachel Sieder, Line Schjolden, and Alan Angell, 231–62. New York: Palgrave Macmillan.

Ballestrin, Luciana Maria de Aragão. 2010. "Com Quantas Armas Se Faz Uma Sociedade 'Civil'? Controles Sobre Armas de Fogo Na Governança Global, Brasil e Portugal (1995 - 2010)." Universidade Federal de Minas Gerais.

Blofield, Merike, and Juan Pablo Luna. 2011. "Public Opinion in Income Inequalities in Latin America." In *The Great Gap: Inequality and the Politics of Redistribution in Latin America*, ed. Merike Blofield, 147–73. University Park: The Pennsylvania State University Press.

BRAZIL: MS/SVS/CGIAE. "DATASUS." http://datasus.saude.gov.br (January 12, 2019).

Cheibub, José Antonio, Zachary Elkins, and Tom Ginsburg. 2011. "Latin American Presidentialism in Comparative and Historical Perspective." *Texas Law Review* 89 (7): 1707–39.

Chen, Linda. 2018. "Corporatism Reconsidered: Howard J. Wiarda's Legacy." *Polity* 50 (4): 601–11.

Costa, Gilberto. 2019. "Defensores Do Porte de Arma Aguardam Aprovação Do Novo Texto." *Agência Brasil*.

Cukier, Wendy, and Victor W. Sidel. 2006. *The Global Gun Epidemic: From Saturday Night Specials to AK-47s*. Westport: Praeger Security International.

Datafolha. 2015. *Avaliação Da Presidente Dilma Rousseff.* Instituto de Pesquisa Datafolha. http://media.folha.uol.com.br/datafolha/2015/11/30/avaliacao_dilma.pdf (April 14, 2020).

Datafolha. 2019. *Posse e Porte de Armas.* Sao Paulo: Instituto de Pesquisa Datafolha, Folha de S. Paulo. http://datafolha.folha.uol.com.br/opiniaopublica/2019/07/1988232–66-sao -contra-posse-de-armas.shtml (April 27, 2020).

Datafolha.. 2022. *ELEIÇÕES 2022.* Sao Paulo: Instituto de Pesquisa Datafolha, Folha de S. Paulo. https://bit.ly/3sLFurj.

Desposato, Scott W. 2006. "How Informal Electoral Institutions Shape the Brazilian Legislative Arena." In *Informal Institutions and Democracy. Lessons from Latin America*, eds. Gretchen Helmke and Steven Levitsky. Baltimore, 56–68. The John Hopkins University Press.

Dreyfus, Pablo, Benjamin Lessing, and Júlio Cesar Purcena. 2010. "The Brazilian Small Arms Industry: Legal Production and Trade." In *Small Arms in Brazil: Production, Trade, and Holdings*, eds. Pablo Dreyfus, Benjamin Lessing, Marcelo de Sousa Nascimento, and Júlio Cesar Purcena, 30–83. Geneva: Small Arms Survey.

Faganello, Marco Antonio. 2015. "Bancada Da Bala: Uma Onda Na Maré Conservadora." In *DIREITA, VOLVER! O Retorno Da Direita e o Ciclo Político Brasileiro*, eds. Sebastião Velasco e Cruz, André Kaysel, and Gustavo Codas, 145–61. Sao Paulo: Fundação Perseu Abramo.

Fonseca, Francisco et al. 2006. "O Sistema Nacional de Armas (SINARM) Como Sistema de Gerenciamento Do Estoque Legal de Armas No Brasil: Uma Contribuição Às Políticas Públicas." *Cadernos Gestão Pública e Cidadania* 11 (48): 15–41.

Franceschet, Susan, and Jordi Díez. 2012. "Thinking about Politics and Policy-Making in Contemporary Latin America." In *Comparative Public Policy in Latin America*, eds. Susan Franceschet and Jordi Díez, 3–33. Toronto: University of Toronto Press.

Goertzel, Ted, and Tulio Kahn. 2009. "The Great São Paulo Homicide Drop." *Homicide Studies* 13(4): 398–410.

Hagopian, Frances, Carlos Gervasoni, and Juan Andres Moraes. 2009. "From Patronage to Program: The Emergence of Party-Oriented Legislators in Brazil." *Comparative Political Studies* 42 (3): 360–91.

Hellman, Joel, Geraint Jones, and Daniel Kaufmann. 2003. "Seize the State, Seize the Day: State Capture and Influence in Transition Economies." *Journal of Comparative Economics* 31 (4): 751–73.

Herweg, Nicole, Christian Huß, and Reimut Zohlnhöfer. 2015. "Straightening the Three Streams: Theorising Extensions of the Multiple Streams Framework." *European Journal of Political Research* 54 (3): 435–49.

Hinz, Kristina, Juliana Vinuto, and Aline Beatriz Coutinho. 2020. "Por Dios y Por Las Armas: El Ascenso Neopentecostal y Securitario En Brasil (2003–2019)." *Revista CIDOB d'Afers Internacionals* 126: 185–214.

Hochstetler, Kathryn, and Elisabeth Jay Friedman. 2008. "Can Civil Society Organizations Solve the Crisis of Partisan Representation in Latin America?" *Latin American Politics and Society* 50 (2): 1–32.

Hunter, Wendy, and Timothy J. Power. 2019. "Bolsonaro and Brazil's Illiberal Backlash." *Journal of Democracy* 30 (1): 68–82.

Instituto Igarapé. 2021. *A Flexibilização Do Acceso a Armas e Munições Em Análise Pelo STF: Um Panorama Geral Da Votação.* Rio de Janeiro.

Instituto Igarapé & Instituto Sou da Paz. 2020. *Balanço Preliminar Das Principais Mudanças Na Política de Controle de Armas e Munições No Brasil Em 2019.* Instituto Igarapé & Instituto Sou da Paz.

ipea (Instituto de Pesquisa Econômica Aplicada). 2021. *Atlas Da Violência 2021.* ed. Daniel Cerqueira. Sao Paulo: IPEA, FBSP & IJSN.

ipea (Instituto de Pesquisa Econômica Aplicada), and FBSP (Forum Brasileiro de Segurança Pública). 2022. "Atlas Da Violência - Estatísticas." https://www.ipea.gov .br/atlasviolencia/filtros-series (May 17, 2022).

Kingdon, John W. 1995. *Agendas, Alternatives, and Public Policy.* 2nd edition. New York: HarperCollins College Publishers.

Klimovich, Kristina, and Clive S. Thomas. 2014. "Power Groups, Interests and Interest Groups in Consolidated and Transitional Democracies: Comparing Uruguay and Costa Rica with Paraguay and Haiti." *Journal of Public Affairs* 14 (3): 183–211.

Kline, Harvey F., and Christine J. Wade. 2018. "The Latin American Tradition and Process of Development." In *Latin American Politics and Development*, eds. Harvey F. Kline, J. Wade, Christine, and Howard J. Wiarda. New York: Routledge.

Knaggård, Åsa. 2015. "The Multiple Streams Framework and the Problem Broker." *European Journal of Political Research* 54 (3): 450–65.

Lissovsky, Mauricio. 2006. "A Campanha Na Tevê e a Desventura Do Sim Que Era Não." In *Referendo Do Sim Ao Não: Uma Experiência Da Democracia Brasileira - Comunicaçoes N° 62*, Rio de Janeiro: Instituto de Estudos da Religião ISER, 27–42.

Lott, John R. 1998. *More Guns, Less Crime: Understanding Crime and Gun Control Laws.* Chicago: University of Chicago Press.

Lourenço, Luana. 2015. "O Estatuto Do Desarmamento Sob Ameaça: Projeto Que Deixa a Legislação Brasileira de Controle de Armas Mais Permissiva Está Pronto Para Ser Votado No Plenário Da Câmara Dos Deputados." *Agência Brasil.* http:// www.ebc.com.br/estatutododesarmamento (December 11, 2016).

Lucas, Peter. 2008. "Disarming Brazil: Lessons and Challenges." *NACLA Report on the Americas* 41 (2): 27–31.

Macaulay, Fiona. 2017. "Presidents, Producers and Politics: Law-and-Order Policy in Brazil from Cardoso to Dilma." *Policy Studies* 38 (3): 248–61.

Macaulay, Fiona. 2019. "Bancada Da Bala: The Growing Influence of the Security Sector in Brazilian Politics." In *In Spite of You: Bolsonaro and the New Brazilian Resistance*, ed. Conor Foley, 56–70. New York: OR Books.

Mainwaring, Scott, Timothy J. Power, and Fernando Bizzarro. 2018. "The Uneven Institutionalization of a Party System: Brazil." In *Party Systems in Latin America: Institutionalization, Decay, and Collapse*, ed. Scott Mainwaring, 164–200. Cambridge: Cambridge University Press.

Mainwaring, Scott, and Timothy Scully. 1995. *Building Democratic Institutions. Party Systems in Latin America.* Stanford: Stanford University Press.

Murray, Joseph, Daniel Ricardo de Castro Cerqueira, and Tulio Kahn. 2013. "Crime and Violence in Brazil: Systematic Review of Time Trends, Prevalence Rates and Risk Factors." *Aggression and Violent Behavior* 18 (5): 471–83.

Nowak, Tobias. 2010. "Of Garbage Cans and Rulings: Judgments of the European Court of Justice in the EU Legislative Process." *West European Politics* 33 (4): 753–69.

O'Donnell, Guillermo A. 1994. "Delegative Democracy." *Journal of Democracy* 5 (1): 55–69.

Oliva, Gabriela. 2022. "PoderData: Para 33%, Governo Deveria Facilitar Compra de Armas." *Poder360.* https://bit.ly/3PIrTec.

Oliveira Gozetto, Andréa Cristina, and Clive S. Thomas. 2014. "Interest Groups in Brazil: A New Era and Its Challenges." *Journal of Public Affairs* 14 (3–4): 212–39.

Oxhorn, Philip. 2003. "Social Inequality, Civil Society, and the Limits of Citizenship in Latin America." In *What Justice? Whose Justice?: Fighting for Fairness in Latin America*, eds. Susan Eva Eckstein and Timothy P. Wickham-Crowley, 35–63. Berkeley: University of California Press.

Pekny, Ana Carolina et al. 2015. *Controle de Armas No Brasil: O Caminho a Seguir*. Sao Paulo: Friedrich Ebert Stiftung (FES) Brasil.

Quadros, Marcos, and Rafael Machado Madeira. 2018. "Fim Da Direita Envergonhada? Atuação Da Bancada Evangélica e Da Bancada Da Bala e Os Caminhos Da Representação Do Conservadorismo No Brasil." *Opinião Pública* 24 (3): 486–522.

Quintela, Flavio, and Bene Barbosa. 2015. *Mentiram Para Mim Sobre o Desarmamento*. Campinas, SP: Vide Editorial.

Roberts, Kenneth M. 2015. "Parties, Party Systems, and Political Representation." In *Routledge Handbook of Latin American Politics*, eds. Peter Kingstone and Deborah J. Yashar, 48–60. Routledge.

Rose-Ackerman, Susan, and Raquel de Mattos Pimenta. 2020. "Corruption in Brazil: Beyond the Criminal Law." In *Corruption and the Lava Jato Scandal in Latin America*, eds. Paul Lagunes and Jan Svejnar, 199–212. Abingdon: Routledge.

RT. 2021. "'Everybody Has to Buy a Rifle, Damn It!' Brazilian President Bolsonaro Tells His Supporters." *RT*. https://bit.ly/3u5eDX6.

Russo, Guilherme A. 2020. *Shaping Public Opinion: Political Messages and Attitudes Toward Firearms*. Sao Paulo. https://bit.ly/3ytdPyY.

Sanjurjo, Diego. 2019. "Gun Violence and Defensive Firearm Use in the Governance of Security of Latin America." In *Gun Studies: Interdisciplinary Approaches to Politics, Policy, and Practice*, eds. Jennifer D. Carlson, Kristin A. Goss, and Harel Shapira, 271–93. New York: Routledge.

Sanjurjo, Diego. 2020a. *Gun Control Policies in Latin America*. New York: Palgrave Macmillan.

Sanjurjo, Diego. 2020b. "Taking the Multiple Streams Framework for a Walk in Latin America." *Policy Sciences* 53 (1): 1–17.

Sanjurjo, Diego. 2021. "Why Are Brazilians so Interested in Gun Control? Putting the Multiple Streams Framework to the Test." *Opinião Pública* 27 (3): 730–56. https://bit.ly/3JXjwbw (January 9, 2022).

Scartascini, Carlos, Pablo Spiller, Ernesto Stein, and Mariano Tommasi. 2010. "¿Cómo Se Juega En América Latina? Instituciones Políticas, Procesos de Negociación y Políticas Públicas." In *El Juego Político En América Latina: ¿Cómo Se Deciden Las Políticas Públicas?*, eds. Carlos Scartascini, Pablo Spiller, Ernesto Stein, and Mariano Tommasi, 01–31. Banco Interamericano de Desarrollo (BID).

Schmitter, Philippe C. 1974. "Still the Century of Corporatism?" *The Review of Politics* 36 (1): 85–131.

Silveira Campos, Marcelo da, and Ghiringhelli de Azevedo. 2020. "A Ambiguidade Das Escolhas: Política Criminal No Brasil de 1989 a 2016." *Revista de Sociologia e Política* 28 (73).

de Souza, Maria De Fátima Marinho et al. 2007. "Reductions in Firearm-Related Mortality and Hospitalizations in Brazil After Gun Control." *Health Affairs* 26 (2): 575–84.

Waiselfisz, Julio Jacobo. 2015. *Mapa Da Violência 2016: Homicídios Por Armas de Fogo No Brasil*. Brasília, D.F.: FLACSO Brasil.

Wiarda, Howard J. 2001. *The Soul of Latin America: The Cultural and Political Tradition*. New Haven, CT: Yale University Press.

Zahariadis, Nikolaos. 1995. *Markets, States and Public Policy: Privatization in Britain and France*. Ann Arbor, MI: University of Michigan Press.
Zohlnhöfer, Reimut, and Christian Huß. 2016. "How Well Does the Multiple-Streams Framework Travel? Evidence from German Case Studies." In *Decision-Making under Ambiguity and Time Constraints*, eds. Reimut Zohlnhöfer and Friedbert W. Rüb, 169–88. Colchester: ECPR Press.

10. Turkey's pandemic management: Insights from the Multiple Streams Framework perspective

Lacin Idil Oztig

INTRODUCTION

Turkey's pandemic management took different forms depending on the dynamics of the Covid-19 pandemic. Turkey adopted preventive measures before the virus entered the country (between January and March 2020). The Emergency Operations Centre in Ankara began to monitor virus-related developments in the world, flights to and from various countries including China were suspended, the Scientific Advisory Board (SAB) was established,which consisted of medical scientists assigned to develop measures combatting the Covid-19 pandemic, and a Covid-19 disease guide was prepared. After the World Health Organization (WHO) announced the Covid-19 outbreak as a pandemic and the first Covid-19 case was reported in the country on March 11, restrictive measures were enforced that included international and inter-city travel restrictions, the shutdown of schools, universities, businesses, and other public places, and lockdowns. Even though restrictions were gradually loosened after June 2020, lockdowns continued intermittently from October 2020 until May 2021. Turkey moved to the full normalization stage with the start of face-to-face education in schools and universities in September 2021. On March 2, 2022, the outdoor mask-wearing requirement was lifted.

This chapter examines Turkey's response to the Covid-19 pandemic from January 2020 to March 2022 through the lens of the Multiple Streams Framework (MSF). In contrast to the traditional decision-making theory that assumes that policy preferences are fixed and exogenously given, the MSF is built upon the assumptions that policy-making processes are characterized by ambiguity and randomness and that policymakers operate under severe time constraints and with limited information which causes stress, vagueness, and confusion (Zahariadis 2007; Herweg, Zahariadis, and Zohlnhöfer 2018). According to the MSF, policy-making processes do not operate linearly.

Rather, they are characterized by multifaceted dynamics in which problems, ideas, and politics get entangled and then move on top of the government's agenda (McLendon 2003). From this perspective, problems, policies, and politics can develop independently of one another and be coupled following the opening of a policy window (Cairney and Zahariadis 2016; Koebele 2021).

Using the MSF, this chapter examines the impact of the Covid-19 pandemic (2020–22) on Turkey's agenda-setting. Through process tracing, this chapter shows how the MSF's three streams operated, interacted with one another throughout the pandemic, and which role policy entrepreneurs played in the coupling process. The WHO's announcement of the Covid-19 pandemic and the confirmation of the first virus case in the country on March 11, 2020 are identified as two critical moments that led to a window opening in the problem stream. Further, the chapter explains how solutions to the public health problem were coupled through the SABs recommendations and the roles played by the Health Minister, the SAB, and the President in joining the three streams. It also discusses the activities of advocacy groups in the problem and policy streams.

This chapter is organized as follows. The first section explains the research design. It discusses the applicability of the MSF framework to the Turkish case in view of the country's political dynamics and explicates the method of analysis: process tracing. The second section provides the case study. Turkey's agenda-setting during the pandemic is explained through the lens of the MSF framework. The third section summarizes the findings and discusses their implications.

RESEARCH DESIGN

As noted in the Introduction, this chapter analyzes the impact of the Covid-19 pandemic on Turkey's agenda-setting between 2020 and 2022 using the MSF framework. While some attention is devoted to policy adoption, this chapter leaves out the implementation output from the analysis due to space restrictions.

The problem, policy, and politics streams are examined at the national level. Importantly, Turkey is a non-democracy (see Freedom House Index 2022). Differing from many functioning democracies, the mode of interaction is not bargaining in Turkey's politics stream (Bolukbasi and Ertugal 2019). The state-society relationship is hierarchical, and the policy-making process is not characterized by consensus (Bolukbasi and Ertugal 2019). Turkey's top-down approach to policy-making has been bolstered under the Justice and the Development Party (JDP) rule through increased political control over the bureaucracy and deliberate exclusion of a wide range of societal actors from decision-making processes. After Turkey switched to the presidential system in 2018, the President's powers have substantially increased (Ustuner and Yavuz 2017), paving the way for one-man rule. Under the new system, the power of the executive has been expanded at the expense of the non-core executive and the legislature (Bolukbasi and Ertugal 2019).

This chapter takes note of the differences between liberal democracies and non-democracies in general and how Turkey's policy-making process differs from those of western democracies in particular. That being said, this chapter proceeds with the assumption that the MSF can travel to non-democratic settings despite the distinctions between regime types regarding the way the problem, policy, and politics streams operate (see Herweg, Zahariadis, and Zohlnhöfer 2022), the size of the policy communities, and the criterion of survival (Herweg, Zahariadis, and Zohlnhöfer 2018).

While Turkey has become an electoral authoritarian state under the JDP, it is still different from single-party regimes or military dictatorships. Notwithstanding the curtailment of political and civil liberties, this chapter takes into consideration advocacy groups and the national mood in conducting an MSF-led analysis. Advocacy groups (more specifically health associations) played active roles both in the problem and policy streams during the pandemic by presenting data-related issues as problems and through their policy proposals respectively. While standard MSF-reasoning expects to find advocacy groups in the politics streams (Kingdon 2011), this chapter brings a novel perspective to the MSF literature by highlighting the active role played by advocacy groups in the policy stream through their systematic attempts at proposing Covid-19 related policies. In other words, these groups acted as policy entreprenueurs with their aspiration to promote their alternative policy solutions. Furthermore, this chapter sheds light on how the government limited these groups' range of maneuverability and adopted a top-down approach in agenda setting, mirroring Turkey's general political tendencies.

The link between the Covid-19 pandemic and Turkey's agenda-setting is tested through the method of process tracing. The method selection is compatible with Dolan and Blum's arguments (chapter 5 in this volume) that the dynamics of coupling should be studied as a process and that methodological pluralism might lead to the development of rich empirical studies through the MSF. In this context, rather than developing falsifiable hypotheses, this chapter aims to identify the relationship between the Covid-19 pandemic and Turkey's agenda-setting through process-tracing and couple them with theory laden explanations (see Copeland and James 2014; Dolan 2021).

Process tracing refers to "the analysis of evidence on processes, sequences, and conjunctures of events" in a way that unpacks causal processes (Bennet and Checkel 2015, 7). The main idea of process tracing is concatenation, which "is the state of being linked together, as in a chain or linked series" (Waldner 2012, 68). The chapter relies on the primary data (newspaper articles, the reports of health associations, Our World in Data, and ministerial reports) and the secondary literature.

TURKEY'S PANDEMIC MANAGEMENT FROM A MSF PERSPECTIVE

The Problem Stream

Notwithstanding that not all focusing events bring about agenda change, they share a commonality as they increase the probability of agenda change (Birkland 1997; Herweg, Zahariadis, and Zohlnhöfer 2018). The intertwinement between the Covid-19 crisis and agenda change throughout the world is so strong that the Covid-19 pandemic fits into Kingdon's (2011, 96) definition of a grave crisis that "…bowl[s] over everything standing in the way of prominence on the agenda".

The WHO's announcement of pneumonia-like cases in Wuhan on January 9, 2020, aggravated Turkish policymakers' threat perception. For example, according to an analysis conducted by Sentoregil and Akinci (2021), Health Minister Fahrettin Koca's first tweet concerning Covid-19 dates back to January 22, 2020. As of February 2020, most of his tweets were coronavirus-related (Sentoregil and Akinci 2021).

On March 11, the declaration of a pandemic by the WHO as well as the announcement of the first Covid-19 case in Turkey became two focusing events, leading to the opening of an agenda window. A glance at policymakers' speeches in March 2020 reveals how Covid-19 was framed as a major public health problem in Turkey. For example, in his speech immediately after the detection of the first Covid-19 case in Turkey, Health Minister Koca stated that Turkey had a plan to fight the pandemic (Anadolu Agency 2020). A week later, President Erdogan stated that Turkey mobilized all its means to eliminate the virus threat (The Presidency of Turkish Republic 2020). Later, he promised that Turkey would go through the pandemic with minimum damage (Mutlu, Alyanak, and Orkan 2020). These statements point to the fact that as of March 2020, Turkish policymakers went on high alert and urgently contemplated combating the virus. With the recognition of the Covid-19 virus as a pressing problem, the pandemic moved to the top of policymakers' agenda (see Kingdon 2011).

Taken together, while the spread of Covid-19 throughout the world prompted the attention of Turkish policymakers, after Covid-19 reached the pandemic stage and the first virus case was reported in Turkey, the issue quickly turned into a "serious public health crisis" or "the problem of Covid-19". Importantly, with policymakers' framing the virus as a major public health problem that necessitated urgent policy action, an agenda window in the problem stream

(Zahariadis 2003) opened that eventually paved the way for the coupling of the problem and policy streams.

The Turkish Medical Association and Ankara Doctors Association played active roles in the problem stream. For example, since the start of the pandemic, the Turkish Medical Association repeatedly called the Ministry of Health to reveal data on Covid-19 cases in terms of sex, age, and occupation (The Turkish Medical Association 2021). On March 31, 2020, it claimed that people who tested negative, but needed to go through Covid-19 treatment, were not classified as Covid-19 patients and argued that this caused a huge difference between the number of Covid-19 patients and the number of people who tested positive (DW Turkiye 2020). The Ankara Doctors Association raised questions regarding data transparency by noting that the information shared with the public is different from that of the field (DW Turkiye 2020). While these two advocacy groups framed the date-related issues as public health problems, they were not able to persuade policymakers to accept these frames. In other words, due to the dynamics of the problem stream, these groups could not act as successful problem brokers.

The government's problem perception regarding the pandemic did not fit with that of these groups. More specifically, while the government and these advocacy groups saw the pandemic as a threat, these advocacy groups perceived Covid-19 more dangerous than the government and pressured the government to announce the precise magnitude of the threat by presenting accurate data to the public. All in all, the activities of the advocacy groups in the problem stream did not influence problem recognition (see Zohlnhöfer, Herweg, and Zahariadis 2022). This result is consistent with the argument that in non-democratic regimes, successful problem brokers are likely to be people close to the autocrat or public officials (Herweg, Zahariadis, and Zohlnhöfer 2022; Wu 2022).

The Policy Stream

In the policy stream, policy solutions to problems are generated. A policy community "is mainly a loose connection of civil servants, interest groups, academics, researchers and consultants (the so-called hidden participants), who engage in working out alternatives to the policy problems of a specific policy field" Herweg 2016, 132). In general, civil servants, advocacy groups, and scientists do not play key roles in Turkey's policy stream (Bolukbasi and Ertugal 2019). The traditional hierarchical state-society relationship is maintained by the Turkish constitutional system through the protection of the state against individuals (Ozbudun 2011). Civil servants work in a culture in which subservience and loyalty are encouraged; as such, they are unwilling to take the initiative (Ertugal 2021) . The agency of the bureaucracy has been severely undermined following the Justice and Development Party's (JDP) ascendency to power (Ustuner and Yavuz 2017). Professional organizations, such as bar associations, engineers and architects, associations, and medical associations are strictly controlled by the political authority (Ozbudun 2011). In general, criticisms and alternative policy proposals generated by advocacy groups do not receive serious consideration from the government (Ertugal 2021). In other words, advocacy groups' recommendations do not generally pass the criteria of survival due to Turkey's centralized and authoritarian decision-making tendencies.

In the past, professional organizations did take legal actions for the reversal of the government's decisions in urban, energy, and climate domains. However, these actions failed due to the politicization of the judiciary (Eraydin 2012; Esen and Gumuscu 2017). In Ertugal's words (2021, 17), Turkey's current policy style "undermines policy expertise, reduces the possibility for the emergence of bureaucratic policy entrepreneurs, discourages initiative-taking, and encourages passivity and loyalty".

It is important to note that during the pandemic, a number of major health associations played an active role in the policy stream. Among the health associations, the Turkish Medical Association played the most active role by advocating solutions to the Covid-19-related problems. Being health experts, both members of the SAB and the Turkish Medical Association share a commonality by being part of the same epistemic community, "a network of professionals with recognized expertise and competence in a particular domain and an authoritative claim to policy-relevant knowledge within that domain or issue-area" (Haas 1992, 3). While the SAB was created within the Ministry of Health, the Turkish Medical Association remains outside of the formal policy-making process.

However, as mentioned previously, advocacy groups are not integrated into the formal policy-making process. Adding to that, the anti-government stance of the Turkish Medical Association has further obstructed its access to the government. The Ministry of Health has not responded to its request for a meeting for more than a year. It has also been systematically excluded from Turkey's policy-making processes regarding the pandemic.

For example, on March 17, 2020, the Turkish Medical Association along with five major health associations published a declaration calling for the inclusion of the Turkish Medical Association and Turkish Pharmacy Association in the SAB (TJOD 2020). In addition to these associations, the Association of Public Health Experts was also excluded from the SAB (Kisa and Kisa 2020). Furthermore, major health associations were not invited to participate in the SAB and the Covid-19 coordination meeting (headed by President Erdogan in his presidential palace on March 18, 2020) after which important decisions related to the pandemic were announced (TRT Haber 2020).

The Turkish Medical Association repeatedly called the government to launch an effective, coordinated communication campaign to deal with vaccine hesitancy. It criticized the government for not allowing professional chambers such as the Union of Chambers of Turkish Engineers and Architects (UCTEA), universities, and independent organizations to provide inspection on the provision of free masks, the quality of mask production, and ventilation (The Turkish Medical Association 2021). It went so far as to argue that the exclusion of major health associations became a part of the government's pandemic management strategy (Erdogan 2020). Yet, so far, its proposals did not lead to a policy change.

That said, some advocacy groups were able to affect policies in the policy stream. For example, a few days after the President of the Turkish Dental Association, Atilla Atac, criticized the absence of a dentist within the SAB, a professor, who specialized in jaw surgery, was appointed as a member of the SAB (The Turkish Dental Association 2020). The President of the Mental Health Association (MHA), Omer Akgul, emphasized the importance of the psychological fight against the pandemic and advised the inclusion of psychology and sociology experts in the SAB or the creation of a psychosocial coronavirus board (Cumhuriyet 2020). This recommendation appears to have played an important role in the establishment of the Social Sciences Board by the Ministry of Health which examines the social and psychological impacts of the pandemic. The Board consists of experts specialized in sociology, psychology, and communication (The Turkish Ministry of Health 2020).

Taken all together, the composition of the SAB was changed, and the Social Sciences Board was created following the advocacy of public health associations. However, apart from a few exceptions, major health associations could not play a pivotal role in agenda-setting. The exclusion of the Turkish Medical Association and other major health associations is consistent with the general finding in the MSF literature that the access to policymakers is crucial in coupling the streams (Herweg, Zahariadis, and Zohlnhöfer 2018). Due to its anti-government stance, the Turkish Medical Association could not act as a successful policy entrepreneur.

The SAB stands out as the most relevant actor in the policy stream. Differing from Turkey's general policy-making characteristics, the SAB emerged as a pivotal actor in Turkey's policy stream during the pandemic. The SAB was established by the Ministry of Health on January 10, 2020. Health Minister Fahrettin Koca played an active role in its creation. The members of the SAB were selected and invited based on the recommendations of Mr Koca (Milliyet 2020). Mr Koca heads the SAB which consists of university professors and medical experts specialized in pulmonology, virology, infectious diseases, clinical diseases, and a legal advisor. The SAB was initially created with 26 members which was later increased to 38. The creation of the SAB led to the softening-up process, as policy proposals were discussed and finalized within the SAB meetings headed by the Minister of Health (Milliyet 2020). The following paragraphs summarize those SAB proposals that played a pivotal role in Turkey's response to the pandemic.

Before the virus hit the country, the SAB published a Covid disease guide that revealed information about the virus, infection control/isolation, treatment, etc. In conformity with the recommendations of the SAB, flights to and from China, Italy, Iraq, Iran, and South Korea were suspended, Covid-19-related measures were taken at border gates, thermal cameras were placed in airports, and Turkish citizens in Wuhan were evacuated. On March 2, information leaflets prepared by the Ministry of Health were distributed to 81 provincial health directorates and all health and public institutions (Hurriyet 2020a).

After the first Covid-19 case was announced on March 11, the SAB played a pivotal role in Turkey's shift towards restrictive measures (Oztig 2022). In line with the SAB's recommendations, people who came from abroad were placed in quarantine for two weeks. Civil servants were prohibited from traveling abroad. Cafes, restaurants, theatres, shopping malls, and gyms were shut down. Hospital visits, court hearings, cultural and sports activities, and prayer gatherings in mosques were suspended. Civil servants switched to flexible working hours. Civil servants suffering from chronic diseases were allowed to take administrative leave. All international and inter-city travel was suspended. Inter-city travel was only allowed with special permission from the governor's office. Schools and universities suspended face-to-face education and moved classes online (TRT Haber 2021). A curfew was imposed on people who were above 65 and who had chronic diseases, later it was extended to those under 20 years old (Karaaslan 2021a).

Turkey's Covid-19 cases rapidly increased in the first weeks of April 2020 with 5,138 new cases on April 11 (Our World in Data 2021). In parallel with the increase in cases, full lockdowns started to be implemented. Turkey's first general (two-day) lockdown was implemented on April 11. Two-day and four-day lockdowns were intermittently imposed until June 1. Against the backdrop of a decrease in new cases in May (Our World in Data 2021), restrictions were gradually reduced. From June 1 onwards, a period called "new normalization" commenced. Inter-city travel restrictions ended, and restaurants, cafes, and gyms were reopened. International flight restrictions gradually eased. However, some additional measures were implemented. For instance, mask-wearing outdoors became obligatory in Istanbul, Ankara, and Bursa. In July, cinemas and theaters were reopened, and working hour limitations for shopping centers, restaurants, etc. were lifted (Karaaslan 2021a).

However, the loosening of restrictions correlated with increases in cases (Our World in Data 2021). Consequently, more precautionary measures were taken. Mask-wearing became mandatory in September 2020. In November

2020, new restrictions were implemented, such as the closure of businesses and public places; partial weekend curfews; limited-hour curfews for people who were under 20 years old and over 65. The Ministry of Education announced the continuation of online education for schools and universities (BBC Turkce 2020). In November, Turkey reached an agreement with China for the supply of Sinovac, an inactivated Covid-19 vaccine. A month later, a contract was signed with a Germany-based BioNTech company for the procurement of additional vaccine doses (Hurriyet 2020b).

Partial curfews were imposed in November 2020, and they continued inter-mittently until June 2021. In March 2021, the Ministry of Health published a risk map that split provinces into four tiers by Covid-19 risk low, middle, high, and very high risk. This month also witnessed the beginning of the period of controlled normalization. Restaurants and cafes were opened under certain conditions. Depending on their risk status, in certain provinces, face-to-face education started. Lockdowns were imposed during certain hours on weekdays while full lockdowns were implemented on weekends. Inter-city restrictions were partially enforced. Nevertheless, based on their risk status, provinces could adopt additional measures (Oztig 2022).

Turkey's highest number of Covid-19 cases throughout the pandemic was observed on April 16, 2021, with 63,082 cases (Our World in Data 2021). After this sharp increase in cases, the country went into a full lockdown between 29 April and 17 May 2021. All businesses were closed. Public transportation started to operate at 50 percent capacity. Curfews and inter-city travel restric-tions were enforced. On May 16, "gradual normalization measures" were announced by the Ministry of Interior. From May 17 until June 1, curfews were imposed at certain hours. Curfews no longer applied to people under 18 and over 65 who received two doses of the vaccine. Inter-city travel was allowed except during curfew hours (The Turkish Ministry of Interior 2021a).

The period from late April until June 2021 is characterized by a sharp drop in Covid-19 cases albeit with some fluctuations (Our World in Data 2021). The second stage of the gradual normalization commenced on June 1. Slight changes were made to the curfew hours. Restaurants and cafes were permitted to open every day except Sunday, under certain conditions. Cinemas were opened with limited capacity. Inter-city travel restrictions during curfew hours continued (The Turkish Ministry of Interior 2021b). The normalization process gathered pace from July 1 onwards. Curfews and inter-city restrictions were lifted. Capacity limitations for public transportation were lifted (The Ministry of Interior 2021c). In September, schools and universities switched to face-to-face education.

On September 7, 2021, the Mu variant was reported in two individuals. Health Minister Koca noted that no additional measures would be taken with respect to this variant. Specifying that more than 90 percent of the Covid-19 cases in Turkey were Delta or Delta plus variants, he argued that there was a high probability that the number of cases would decrease after two shots of the Covid-19 vaccine, and the threshold of the herd immunity would eventually be at 85 percent (Euronews 2021). Proffesor Mustafa Necmi İlhan, the SAB member, noted that against the backdrop of large-scale vaccination, new restrictions are not on the agenda. However, he urged people to get vaccinated and receive booster shots (TRT 2021b).

The Turkish Medicines and Medical Devices Agency gave emergency approval for Turcovac, Turkey's locally developed vaccine, in December 2021. As of February 2022, Turcovac started to be rolled out in 81 provinces (Usul 2022). The SAB member and the President of Turkey's Vaccination Institute Professor Ates Kara underlined Turkovac's effectiveness in preventing hospitalization and death (Maltas 2022).

On March 2, 2022, following the SAB meeting, Health Minister Koca announced that the requirement to wear masks outdoors was lifted. The requirement to wear masks indoors was also lifted on certain conditions (Bianet 2022). Mr Koca justified these decisions on the grounds that the pandemic currently affected social life much lesser as compared to before and noted that the fight against the pandemic would continue through vaccination (Usul, Karaaslan, and Sahin 2022).

The Politics Stream

The politics stream consists of factors that influence the body politic (Béland and Howlett, 2016). This chapter examines the dynamics of the politics stream by focusing on the national mood and the government (see Kingdon 2011). While interest group campaigns are another element of the politics stream (Herweg, Zahariadis, and Zohlnhöfer 2018), this chapter leaves them out from the analysis as the Turkish Government systematically turns a blind eye to such campaigns.

The national mood
The national mood refers to perceptions held by the majority of citizens in a country. While it is an elusive concept, it can be concretized by looking at opinion polls (Dolan 2019; Sanjurjo 2020; Zahariadis 2015). This chapter operationalizes the national mood by looking at Turkish citizens' political trust in the government. In Turkey, politicians and the government are seen as the least trustworthy. This is in sharp contrast to scientists and doctors who are seen as the most trustworthy professionals (Trustworthiness Index 2019). According to an OECD report, during the early stages of the Covid-19 pandemic in 2020, only 55 percent of the Turkish respondents indicated their trust

in the government while 63 percent and 61 percent of the respondents indicated their trust in the civil service and Parliament respectively (OECD 2021).

The survey conducted by European Social Survey in 2016 shows that 36.8 percent of the respondents believed that they have a say in what the government does (OECD 2019). According to the Pew Research Survey, conducted in 2015, 54 percent of the people were dissatisfied with the way things are going in Turkey, while 44 percent were satisfied. Between 2012 and 2015, while favorable opinions of Erdogan decreased from 59 to 39 percent, negative views increased from 33 to 39 percent (Poushter 2015) .

It is important to note that even though Turkey's authoritarian tendencies have increased over the years, President Erdogan is concerned about his public image. He takes into consideration and tries to manipulate the national mood through his populist discourse (see Yılmaz 2021). He frequently employs "the national will" discourse in justifying his decisions (Oral 2015). In other words, in view of his electoral incentives, he aims to increase his popularity by portraying his decisions in accordance with the utmost interests of the general populace.

This chapter posits that the national mood played an important role in Turkey's politics stream during the pandemic. A poll conducted by Yontem (2020) in March 2020 among 360 individuals reveals that the Ministry of Health was seen as the most responsible institution during the pandemic. Against the backdrop of high trust in medical professionals, low trust in the government, along with sharp decreases in Erdogan's popularity, the government's policies in compliance with the recommendations of SAB and the major role played by the Health Minister can be evaluated as strategies to increase the legitimacy of the government's decisions and ensure the maximum level of public compliance to the restrictive measures (see Zahariadis, Petridou, and Oztig 2020). It is reasonable to argue that in a public health crisis on such a scale, policy actions become more impactful when political actors draw on research and science (Amri and Logan 2021).

The government
Under the ruling JDP, especially after new institutional and administrative arrangements were introduced following the 2017 constitutional amendments, which abolished the parliamentary system and introduced the presidential system (Bolukbasi and Ertugal 2019), the President has become the most relevant actor in Turkey's political stream. The prime minister's office was dissolved. The President appoints ministers, high-level civil servants, and four members of the Board of Judges and Prosecutors and selects more than half of the judges of the Constitutional Court. He has the option of bypassing legislation, sending laws back to the Parliament, and dissolving the Parliament (Yilmaz 2020). Presidential decrees and bylaws dominate

Turkey's policy-making processes (Ertugal 2021). Turkey's new system can be described as "the presidentialisation of the executive branch" and "presidential bureaucracy" (Bakir 2020).

The Coupling of the Streams

As mentioned previously, during the pandemic, the SAB generated policy solutions and coupled them with problems (see Herweg, Zahariadis, and Zohlnhöfer 2018; Knaggard 2015). Following the SAB's recommendations, the problem and policy streams were coupled. The SAB's recommendations including restrictions, loosening restrictions, gradual normalization, and full normalization shaped policymakers' pandemic-related decisions.

The reality of the policy-making world rarely fits the rational viewpoint of policymakers who are challenged with a clear-cut problem and come up with an appropriate solution to it (Möck et al. 2022). Kingdon's (2011) portrayal of policymakers as deficient individuals stands in sharp contrast to the rationalistic perspective that depicts them as capable and well-informed actors (Möck et al. 2022). Most of the time, policymakers make decisions in the face of uncertainty. In addition, they have limited time and resources to understand all technicalities of policy problems (Cairney and Zahariadis 2016; Zahariadis 2007). Making the right decisions on time and communicating these decisions effectively are of immense importance for policymakers (Bull 2012).

Like in many countries, the Covid-19 crisis caught Turkish policymakers off guard. Even though the Ministry of Health had been preparing for large-scale outbreaks and pandemics since 2004 and published the "National Pandemic Influenza Preparedness Plan" in 2019 (The Turkish Ministry of Health 2019), Turkish policymakers urgently needed expert opinion to handle this novel, unprecedented crisis.

By creating the SAB, Turkish policymakers aimed to reduce uncertainty and make informed decisions in an extremely dynamic and shifting environment. Under increased uncertainty and time pressure regarding the Covid-19 crisis, the SAB provided a roadmap for the government with its expert opinion on the management of the health crisis. For example, in the initial phase of the pandemic, the SAB recommended strict measures including nationwide quarantine, travel restrictions, border closures, lockdowns, and physical and social distancing. In the later stages of the pandemic, the SAB recommended a gradual loosening of the restrictions. It recommended an end to all restrictions on March 2, 2022 (Oztig 2022).[1] It is important to highlight that in view of severe uncertainty during the pandemic, the SAB's recommendations passed the criteria of survival that consist of technical feasibility, value acceptability, tolerable costs, receptivity among decision-makers, and public acquiescence (Kingdon 2011). President Erdogan's Covid-19-related instructions outlined in presidential cabinet meetings were informed by the SAB's recommendations. The Ministry of Interior issued decisions based on the President's instructions and sent them to 81 provinces of Turkey (Oztig 2022).

The Minister of Health and the SAB members played key roles in coupling all the streams. Their statements and explanations played a pivotal role in persuading the Turkish public about Covid-19 precautions, health and hygiene practices, and vaccination. After the SAB meetings, the Minister of Health, Mr Fahrettin Koca, hosted press conferences and communicated the SAB's recommendations to the public. He frequently emphasized his medical profession in communicating with the public. He aimed to generate popular support for the SAB's recommendations by emphasizing the severity of the problem. He adopted the motto that "coronavirus is not stronger than the precautions we will take". While informing the public about the pandemic and the precautions to be observed to minimize the spread of the virus, he gave an utmost attention not to cause panic in the society (The Ministry of Health 2020).

Mr Koca also effectively used his Twitter account to reach out to the public during this unprecedented health crisis. His Twitter followers increased from 391,000 in March 2020 to 6.7 million in December 2020. With the way he communicated with the public, Mr Koca became a popular figure even among the opposition. The Ministry of Health also launched communication campaigns and prepared public announcements to inform the public and ensure maximum compliance (Arslantas, Schulz, and Karadag 2021) .

The SAB members also played an active role in informing citizens about the virus and fighting perceived disinformation on TV, social media, and newspapers (Arslantas, Schulz, and Karadag 2021). Among them, Prof. Ates Kara was the most popular one. He often appeared on TV and gave information and answered people's questions related to the virus, its treatment, the pandemic dynamics, and vaccination (such as the difference between activated and inactivated vaccines, the side effects of Covid-19 vaccines, etc.).

As mentioned previously, the SAB enabled the President to increase the legitimacy of his decisions amidst low trust in the political leadership. Importantly, to improve his public image, President Erdogan also engaged in credit claiming during the pandemic (Zahariadis, Petridou, and Oztig 2020). The health crisis represented an opportunity for Erdogan to increase his popularity. In other words, he aimed to turn the Covid crisis into an opportunity by showcasing Turkey's handling of the pandemic as a success story. By framing Turkey's pandemic management as a success, Erdogan took part in the coupling of the problem, policy, and politics streams.

For example, he noted that Turkey was able to control the spread of the disease while developed countries were still struggling (Anadolu Agency 2021). He argued that the local production of masks and test kits and the number of health personnel gave Turkey a competitive advantage in pandemic management (Euronews Turkiye 2020). For example, in 2021, the Directorate of Communications of the Presidency of the Republic of Turkey[2] published a book outlining Turkey's success in handling the Covid-19 crisis (Anadolu Agency 2021). In the same year, it opened a website named "Turkey Stops Covid" which highlights Turkey's achievements in the contexts of foreign aid, contact tracing teams, vaccination, pandemic and emergency hospitals, support groups (The Directorate of Communications of the Presidency of the Republic of Turkey 2023).

In his speech at the Shanghai Cooperation Organization in 2022, Erdogan indicated that Turkey gave aid to 161 countries and 12 international organizations during the pandemic and defined Turkey as the most generous country in the world (Hurriyet 2022a). In his speech at the 8th Turkish Medical World Congress in 2022, he identified healthcare as one of the most ambitious domains of his leadership. He stated that with TURCOVAC, Turkey has become one of the nine countries in the world capable of producing a Covid-19 vaccine (Dogru Haber 2022).

By downplaying the criticisms of major health associations and emphasizing the number of hospitals, Turkey's medical aid to many countries during the pandemic, and TURCOVAC (Anadolu Agency 2021), Erdogan used Covid-19-related information strategically and selectively to increase his popularity among the Turkish public. His repeated stress on Turkey's efficient handling of the crisis aimed to make a persuasive case for his strong leadership.

CONCLUSION AND DISCUSSION

This chapter drew on the MSF in explaining Turkey's agenda-setting regarding the Covid-19 pandemic. It identifies the WHO's classification of the Covid-19 outbreak as a pandemic and the report of the first virus case in the country on 11 March 2020 as two focusing events that led to a window opening in the problem stream. Against the backdrop of aggravated concerns following the focusing events, Covid-19 moved to the top of policymakers' agenda and a policy window was opened in the problem stream. Turkish Medical Association and Ankara Doctors Association were active in the problem stream. Yet, they were not able to push the issues related to Covid-19 onto the agenda. In other words, the activities of the problem brokers in the problem stream did not have an impact on agenda-setting.

The problem and policy streams were coupled following the SAB's policy proposals to combat the pandemic. The SAB attached solutions to the problem in the policy stream. In the face of severe uncertainty, the SAB generated policies that led to the adoption of drastic measures to contain the spread of the virus. As the pandemic progressed, the SAB recommended the loosening of restrictive measures, the reintroduction of restrictions, gradual normalization, and full normalization. The SAB's pandemic-related recommendations were translated into the President's instructions and ministerial decisions. Several public health associations were also active in the policy stream. Nonetheless, apart from a few exceptions, their proposals did not gain agenda status.

Health Minister Koca, the SAB members, and President Erdogan were instrumental in coupling the problem, the policy, and politics streams. With their medical professional identity, Health Minister Koca and the SAB members played key roles in increasing the legitimacy of the government's strategy in handling the pandemic and persuading the public to take preventive measures to minimize the spread of the virus. Importantly, Erdogan benefited from the SAB's role in the policy stream to make a success story for himself amidst his declining popular support. Building on the hard work of the Health Minister and the SAB, President Erdogan framed Turkey's pandemic management in the context of his successful political leadership. In other words, while Health Minister Koca and the SAB relied on medical science, especially epidemiology in coupling the three streams, President Erdogan relied on credit-claiming.

NOTES

1. In the SAB meetings, not all decisions were taken unanimously. For example, the lifting of final restrictions at the SAB meeting on March 2, 2022, was decided even though some SAB members showed reservations (Hurriyet 2022b).
2. This institution is directly tied to the Presidency. It was established in 2018 to promote Turkey's brand both at the national and international levels (The Directorate of Communications of the Presidency of the Republic of Turkey 2019).

REFERENCES

Amri, Michelle M. and Dilani Logan. 2021. "Policy responses to Covid-19 present a window of opportunity for a paradigm shift in global health policy: An application of the Multiple Streams Framework as a heuristic." *Global Public Health* 16 (8–9): 1187–97. https://doi.org/10.1080/17441692.2021.1925942.

Anadolu Agency. 2020. "The Health Minister Koca announced the first Covid-19 case in Turkey," March 11. https://www.aa.com.tr/tr/koronavirus/saglik-bakani-koca-turkiyede-ilk-koronavirus-vakasinin-goruldugunu-acikladi/1761466.

Anadolu Agency. 2021. "President Erdoğan wrote an introduction to the book 'Turkey's Successful Struggle against Coronavirus." March 15. https://www.aa.com.tr/tr/turkiye/cumhurbaskani-erdogan-turkiyenin-koronavirusle-basarili-mucadelesi-kitabina-takdim-yazisi-kaleme-aldi/2176736.

Arslantas, Duzgun, Ludwig Schulz, and Roy Karadag. 2021. "Sustainable Governance in the context of the Covid-19 crisis." Bertelsmann Stiftung, https://www.bertelsmann-stiftung.de/index.php?id=5772&tx_rsmbstpublications_pi2%5bdoi%5d=10.11586/2021108&no_cache=1.

Bakir, Caner. 2020. "The Turkish State's Responses to Existential Covid-19 Crisis." *Policy and Society* 39 (3): 424–41. https://doi.org/10.1080/14494035.2020.1783786.

BBC Turkce. 2020. "*New Prohibitions,*" (in Turkish) November 17. https://www.bbc.com/turkce/haberler-turkiye-54977340.

Béland, Daniel and Michelle Howlett. 2016. "The Role and Impact of the Multiple-Streams Approach in Comparative Policy Analysis." *Journal of Comparative Policy Analysis: Research and Practice* 18 (3): 221–27. https://doi.org/10.1080/13876988.2016.1174410.

Bennett, Andrew and Jeffrey T. Checkel. 2015. "Process tracing: from philosophical roots to best practices." In *Process Tracing: From Metaphor to Analytical Tool*, eds. Andrew Bennett and Jeffrey T. Checkel, 3–38. Cambridge: Cambridge University Press.

Bianet. 2022. "Turkey lifts outdoor mask mandate, contact tracing code requirement." March 2. https://bianet.org/english/health/258511-turkey-lifts-outdoor-mask-mandate-contact-tracing-code-requirement.

Birkland, Thomas A. 1997. *After Disaster: Agenda-Setting, Public Policy and Focusing Events*. Washington, DC.: Georgetown University Press.

Bolukbasi, H. Tolga and Ebru Ertugal. 2019. "Napoleonic Traditions, Majoritarianism, and Turkey's Statist Policy Style." In *Policy Styles and Policy-making Exploring the Linkages*, eds. Michael Howlett and Jale Tosun, 351–74. New York: Routledge.

Bull, Peter. 2012. "What makes a successful politician? The social skills of politics." In *The Psychology of Politicians*, eds. Ashley Weinberg, 61–76. Cambridge: Cambridge University Press.

Cairney, Paul and Nikolaos Zahariadis. 2016. "Multiple streams approach: a flexible metaphor presents an opportunity to operationalize agenda-setting processes." In *Hanbook of Public Policy Agenda Setting*, eds. Nikolaos Zahariadis, 87–105. Cheltenham: Edward Elgar Publishing.

Copeland, Paul, and Scott James. 2014. "Policy Windows, Ambiguity and Commission Entrepreneurship: Explaining the Relaunch of the European Union's Economic Reform Agenda." *Journal of European Public Policy* 21 (1): 1–19.

Cumhuriyet. 2020. "A Recommendation of a psychosocial coronavirus board from the Mental Health Association." (in Turkish) March 28. https://www.cumhuriyet.com.tr/haber/ruh-sagligi-derneginden-psikososyal-koronavirus-kurulu-onerisi-1729974.

Dogru Haber. 2022. "Erdogan attends 8th Turkish Medical World Congress." October 31, https://dogruhaber.com.tr/haber/873096-erdogan-attends-8th-turkish-medical-world-congress/.

Dolan, Dana A. 2019. "Multiple Partial Couplings in the Multiple Streams Framework: The Case of Extreme Weather and Climate Change Adaptation." *Policy Studies Journal* 49 (1): 164–89. doi: 10.1111/psj.12341.

Durant, Robert F. and Paul F. Diehl. 1989. "Agendas, Alternatives, and Public Policy: Lessons from the U.S. Foreign Policy Arena." *Journal of Public Policy* 9 (2): 179–205. doi: https://doi.org/10.1017/S0143814X00008114.

DW Turkiye. 2021. "The opposition and professional organizations want more transparency" (in Turkish) March 31. https://www.dw.com/tr/muhalefet-ve-meslek-%C3%B6rg%C3%BCtleri-daha-fazla-%C5%9Feffafl%C4%B1k-istiyor/a-52958754.

Eraydın, Ayda and Tuna Tasan-Kok. 2014. "State response to contemporary urban movements in Turkey: A critical overview of state entrepreneurialism and authoritarian interventions." *Antipode* 46 (1): 110–29. https://doi.org/10.1111/anti.12042.

Erdogan. 2020. "Criticism from TMA: "The Process Is Not Managed Transparently."" *VOA*, May 14. https://www.amerikaninsesi.com/a/turk-tabipleri-birliginden-salgin -yonetimi-elestirisi-surec-seffaf-yonetilmiyor/5419813.html.

Ertugal, Ebru. 2021. "Does policy style shift when the political regime changes? Insights from Turkey." *Contemporary Politics*, https://doi.org/10.1080/13569775 .2021.1976941.

Esen, Berk and Sebnem Gumuscu. 2017. "Building a competitive authoritarian regime: State-business relations in the AKP's Turkey." *Journal of Balkan and Near Eastern Studies* 20 (4): 349–72. https://doi.org/10.1080/19448953.2018.1385924.

Euronews Turkiye. 2020. "President Erdoğan announced the new measures taken against the Covid-19 pandemic" (in Turkish), April 4. https://tr.euronews.com/ 2020/04/03/cumhurbaskan-erdogan-covid-19-salg-n-na-kars-al-nan-yeni-onlemleri -ac-klad.

Euronews Turkiye. 2021. "Fahrettin Koca: The Mu variant was detected in two people in Turkey." September 7. https://tr.euronews.com/2021/09/07/fahrettin-koca-turkiye -de-2-kiside-mu-varyant-goruldu.

Freedom House Index. 2022. "Turkey" https://freedomhouse.org/country/turkey/ freedom-world/2022.

Haas, Peter M. 1992. "Introduction: Epistemic Communities and International Policy Coordination." *International Organization* 46 (1): 1–35. doi: https://doi.org/10 .1017/S0020818300001442.

Herweg, Nicole. 2016. "Clarifying the Concept of Policy Communities in the Multiple Streams Framework." In *Decision- Making under Ambiguity and Time Constraints: Assessing the Multiple Streams Framework*, eds. Zohlnhöfer, Reimut and Rüb Friedbert, 125– 45. Colchester: ECPR Press.

Herweg, Nicole, Nikolaos Zahariadis, and Reimut Zohlnhöfer. 2018. "The Multiple Streams Framework: Foundations, Refinements, and Empirical Applications." In *Theories of the Policy Process,* eds. Christopher M. Weible and Paul A. Sabatier, 65–93. New York: Routledge.

Herweg, Nicole, Nikolaos Zahariadis, and Reimut Zohlnhöfer. 2022. "Travelling Far and Wide? Applying the Multiple Streams Framework to Policy-Making in Autocracies." *Polit Vierteljahresschr* 63: 203–23.

Hurriyet.2020a. "Coronavirus information leaflets were sent to 81 provinces." March 2. https://www.hurriyet.com.tr/gundem/corona-virus-bilgilendirme-brosuru-81-ile -gonderildi-41459026.

Hurriyet. 2020b. "The Ministry of Health signed a contract related to the BioNTech vaccine" (in Turkish), December 25) https://web.archive.org/web/20201225182543/ https:/www.indyturk.com/node/290931/haber/sağlık-bakanlığı-biontech-aşısı-ile -ilgili-anlaşmayı-imzaladı-yıl-sonuna-kadar-550.

Hurriyet. 2022a. "President Erdoğan: We are proud to be the most generous country in the world" (in Turkish) September 16, https://www.hurriyet.com.tr/dunya/son -dakika-cumhurbaskani-erdogandan-onemli-mesajlar-42138360.

Hurriyet. 2022b. "The Coronavirus restrictions were lifted" (in Turkish) March 2, https://www.hurriyet.com.tr/gundem/son-dakika-bakan-koca-acikliyor-turkiyenin -corona-virusuyle-mucadelesinde-kritik-gun-42014576.

Karaaslan, Yesim S. 2021a. "A report on Turkey's 1-year fight against Covid-19" (in Turkish) *Anadolu Agency*, March 10. https://www.aa.com.tr/tr/koronavirus/ turkiyenin-1-yillik-kovid-19la-mucadele-surecinin-tedbir-karnesi/2171001#.

Karaaslan, Yesim S. 2021b. "In the fight against the Covid-19 pandemic, the period of localized decision starts" (in Turkish) *Anadoly Agency*, January 15. https://www

.aa.com.tr/tr/koronavirus/kovid-19la-mucadelede-yerinden-karar-donemi-basliyor/ 2144940.

Kingdon, John W. 2011. *Agendas, Alternatives, and Public Policies*. New York: Longman.

Kisa, Sezer and Adnan Kisa. 2020. "Under-reporting of Covid-19 cases in Turkey." *The International Journal of Health Planning and Management* 35 (5): 1009–13. doi: 10.1002/hpm.3031.

Knaggard, Asa. 2015. "The Multiple Streams Framework and the problem broker." *European Journal of Political Research* 54 (3): 450–65.

Koebele, Elizabeth A. 2021. "When multiple streams make a river: analyzing collaborative policy-making institutions using the multiple streams framework." *Policy Sciences* 54: 609–28. doi: https://doi.org/10.1007/s11077–021–09425–3.

Maltas, Rauf. 2022. "Prof.Dr. Ates Kara: The effectiveness of the Turcovac vaccine in preventing hospital admissions is very high." *Anadolu Agency*, February 28. https://www.aa.com.tr/tr/koronavirus/prof-dr-ates-kara-turkovac-asisinin-hastaneye -basvuruyu-onlemede-etkinligi-cok-yuksek/2518119.

McLendon, Michael K. 2003. "State governance reform of higher education: Patterns, trends, and theories of the public policy process." In *Higher education: Handbook of theory and research*, eds. John C. Smart, 57–144. London: Kluwer.

Milliyet. 2020. "The members of the Scientific Board." April 7. https://www.milliyet .com.tr/gundem/bilim-kurulu-uyeleri-kimlerdir-isimleri-ne-2020-bilim-kurulu -uyeleri-kimlerden-olusuyor-6180779.

Möck, Malte, Colette S. Vogeler, Nils C. Bandelow, and Johanna Hornung. 2022. "Relational coupling of multiple streams: The case of Covid-19 infections in German abattoirs." *Policy Studies Journal*, doi: 10.1111/psj.12459.

Mutlu, Sefa, Cigdem Munibe Alyanak, Semra Orkan. 2020. "President Erdoğan: We will emerge from the coronavirus epidemic with minimum damage." *Anadolu Agency*, March 25. https://www.aa.com.tr/tr/koronavirus/cumhurbaskani-erdogan -koronavirus-salginindan-olabilecek-en-az-hasarla-cikacagiz/1779565.

OECD. 2019. "Country Fact Sheet: Turkey." https://www.oecd.org/gov/gov-at-a -glance-2019-turkey.pdf.

OECD. 2021. "Government at a Glance: 2021 Country Fact Sheet." https://www.oecd .org/gov/gov-at-a-glance-2021-turkey.pdf.

Oral, Bahar. 2015. "An Analysis of the National Will Discourse of Erdogan: From 'Nation-as-One' to 'Nation as Us." A thesis submitted to the graduate school of social science of Middle East Technical University, https://etd.lib.metu.edu.tr/ upload/12619484/index.pdf.

Our World in Data. 2021. "Turkey: Coronavirus Pandemic Country Profile," https:// ourworldindata.org/coronavirus/country/turkey.

Ozbudun, Ergun. 2011. *The Constitutional System of Turkey: 1876 to the Present*. New York: Palgrave Macmillan.

Oztig, Lacin Idil. 2022. "Policy styles and pandemic management: The case of Turkey." *European Policy Analysis* 8 (3): 261–76.

Poushter, Jacob. 2015. "Deep Divisions in Turkey as Elections Nears." *Pew Research*. October 15. https://www.pewresearch.org/global/2015/10/15/deep-divisions-in-turkey-as-election-nears/.

Sanjurjo, Diego. 2020. *Gun Control Policies in Latin America*. Cham: Palgrave.

Sentoregil, Merve and Semra Akinci. 2021. "The Use of Social Media in Crisis Communication: An Analysis on Fahrettin Koca's Use of Twitter In The First Six Months Of Coronavirus." *Usak University Journal of Social Sciences* 14 (1): 223–38.

The Directorate of Communications of the Presidency of the Republic of Turkey. 2019. "About DoC" https://www.iletisim.gov.tr/english/kurum-hakkinda.

The Directorate of Communications of the Presidency of the Republic of Turkey. 2023. "Turkiye Stops Covid," https://www.turkiyestopscovid.com/what-we-are-doing.

The Ministry of Health. 2020. "The Coronavirus is not stronger than the precautions we will take" (in Turkish) March 11, https://www.saglik.gov.tr/TR,64383/koronavirus -alacagimiz-tedbirlerden-guclu-degildir.html.

The Turkish Dental Association. 2020. "Our Colleague Prof.Dr. Fizen Cizmeci was appointed as a member of the Coronavirus Scientific Board" (in Turkish) March 25. https://web.archive.org/web/20200329110914/http://www.tdb.org.tr/icerik_goster .php?Id=3429.

The Turkish Medical Association. 2021. "The Covid-19 Pandemic First Year Evaluation Report" March 29. https://www.ttb.org.tr/yayin_goster.php?Guid=d5039d20-9082 -11eb-bd87-a1e3902714ed.

The Turkish Ministry of Health. 2019. "Pandemic Influenza National Preparedness Plan" (in Turkish). https://grip.gov.tr/depo/saglik-calisanlari/ulusal_pandemi_plani .pdf.

The Turkish Ministry of Health. 2020. "Social Sciences Board convened under the chairmanship of Health Minister Koca" (in Turkish) June 8. https://www.saglik.gov .tr/TR,65907/toplum-bilimleri-kurulu-saglik-bakani-koca-baskanliginda-toplandi .html.

The Turkish Ministry of Interior. 2021a. "A Circular on Gradual Normalization Measures" (in Turkish) May 16. https://www.icisleri.gov.tr/kademeli-normallesme -tedbirleri-genelgesi.

The Turkish Ministry of Interior. 2021b. "A Circular on Normalization Measures in June" (in Turkish) June 1, https://www.icisleri.gov.tr/haziran-ayi-normallesme -tedbirleri-genelgesi.

The Turkish Ministry of Interior. 2021c. "A Circular on Gradual Normalization Measures was sent to 81 Governorship" (in Turkish) June 27. https://www.icisleri .gov.tr/81-il-valiligine-kademeli-normallesme-tedbirleri-genelgesi-gonderildi.

The Presidency of Turkish Republic. 2020. "We mobilized all our means to eliminate the virus threat our country is exposed to as soon as possible" March 18. https://www .tccb.gov.tr/haberler/410/117037/-ulkemizin-maruz-kaldigi-virus-tehdidinin-en -kisa-surede-bertaraf-edilmesi-icin-devlet-olarak-tum-imk-nlarimizi-seferber-ettik-.

TJOD. 2020. "About Final Declaration of Istanbul Meeting" (in Turkish), March 17. https://www.tjod.org/17-mart-istanbul-toplantisi-sonuc-bildirgesi-hakkinda/.

TRT Haber. 2020. "The Covid-19 meeting ended" (in Turkish), March 18. https://www .trthaber.com/haber/gundem/koronavirusle-mucadele-esgudum-toplantisi-sona-erdi -468163.html.

TRT Haber. 2021a. "Scientific boards played effective roles in the fight against Covid-19" (in Turkish) January 31. https://www.trthaber.com/haber/gundem/bilim -kurullari-covid-19la-mucadelede-etkin-rol-oynadi-552292.html.

Trustworthiness Index. 2019. "Global Trust in Professions: Who Do Global Citizens Trust?" https://www.ipsos.com/sites/default/files/ct/news/documents/2019-09/global -trust-in-professions-ipsos-trustworthiness-index.pdf.

Üstüner, Yilmaz and Nilay Yavuz. 2017. "Turkey's Public Administration Today: An Overview and Appraisal." *International Journal of Public Administration* 41 (10): 820–31. doi: https://doi.org/10.1080/01900692.2017.1387147.

Usul, Ahmet S. 2022. "Health Minister Koca stated that TURKOVAC has started to be administered in 81 provinces" (in Turkish), *Anadolu Agency*, February 8. https://

www.aa.com.tr/tr/koronavirus/saglik-bakani-koca-turkovacin-81-ilde-uygulanmaya
-baslandigini-bildirdi/2496616.

Usul, Sertan, Yesim S. Karaaslan, and Sefa Sahin. 2022. "The Minister of Health: Our-door mask wearing is no longer necessary." *Anadolu Agency*, March 2. https://www.aa.com.tr/tr/koronavirus/saglik-bakani-koca-artik-acik-havada-maske
-kullanmak-zorunda-degiliz/2521327.

Waldner, David. 2012. "Process Tracing and Causal Mechanisms." In *Handbook of the Philosophy of Social Science*, eds. Harold Kincaid, 65–84. Oxford: Oxford University Press.

Wu, Yipin. 2020. "Dynamics of policy change in authoritarian countries: a multiple-case study on China." *Journal of Public Policy* 40: 236–58.

Yilmaz, Ihsan. 2021. "Erdogan's Political Journey: From Victimised Muslim Democrat to Authoritarian, Islamist Populist." *ECPS Leader Profiles. European Center for Populism Studies (ECPS)*. February 14, 2021. https://doi.org/10.55271/lp0007.

Yılmaz, Zafer. 2020. "Erdoğan's presidential regime and strategic legalism: Turkish democracy in the twilight zone." *Southeast European and Black Sea Studies* 20 (2): 265–87. doi: https://doi.org/10.1080/14683857.2020.1745418.

Yontem. 2020. "Life in the Time of Corona: A Social Research." April, https://yontemresearch.com/Uploads/Life_in_the_Time_of_Corona.pdf.

Zahariadis, Nikolaos. 2003. *Ambiguity and Choice in Public Policy: Political Manipulation in Democratic Societies*. Washington, DC: Georgetown University Press.

Zahariadis, Nikolaos. 2007. "The Multiple Streams Framework: Structure, Limitations, Prospects." In *Theories of the Policy Process*, eds. Paul A. Sabatier, 65–93. Boulder, CO: Westview Press.

Zahariadis, Nikolaos. 2015. "The Shield of Heracles: Multiple Streams and the Emotional Endowment Effect." *European Journal of Political Research* 54 (3): 466–481. doi: https://doi.org/10.1111/1475–6765.12072.

Zahariadis, Nikolaos, Evangelia Petridou, and Lacin Idil Oztig. 2020. "Claiming credit and avoiding blame: political accountability in Greek and Turkish responses to the Covid-19 crisis." *European Policy Analysis* 6 (2): 159–169. doi:https://doi.org/10.1002/epa2.1089.

Zohlnhöfer, Reimut, Nicole Herweg, and Nikolaos Zahariadis. 2022. "How to Conduct a Multiple Streams Study." In *Methods of the Policy Process*." eds. Christoper M. Weible and Samuel Workman, 23–50. New York/Abingdon: Routledge.

11. The Multiple Streams Framework in an autocracy: China's long-awaited Soil Pollution Law

Annemieke van den Dool

INTRODUCTION

While the Multiple Streams Framework (MSF) has greatly advanced our understanding of the policy process in democracies (Cairney and Jones 2016), this is much less the case for autocracies (Herweg et al. 2018; Herweg et al. 2022; Zohlnhöfer et al. 2015).[1] Since Kingdon's work in the 1980s, hundreds of journal articles have applied the MSF to democracies (Jones et al. 2016). However, a systematic search using Google Scholar, JSTOR, Scopus, Web of Science, and WorldCat results in only 88 unique English-language peer-reviewed journal articles that use the MSF in the context of autocracies, covering 20 different countries.[2]

The dearth of MSF studies in autocracies is part of a broader gap in our understanding of the policy process in autocracies. From an applied perspective, this is problematic because, as of 2020, the majority of the world population (68 percent) lives in autocracies (Alizada et al. 2021). Policy decisions taken in such contexts affect the daily lives of billions of people, which in and of itself warrants a better understanding of the policy process in autocracies. Moreover, a better understanding of the policy process across political systems helps us identify ways to monitor, anticipate, explain, and engage in policy-making in autocracies. This is especially important because problems in one country, if left unaddressed, can easily affect other parts of the world (Boin 2019). From a theoretical perspective, the lack of MSF studies on autocracies hampers theory development, especially regarding the framework's external validity and the identification of potentially universal mechanisms that underly the policy process across different political systems. Comparative research contributes to theory and methodological development as it forces scholars to refine hypotheses and to be more explicit in their operationalization.

In response, this chapter applies the MSF to China, the world's largest non-democracy, through a case study of the Soil Pollution Prevention and Control Law. Even though soil pollution had threatened food security (NEPA 1990) and public health for decades and even though 15 other environmental laws were passed during 1979–2009, it was not until 2013 that the Soil Pollution Law was included in the formal legislative agenda of the National People's Congress (NPC) – China's legislature. The law was eventually adopted in 2018. This chapter aims to identify the obstacles to and driving forces behind the inclusion of the Soil Pollution Law in the legislative agenda. The research question is: Why did it take until 2013 for China's Soil Pollution Law Prevention and Control Law to be included in the NPC's legislative plan?

Using qualitative content analysis and a dataset consisting of approximately 200 documents (mostly Chinese-language, including government reports, policy documents, legislative records, and news articles), the chapter argues that lack of soil pollution data and disagreement about the need for a soil pollution law slowed down agenda setting. Initially there was a lack of soil pollution data. Once such data had been collected by the government, it was considered a state secret and data were not released until 2013. Disagreement between the Ministry of Agriculture and the Ministry of Environmental Protection about the need for a soil pollution law was overcome after top-level political leaders started to pay serious attention to soil pollution, which happened after the completion of the soil pollution survey. By testing a set of China-specific MSF hypotheses, the chapter illustrates how the framework can be used to gain a better understanding of the policy process in autocracies.

THEORETICAL FRAMEWORK

The Multiple Streams Framework in China

A growing body of literature applies the MSF to China. Since Kingdon's (1984) seminal book, a total of 28 English-language peer-reviewed journal articles on the MSF in China have been published up until 2021.[3] This is a small number compared to the English-language MSF literature on North America and Europe. In their literature review, Jones et al. (2016) found that 78 percent of all English-language journal articles on the MSF examine democracies in North America and Europe.

Similar to the broader MSF literature (Cairney and Jones 2016), existing English-language MSF studies on China mainly explain single cases of policy-making (van den Dool 2022). Most articles start by describing a specific policy problem, e.g., HIV/AIDS or education reform, rather than taking the MSF as starting point. Very few English-language MSF journal articles (Van den Dool 2022; Zhu 2008) explicitly aim to contribute to MSF theory development.

To move from merely explaining specific cases of policy change towards systematically deepening our understanding of China's policy process using the MSF, we need to review and possibly refine existing hypotheses to fit China's political context (Zohlnhöfer et al. 2022). China is a closed autocracy (Alizada et al. 2021), meaning that it lacks competitive, free, multi-party elections (Lührmann et al. 2018). The Communist Party controls the appointment of key positions in legislative and executive bodies and thus plays a dominant role in all aspects of policymaking (Saich 2015). Moreover, in authoritarian regimes there is limited space for political mobilization (Linz 2000). Information flows in China are controlled by high-level bureaucratic and political units through, inter alia, a licensing system for media outlets, mandatory real-name registration for internet users, blocked websites and platforms (e.g., Google and Twitter), bans on specific content, and (paid) online propaganda commentators (Roberts 2018). Censorship is especially common for issues deemed politically sensitive (Wade 2016). Based on these features, Van den Dool (2022) proposed a set of China-specific MSF hypotheses that build on Herweg et al. (2018) and overlap with expectations for the MSF in autocracies developed by Herweg et al. (2022). To allow for cross-case comparisons and to develop a consistent research program, the same China-focused MSF hypotheses will be used in this chapter. The hypotheses are listed in Table 11.1.

Compared to the generic hypotheses listed in Herweg et al. (2018), the first China-specific refinement is that whether a condition is considered a problem by policymakers is not just the product of an indicator changing to the negative, a harmful focusing event, or feedback, but is also shaped by the political sensitivity of the condition and subsequent censorship. If individuals try to frame a condition as problematic, but the issue or the frame happens to be or becomes politically sensitive, it will get censored. When this happens, neither policymakers nor other policy actors (including citizens) can publicly acknowledge, monitor, and attempt to address the condition. An example from China is the suppression of news about the adulteration of infant milk powder for several months in 2008, while the number of infants with kidney failure increased over time (Van den Dool 2019).

The second refinement of existing general MSF hypotheses is the need for a policy proposal to be non-regime threatening in addition to being technically feasible, financially viable, and consistent with existing norms and values of policymakers and citizens. Due to China's one-party system, certain policy proposals are off-limits and are likely to be censored quickly. An example is Charter 08, which proposed substantial constitutional change (Shirk 2011).

Third, given the one-party system, policymakers are restricted by the general ideology of the Communist Party. Consequently, I theorize that support by the Communist Party or by the State Council – China's highest administrative authority – contributes to a mature political stream. Likewise, a threat to the survival of the Communist Party (rather than risk of not being re-elected in democracies) opens a problem window, whereas a political window opens in response to a perceived change in the national mood or leadership change in the Politburo (i.e., the Communist Party elite) or State Council (i.e., the executive elite).

METHODOLOGY

To deepen our understanding of the drivers of policy change in China, this chapter applies China-specific MSF hypotheses pertaining to agenda setting to a case study of the Soil Pollution Law, which was selected for several reasons. First, at the outset, this case showed potential to falsify existing MSF hypotheses as the problem, policy, and political streams appeared mature, yet there was no agenda change. China has experienced soil pollution for several decades (NEPA 1990). Fifteen other new environmental laws were passed between 1979 and 2009 , e.g., the Forest Law in 1979, the Marine Environment Protection Law in 1982, the Water Pollution Law in 1984, the Air Pollution Law in 1987, the Solid Waste Law in 1995, the Noise Pollution Law in 1996, and the Desertification Law in 2001. This showed that there was at least some degree of high-level political attention and support for environmental protection throughout the 1980s, 1990s, and 2000s, yet the soil pollution law was not included in the official decision agenda until 2013 and was not passed until 2018. Consequently, China's Soil Pollution Law can be considered an influential case (Gerring and Cojocaru 2016) in the sense that it has potential to falsify the MSF agenda setting hypothesis. The case also has empirical relevance as soil pollution is a tremendously important problem, threatening health and food security of more than a billion people. Applying the MSF to the Soil Pollution Law helps us understand the politics behind environmental policy-making in China, which may also be relevant for other urgent environmental issues such as climate change.

Data collection on policy processes in autocracies comes with several challenges, which shape the scope of this chapter. First, government transparency is limited: data that is available in democracies is not necessarily available in autocracies. An example is legislative proposals by members of Parliament. In China, only the topic (and sometimes excerpts) of such proposals is available, not the full content. Second, data may have been censored, manipulated, or deleted. For example, on social media, citizens may have discussed a scandal involving soil pollution, but if the content is considered a political threat, it may get deleted by the authors or by the internet platform. Third, while interviews are not impossible, such fieldwork has become increasingly difficult in recent years (Greitens and Truex 2020), especially during the Covid-pandemic which was ongoing at the time of writing this chapter. Fourth, data is often scattered among different and ever-changing websites and databases, making data collection a time consuming and laborious process. For these reasons, I limit the scope of this chapter to the three streams, the policy window, and agenda setting. I thus exclude the coupling process and the role of the policy entrepreneur, both of which require much more extensive data collection, which goes beyond the resources available for the current study.

Table 11.1 operationalizes the selected hypotheses and lists relevant data. Almost all the data is in Chinese. To analyze the problem stream, I use the following variables and data. First, to identify relevant indicators, I use annual State of the Environment Reports published between 1989–2018, collected from the website of the Ministry of Ecology and Environment. Second, to analyze policy feedback, I rely on legislator complaints (Kingdon 1984) in the form of legislative proposals (*yi'an*), which are expressions of dissatisfaction with existing policies. I collected legislative proposals (n = 10,644) put forward by delegates of the National People's Congress (NPC) as documented in annual legislative reports (*daibiao tichu de yi'an de chuli yijian baogao*) and the response to such proposals as documented in the annual reports (n = 25) by the NPC Environment and Resource Protection Committee (*huanjing yu ziyuan baohu weiyuanhui*). This is one of the NPC special committees that reviews proposals for inclusion in the NPC legislative plan. Both datasets cover the period 1994 (which is the first year for which this data is digitally available) until 2018 (which is the year in which the Soil Pollution Law was adopted) and were collected through CNKI, which is a widely used database for academic and non-academic periodicals in China. Third, data on focusing events and censorship is sourced from China Digital Times, which is a California-based website that publishes content that "has been or is in danger of being censored in China" (China Digital Times n.d.). I use this source because of the sensitivity of environmental issues in China and soil pollution in particular. Even if sensitive news gets published, it is not uncommon for previously published news on sensitive topics to be no longer available. Therefore, instead of using Chinese newspapers' archives, I use China Digital Times to identify focusing events and evidence of censorship.

To analyze the policy stream, I rely on two datasets. To identify proposals, I use the abovementioned dataset of legislative proposals. To assess whether proposals were perceived as financially viable, technically feasible, and consistent with existing norms and values of policymakers, I rely on the annual NPC-ERPC reports and official legislative records pertaining to the Soil Pollution Law, including the official justification of the bill (NPC-ERPC 2017a), reports on the drafting progress (NPC-ERPC 2017b, 2018), and two drafts (NPC 2017a, 2017b).

To analyze the political stream and to identify political windows, I rely on Government Work Reports (*zhengfu gongzuo baogao*) and State Council

Legislative Plans from 2000–18, both of which are available on the State Council website. To assess Party support, I analyze reports presented at the five-year Party Congress in 2002, 2007, 2012, and 2017. I complement this with the abovementioned annual reports by the NPC Environment and Resource Protection Committee to unpack the legislative process and identify obstacles that prevent the Soil Pollution Law from inclusion in the formal legislative agenda.

To identify problem windows, which are theorized to open if a condition puts the survival of the Communist Party at risk, I analyze the official problem description by legislators, government, and the Party. I do so using the aforementioned NPC delegate proposals, the annual NPC-ERPC reports, China State of the Environment Reports, Government Work Reports, and Party Congress reports.

While it is difficult to verify the accuracy of the information in the documents listed in Table 11.1, given the nature of MSF hypotheses and the case study as well as the data collection strategy, there is limited risk that this will affect the chapter's conclusions. As pointed out by Zohlnhöfer et al. (2022), in analyzing the problem stream, the focus is on how the problem is *perceived* by policymakers. Therefore, the fact that we cannot verify the exact scale and nature of soil pollution in China does not matter for this chapter. Second, the case study does show disagreement regarding the making of the Soil Pollution Law, which signals that it was possible to criticize or object to this proposal, at least to some extent. Third, for data that is likely to be censored, I use China Digital Times to identify focusing events and evidence of censorship.

FINDINGS

Problem Stream: Policymakers Acknowledge Severe Soil Pollution

The annual State of the Environment reports show that policymakers in China considered soil pollution to be a problem at least as early as 1989, when the National Environmental Protection Agency (NEPA) published the first State of the Environment Report. Throughout the 1990s, the reports stated that 6–10 million hectares of farmland suffered from industrial and urban waste pollution, which accounted for 6–10 percent of China's total farmland. This is considerable given that some of the reports also mentioned that China's population far exceeds its available arable land. Soil pollution was described as "increasing in severity day by day. It has become a restriction for the sustainable development of China's rural economy and society" (SEPA 2007, 83). However, in the 2000s, these reports no longer specified the hectares of polluted land.

Table 11.1   Operationalization of MSF hypotheses[4]

Hypotheses	Variables (and data)
Problem stream A condition reaches the policymaking agenda if an indicator changes to the negative, a harmful focusing event occurs, or if a government program does not work as expected, unless the condition is politically sensitive and censored.	Indicator(s): China State of the Environment Reports 1989–2018 (*Zhongguo huanjing zhangkuang gongbao*). Policy feedback: NPC delegate proposals (*yi'an*) and NPC-ERPC reports (1994–2018). Focusing events: China Digital Times (2004–18). Censorship: China Digital Times (2004–18).
Policy stream A proposal reaches the policymaking agenda if the proposal is non-regime threatening, financially viable, technically feasible, and consistent with existing norms and values of policymakers.	Proposals: NPC delegate proposals (*yi'an*) and NPC-ERPC reports (1994–2018). Tone surrounding policy proposals: NPC-ERPC reports (1994–2018) and legislative records (i.e., official justification of the law, drafting reports, and drafts).
Political stream A policy proposal reaches the policymaking agenda if it fits the general ideology of top leaders in the Communist Party or the State Council.	Identification of support from the State Council and the Communist Party: Government Work Reports (2000–18), State Council Legislative Plans (2000–18), Party Congress reports (2002, 2007, 2012, 2017).
Problem window A policy window opens in the problem stream if a condition puts the survival of the Communist Party at risk.	Tone of problem description and proposals: NPC delegate proposals (*yi'an*) and NPC-ERPC reports (1994–2018); China State of the Environment Reports 1989–2018; Government Work Reports; Party Congress Reports.
Political window A policy window opens in the political stream as a result of a perceived change in the national mood or leadership change in the Politburo or State Council.	State of the Environment Reports, annual speeches by high-level political leaders.
Agenda-setting An issue reaches the agenda if (a) a problem or political window opens; (b) the streams are ready for coupling; and (c) a policy entrepreneur promotes policy change.	See above-mentioned datasets for problem and political windows as well as the three streams. Note: policy entrepreneur and coupling are not included in the analysis due to limited data availability.

Source: Herweg et al.,2018; Van den Dool, 2022.

In addition to NEPA and the State Environmental Protection Administration (NEPA's successor), delegates to the National People's Congress (NPC) – China's legislature – repeatedly raised the problem of soil pollution. Evidence of this is provided in annual reports of proposals put forward by NPC delegates and by the annual reports of the NPC Environment and Resource Protection Committee. In the context of the MSF, these proposals serve as government feedback in the sense that legislators supposedly bring forward societal concerns (Kingdon 1984). NPC delegates first raised soil pollution in 2006, when several delegates stated that "China's soil pollution situation is already quite severe" (NPC-ERPC 2007a, 89). In 2007, delegate Jinglong Yu stated that "soil pollution in China is intensifying, seriously threatening ecological safety, food safety, and human safety" (NPC-ERPC 2007b). Likewise, in 2008, delegate Xihua Huang stated that "along with population increase and rapid economic development, China's soil pollution problem is rather prominent and already threatens human health and life safety. It seriously impacts rural industrial production and land resources usage. It restricts the sustainable development of the economy, society, and the environment" (NPC-ERPC 2009, 121). From 2011 until 2018, every year, NPC delegates stretched the severity of soil pollution in China and the number of delegates involved in expressing these concerns grew over time (see Figure 11.1).

In response to these proposals, the NPC Environment and Resource Protection Committee repeatedly acknowledged the severity of soil pollution. In 2006, the committee stated that "China's soil, especially rural areas, is exposed to multiple pollution threats and is not yet subject to law" (NPC-ERPC 2007a, 90). In 2008, the committee wrote that soil pollution prevention and control was a "weak link in China's environmental protection work" (NPC-ERPC 2009, 121). In 2011, the committee stated that "the overall situation of China's soil pollution is severe and should be paid attention to" (NPC-ERPC 2012, 112). In 2014, the committee argued that "the soil pollution problem is a key difficulty of deep societal concern and a concern of the people" (NPC-ERPC 2015, 112). Likewise, in 2015, the committee stated that "China's current soil environment situation is not hopeful. Pollution incidents are frequently occurring, which constitutes a threat to the people's health and the nation's ecological safety" (NPC-ERPC 2016, 169).

There have been multiple incidents involving soil pollution that fit the definition of focusing events as sudden, rare, harmful events that are concentrated to a specific area and known to national-level policymakers and the public virtually simultaneously (Birkland 1997). During the 2000s, the State of the Environment Reports included statistics on the number of "soil pollution incidents". The number fluctuated between 0 and 16 per year. However, the reports do not provide details regarding the scale, location, or nature of these incidents. Nevertheless, the China Digital Times dataset includes several focusing events. In May 2013, government authorities in southern China's Guangdong province found excessive amounts of cadmium in rice from Hunan province, which sparked widespread concern over food safety (China Digital Times 2013a). In August the same year, news media reported that over the course of just a few years, 26 people had died from cadmium poisoning in a village in Hunan province (China Digital Times 2013b). In 2016, state media reported that hundreds of children at a school in Changzhou, Jiangsu province, fell ill due to soil pollution (China Digital Times 2016).

The 2013 soil pollution focusing events may have contributed to increased attention from NPC delegates to soil pollution. The number of proposals for a soil pollution law increased from two (supported by 69 delegates) in 2013 to seven (supported by 215 delegates) in 2014. However, the 2013–18 legislative agenda was approved in September 2013. Hence, the increase in proposals in 2014 cannot explain legislative agenda setting. Moreover, the NPC Environment and Resource Protection Committee reports and legislative records pertaining to the Soil Pollution Law do not refer to any specific soil pollution incident.

Importantly, although soil pollution was widely considered a problem, for a long time there was no consistent indicator that captured its scale, nature, and severity. Therefore, in 2005, the State Environmental Protection Administration launched a national soil pollution survey. In the years during which the survey was ongoing, rather than sharing survey results, the State Environmental Protection Agency included the number of soil samples taken in its annual State of the Environment Reports. While the survey was finished in 2010 (Ministry of Environmental Protection 2010), the results were not published.

The soil survey results were initially considered a state secret. A lawyer named Zhengwei Dong requested the survey results under China's Government Information Openness Regulations in January 2013 (Dong 2013a), but the Ministry of Environment denied the request, stating that the data were state secrets. Dong subsequently filed an Administrative Reconsideration Request. However, in May 2013, the Ministry responded that the data were "temporarily managed as state secret" because it needed more time to verify the data, without providing a timeline for data release (Dong 2013b).

When some of the soil pollution data were finally released, the indicators were worse than previously reported. In December 2013, the State Council (i.e., China's highest executive government organization) held a press conference on the survey, during which it was revealed that 3.33 million hectares were affected by medium or severe soil pollution (State Council Information Office 2013). However, when the official soil pollution report was finally released in April 2014, the problem turned out to be even larger. The report stated that 16.1 percent of all soil samples and 19.4 percent of *farmland* samples exceeded pollution standards. The report described this situation as "not optimistic, with rather serious pollution in some areas. The soil environment and quality of farmland are bleak" (Ministry of Environmental Protection 2014, 1). Yet, the five-page report only provided a general overview of the survey and did not detail the severity and type of pollution per location.

Additional research is needed to explain why the Ministry of Environmental Protection changed its attitude towards the data as being a "state secret" to "temporary state secret" to partial release. Several plausible explanations are worth exploring further. First, there was societal pressure to release the data. The aforementioned lawyer announced in news media that he considered filing an administrative lawsuit to force the government to release the data. Second, under China's existing legal framework, there was no legal basis for classifying the survey results as a (temporary) state secret. Third, if the reluctance of the Ministry of Environmental Protection to release the data was due to survey verification issues, these may have been addressed over time, increasing the willingness of the Ministry of Environmental Protection to release the data.

In sum, the severity of soil pollution in China has been known and acknowledged by ministerial-level government officials at least since 1989. However, compared to other environmental problems such as water pollution and air pollution, as evidenced by the annual State of the Environment Reports, the issue of soil pollution received relatively little government attention. This and the fact that soil pollution is not as easy to notice as other forms of pollution may have slowed down the agenda setting process. Members of the legislature had raised the issue of soil pollution since 2006. However, there was no consistent indicator for soil pollution and soil pollution was considered a politically sensitive problem. It was not until 2013–14 that some basic data about the scale and nature of the problem was released.

Policy Stream: Proposals for a Soil Pollution and Prevention Law

To address the problem of soil pollution, since the mid-2000s, proposals have been made to draft a new law on the issue. The making of a soil pollution and prevention law has been proposed by NPC delegates at least as early as 2007. As shown in Figure 11.1, delegates submitted proposals for such a law in 2007, 2008, and yearly from 2011 until 2018. The number of proposals (displayed as column) and the number of delegates (displayed as line) supporting these proposals increased over time.[5] No proposals for a soil pollution law were put forward in 2009 and 2010.

Based on the MSF, the likelihood of a policy proposal to reach the agenda is shaped by the proposal's financially viability, technically feasibility, and consistency with existing norms and values. In the context of China, an additional requirement is that a proposal needs to be non-regime threatening. The fact that proposals for a soil pollution law were included in publicly available records of the NPC shows that it is not considered regime threatening. Perceived financial viability, technical feasibility, and consistency with existing norms and values can be assessed by reviewing records of the legislative process. Based on the legislative history of the law, several general themes are apparent.

A theme that emerged prior to and throughout the formal legislative process was who should be responsible for soil pollution and soil restoration. Before the draft was reviewed by the NPC, in academic publications, scholars had proposed to held polluters responsible for pollution, which would require a clear scope of responsibilities, standards, and penalties (e.g., Hu 2008). During the

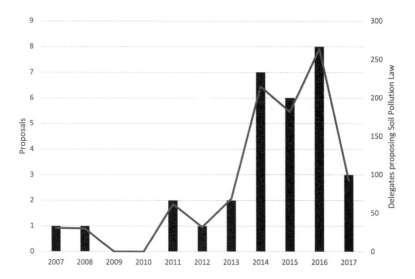

Figure 11.1   Proposals (columns) by NPC delegates (line) to draft a soil pollution law (2007–2017)

legislative process, the NPC Environment and Resource Protection Committee (2017a) stated that the law should "clarify the responsibility of each party" and "solve and assign expenses for prevention and cure". Nevertheless, experts and delegates advocated for further clarification of responsibility, especially in case of pollution of agricultural land (NPC-ERPC 2017b; NPC-ERPC 2018). Moreover, there were requests for increasing the monetary penalties for soil pollution. A related point of contention was funding for soil remediation. Given that soil pollution threatens food security and food safety, it is important to restore polluted farmland, but doing so is costly. Early drafts of the law contained an article on funding. However, during the NPC reviews, some NPC delegates and the Ministry of Finance requested changes to the funding mechanism.

Other themes that were discussed before and during the legislative process include standard setting and coordination between different government actors. Standard setting is important if polluters are to be held responsible and if public health is to be protected, yet local variation in soil conditions and soil pollution made standard setting difficult. Because soil pollution is a complex issue that involves government agencies working on environment, agriculture, land management, and other areas, delegates called for clarifying implementation and enforcement tasks.

Thus, despite some substantive challenges, NPC delegates and the NPC Environment and Resource Protection Committee repeatedly advocated for the drafting of a soil pollution law. None of the challenges encountered seemed unsolvable or decreased the enthusiasm for the creation of a soil pollution law. Moreover, scholars actively searched for solutions to these challenges, especially through comparative research of other legal systems elsewhere in the world, especially Japan, the US, and European countries. Some of these solutions later emerged in the draft law, e.g., the polluter pays principle and government funding for soil remediation.

Political Stream: Support by Top-level Leaders After Completion of Soil Pollution Survey

As theorized above, agenda setting is more likely if a policy proposal fits the general ideology of top leaders in the Communist Party or the State Council. In China, most laws are drafted by the State Council and national-level ministries and commissions (Van den Dool 2019). The State Council is chaired by the premier and consists of the heads of national-level departments (which includes ministries and commissions), most of whom are Communist Party members. To assess the degree to which the proposed soil pollution law was consistent with the general ideology of the State Council and the Communist Party, I analyzed Government Work Reports (2000–18), State Council Legislative Plans (2000–18), and official reports presented at the National Congress of the Chinese Communist Party (2002–17).

Based on Government Work Reports and State Council Legislative Plans, the State Council started to pay serious attention to soil pollution from 2012. Government Work Reports (*zhengfu gongzuo baogao*), which summarize government activities of the past year and identify tasks for the coming year, mentioned environmental pollution throughout the period 2000–20, but it was not until 2012 that *soil* pollution was briefly mentioned. Soil pollution was subsequently mentioned in the Government Work Report every year from 2012–18. Likewise, the State Council Legislative Plan does not include the Soil Pollution Law until 2012.

One plausible explanation why it took until 2012 for increased State Council attention to the issue of soil pollution is disagreement among the departments under the State Council about the necessity of a soil pollution law. Initially, the NPC Environment and Resource Protection Committee supported proposals for a soil pollution law. In fact, as early as 2004, the Committee proposed that "relevant departments strengthen research on soil pollution prevention and control legislation" (NPC-ERPC 2005, 80). In 2007, the Committee stated that the State Environmental Protection Administration had established a drafting group and that legislative work was ongoing (NPC-ERPC 2007b). Moreover, it proposed to include the soil pollution law in the official legislative plan. This is significant because the majority of bills in the NPC legislative plan is passed at some point (Van den Dool 2019). In 2008, the Committee reported that the State Environmental Protection Agency was conducting research on drafting a soil pollution law and it proposed that the relevant State Council department put forward relevant legislative suggestions (NPC-ERPC 2009). In 2009–10, no proposals for drafting a soil pollution law were reported and the issue was not mentioned in the NPC Environment and Resource Protection Committee reports.

However, in 2011 and 2012, the Committee reported that the Ministry of Environmental Protection and the Ministry of Agriculture disagreed about the need for a soil pollution law (NPC-ERPC 2012, 2013). The former supported the drafting of a dedicated law on soil pollution, but the Ministry of Agriculture argued that "although strengthening soil pollution is very necessary and important for ensuring the quality and safety of agricultural products and the sustainable development of agriculture", it disagreed about how to address the issue (NPC-ERPC 2012, 111–12). It argued that "the key to prevent and control soil pollution is to make great efforts to manage the different sources of pollution" and therefore the ministry proposed to "seriously enforce super-vision and improve relevant rules" and to "not formulate a soil pollution law" (NPC-ERPC 2012, 111–112).

The aforementioned 2012 shift in State Council attention to soil pollution is most likely the result of the soil pollution survey results. In October 2012, the State Council convened a meeting on the soil pollution survey results, during which it was stated that "China's soil environment situation must give rise to high level attention" (State Council General Office 2012). From late 2012, top-level political attention to the development of a soil pollution law increased. An official drafting group consisting of environmental and legal experts was established in November 2012 (Cheng 2013). In January 2013, the State Council General Office (2013) released a soil protection work plan, which opened by referring to the soil pollution survey and which included as one of the main tasks to "research and draft specialized legislation on soil environmental protection".

The Soil Pollution Law was subsequently included in the NPC legislative plan (2013–18). In 2014, the NPC Environment and Resource Protection Committee – which was in charge of overseeing the drafting process – reported that legislative work was making progress and that the Committee would "earnestly listen to opinions from different sides, actively take in views and suggestions from NPC delegates, and finish the drafting work as soon as pos-sible" (NPC-ERPC 2015, 109). The Committee also requested that selected provincial governments develop local-level legislation, which would serve as input for the national-level soil pollution law (NPC-ERPC 2015, 109).

While the data show a State Council attention shift in 2012, there is no evidence of a similar shift of attention within the Communist Party. Soil pollution was very briefly mentioned in President's Hu Jintao's report to the National Congress of the Chinese Communist Party in 2007. However, in his 2012 report presented at the National Congress of the Chinese Communist Party, soil pollution was briefly mentioned again, with almost identical phrasing, suggesting that there is no evidence of increased attention by the Party Congress in 2012.

Regarding the political window, there is no evidence that a leadership change triggered increased attention for the soil pollution law in 2012. The Ministry of Environmental Protection – and its predecessor the State Environmental Protection Administration – was headed by Shengxian Zhou from 2005 until 2015. Under Zhou, especially during 2006–08, the ministry increased its attention to soil pollution, which is evidenced not only by more text dedicated to soil pollution in the annual State of the Environment Reports, but also by the launch of the first soil pollution survey and the establishment of the aforementioned legislative drafting group. While the Ministry of Agriculture did change leadership in 2006 and 2009, there is no evidence that leadership change triggered increased attention to soil pollution. In 2006, Zhengcai Sun became Minister of Agriculture. There is no evidence that Sun paid attention to soil pollution during this appointment. His successor Changfu Han initially barely mentioned "soil" or "pollution" in his annual reports, but this changed in 2012, when he mentioned "pollution" five times, including heavy metal soil pollution.

Eventually, the draft law was submitted to the NPC Standing Committee (NPC-SC) for review. In China, consistent with the Legislation Law, most laws are deliberated three times before voting. The NPC-SC usually meets every other month. Figure 11.2 shows how the draft moved through the NPC. It was reviewed in June 2017, December 2017, and August 2018 and adopted in August 2018.

Figure 11.2   *Review of the Soil Pollution Law by the NPC Standing Committee (NPC-SC)*

CONCLUSION AND DISCUSSION

This chapter applied a set of China-specific MSF hypotheses to a case study of China's Soil Pollution Law to illustrate how the framework can be used in an autocracy while providing insight into China's policy process. In particular, the chapter aimed to explain why it took until 2013 for the Soil Pollution Law to be included in the official legislative plan. The chapter identifies obstacles to and driving forces of legislative agenda setting by China's National People's Congress. I use the Multiple Streams Framework because it provides a systematic approach and considers a wide range of explanatory factors, including indicator deterioration, focusing events, feedback on government policy, availability of feasible solutions, party ideology, national mood, and leadership change.

Through document analysis, the chapter showed that although the problem of soil pollution had been acknowledged by policymakers since the 1990s and by legislators since the mid-2000s, it was not until 2013 that the Soil Pollution Law was included in the official legislative agenda. The case study identifies obstacles to agenda setting. First, initially there was a lack of soil pollution data. Once such data had been collected by the government, it was considered a state secret. Data were not released until 2013. Second, there was disagreement between policymakers at the Ministry of Agriculture and the Ministry of Environmental Protection about the need for a soil pollution law. This impasse was overcome after top-level political leaders started to pay serious attention to soil pollution, which happened after the completion of the soil pollution survey. Table 11.2 summarizes the findings.

At first sight, these results do not seem very different from what we expect to see in democracies. First, the case study illustrates the importance of data, or indicators, in the context of the MSF. As shown by DeLeo and Duarte (2021), while worsening indicators can lead to agenda setting, increased politicization decreases attention from policymakers. The case of China's Soil Pollution Law is similar in the sense that soil pollution data was perceived by policymakers to threaten their interests. As a result, such data was not released, which facilitated high-level political leaders to ignore the issue and contributed to the lack of sustained high-level political attention. Second, the case study shows internal disagreement among policy makers that likely slowed down the Soil Pollution Law from being included in the NPC legislative agenda. Like in democracies, such impasses are not uncommon in China (Truex 2018). One of the reasons for such gridlocks in China is departmentalism (*benwei zhuyi*), i.e., a tendency to and even an expectation that government departments focus on their own mission and agenda (Shirk 1993; Tanner 1994).

However, a major difference with democracies is that, generally speaking, in democracies, there are multiple ways for news media, industry, citizens, NGOs, and other non-official policy actors to either collect data themselves or request access to government data. As shown in the case study, soil pollution was considered a politically sensitive issue and the soil pollution survey results were treated as state secrets. Although the soil pollution survey started

Table 11.2   Case study results: Hypotheses and evidence

Hypotheses	Evidence
Problem stream A condition reaches the policymaking agenda if an indicator changes to the negative, a harmful focusing event occurs, or if a government program does not work as expected, unless the condition is politically sensitive and censored.	• Soil pollution law included in legislative agenda in 2013. • Indicator: In the 1990s, 6–10% of farmland reported as polluted; 2014 survey results show 19.4% of farmland samples exceed standards. • Focusing events: In the 2000s, 0–16 incidents/year; 2013 cadmium rice; 2016 Changzhou soil pollution incident. • Policy feedback: Concerns expressed by legislators in 2006–2008 and 2011–18. • Censorship: Soil pollution survey from 2005–10, results not released until 2013–14; results treated as state secret.
Political stream A policy proposal reaches the policymaking agenda if it fits the general ideology of top leaders in the Communist Party or the State Council.	• Policy proposal included in the legislative agenda in 2013 after expression of high-level support. • Ideological fit: High-level attention to soil pollution from March 2012 when issue is mentioned in Government Work Report.
Policy stream A proposal reaches the policymaking agenda if the proposal is non-regime threatening, financially viable, technically feasible, and consistent with existing norms and values of policymakers.	• Proposal did not reach legislative agenda until 2013, despite meeting the policy stream criteria. • Non-regime threatening: Since mid-2000s, soil pollution law discussed in publicly available legislative reports. • Financial viability and technical feasibility: Substantive issues, but not discussed as insurmountable. • Value consistency: Law proposed by policymakers and legislature, but resistance by Ministry of Agriculture.
Political window A policy window opens in the political stream as a result of a perceived change in the national mood or leadership change in the Politburo or State Council.	• No political windows have been observed. • Leadership change: Leadership change in 2013, but shift in attention happened in 2012.
Problem window A policy window opens in the problem stream if a condition puts the survival of the Communist Party at risk.	• No problem windows have been observed. • Soil pollution described as severe, but no evidence of threat to Party survival.
Agenda-setting An issue reaches the agenda if (a) a problem or political window opens; (b) the streams are ready for coupling; and (c) a policy entrepreneur promotes policy change.	• Soil Pollution Law reached the decision agenda in 2013. • No open window. • Streams all mature: severe problem, soil pollution law proposal, high-level political support. • No evidence of policy entrepreneur.

around 2006, partial results were not released until late 2013. If more effective mechanisms had existed that allowed the public to either collect data or exert pressure to get access to government data, it is plausible that the Soil Pollution Law would have reached the official NPC legislative plan several years earlier.

This case study is among the first to systematically test China-specific MSF hypotheses developed in Van den Dool (2022). Although the case study's findings contribute to a better understanding of China's policy process, the chapter does have limitations. Most importantly, due to lack of data, I have not examined policy entrepreneurship and coupling. Future studies could explore this through network analysis using policy documents, news articles, social media data, and/or journal articles. Moreover, given that this is a single case, additional studies are needed to establish the generalizability of the findings, especially regarding the role of data (i.e., indicators) and censorship in policymaking.

NOTES

1. I have presented this chapter at several conferences. I am grateful for comments that I received on these occasions. This research project has benefited from research assistance provided by W. Zhang, which has been funded by the Undergraduate Studies Office Summer Research Scholars Program and the Center for the Study of Contemporary China at Duke Kunshan University.
2. Search conducted in May 2022.
3. Search conducted in May 2022, using Google Scholar, JSTOR, Scopus, Web of Science, and WorldCat. Search terms: "multiple streams framework", "multiple streams analysis", and "multiple streams approach".
4. Except from some data collected from China Digital Times, all documents are in Chinese. Quotes used from these documents in the findings section have been translated to English by the author.
5. The total number of NPC delegates varies slightly over time, but is just below 3,000 individuals.
6. Except from some data collected from China Digital Times, all documents are in Chinese. Quotes used from these documents in the findings section have been translated to English by the author.

REFERENCES

Alizada, N., R, Cole, L. Gastaldi, S. Grahn, S. Hellmeier, P. Kolvani, J Lachapelle, A. Lührmann, S. F. Maerz, S. Pillai, and S. I. Lindberg. 2021. *Autocratization Turns Viral. Democracy Report 2021*. University of Gothenburg: V-Dem Institute.

Birkland, T. A. 1997. *After disaster: Agenda setting, public policy, and focusing events*. Georgetown University Press.

Boin, A. 2019. The Transboundary Crisis: Why we are unprepared and the road ahead. *Journal of Contingencies and Crisis Management 27* (1): 94–99.

Cairney, P., & M. D. Jones. 2016. Kingdon's multiple streams approach: what is the empirical impact of this universal theory? *Policy Studies Journal 44* (1): 37–58.

Cheng, X. 2013, May 24. Zhuanfang Wang Shuyi: Turang wuran fangzhi fa yuji 3 nian nei chutai [Exclusive interview with Wang Shuyi: Soil pollution prevention and control law is predicted to be launched within 3 years]. *Nanfang Ribao.*

China Digital Times. (n.d.). *About China Digital Times.* https://chinadigitaltimes.net/about/.

China Digital Times. 2013a, May 30. Meizhou zhuanzai: Guanyu du dami he turang wuran [Weekly forwarding: About poisonous rice and soil pollution]. https://chinadigitaltimes.net/chinese/296073.html.

China Digital Times. 2013b, August 1. Cadmium Poisoning from Hunan Factory Kills 26. https://chinadigitaltimes.net/2013/08/cadmium-poisoning-from-hunan-factory-kills-26/.

China Digital Times. 2016, April 18. Hundreds Ill at "Toxic School" Near Chemical Plants. https://chinadigitaltimes.net/2016/04/hundreds-fall-ill-toxic-school-near-chemical-plants/.

DeLeo, Rob. A., & Alex Duarte. 2022. "Does data drive policymaking? A multiple streams perspective on the relationship between indicators and agenda setting." *Policy Studies Journal* 50 (3): 701–24.

Dong, Zhengwei. 2013a, February 2. Shenqing huanbaobu xinxi gongkai quanguo turang wuran zhuangkuang diaocha shuju he fangzhu fangfa [Application at the Ministry of Environmental Protection to publish the national soil pollution situation survey data and methods for prevention and cure]. Dong Zhengwei lüshi - xinlang boke. https://blog.sina.com.cn/s/blog_57a1cb0701019k1s.html.

Dong, Zhengwei. 2013b, May 9. Huanbaobu queren quanguo turang wuran zhuangkuang diaocha shuju yingdang xiang shehui gongkai [Ministry of Environmental Protection confirms that the national soil pollution situation survey data should be made public]. Dong Zhengwei lüshi - xinlang boke. https://blog.sina.com.cn/s/blog_57a1cb070101bj1s.html.

Gerring, J., & L. Cojocaru2016. "Selecting cases for intensive analysis: A diversity of goals and methods." *Sociological Methods & Research* 45 (3): 392–423.

Greitens, S. C., & R. Truex. 2020. "Repressive experiences among China scholars: New evidence from survey data." *The China Quarterly* 242: 349–75.

Herweg, Nicole, Nikolaos Zahariadis, and Reimut Zohlnhöfer. 2018. "The Multiple Streams Framework: Foundations, Refinements, and Empirical Applications." In *Theories of the Policy Process*, 4th edition, eds. Christopher M. Weible and Paul A. Sabatier, 17–53. Boulder, CO: Westview Press.

Herweg, Nicole, N. Zahariadis, & R. Zohlnhöfer. 2022. "Travelling far and wide? Applying the multiple streams framework to policy-making in autocracies." *Politische Vierteljahresschrift* 63 (2): 203–23.

Hu, L. 2008. "Fada guojia turang wuran fangzhi falü zhidu de jingyan jiqi jiejin [Experience and lessons from developing countries' legal systems for soil pollution prevention and control]." *Fazhi yu shehui* 3: 259–60.

Huang, Y. 2006. "The politics of HIV/AIDS in China." *Asian Perspective* 95–125.

Jones, Michael D., Holly L. Peterson, Jonathan J. Pierce, Nicole Herweg, Amiel Bernal, Holly Lamberta Raney, and Nikolaos Zahariadis. 2016. "A River Runs Through It: A Multiple Streams Meta-Review." *Policy Studies Journal* 44 (1): 13–36.

Kingdon, John W. 1984. Agendas, *Alternatives, and Public Policies.* Boston: Little, Brown.

Linz, J. J. 2000. *Totalitarian and authoritarian regimes.* Boulder, CO: Lynne Rienner Publishers.

Ministry of Environmental Protection. 2010. Zhongguo huanjing zhuangkuang gongbao [China State of the Environment Report for 2010].

Ministry of Environmental Protection. 2014. Quan guo turang wuran zhuangkuang diaocha gongbao [Report on the national soil pollution situation survey].

Lührmann, A., M. Tannenberg, & S. I. Lindberg. 2018. "Regimes of the world (RoW): Opening new avenues for the comparative study of political regimes." *Politics and Governance* 6 (1): 60.

National Environmental Protection Agency (NEPA). 1990. *1989 nian huanjing zhuangkuang gongbao* [State of the Environment Bulletin 1989].

NPC Environment and Resource Protection Committee (NPC-ERPC). 2005. Quanguo renda huanjing yu ziyuan baohu weiyuanhui guanyu di shi jie quanguo renmin daibiao dahui di er ci huiyi zhuxituan jiaofu shenyi de daibiao tichu de yi'an shenyi jieguo de baogao [Report by the NPC Environment and Resource Protection Committee about the deliberation results regarding the proposals put forward by delegates and handed over by the Presidium of the 2nd Meeting of the 10th NPC]. *Quanguo renmin daibiao dahui changwu weiyuanhui gongbao* 1, 77–86.

NPC Environment and Resource Protection Committee (NPC-ERPC). 2007a. Quanguo renda huanjing yu ziyuan baohu weiyuanhui guanyu di shi jie quanguo renmin daibiao dahui di si ci huiyi zhuxituan jiaofu shenyi de daibiao tichu de yi'an shenyi jieguo de baogao [Report by the NPC Environment and Resource Protection Committee about the deliberation results regarding the proposals put forward by delegates and handed over by the Presidium of the 4th Meeting of the 10th NPC]. *Quanguo renmin daibiao dahui changwu weiyuanhui gongbao* 1, 83–95.

NPC Environment and Resource Protection Committee (NPC-ERPC). 2007b. Quanguo renda huanjing yu ziyuan baohu weiyuanhui guanyu di shi jie quanguo renmin daibiao dahui di wu ci huiyi zhuxituan jiaofu shenyi de daibiao tichu de yi'an shenyi jieguo de baogao [Report by the NPC Environment and Resource Protection Committee about the deliberation results regarding the proposals put forward by delegates and handed over by the Presidium of the 5th Meeting of the 10th NPC]. http://www.npc.gov.cn/zgrdw/pc/xwzx_2/dblz/2007–12/03/content_13.

NPC Environment and Resource Protection Committee (NPC-ERPC). 2009. Quanguo renda huanjing yu ziyuan baohu weiyuanhui guanyu di shiyi jie quanguo renmin daibiao dahui di yi ci huiyi zhuxituan jiaofu shenyi de daibiao tichu de yi'an shenyi jieguo de baogao [Report by the NPC Environment and Resource Protection Committee about the deliberation results regarding the proposals put forward by delegates and handed over by the Presidium of the 1st Meeting of the 11th NPC]. *Quanguo renmin daibiao dahui changwu weiyuanhui gongbao* 1, 117–25.

NPC Environment and Resource Protection Committee (NPC-ERPC). 2012. Quanguo renda huanjing yu ziyuan baohu weiyuanhui guanyu di shiyi jie quanguo renmin daibiao dahui di si ci huiyi zhuxituan jiaofu shenyi de daibiao tichu de yi'an shenyi jieguo de baogao [Report by the NPC Environment and Resource Protection Committee about the deliberation results regarding the proposals put forward by delegates and handed over by the Presidium of the 4th Meeting of the 11th NPC]. *Quanguo renmin daibiao dahui changwu weiyuanhui gongbao* 1, 106–21.

NPC Environment and Resource Protection Committee (NPC-ERPC). 2013. Quanguo renda huanjing yu ziyuan baohu weiyuanhui guanyu di shiyi jie quanguo renmin daibiao dahui di wu ci huiyi zhuxituan jiaofu shenyi de daibiao tichu de yi'an shenyi jieguo de baogao [Report by the NPC Environment and Resource Protection Committee about the deliberation results regarding the proposals put forward by delegates and handed over by the Presidium of the 5th Meeting of the 11th NPC]. *Quanguo renmin daibiao dahui changwu weiyuanhui gongbao* 1, 155–76.

NPC Environment and Resource Protection Committee (NPC-ERPC). 2015. Quanguo renda huanjing yu ziyuan baohu weiyuanhui guanyu di shi'er jie quanguo renmin daibiao dahui di san ci huiyi zhuxituan jiaofu shenyi de daibiao tichu de yi'an shenyi jieguo de baogao [Report by the NPC Environment and Resource Protection Committee about the deliberation results regarding the proposals put forward by delegates and handed over by the Presidium of the 2nd Meeting of the 12th NPC]. *Quanguo renmin daibiao dahui changwu weiyuanhui gongbao* 1, 108–21.

NPC Environment and Resource Protection Committee (NPC-ERPC). 2016. Quanguo renda huanjing yu ziyuan baohu weiyuanhui guanyu di shi'er jie quanguo renmin daibiao dahui di er ci huiyi zhuxituan jiaofu shenyi de daibiao tichu de yi'an shenyi jieguo de baogao [Report by the NPC Environment and Resource Protection Committee about the deliberation results regarding the proposals put forward by delegates and handed over by the Presidium of the 3rd Meeting of the 12th NPC]. *Quanguo renmin daibiao dahui changwu weiyuanhui gongbao* 1, 165–82.

NPC Environment and Resource Protection Committee. 2017a. Guanyu "Zhonghua renmin gongheguo turang wuran fangzhifa (cao'an)" de shuoming [Explanation about the PRC's soil pollution and prevention law (draft)]. http://www.npc.gov.cn/zgrdw/npc/xinwen/2018-08/31/content_2060169.htm.

NPC Environment and Resource Protection Committee. (2017b). Quanguo renmin daibiao dahui falü weiyuanhui guanyu "Zhonghua renmin gongheguo turang wuran fangzhi fa (cao'an)" xiugai qingquang de huibao [Report by the NPC Legal Committee on the revision situation of the PRC's soil pollution and prevention law (draft)]. http://www.npc.gov.cn/zgrdw/npc/xinwen/2018-08/31/content_2060165.htm.

NPC Environment and Resource Protection Committee. (2018). Quanguo renmin daibiao dahui falü weiyuanhui guanyu "Zhonghua renmin gongheguo turang wuran fangzhi fa (cao'an)" xiugai qingquang de huibao [Report by the Constitution and Legal Committee on the results of the review of the PRC's soil pollution and prevention law (draft)]. http://www.npc.gov.cn/zgrdw/npc/xinwen/2018-08/31/content_2060165.htm.

Roberts, Margaret E. 2018. *Censored: Distraction and Diversion Inside China's Great Firewall*. Princeton: Princeton University Press.

Saich, Tony. 2015. *Governance and Politics of China*. London: Palgrave Macmillan.

Shirk, S. L. 1993. *The Political Logic of Economic Reform in China*. Berkeley: University of California Press.

Shirk, S. L. 2011. "Changing media, changing China." In *Changing Media, Changing China*, ed. S. L. Shirk 1–37. New York: Oxford University Press.

State Council General Office. (2012, October 31). Wen Jiabao zhuchi zhaokai Guowuyuan changwu huiyi yanjiu bushu turang huanjing baohu he zonghe zhili gongzuo [Wen Jiabao presides State Council Standing Committee meeting to research the deployment of soil environmental protection and comprehensive governance work]. http://www.gov.cn/ldhd/2012-10/31/content_2254955.htm.

State Council General Office. (2013, January 23). Guowuyuan bangongting guanyu yinfa jinqi turang huanjing baohu he zonghe zhili gongzuo anpai de tongzhi [State Council General Office notice about the publication of a soil environmental protection and comprehensive governance work plan for the nearby future]. http://www.gov.cn/zhengce/content/2013-01/28/content_4574.htm.

State Council Information Office. (2013, December 30). Xinwenban jieshao di er ci quanguo tudi diaocha zhuyao shuju chengguo [Press office gives a presentation about the main data results of the second national land survey]. http://www.gov.cn/wszb/zhibo597/wzsl.htm.

State Environmental Protection Administration (SEPA). (2007). 2006 Zhongguo huanjing zhuangkuang gongbao [China State of the Environment Report for 2006].

Tanner, M. S. 1994. "Organizations and Politics in China's Post-Mao Law-Making System." In *Domestic Law Reforms in Post-Mao China*, ed. P. B. Potter, 56–96. Armonk, N.Y.: M.E. Sharpe.

Truex, R. 2018. "Authoritarian Gridlock? Understanding Delay in the Chinese Legislative System." *Comparative Political Studies* 0(0): 1–38.

van den Dool, A. 2019. "Never Again: Legal Change after Public Health Crises in China." PhD diss. University of Amsterdam. UvA-DARE. https://hdl.handle.net/11245.1/eb205 b8a-c022–4f89–9961-c07117766c34.

van den Dool, A. 2022. "The multiple streams framework in a Nondemocracy: The Infeasibility of a national ban on live poultry sales in China." *Policy Studies Journal*.

Wade, S. 2016. "Minitrue: 21 rules on coverage of the two sessions." https://chinadigitaltimes.net/2016/03/minitrue-important-notices-coverage-two-sessions/.

Zhu, Xufeng. 2008. "Strategy of Chinese Policy Entrepreneurs in the Third Sector: Challenges of 'Technical Infeasibility'." *Policy Sciences* 41(4): 315–34.

Zohlnhöfer, R., N. Herweg, & F. Rüb. 2015. "Theoretically refining the multiple streams framework: An introduction." *European Journal of Political Research* 54 (3): 412–18.

Zohlnhöfer, R., N. Herweg, and N. Zahariadis. 2022. "How to conduct a multiple streams study." In *Methods of the Policy Process*, eds. Christopher M. Weible and Samuel Workman. Routledge: New York.

PART III

Subnational and international levels

12. Subnational focusing events and agenda change: The case of toxic algae bloom and contaminated drinking water in Toledo, Ohio

Kristin Taylor, Rob A. DeLeo, Stephanie Zarb, Nathan Jeschke, and Thomas A. Birkland

OVERVIEW

Under what conditions do potential focusing events produce agenda change in subnational contexts?[1] Potential focusing events (Birkland 1997) can help promote stream coupling by drawing policymaker attention to previously ignored issues (Kingdon 2011). Focusing events are thus an important element of the problem stream (Kingdon 2011; O'Donovan 2017; Saurugger and Terpan 2016), yet few studies have systematically applied the Multiple Streams Framework (MSF) to the study of focusing events in subnational contexts (Eckersley and Lakoma 2021; Henstra 2010). This omission is significant in the context of a federal system like the US where subnational governments are provided considerable authority to respond to disaster.

We address this gap by applying the MSF to the case of a toxic algae bloom in Toledo, Ohio in 2014. We assess primary data collected from interviews with key informants in Toledo as well as secondary data collected from Toledo's municipal government website (e.g., city council meeting minutes and other government documents), the Ohio State legislature's website (e.g., legislative agenda packets), and publicly available local news sources. Our chapter raises important questions about the assumption of stream independence. Specifically, we show that although the algae bloom did in fact trigger agenda setting and, to some extent policy change, certain policy ideas were effectively vetoed by actors operating within the political stream, specifically the agricultural lobby. Our findings suggest the focal power of disasters is significant but at times incapable of creating substantive policy change.

Additionally, we provide important insights into the analytical challenges associated with studying focusing events within nested systems, like the US, where authority and jurisdiction is shared by actors operating at various levels of government.

THE MULTIPLE STREAMS FRAMEWORK AND POTENTIAL FOCUSING EVENTS

In the MSF, Kingdon (2011) suggests focusing events can help give problems "a little push to get the attention of people in and around government" (p. 94). This is especially true in highly technocratic policy domains, like transportation or emergency management, which lack a highly attentive public meaning there are few organized interests that readily mobilize to support policy change (Birkland 1997). Focusing events have the capacity to "simply bowl over everything standing in the way of their prominence on the agenda" (Kingdon 2011, 96), a testament to their emotive power and the fact that these types of crises often aggregate death and destruction. Kingdon also notes that focusing events include symbols of problems that suddenly catch on, and the personal experience of policy actors.

Birkland (1997) developed a definition of focusing events that was more amenable to empirical testing. He argued that *potential* focusing events are sudden, rare, revealing harm or the potential for harm, are known to the public and policymakers virtually simultaneously and are concentrated in a community of interests (Birkland 1997). His definition concentrates attention on the events that bowl over the agenda, but it does not encompass personal experience of decision makers or sudden symbol uptake, because these processes are idiosyncratic. Birkland's approach, by contrast, allows us to define variables that are associated with the degree to which an event is more or less "focal". Birkland further refined the concept to argue that focusing events reveal evidence of policy failure which can lead to policy learning (Birkland 2006). They have the potential to mobilize interest group activity (Pralle 2006; Birkland 1997), break up policy monopolies (Baumgartner and Jones 2010), and initiate policy learning (O'Donovan 2017a; Crow et al. 2018; 2009; 2006).

A growing research agenda has developed around testing the idea of potential focusing events, including the accuracy of the definition, the conditional nature of focusing events, and the level of analysis in application. The rarity of focusing events appears to be as important as an accumulation of several focusing events in a relatively concentrated period of time (O'Donovan 2017b). Governmental experience with the policy problem revealed by a focusing event helps to advance learning and policy change (O'Donovan 2017a). However, experience with a problem from a single focusing event does not reduce ambiguity about the policy issue, but experience with multiple events does (Taylor, Zarb, and Jeschke 2021). Furthermore, the role of time in focusing events and agenda setting is important. Long-duration, slow-onset crises have similar focal power (DeLeo et al. 2021), despite not adhering to the classic definition of focusing events that emphasizes the suddenness of the crisis and the extent to which the event is known simultaneously to policymakers and the public alike.

Focusing event theory has been applied extensively to national issues (Birkland 1997, 2004, 2009, Birkland and DeYoung 2011). The applicability of focusing events at the subnational level on agenda change requires greater scholarly attention. It is unsurprising that highly localized subnational events, like school shootings, have the ability to focus national attention (Birkland and Lawrence 2009; Lawrence and Birkland 2004). However, the literature on subnational focusing events has focused on other aspects of the policy process, including policy learning (O'Donovan 2017a; Crow et al. 2018) and policy change (O'Donovan 2017b). This literature suggests not only that focusing events can initiate subnational attention and policy change, but that their effect may be proximal, meaning attention upticks are most pronounced with the specific communities stricken by the event (Yeo and Knox 2019; Huber-Stearns, Schultz, and Cheng, n.d.). This dynamic is reinforced by the American system of hazards management, which delegates considerable responsibility to local governments to act as first responders. In short, the smaller the disaster, the less likely the national government is to get involved. In short, the existing literature on subnational focusing events has not directly addressed the matter of subnational agenda change in the MSF.

METHODOLOGY

Following the call for systematic research design for MSF (Zohlnhöfer, Herweg, and Zahariadis 2022), we identify *agenda change* as the dependent variable. Our unit of analysis is a democracy. The level of analysis is subnational governments, specifically the City of Toledo and the State of Ohio. Although we are using MSF outside of its original application it requires minimal, if any adaptation, because the institutions of the US subnational government are similar to those of the national government.

This study is motivated by the following research question:

Under what conditions do potential focusing events initiate subnational agenda change?

We draw from hypotheses devised by Zohlnhöfer, Herweg, and Zahariadis (2022) to underpin our theory of focusing event-initiated agenda change in subnational governments. We are particularly concerned with the content and policy activity in the problem stream that opens a window of opportunity for agenda change, rather than the content of the politics or policy stream. Thus, we first hypothesize:

H1: A policy window opens in the problem stream due to a focusing event.

Whereas previous studies, as noted above, have primarily studied focusing events within the context of national institutions, our focus on subnational institutions necessitates a secondary hypothesis regarding the effect of nested on policy change. We specifically hypothesize:

H1a: Focusing events are more likely to induce policy change within local governments as opposed to state or national government.

To test this hypothesis, we use a case study method to examine the effect of a potential focusing event on subnational agenda and policy change. We examine disruptions in drinking water infrastructure systems to assess the applicability of focusing events to subnational crises. A case study approach allows for in-depth analysis of an issue across multiple jurisdictions (Yin 2018).

To identify an open policy window, we rely on evidence of agenda setting activity. Because policy windows open and close, and can often go unnoticed (Kingdon 2011; Herweg et al. 2018; Zohlnhöfer et al. 2022), we look for prima facie evidence of an open policy window. Reliance on prima facie evidence is useful for identifying other sorts of ex-post policy activity, such as policy learning, and is identified by looking at government documents, news accounts, and other public records (May 1992; Birkland 2006; O'Donovan 2018; Taylor et al. forthcoming). The dependent variable, *agenda change*, is defined as the extent to which issues relating to drinking water safety and the algae bloom rose or fell on subnational policy agendas. We identify agenda change as the dependent variable because although there may be agenda activity in an open policy window, we are concerned about the extent to which focusing events trigger agenda change. Specifically, we focus on the local policy agenda of the City of Toledo and the Ohio State Legislature. Additionally, we also qualitatively explore whether this uptick in agenda activity resulted in policy change, which we conceptualize as the creation of new law or policies aimed at addressing drinking water safety.

We gathered data from city council meeting agenda packets to examine whether the focusing event resulted in agenda activity. Agenda packets contain the meeting agenda, a record of first and second readings of Bills, issues and resolutions formally motioned for consideration or a vote, and a record of how council members voted. While not equivalent to the depth of the congressional record often used in national applications, at the subnational level agenda packets offer the opportunity to examine how often motions discussing drinking water infrastructure and algae bloom were discussed in city council meetings. State level agenda activity could not be measured in the manner

Table 12.1   Agenda activity summary statistics

Problem Definition	N	Sparsity*	Mean	SD	Min.	Max.
Water Infrastructure	49	83%	0.225	0.607	0	5
Algae Public Health	7	97%	0.037	0.211	0	2
Agricultural Runoff	3	99%	0.018	0.165	0	2
Fishing/Tourism	2	99%	0.018	0.165	0	1

Note: *Sparsity indicates the percentage of agenda packets with zero keyword mentions.

because the State's session journals only include Bill titles and many of the policies at the state level discussed in the case study were introduced as line items in the yearly budget.

The city agenda packets were analyzed for frequency of mentions of "drinking water", "algae", "nonpoint" and "fishing" to identify patterns of related policy activity during the study period of September 1, 2013 to December 31, 2021. These keywords generated inductively by identifying keywords that were associated with the problem definitions from the case study. Agenda packets with keyword hits were reviewed and a specific keyword was selected to represent different problem definitions that minimized false positive results. Table 12.1 contains the summary statistics of the presence of the different problem definitions in individual agenda packets.

To examine the algae bloom and subsequent contamination of the drinking water supply in Toledo as a potential focusing event, we present a qualitative discussion of the event using secondary data to assess how well it meets Birkland's definition of a potential focusing event (1997, 1998). We apply the MSF exploring the dynamics of agenda setting and policy change in studies of the City of Toledo and the State of Ohio. This design allows us to examine the nested dynamics of *policy change* after events. Cases were developed using primary data collected from open-ended interviews with key informants in Toledo between April 2018 and February 2020. We interviewed four key informants in the City of Toledo government. These key informants included public works directors, city managers, and public health officials. Key informants were identified through their professional roles and snowball sampling. The case study analysis is supplemented with secondary data collected from publicly available documents, including government documents, media reports, and press releases.

CASE STUDY

Focusing Event

The toxic algae bloom and subsequent drinking water created a crisis in Toledo, Ohio encompassing all of the characteristics of a potential focusing event. The crisis was *rare*. On August 1, 2014, a routine test performed by the City of Toledo indicated microcystin levels, an important indicator of toxic algae blooms, exceeded the drinking water advisory threshold. While algae blooms have plagued Ohio since the 1920s, few have had as significant an impact as the 2014 bloom: the crisis impacted nearly half a million people and resulted in US$65 million worth in economic losses (Steffen et al. 2017). Algae blooms are a common, seasonal occurrence from July to October that are caused by a phosphorus load that occurs in Lake Erie from March to July (National Centers for Coastal Ocean Science n.d.). In this context, algae blooms are not rare, however the algae contamination of the drinking water supply was exceptionally rare, revealing risks that were previously unknown or misunderstood.

Second, the onset of the crisis was *sudden*. The City of Toledo notified the Ohio Environmental Protection Agency (EPA) and performed a second round of testing at 11:00 pm. Shortly after the second round of testing, the Ohio EPA advised Toledo to issue a "Do Not Drink" advisory (Jetoo, Grover, and Krantzberg 2015). Within a matter of hours, the discovery of the algae bloom effectively incapacitated Toledo's drinking water system.

Third, the *public and policy makers learned of the crisis virtually simulta-neously*. The identification of the toxic bloom resulted from routine testing, suggesting policymakers had little to no advance knowledge of problems with the drinking water supply. The crisis was caused by strong winds that pushed a dense plug of the cyanobacterial harmful algae bloom (cHAB's) into the Toledo's water intake system, overwhelming the city's ability to treat the water (Ecowatch 2014).

Fourth, the *crisis revealed significant potential for harm* if people came in contact with the contaminated water. Residents were advised to not drink, boil, or use the water for drinking, cooking, making infant formula, making ice, or brushing their teeth. Parents were also advised to not let their children shower. Local stores quickly sold out of bottled water, and residents drove as far as Detroit and Ann Arbor to purchase bottled water. In response, Ohio Governor Kasich declared a state of emergency in three counties. The National Guard worked with local governments to provide water. Two days later, the advisory was lifted when microcystin levels returned to their normal levels (Ames et al. 2019).

Finally, the crisis had a *direct impact on a geographic community*, and as we will discuss later, organized communities of interest, namely the agricultural, tourism, and fishing industries. The drinking water crisis and the state of emergency declaration centered on three counties comprising the metropolitan Toledo area. In this respect, the crisis was fairly localized, although political fallout from the disaster would be felt across the state of Ohio.

Agenda Change

After examining local city council agendas, it is apparent that there were significant spikes in attention and agenda setting activity around both drinking water and algae bloom after the Toledo Water Crisis. The boxplot in Figure 12.1 shows the variance in the dependent variable. By looking at agenda attention by month and visualizing the distribution within those months it is apparent that drinking water infrastructure typically has little staying power on the agenda. Mentions are sporadic, rarely accumulating across multiple, consecutive council meetings. When drinking water is on the City Council's agenda, that attention does not carry over from one council meeting to the next. The largest change in attention occurs shortly after the 2014 algae bloom. However, the effects of the algae bloom were not contained to drinking water infrastructure, leading to competing problem definitions.

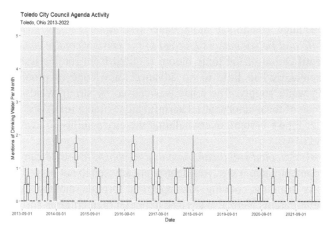

Note: Gray shading indicates the date of the 2014 Toledo algae bloom.
Source: Authors.

Figure 12.1   *Mentions of drinking water on local city council agendas per month*

Subnational Problems, Politics, and Policy Streams

The problem stream: ambiguity and competing definitions of the 2014 algae bloom

Historically, cHAB were caused by large amounts of phosphorus being discharged into Lake Erie. In 1972, the Clean Water Act (CWA)) forced sewage plants and other "point" sources to stop discharging phosphorus into Lake Erie along with a ban on phosphate detergents brought a dramatic improvement to Lake Erie's water quality. However, the CWA does not address runoff from "nonpoint" sources, such as farms, lawns, and failing septic systems. In the case of Lake Erie, the major contributor to the algae growth was identified as chemical fertilizer and manure which washed off farm fields into the surface water, triggering the yearly outbreaks of cyanobacteria. In addition, an increase in heavy rains and temperatures, often attributed to climate change, has made the situation worse. The first extensive Lake Erie cHAB was recorded in 1995 (Steffen et al. 2017). Since then, major cHABs have become annual summertime events, with the largest recorded cHAB occurring in 2011 (Levy 2017; Steffen et al. 2017).

Although there was widespread consensus that the 2014 water crisis represented a significant event worthy of public and policymaker attention, there was considerable ambiguity regarding the cause and implications of the disaster. This ambiguity manifested competing definitions of the problem, which, as we will note later, shaped not only the magnitude of issue expansion within the politics stream and, perhaps more importantly, the types of solutions that emerged within the policy stream.

Algae bloom as a tourism and fishing industry issue

The economic impact of algae blooms on the local fishing and tourism industries is staggering. Local charter boat captains have reported annual losses to their businesses between US$12,000–$15,000 (Glaser 2015; Scarfone, Gill, and Ryan 2019). David Spangler, President of the Lake Erie Charter Boat Association, estimates that charter boat owners have lost 10 percent of their income because of algal blooms ("Five Years Later..." 2019).

In addition to the fishing and charter boat industries, local communities are seeing a significant impact on tourism from the contaminated water. More than 24,000 homeowners have seen the value of their homes decrease as the water becomes increasingly inaccessible for both fisherman and recreational users. Some local lakeside communities, which rely on summer swimmers to maintain their economy, have contemplated installing community pools as a swimming alternative since the beaches are routinely shut down due to the danger posed by swimming in algal blooms (Glaser 2015; Scarfone, Gill, and Ryan 2019).

Algae bloom as infrastructure issue

The Collins Park Water Treatment Plant began operation in 1942 with an 80-million-gallon per day capacity. The last major upgrade to the facility (prior to the water crisis) occurred in 1956 when the plant expanded its capacity to 120 million gallons per day. ("FAQs", n.d., "How Water is Treated", n.d.). The longstanding lack of investment led the Ohio EPA to pressure the Toledo City Council to invest in upgrading the water treatment plant. In 2013, then-Toledo Mayor Michael Bell highlighted many of these concerns and the City Council authorized US$300 million in upgrades. However, the Ohio EPA felt those upgrades would not be sufficient and continued to pressure the city to do more. Letters written to former Mayor Michael Collins in January and June of 2014 warned of the potential for catastrophic failure, and while algae contamination was cited as a potential issue, much of the concern was focused on ongoing infrastructure issues. Mayor Collins was the acting mayor at the time of the 2014 bloom. In a June 2014 letter, the Ohio EPA director warned Mayor Collins that he could not, "...underscore boldly enough the precarious condition of Toledo's drinking water system and the imminent vulnerability to failure" (Henry and Patch 2014) .

In our interviews with public officials in the City of Toledo, it was apparent that they had made significant efforts to bring the situation to the attention of the Mayor and City Council but had failed to garner support. As one respondent reported:

> We were trying prior to 2014 to create a source water protection plan but they couldn't get any teeth behind it. Now everyone is championing the Great Lakes. We have recognized this for years, but we couldn't get support. In our view it [the Toledo Water Crisis] was a bit of a blessing because no one pays attention until it's in your home.

Algae bloom as a public health issue

Exposure to cHAB often results in rashes and blisters, while consuming contaminated water can cause nausea, vomiting, diarrhea, kidney and liver failure. In extreme cases, people have been poisoned via inhalation while swimming in contaminated water. Exposure has also been linked to the death of livestock and family pets (Wynne and Stumpf 2015). Before the 2014 event, cHAB was seen as a nuisance harming the tourism and commercial fishing industry. After the incident, local, state, and federal officials recognized that cHAB posed a significant threat to public health (Steffen et al. 2017). Primarily, the concern centered around the health implications of residents consuming contaminated drinking water. Both the city of Toledo and local utility operators understood that it was likely that the conditions which created the drinking water crisis would occur again. While it was not feasible to change the location of the water intake, it was possible to invest in systems capable of treating cHAB contaminated water.

Algae bloom as an agricultural runoff issue
As noted above, a significant driver of cHAB contamination is agricultural runoff, making this a problem of pollution caused by agricultural activities. Specifically, the unfettered application of certain types of fertilizers and manure can contribute to phosphorous loading within Lake Erie thus making the watershed more susceptible to blooms. This aspect of the problem makes solutions more difficult to develop, as we discuss in this chapter.

Competing Definitions Across Time
Figure 12.2 illustrates how the competing problem definitions held attention on the agenda over the study period. Drinking water infrastructure had superficially spiked on the council's agenda in the months prior to the event as a result of proclamations recognizing National Drinking Water Week. Immediately after the event, drinking water infrastructure was more substantively featured on the agenda as the City Council approved initial funds to improve the city's drinking water treatment. The resulting project (the Collins Park water treatment plant) continues to feature on the council's agenda as the project and requested funding expands over time. Conversely the public health consequences of the algae bloom rise on the agenda immediately after the event but quickly drops off. Agriculture runoff as a nonpoint pollution source for algae blooms only reaches the agenda in the form of a proclamation directed to Congress to federally regulate the agricultural runoff into Lake Erie under the CWA in 2016. Finally fishing/tourism only reaches the agenda twice, peaking with a mention as a Lake Erie use in an economic impact of algae blooms in June 2018. Our analysis of politics and policy stream helps explain why the window created by the 2014 algae bloom only appears to open for drinking water infrastructure.

The Policy Stream

Table 12.2 summarizes policy alternatives in circulating the policy stream in the aftermath of the 2014 bloom. Despite being a fairly localized event that primarily affected Toledo, the 2014 crisis triggered policymaking across all levels of government. The following section briefly details each of these alternatives including their current status.

Upgrade of the collins park water treatment plant
The 2014 algae bloom highlighted existing deficiencies within Toledo's water treatment infrastructure, many of which predated the bloom. Two years after

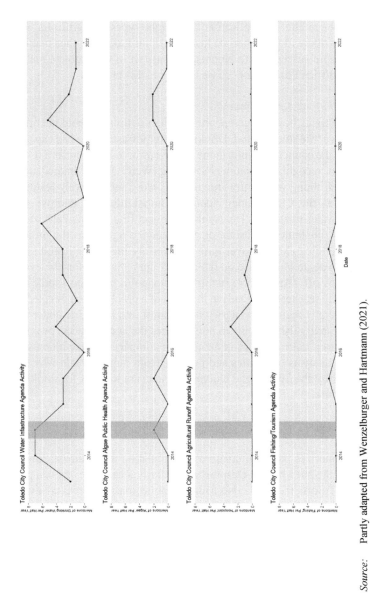

Source:　　Partly adapted from Wenzelburger and Hartmann (2021).

Figure 12.2　　Local city council agenda activity. Gray shading indicates the time period containing the 2014 Toledo algae bloom

Table 12.2   *Policy alternatives for addressing the water crisis*

Policy	Description	Level of Government	Status
Collins Park	Toledo city government authorized funding for major renovations and updates to Toledo's Collins Park Water Treatment Plant	Local	Enacted
LEBOR	The Lake Erie Bill of Rights (LEBOR) is a citizen petition that would amend the Toledo charter and grant rights to Lake Eerie	Local/State/Federal	Rejected
SB1	Enacted in 2015, Senate Bill 1 prohibits spreading of fertilizer Lake Eerie watershed when soil at elevated risk of runoff (e.g., snow covered, chance of rain, frozen) but includes feasibility loopholes.	State	Enacted
EO 2018–09K	Governor Kasich signed executive order (EO 2018–09K) in 2018 mandating regulation of agricultural runoff. Order was delayed by state panel.	State	Delayed
H2Ohio	Governor DeWine created pilot initiative in 2019 incentivizing farmers to manage nutrients responsible for algae blooms	State	Enacted
HB166	Section FY 2021–2022 budget (House Bill 177) barring people from filing lawsuits on behalf of ecosystems	State	Enacted
Impairment	US EPA regulation requiring that states regulate population or be added to impairment list. Lake Eerie was added to list in 2018.	Federal	Added

the disaster, in December 2016, the Toledo City Council indicated that the Division of Water Treatment had identified over US$500 million in needed upgrades ('Formal Agenda' 2016, 31). The upgrade of the Collins Park Water Treatment plant was funded through a series of municipal funds and bonds, the Ohio Water Development Authority, and a loan from the Ohio EPA. Construction began after the December 2016 city council vote to fund phase one of the planned upgrades (Formal Agenda, 2016, 31). Of the total project cost, approximately 20 percent was dedicated to ensuring the plant was capable of treating water contaminated by harmful algal blooms (The Plan 2022). Upgrades were based primarily on the recommendations of a panel of academics, technical experts, and regulatory experts who, among other things, called for the installation of an ozone treatment facility which would be capable of removing the toxins caused by algae blooms. The plan also increased the overall capacity of Collins Park and provided for basic repairs and other upgrades designed to improve safety, security, and general facility restoration. The plan also called for "inspection and rehabilitation" ('Formal Agenda' 2016, 40) of the raw water intake crib and lead detection, inspection, and rehabilitation of the raw water mains ('Formal Agenda' 2016).

Lake Erie Bill of Rights (LEBOR)

Frustrated by the lack of substantive policy change at the local and state levels, a team of environmental interest groups (Toledoans for Safe Water and the Community Environmental Legal Defense Fund) drafted the Lake Erie Bill of Rights (LEBOR). LEBOR, which was proposed as a ballot initiative, effectively gave Lake Erie "personhood," allowing citizens to file lawsuits on behalf of Lake Erie against polluters. LEBOR was designed to reduce agricultural runoff in large-scale animal agriculture and row crop operations and to address other industrial and residential polluters (Toledoans for Safe Water n.d.). The initiative was eventually blocked by the United States District Court.

Senate Bill 1

After the crisis, state legislators introduced legislation aimed at reducing agricultural runoff. Only one of those Bills, Senate Bill 1 (SB1), was enacted. SB1, signed into law on July 3, 2015, attempted to reduce runoff by prohibiting the spreading of fertilizer on frozen, snow-covered, or saturated land, and called for fines for violators. Despite being one of the few legislative attempts to explicitly address runoff arising from fertilizer applications, the final version of the Bill included a series of provisions that undermined its efficacy by providing farmers with various loopholes that allowed them to avoid complying with the new regulations.

Executive order

In July of 2018, Governor Kasich signed Executive Order 2018–09K, "Taking Steps to Protect Lake Erie." The order was designed to designate eight of Ohio's watersheds, including Lake Erie, as being "distressed", a designation that would provide the Ohio Department of Agriculture authority to set requirements for storing, handling, and applying manure. The order would have applied to nearly 7,000 Ohio farms – comprising over two million acres of farmland – and required them to follow nutrient management plans designed to reduce the amount of phosphorus and nitrogen in Lake Erie. The Ohio Soil and Water Conservation Commission delayed implementation of the order amid industry concerns about their ability to comply with the measure (Seewer 2018).

H2Ohio

In 2019, Ohio Governor Mike DeWine introduced H2Ohio, a pilot program aimed at addressing water quality within the state of Ohio. H2Ohio includes measures to reduce harmful algal bloom by providing financial incentives for farmers who voluntarily use nutrient management best practices to reduce runoff and funding for the creation of phosphorus-filtering wetlands. Participating farmers are provided with individualized nutrient management plans for phosphorus and nitrogen reduction. Data on the effectiveness of these plans is collected annually, thereby allowing modification across time. The program is funded through a combination of federal and state funds (H2Ohio Accomplishments for Fiscal Year 2020 | H2Ohio n.d.) .

State budget

Largely in response to the LEBOR, Governor Mike DeWine approved language inserted in the state's FY 2021–2022 budget that explicitly prohibits legal actions on behalf of nature or an ecosystem. The language effectively prevents the State of Ohio from funding a lawsuit for environmental management or conservation.

Impairment

Under the federal Clean Water Act, states are required to protect water from pollution by maintaining a list of all impaired waters within their jurisdiction. Once a body of water is declared impaired, the EPA will work with the state to develop an allowable total maximum daily load (TMDL) of pollutants, from all point and nonpoint sources, found in the body of water. If a body of water exceeds the TMDLs for one or more pollutants based on its intended uses (e.g., drinking water, recreation, aquatic life support), the state must work with the EPA to develop measures to control point and nonpoint source pollution (US EPA 2015). The Ohio EPA declared Lake Erie impaired in March of 2018.

Policymaking in a nested system

Five out of the seven policies proposed in the aftermath of the algae bloom were enacted, suggesting the crisis triggered considerable activity across all three levels of government. However, closer analysis suggests that the policies that survived the post-crisis period were, in many respects, the proverbial "lowest hanging fruit" in that none of them effectively addressed the root cause of the issue, namely agricultural runoff. Indeed, of the various policies introduced during this period only one, LEBOR, included provisions to include the adequate enforcement of the runoff mitigation policies, but this law was struck down by the courts. Moreover, as noted below, counter-mobilization by the agriculture community. And, although the upgrades to the Collins Treatment plant were much needed, demand for these changes predated the bloom.

The Politics Stream

Having outlined the competing definition claims and policy alternatives that emerged as a result of the 2014 crisis, the following section provides a detailed account of activity occurring within the politics stream. Figure 12.3 provides a timeline of major developments. In the years leading up to the Toledo water crisis, the City of Toledo was warned on several occasions that Collins Park Water Treatment plant was in disrepair and required upgrades. Several stakeholders expressed frustration over their inability to induce the local government to create a source water protection plan. One respondent specifically noted that Toledo Mayor Collins was aware of the ongoing issues at Collins Park Water Treatment Plant, but refused to address the issue, "during an election year". Local media reporting substantiated these claims. A story published on August 8, 2014 revealed that the Ohio EPA sent letters to city officials on June 4, 2014 – nearly two months before the algae bloom –warning that the plant was "vulnerable to potential failures that could severely impact the city's ability to provide adequate quantities of safe water to its citizens" (WTOL 2014).

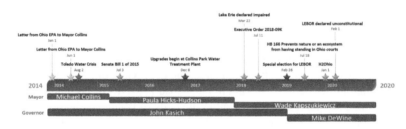

Source: Authors.

Figure 12.3   Timeline of the Toledo water crisis

In addition to the calls to upgrade Collins Park, a number of local interest groups, researchers, and local business owners mobilized to pressure local officials to address algae blooms, which they argued were negatively impacting the local tourism and fishing industries, in the years preceding the 2014 crisis. Interest groups, including water rights and charter fishing groups, were advocating for solutions to non-point phosphorus discharge in Lake Erie for economic and environmental benefits (Henry 2014a). Yet, despite strong pressure from the Ohio EPA and local groups, city officials balked at calls to address the algae issue in Lake Erie in part because of the considerable cost associated with upgrading the plant (Henry 2014b).

The 2014 water crisis disrupted the lack of policymaker attention by creating a widespread water disaster. The crisis redoubled existing efforts by local groups to address existing water safety issues and spawned a push for policy change across multiple levels of government. However, many of these efforts met stiff resistance from both the agricultural lobby and the oil and gas industry.

Of all the policies suggested during this period, the proposal to upgrade the Collins Park Water Treatment Plant was the least politically controversial. The city council worked from the time of the crisis through December 2016 to develop and fund extensive upgrades to the plant. The upgrades were coordinated with academics, technical experts, and regulatory experts who determined that an ozone system would allow Collins Park Water Treatment plant to remove microcystin, the dangerous toxin caused by cHAB. Construction began at Collins Park Water Treatment Plan on December 6, 2016. The ozone system was completed and began service on June 24, 2021 (City of Toledo 2021). Other improvements included increasing the capacity of the plant, improvements to the raw water intake crib and low service pumping station, chemical feed improvements, and a public relations plan to increase public trust in municipal water (Smith, Goetz, and Mazur 2016). The upgrades did not, however, do anything to address agricultural runoff, one of the chief causes of the bloom.

Just over a year after the algae bloom incident, Mayor Collins died unexpectedly in 2015. Then city council President, Paula Hicks-Hudson was appointed interim mayor and went on to win re-election in 2015 against another former Toledo Mayor, Carty Finkbeiner. Neither drinking water nor the 2014 crisis represented prominent issues in the 2015 special election, as both candidates focused on a large city budget shortfall, increasing economic development, and reducing gun violence (MESSINA 2015; Paula Hicks-Hudson will be sworn in as Toledo's next mayor Tuesday 2015).

Frustrated by the seemingly waning policymaker interest in addressing the issue of agricultural runoff, Toledoans for Safe Water and the Community Environmental Legal Defense Fund (CELDF) sought to enact LEBOR through citizen initiative. Proponents of LEBOR collected 10,000 signatures, of which more than 6,000 were validated thereby placing the LEBOR on the November 2016 ballot. However, the Lucas County Board of Elections blocked the measure from the ballot. In response, Toledoans for Safe Water filed a lawsuit in the Ohio Supreme Court. Business and agricultural interests lobbyists countered by filing a series of amicus briefs aimed at keeping the LEBOR off the ballot (Toledoans for Safe Water n.d.).

After a lengthy legal battle, the Lucas County Board of Elections held a special hearing ruling that the LEBOR would move forward to a special election. The special election occurred on February 26, 2019, with 61 percent of voters voting in favor of the measure. In response to the LEBOR, Ohio State University's agricultural law program disseminated information for farmers to defend themselves from lawsuits brought under the LEBOR. A local farmer, with support from Ohio's Agricultural District Program (Right to Farm Law) and the Ohio Farm Bureau, filed a lawsuit against the LEBOR in a federal court. In response to that lawsuit, an injunction was filed blocking LEBOR until the litigation was resolved (Toledoans for Safe Water n.d.).

In July 2019, Governor Mike DeWine signed the FY 2020–2021 operating budget for the State of Ohio. The operating budget included a section stating that "nature or any ecosystem does not have standing to participate in or bring an action in any court of common pleas" (Creates FY 2020–2021 operating budget 2019). This provision specifically prevented private lawsuits brought on behalf of nature or ecosystems. While this Bill was sufficient to nullify the LEBOR, in February 2020, a federal court also ruled that the LEBOR was unconstitutional ("Turning the Tides: Judge Finds Lake Erie Bill of Rights Unconstitutional - National Agricultural Law Center" n.d.).

In addition to LEBOR, proponents of substantive policy change sought to leverage federal statutes as a way to address the runoff issue. Specifically, there were several attempts to have Lake Erie declared impaired under the Clean Water Act. Governor Kasich balked at these attempts, citing concerns that the term "impaired" would discourage tourism and fishing in the lake. In response, the Environmental Law and Policy Center, a legal advocacy group, sued the US EPA in a federal court. In 2018, they prevailed, and Lake Erie was added to the impaired list. The rule was anchored in scientific studies that showed that Lake Erie met the criteria for impaired status as far back as 2010 (Geist n.d.; Henry 2018).

Although he was reluctant to embrace impairment, Governor Kasich did sign an executive order during his last term in office that aimed to initiate the process of reducing agricultural runoff. In signing the order, Governor Kasich acknowledged the lack of legislative progress, a testament to the influence of farmers and the agricultural lobby. However, the state panel responsible for approving the implementation of the order, the Ohio Soil and Water Conservation Commission, ultimately delayed implementation (Board again sidelines Kasich's order on Lake Erie algae 2018; O'Mara 2015; Shields 2014). Months later, Governor DeWine followed in his predecessor's footsteps by using the power of the executive to address the runoff when he launched H2Ohio. H2Ohio pays farmers to voluntarily implement measures that reduce runoff. As of this writing, the program has enrolled nearly 36 percent of farms in the affected area of Lake Erie and marks the first steps toward reducing agricultural runoff in Lake Erie (H2Ohio Accomplishments for Fiscal Year 2020 | H2Ohio n.d.).

Politics in a nested system

Untangling the political dynamics of policymaking in the wake of the algae bloom is incredibly complex, a testament to the nested of the nested structural arrangement associated with the environmental policy domain. While the crisis breathed new life into longstanding calls to control agriculture runoff, a strong – and politically connected – counter-mobilization effort by the state's agricultural interests effectively blocked any attempt to create substantive policy change. Interestingly, farmers, at times, capitalized on the opportunities for venue shifting provided by the nested arrangement. This was most clearly evidenced in the legal injunctions used to block LEBOR from advancing on the local ballot. In this we see evidence of complex multi-faceted efforts of agenda denial that spans venues and levels of government by established interests in the agricultural lobby that sought to maintain the status quo.

DISCUSSION AND FINDINGS

To what extent did the 2014 algae bloom and subsequent drinking water crisis shape agenda setting and policy change? Our study suggests the crisis opened a policy window but only for a select number of issues. Specifically, the disaster triggered a marked uptick in issue attention at both the state and local levels, as illustrated by the observed changes in agenda activity as well as the proliferation of policymaking that occurred in the years following the crisis. However, policymakers at both the local and state levels were reluctant to endorse solutions threatening the entrenched interests of the agriculture industry, especially those regulating runoff. At the local level, this manifested in the willingness to make considerable – and no doubt important – investments in upgrading the Collins Treatment Plant while refusing to endorse LEBOR. At the state level, this manifested in the final version of SB 1, which was effectively gutted of any provisions that would prevent farmers from violating the new runoff regulations, as well as HB 166, which, alongside the federal court ruling, dashed environmental groups' ability to take legal action on behalf of the watershed. Existing solutions that addressed problems that were already known in the policy community – like infrastructure improvements – easily made their way through the window of opportunity and onto the agenda. To expand upon the metaphor-rich parlance of MSF, the 2014 algae bloom opened a window wide enough to accommodate fresh air but not so wide as to allow a bird to fly into the house.

Second, our analysis underscores the challenges associated with assessing coupling within, for lack of better term, a nested system like the US In many respects, there were three distinct sets of streams of activity operating across the local, state, and federal levels of government. At times these streams operated in a relative vacuum with little influence from the other levels of government. The Collins Park upgrade package was, more or less, a local initiative resulting from a compelling issue in the problem stream revealing a crisis that was in need of a solution. Similarly, SB 1 was primarily the product of legislative activity. However, in other instances, activity at one level effectively foreclosed the possibility of change at another level. The most notable example is the LEBOR, which aimed to amend a local city chart but was ultimately blocked by a federal court and the state legislature. Whereas most applications of the theory focus on the change within a single level of government, this finding points to the need for more multilevel studies that account for the dynamic nature of policymaking in federal systems like the US (see Knaggård and Hildingsson n.d.).

This finding of course stands in contrast to our second hypothesis regarding the proximal nature of focus event. Contrary to our original expectation we did, in fact, find some evidence of policy change across all three levels of government. However, the scope or magnitude of that change was ultimately minimized by the agriculture lobby, which, in some instances, capitalized on the venue shifting opportunities provided by the US's nested system.

Third, we find that in the MSF, conceptualizing policy change is complicated. Based on the case, we find that it is fairly simple to characterize change when we look at the new water treatment plant investment. However, this is misleading because the change that occurs is superficial. Building a new water treatment plant is not a policy change that addresses the problem of algae contaminated drinking water completely. In contrast, reducing agricultural runoff would address the source of the problem. For the MSF, the implication is that conceptualizing policy change requires a deep examination of the politics stream. Strong organized interests such as the agricultural interest groups in Ohio have the influence to make certain policy alternatives not viable. In the case of Toledo, the solution that was the most innovative in addressing the water contamination caused by agricultural runoffs was ultimately adopted on a voluntary basis by individual farms.

This finding reflects ongoing debates regarding stream independence prior work in the MSF that critiques the assumption of stream independence (see, e.g., Robinson and Eller 2010; Herweg et al. 2015). In our case, the agricultural lobby was clearly an integral part of the larger environmental policy community, however they were also inextricably linked to the policy stream and, in many respects, drove mobilization efforts. While it is tempting to conclude that the overlapping members undermine the contention that the streams are independent, closer analysis reveals the agriculture community effectively wore two hats: as issue experts generating solutions to aimed at bolstering their industry while reducing runoff and as lobbyists actively working to protect their economic interests. This duality is consistent with Kingdon's (2011) contention that participants can straddle multiple streams; however, future research should consider whether these types of actors tend to privilege certain responsibilities over others. For example, to what extent do the financial goals of agriculture interests bias the types of solutions they may or may not support within the policy stream? In short, our study suggests that stream independence is conditional based on the actors and organized interests of the policy community in the political stream.

Fourth, the case of Toledo as a subnational focusing event raises questions about the duration of policy windows. It seems to be completely unrealistic to argue that the window of opportunity remained completely open for all the eight years of our study period. Indeed, as noted above, it was never open for some issues. However, policy and political activity persisted during this time. We argue that the 2014 algae bloom and drinking water contamination meets the threshold for a potential focusing event (Birkland 1997). However, the case presented evidence that the algae bloom is seasonal, occurring in the years prior to 2014 and the years following the contamination. We are very reluctant to characterize those algae blooms as focusing events because they did not reveal risk or harm in the same way that the 2014 event did, nor were the effects of the algae contamination in drinking water so sudden. This finding echoes recent work by Huber-Stearns, Schultz, and Cheng (2019), who found windows of opportunity remained open for longer in the aftermath of damaging wildfires in Colorado.

The cyclical nature of the crisis kept the problem relevant without the same bowl over effect of the first one. This is the third piece of empirical evidence suggesting that repeated hazards are important factors for agenda setting in the MSF (DeLeo et al 2021 and O'Donovan 2017). Specifically, our study provides further evidence that repeated events or hazards can keep an item on the agenda on some level across time. Prior to the initial event, the algae blooms were not perceived as a risk public health, rather they were viewed as a nuisance preventing recreational and fishing use of Lake Erie (Steffen et al. 2017). This suggests that awareness and understanding of risks can be influential in agenda setting. Furthermore, we find evidence of repeated events functioning in the same way that focusing events do in the MSF: they reveal harms that were previously unknown or understood (in the policy stream), they allow for definition and framing of a policy problem in the problem stream, and they initiate interest group mobilization in the politics stream.

Lastly, our study uncovers a potential methodological roadblock to investigating agenda change within US state legislatures. Policy scientists have long used the number of entries in the *Congressional Record*, a running record of everything said on the floor of the US Congress, as well as committee hearing activity as indicators of issue attention within the national government. While the Toledo City Council agenda packets include substantive details about the motions discussed, state legislative journals only listed the titles of bills being voted on. It is plausible that this was simply an artifact of the Ohio legislature's reporting system, however future research should explore the possibility of alternative data sources for state legislative contexts.

CONCLUSION

This chapter examined the extent to which subnational focusing events lead to agenda change. It contributes to the empirical development of the MSF by extending the application of focusing events to subnational levels of policy making. It presented a qualitative case study of the 2014 drinking water crisis in Toledo, Ohio. A toxic algae bloom contaminated the drinking water supply and system functioned as a focusing event that initiated agenda change and prolonged agenda activity in the City of Toledo and the State of Ohio. The findings suggest that in subnational contexts, similar to national contexts, the politics and policy streams may not necessarily be independent, focusing events can signal problems that occur repeatedly and over a long duration, and coupling results in windows of opportunity but the opportunities for substantive policy change are often undermined by various veto points that exist at other levels of government, particularly those with the authority to override, or at least interrupt, decisions rendered at a lower level of government.

NOTE

1.   This research is supported by a CRISP 2.0 Type 2 grant from the Division of Civil, Mechanical and Manufacturing Innovation Program (CMMI) at the National Science Foundation. The project is entitled, CRISP 2.0 Type 2: Collaborative Research: Water and Health Infrastructure Resilience and Learning (WHIRL). This work was performed in accordance with Wayne State University's Institutional Review Board policies (IRB# 055119B3X, Protocol# 1905002290).

REFERENCES

Baumgartner, Frank R., and Bryan D. Jones. 2010. *Agendas and Instability in American Politics, Second Edition.* Chicago, University of Chicago Press.

Birkland, Thomas A. 1997. *After Disaster: Agenda Setting, Public Policy, and Focusing Events.* Washington, DC: Georgetown University Press.

Birkland, Thomas A. 2004. "Learning and Policy Improvement after Disaster - The Case of Aviation Security." *American Behavioral Scientist* 48 (3): 341–64. https://doi.org/10.1177/0002764204268990.

Birkland, Thomas A. 2006. *Lessons of Disaster.* Washington, D.C.: Georgetown University Press.

Birkland, Thomas A. 2009. "Disasters, Lessons Learned, and Fantasy Documents." *Journal of Contingencies and Crisis Management* 17 (3): 146–56.

Birkland, Thomas A., and Sarah E. DeYoung. 2011. "Emergency Response, Doctrinal Confusion, and Federalism in the Deepwater Horizon Oil Spill." *Publius-The Journal Of Federalism* 41 (3): 471–93. https://doi.org/10.1093/publius/pjr011.

Birkland, Thomas A., and Regina G. Lawrence. 2009. "Media Framing and Policy Change After Columbine." *American Behavioral Scientist* 52 (10): 1405–25. https://doi.org/10.1177/0002764209332555.

Burris, Keith C. 2013. "Collins Wants to Go Back to Strong Mayor." *The Blade.* December 23. https://www.toledoblade.com/opinion/keithburris/2013/12/20/Collins-wants-to-go-back-to-stro ng-mayor/stories/20131219222. Accessed June 13, 2022.

Burris, Keith C. 2014. "Toledo Mayor Collins Needs to Change - and Quickly." *The Blade.* https://www.toledoblade.com/opinion/keithburris/2014/08/09/Collins-needs-to-change-and-quickly/stories/20140808197. Accessed June 13, 2022.

City of Toledo. 2021. "Ozone Treatment Begins at Collins Park Water Treatment Plant." July 1. https://toledo.oh.gov/news/2021/07/01/ozone-treatment-begins-at-collins-park-water-treatment-plant#:~:text=The%20ozone%20treatment%20facilities%20for,with%20ozone%20since%20that%20date. Accessed June 13, 2022.

Crow, Deserai A., Elizabeth A. Albright, Todd Ely, Elizabeth Koebele, and Lydia Lawhon. 2018. "Do Disasters Lead to Learning? Financial Policy Change in Local Government." *The Review of Policy Research* 35 (4): 564–89. https://doi.org/10.1111/ropr.12297.

DeLeo, Rob A, Kristin Taylor, Thomas A. Birkland, and Deserai A. Crow. 2021. "During Disaster: Refining the Concept of Focusing Events to Better Explain Long-Duration Crises." *International Review of Public Policy* 3 (1).

Eckersley, Peter, and Katarzyna Lakoma. 2021. "Straddling Multiple Streams: Focusing Events, Policy Entrepreneurs and Problem Brokers in the Governance of English Fire and Rescue Services." *Policy Studies*, March, 1–20. https://doi.org/10.1080/01442872.2021.1892620.

Ecowatch. 2014. "Toledo Water Ban Lifted, But Is the Water Safe and What Caused the Toxic Algae Bloom?" August 5. https://www.ecowatch.com/toledo-water-ban-lifted-but-is-the-water-safe-and-what-caused-the-toxi-1881940622.html, retrieved June 13, 2022.

Elms, Sarah. 2019. "LEAD SAFETY; Coalition Wants Lead-Safe Ordinance; Pressure is on Elected Officials." *The Blade*, Oct 21. Accessed via ProQuest, June 14, 2022.

Gruber-Miller, Stephen. 2014. "LAKE ERIE ALGAE BLOOMS; Treatment Plants Voluntarily Test for Microcystin; But Tracking Toxin Not Mandated." *The Blade.* June 14. https://www.toledoblade.com/news/state/2014/06/30/Lake-Erie-algae-blooms-Treatment-plants-voluntarily-test-for-microcystin/stories/20140618189. Accessed June 14, 2022.

Henry, Tom. 2014a. "Activists Hope Algae Report Spurs Action: Collaboration Results in 16 Recommendations." *The Blade* March 3. https://www.toledoblade.com/news/state/2014/03/03/Activists-hope-algae-report-spurs-action/stories/20140202198. Accessed June 14, 2022

Henry, Tom. 2014b. "Senate Reauthorizes Algae Act." *The Blade.* Feb. 14. https://www.toledoblade.com/local/politics/2014/02/15/Senate-reauthorizes-algae-act/stories/20140214277. Accessed June 14, 2022.

Henstra, Daniel. 2010. "Explaining Local Policy Choices: A Multiple Streams Analysis of Municipal Emergency Management: Municipal Emergency Management." *Canadian Public Administration* 53 (2): 241–58. https://doi.org/10.1111/j.1754-7121.2010.00128.x.

Herweg, Nicole, Huß, Christian, and Zohlnhöfer, Reimut. 2015. "Straightening the Three Streams: Theorizing Extensions of the Multiple Streams Framework." *European Journal of Political Research* 54 (3): 435–49.

Herweg, Nicole, Nikolaos Zahariadis, and Reimut Zohlnhöfer. 2018. "The Multiple Streams Framework: Foundations, Refinements, and Empirical applications." In *Theories of the Policy Process*, 4th edition, eds. Christopher M. Weible and Paul A. Sabatier, 17–53. Boulder, CO: Westview Press.

Huber-Stearns, Heidi R., Courtney Schultz, and Antony S. Cheng. n.d. "A Multiple Streams Analysis of Institutional Innovation in Forest Watershed Governance." *Review Of Policy Research*. https://doi.org/10.1111/ropr.12359.

Kingdon, John W. 2011. *Agendas, Alternatives, and Public Policies*. Updated 2nd edition. Longman Classics in Political Science. Boston: Longman.

Lawrence, Regina G., and Thomas A. Birkland. 2004. "Guns, Hollywood, and School Safety: Defining the School-Shooting Problem across Public Arenas." *Social Science Quarterly* 85 (5): 1193–1207. https://doi.org/10.1111/j.0038-4941.2004.00271.x.

Markey, Matt. 2013a. "Erie Issues Easy to See for an Angling Portman: U.S. Sen. Rob Portman Fishes for, and on Lake Erie." *The Blade*. Aug. 20. https://www.toledoblade.com/MattMarkey/2013/08/20/Erie-issues-easy-to-see-for-an-angling-Portman/stories/20130820053. Accessed June 14, 2022.

Markey, Matt. 2013b. "Port Clinton Angler Captures Walmart Bass Event." *The Blade*. Sept. 3. https://www.toledoblade.com/MattMarkey/2013/09/03/Port-Clinton-angler-captures-Walmart-bass-event-1/stories/20130903026. Accessed June 14, 2022.

"Mayor Hicks-Hudson's Victory." 2015. *The Blade*. https://www.toledoblade.com/Editorials/2015/11/05/Mayor-Hicks-Hudson-s-victory.html. Accessed June 14, 2022.

McNabb, David E. 2016. *Public Utilities: Old Problems, New Challenges*. 2nd edition. Cheltenham, UK Northampton: Edward Elgar Publishing.

Messina, Ignazio. 2015. "Mayor Will Run to Keep Job in Nov.; She Wants to 'Move Forward.'" *The Blade*. Mar. 18. https://www.toledoblade.com/Politics/2015/03/18/Mayor-will-run-to-keep-job-in-Nov.html. Accessed June 14, 2022.

Messina, Ignazio. 2016. "City Administration to Seek Federal Help with Lake Algae: Plans to Urge Congress to Strengthen 1972 Water Act." *The Blade* (Toledo, Ohio).

Messina, Ignazio. 2017. "Candidate Says He'd Hire 40 Police Officers a Year" *The Blade*. May 30. https://www.toledoblade.com/local/politics/2017/05/31/Toledo-mayor-Candidate-Wade-Kapszukiewicz-says-he-d-hire-40-police-officers-a-year/stories/20170530297. Accessed June 14, 2022

National Centers for Coastal Ocean Science. n.d. "Lake Erie Harmful Algal Bloom FAQs." Washington, D.C: United States Department of Commerce, National Oceanic and Atmospheric Administration. https://coastalscience.noaa.gov/research/stressor-impacts-mitigation/hab-forecasts/lake-erie/faqs/. Accessed June 14, 2022.

O'Donovan, Kristin. 2017a. "Policy Failure and Policy Learning: Examining the Conditions of Learning after Disaster." *Review of Policy Research* 34 (4): 537–58. https://doi.org/10.1111/ropr.12239.

O'Donovan, Kristin. 2017b. "An Assessment of Aggregate Focusing Events, Disaster Experience, and Policy Change." *Risk Hazards & Crisis In Public Policy* 8 (3): 201–19. https://doi.org/10.1002/rhc3.12116.

"Paula Hicks-Hudson Will Be Sworn in as Toledo's next Mayor Tuesday." 2015. *The Blade*. February 13. https://www.toledoblade.com/local/2015/02/13/Paula-Hicks-Hudson-will-be-sworn-in-as-Toledo-s-next-mayor-Tuesday/stories/20150213155. Accessed June 14, 2022.

Pralle, Sarah B. 2006. *Branching out, Digging in: Environmental Advocacy and Agenda Setting*. Georgetown University Press.

Provance, Jim. 2014. "Ohio Bill Attempts to Prevent Toxic Algae: Findlay Senator Looks to Reduce Harmful Runoff in Lake Erie." *The Blade* (Toledo, Ohio).

Robinson, Scott E., and Warren S. Eller. 2010. "Participation in Policy Streams: Testing the Separation of Problems and Solutions in Subnational Policy Systems." *Policy Studies Journal* 38 (2): 199–216. https://doi.org/10.1111/j.1541-0072.2010 .00358.x.

Seewer, John. 2018. "Board again sidelines Kasich's order on Lake Erie algae." *Associated Press*, Nov. 1. https://apnews.com/article/cd0c0e63d5da4039a58d75 ec39272df5. Accessed June 14, 2022.

Taylor, Kristin, Stephanie Zarb, and Nathan Jeschke. 2021. "Ambiguity, Uncertainty and Implementation." *International Review of Public Policy* 3 (1). https://doi.org/10 .4000/irpp.1638.

WTOL. 2014. "Ohio EPA warned city officials about water treatment plant," WTOL News, Toledo, Ohio, Aug. 8. https://www.wtol.com/article/news/ohio-epa-warned -city-officials-about-water-treatment-plant/512-dd71825c-9931-46ea-a2f0 -ed5238b1d6e4. Accessed June 13, 2022.

Yeo, Jungwon, and Claire Connolly Knox. 2019. "Public Attention to a Local Disaster versus Competing Focusing Events: Google Trends Analysis Following the 2016 Louisiana Flood." *Social Science Quarterly* 100 (7): 2542–54.

Yin, Robert K. 2018. *Case Study Research and Applications: Design and Methods*. 6th edition. Los Angeles: SAGE.

Zohlnhöfer, Reimut, Nicole Herweg, and Nikolaos Zahariadis. 2022. "How to Conduct a Multiple Streams Study." In *Methods of the policy process*, 23–50. New York/ Abingdon: Routledge.

13. Policy development in Swedish crisis management: Restructuring of fire and rescue services

Kerstin Eriksson, Gertrud Alirani, Roine Johansson[1] and Lotta Vylund

INTRODUCTION

This chapter focuses on the policy field of crisis management, and more specifically on the organizational restructuring of the fire and rescue services that is currently taking place in Sweden. Viewed from an Multiple Streams Framework (MSF) perspective, a political system is conceptualized as consisting of three streams – the problem, the policy and the political stream – and a characteristic trait of crisis management as a policy field is its dependence on developments in the problem stream. Such developments often consist of focusing events. A focusing event has been defined as "an event that is sudden; relatively uncommon; can be reasonably defined as harmful or revealing the possibility of potentially greater future harms; has harms that are concentrated in a particular geographical area or community of interest; and that is known to policymakers and the public simultaneously" (Birkland 1998, 54). Further, "focusing events are 'focal' because they do obvious damage" (Birkland 1998, 55). Disasters resulting from natural hazards, such as fires, floods and hurricanes, seem to fit the description of focusing events rather well. Such focusing events tend to serve as drivers of policy change within the field (Birkland 1996).

In the present chapter, the focusing events consist of forest fires, uniquely large-scale, by Swedish standards. The first one, the largest fire in Sweden in modern times, occurred in the summer of 2014, and four years later, 2018, several large-scale fires once again devastated large areas of Swedish woodland. Drawing from a case study of policy changes after these forest fires, we use MSF as a tool of analysis to derive hypotheses regarding post-disaster policy development.

The aim of this chapter is to investigate the policy changes that occurred after the forest fires that took place in Sweden during the summers of 2014 and 2018. Changes occurred both on the local and the national levels. In this chapter we will study both levels. The investigation is guided by the following questions:

- How can differences regarding the focal power of the forest fires of 2014 and 2018 on the local and national levels, respectively, be explained?
- What was the effect of the forest fires on the subsequent policy changes regarding fire and rescue services at the local and national levels?

The scientific contribution of this chapter is: (1) to include both the local and the national level in the same analysis; and (2) to study the effects of a single *rare* focusing event as well as effects of the *aggregation* of a chain of similar focusing events.

BACKGROUND

The Swedish Forest Fires in 2014 and 2018: The Focusing Events

The forest fire that struck the county of Västmanland in 2014 came as a shock. It developed into the largest Swedish forest fire in modern times, and it stretched over the municipalities Sala, Surahammar, Fagersta and, Norberg. Nobody had seriously expected a fire of this magnitude to occur in Sweden. Thus, there was a strong element of surprise for the whole country. As one of our informants describe, with an understatement: "I can only state that we are not used to such large fires in Sweden" (I5).

On Thursday, July 31, 2014 a forest fire broke out in Västmanland. In the first days, the fire was not considered an extraordinary event. Three municipal rescue services worked in parallel in two separate response operations to the situation. After a few days, when it was realized that the municipal rescue services were unable to handle the situation, the county administrative board took over the response to the fire (Asp et al. 2015). In Sweden the county administrative board may take over the responsibility of an extensive rescue effort if the municipal rescue services cannot handle the situation themselves. Several national public agencies, volunteer organizations, and private firms were also involved, as well as support from EU (MSB 2016).

The summer of 2018, four years later, was a particularly intense forest fire season, with a large number of fires burning throughout the country threatening lives, property and forest. The largest fires occurred in the counties of Jämtland, Gävleborg, and Dalarna, and it took several weeks to take control over the fires. A number of national agencies, the Swedish Armed Forces and volunteer organizations mobilized to combat the fires in addition to international support with aerial firefighters, helicopters, personnel, equipment and vehicles (SOU 2019:7).

The Swedish Fire and Rescue Services

Swedish municipalities are granted much self-determination (Nilsson and Forsell 2013). Each municipality is responsible for the fire and rescue services and for crisis preparedness and management generally within its own boundaries, but municipalities are also responsible to coordinate their activities and collaborate, when needed, with others (SFS 2003:778). The municipal fire and rescue services can organize itself in several different ways to collaborate with other municipal fire and rescue services (Fredholm and Johansson 2003; Nilsson and Forsell 2013; Swedish Association of Local Authorities and Regions 2015). Such collaboration is governed by the Local Government Act (SFS 2017:725).

The discussion about collaboration between different fire and rescue services is not new. In fact, the possibility of merging and creating municipal associations, e.g., for fire and rescue services, has existed in the Swedish legislation since 1919. During the last 45 years the fire and rescue services have collaborated to a larger extent. In 1974, two municipalities had a municipal association, 20 years later there were seven associations and 2014 there were 47 associations (Swedish Association of Local Authorities and Regions 2015).

In 2006, the term *system command* (Sw.: systemledning) was introduced (Svensson, et al. 2009). For a municipal fire and rescue service it commonly implies that it is not a stand-alone, autonomous organization, but a component of a larger constellation/system with an overall system command. However, the pooled resources only concern the operational resources. The introduction of the term was linked to the discussion about collaboration where a need was identified to quickly be able to gather resources during major events. As one of our informants describe, "in order to cope with the upshifting to larger rescue efforts, the [earlier] model ran out of components" (I7) and needed a level/ component for an overall system command for the fire and rescue service.

At the national level, the Swedish Civil Contingencies Agency (MSB) is responsible for helping society prepare for major accidents, crises and the consequences of war. The authority has no responsibility for the fire and rescue service, it is a municipal responsibility, but the MSB's role is to support the municipalities' capacity to handle different types of situations in an efficient manner, for example, through research and development projects, guidelines and education activities. During larger incidents, MSB's could also support with coordination activities.

In summary, the structure of collaboration between fire and rescue services has been intermittently discussed for about a century. However, during recent times this debate has intensified, and a legal framework as well as actual organizational change has been decided upon and is currently in its implementation stage. Thus, what used to be a rather slow process of change has recently been speeded up considerably, and in the present chapter this intensification of the process of change is interpreted as a result of focusing events.

THEORETICAL FRAMEWORK

The MSF is applied to understand public policy, and particularly policy change, at the system level, by studying under what conditions political issues reach the political agenda and how they become decided upon. The political system is conceptualized as consisting of three streams – the problem stream, the policy stream and the political stream – that operate largely independently of each other but may converge periodically. Such coupling processes are crucial to MSF "as it is the occurrence of a successful coupling that leads to an agenda change" (Herweg, Huß, and Zohlnhöfer 2015, 443).

The *problem stream* refers to the sum of environmental conditions that citizens and policy makers currently define as public problems for which they seek solutions. Here, problems are not viewed as objective facts (Herweg, Zahariadis and Zohlnhöfer 2018). For a condition to be regarded as a public problem policy makers must pay attention to it *as* a problem. In that sense, problems are phenomena that exist in the eyes of the beholder. Some phenomena, regarded as core issues in political competition – because voters regularly care about them – are deemed important and are dealt with relatively regularly, without necessarily being regarded as major problems. Other, non-core issues, receive attention relatively rarely and may need a dramatizing event to be perceived as a problem. Crisis management as a policy field consists of non-core issues. It has been described as a "policy without a public" (May 1991, 190): crisis preparedness and management seldom become salient policy issues until a crisis strikes.

Therefore, crises and disasters may serve as *focusing events,* as salient phenomena in the problem stream that shed light on particular conditions as problems. Their role is to draw the attention of citizens and policy-makers to crisis management-related issues as problems in need of solutions. Therefore, crisis management as a policy field is largely event-driven. However, the focal power of focusing events cannot be determined a priori (Birkland 1996; 1998); policy change does not occur automatically after an event (Petridou and Sparf 2017). Two important factors may contribute to the focal power: it may be *the rarity* of an uncommon focusing event or *the aggregation* of a chain of similar events over time that triggers policy change. A recent study concludes that "major events alone are important in affecting policy change", and "aggregate focusing events coupled with experience are also important predictors" (O'Donovan 2017; cf. Giordono, Boudet and Gard-Murray 2020).

The *policy stream* consists of ideas regarding problem definitions and preferred solutions that are proposed and discussed in policy communities whose members share a common interest in a policy field. The members of such communities may consist of elected officials and policy experts of political parties, but also of specialized experts such as academics, consultants, lobbyists and professionals. A policy researcher has noted that, in the policy field of crisis management "elected officials are quite willing to defer policy formulations to experts who have the training, experience and apparent mastery of emergency management" (Henstra 2010, 249). The degree of integration of policy communities, as well as the types of ideas under consideration, may vary. This affects how potential solutions to problems are treated. The gestation period of ideas in the policy stream varies from rapid to gradual, and the content of ideas may be old or new. When the former is rapid and the latter is old, the situation has been characterized as convergent (Herweg et al. 2018). This means that policy communities are not necessarily characterized by diversity, and conflict. Sometimes a particular problem is framed in a similar manner by all actors in the relevant policy community, and a solution may already exist. Then the community is marked by consensus, and the people involved may agree on what an appropriate solution should look like and who should be commissioned with the task of working out the details of the solution (Petridou, et al. submitted). Absence of political controversy in a policy community may be due to such a convergent situation.

Public policy choices are ultimately made by elected decision-makers, and party leadership is concerned with adopting policies in the *political stream.* In doing so, at least two factors need to be taken into consideration: interest groups and the national mood. However, elected officials as well as interest groups may play a less important role than expected in the policy field of crisis management: even though formal decisions are generally made by elected officials, as shown above they are "quite willing to defer policy formulations to experts" (Henstra, 2010, 249), and "in the policy field of emergency management… there is little reason for pressure groups to form because there is no obvious unifying interest or objective around which to rally" (ibid, 250). The national mood, a concept that "is notoriously difficult to pin down empirically" (Herweg et al., 2015, 438), is a comprehensive concept that comprises things like the current public opinion, or the *Zeitgeist* generally. An important event in the political stream that could result in policy change is political elections leading to a change in government. In order for emergency management issues to take a prominent position in the national mood, it would most likely have to be triggered by a focusing event in the problem stream.

On relatively rare and short-lived occasions *policy windows* open in the problem stream or the political stream. Problem windows may open as the effect of a focusing event. Political windows primarily open as a result of elections or changes in government. Such windows of opportunity may be of two different kinds. The issue under consideration may come up on the political agenda, and the issue may be subject to actual decision-making. Thus, two windows, the *agenda* window and the *decision* window, are under consideration here (Herweg et al. 2015). To take advantage of an open window and couple the streams, a certain amount of agency is required, and the actor that may provide such agency is the *policy entrepreneur* (Petridou 2017). The coupling process is crucial in the political system, as it is successful coupling that leads to agenda change (Herweg et al. 2015) and successful coupling is more likely if policy entrepreneurs have access to core policymakers (Herweg et al. 2018).

Focusing events and their effects in a crisis management field have mostly been studied on a national or a federal level (Jones et al. 2016). Some researchers have emphasized the need to study policymaking at the local level (Albright and Crow 2021; Henstra 2010). Even though being an understudied area, the effects of focusing events on policy development may most likely differ between the local and the national level.

The empirical focus of this chapter is on the restructuring of the fire and rescue services in Sweden after the large forest fires 2014 and 2018 as a case of policy change in response to several focusing events. And in accordance with our theoretical assumption that the effects may differ between local and national level we study policy change at both the national level and at the local level. We use qualitative data collected during a period from 2014 to 2022. The main empirical material consists of documents (evaluations, policy documents and governmental reports) and a number of semi-structured interviews with representatives from national, regional and local authorities engaged in Swedish crisis management.

A total of 10 respondents were interviewed (see Table 13.1). The interviews were conducted in Swedish and lasted around 60 minutes. They followed an interview guide that covered questions related to the three streams in MSF. Follow-up questions were asked for clarification. All interviews were recorded and transcribed. The quotations in the text were translated by the authors. The respondents will be identified using the letter "I" followed by a number (e.g., "I5").

The empirical material was then coded thematically based on the concepts of the MSF. During the analysis four themes emerged, describing the nature and effects of the events. Two of the themes describe the differential focusing power of the events: the rare event and the aggregation of events. The other two themes describe different effects of the focusing events: the opening

Table 13.1   *A description of the informants and their number*

I1	Manager of a fire and rescue services
I2	Manager of a fire and rescue services
I3	Public servant at the county administrative board working with fire and rescue issues
I4	Public servant at the county administrative board working with fire and rescue issues
I5	Involved in the work at the county administrative board after the forest fire in 2014
I6	Public servant involved in the work with developing command issues a MSB (employed at MSB)
I7	Public servant involved in the work with developing command issues a MSB (not employed by MSB)
I8	Public servant, author of an evaluation of the 2014 forest fire
I9	Politician at the local municipal level
I10	Former director general of MSB

of an agenda window and a decision window, respectively. The study is hypothesis-generating (Levy 2008), where an examination of the forest fires in 2014 and 2018 is designed to result in new variables and causal claims that may be tested in other cases.

RESULTS AND ANALYSIS

The Rare Event of 2014

The fire of 2014 was large-scale and resulted in an equally large-scale response operation. The ensuing policy development clearly demonstrated that the fire of 2014 fit well into the description of a focusing event, with considerable focal power, at the local as well as the national level. However, the development looked somewhat different at the different levels.

The local level: Agenda-setting and decision-making without politicization

Four municipalities were directly affected by the fire. We have studied Sala municipality, the one most heavily affected (in terms of burnt area). The fire was regarded as an extreme event that demanded action at the local level. It resulted in a post-crisis "we have to do something" attitude. Or expressed in MSF terms: The fire functioned as a focusing event, and a policy window opened in the problem stream in Sala municipality. As expressed by a politician in Sala:

> You know, the forest fire in itself was a shock – ten percent of the area of the municipality burned. It's like, you cannot fathom it. So many people affected by it. So many animals evacuated. So much burnt, so many problems with the companies when the forest burned. People are that way, that before something happens, they cannot imagine what it's really like. So, I'm glad about this, that we could take the

effects seriously and put so much energy in the year right after the crisis with the fire to set up this structure – that's how I see things. (I9)

Thus, the issue of crisis management, and specifically fire-fighting, became an item on the political agenda in the municipality in the sense that everybody agreed that something must be done. However, the issue did not become a matter of political controversy. It has to do with the way the problem was framed. The forest fire, and particularly the response to it, was largely framed as a problem of resources and coordination. The response operation was generally considered to have been a failure, and the realization that unless something changed the next large fire would result in a similar response failure, provided a strong incentive for change. As expressed by the manager of the municipal fire and rescue services:

> If something has happened to somebody once and things didn't turn out well, then it becomes really hard to explain why it didn't turn out so well the second time either. "What the heck, have you not done anything?" Rarely is one criticized for not learning from the mistakes of others, but one is criticized for not learning from one's own. (I1)

The policy community in Sala – which here consisted of public servants, politicians, timber company officials, consultancies and elected officials with the Swedish Federation of Farmers – converged around this interpretation of the problem. Few, or no, divergent views were expressed (Petridou et al. submitted).

None of the actors involved at the municipal level exploited the crisis, and no framing contests occurred (Boin, t'Hart and McConnell, 2009), even though there was a parliamentary election, at the national, regional and local levels, coming up less than a month after the fire. Thus, in spite of the focusing event having opened a policy window in the problem stream, and an election at the local level was coming up, no policy window opened in the political stream in Sala municipality. Solutions suggested were expressed in technical and administrative terms, and it was solutions aimed at improving the response capacity, rather than preventing large-scale fires from occurring again.

Previous research has concluded that, in the policy field of emergency management, elected officials are quite willing to defer policy formulations to experts (Henstra, 2010), and this happened in Sala. Civil servants (the municipality manager, the crisis management director, and above all the manager of the fire and rescue services) had prominent roles in the formulation of the policy solutions after the 2014 fire. The manager of the fire and rescue services clearly felt the necessity to do something: "We realized during the event [the 2014 fire] that the organizational solution we had, especially in terms of leadership, failed" (I1). Therefore he acted as policy entrepreneur (Petridou, et al. submitted). He was also in a position that allowed him to do that. As confirmed by our informants, the fire and rescue services in Sala was respected and held in high esteem by the local politicians. The failure to respond properly to the 2014 fire did not change that, because the fire came as a total surprise, and it was generally considered that a fire of this extent would have caused insurmountable problems for *any* municipality of Sala's size. Therefore, the blame for the failure was not put specifically on the fire and rescue services in Sala. Thus, the manager of the fire and rescue services could rely on his status and the respect of the politicians. First, he urged the local politicians to assign him the task of finding an organizational solution that would improve the capacity of the fire and rescue services to manage future large-scale events. After the politicians commissioned him to find an appropriate solution, he used his knowledge and experience in the field of emergency management as well as his extensive professional network to that end. His preferred solution was a major organizational change, a contractual agreement of collaboration between the fire and rescue services of Sala and a large number of other municipal fire and rescue services in the Stockholm area (i.e., in another county). It was an agreement to pool their operative resources, without being part of a common organization in other respects. This organizational arrangement (system command) was not a new solution, but at the time of the 2014 fire it was not known in Sala and not widely implemented in Swedish municipalities. It was suggested by the manager of the fire and rescue services, and it was accepted by the local politicians without much discussion (Petridou et al. submitted). Thus, this process can be described, in the terms of Herweg and colleagues (2018), as convergent: characterized by rapid gestation of old ideas.

However, at this point in time, the solution was just a proposal. The preferred solution of the policy entrepreneur opened a policy window in the political stream in the entrepreneur's own county. His proposal turned out to be less than optimal from a local political point of view, because the politicians in Sala came under pressure from the county of Västmanland to choose a solution that stayed within county lines. Therefore, in order to demonstrate the lack of consensus in the county of Västmanland, our policy entrepreneur arranged a meeting, to which politicians were invited, with the other managers of the municipal fire and rescue services in Västmanland to discuss the matter. As he expected, the meeting disintegrated into chaos and intense disagreements over finances and a lot of practical details. This gave the manager of the fire and rescue services in Sala an opportunity to try his own preferred solution a second time: "So I went to the municipal commissioner [in Sala] again and said 'this is not going to work … It will go sideways whatever we do. Can I contact Stockholm again?'" The local politician agreed, and eventually the manager of the fire and rescue services was able to negotiate to attach Sala to the large consortium of municipal fire and rescue services in the Stockholm area. Thus, the policy entrepreneur managed to overcome the resistance from the county and close the policy window in the political stream of the county of Västmanland. Instead, his actions went a long way to opening a decision window in the political stream of Sala. He acted as a policy entrepreneur (cf. Petridou 2017), using his professional knowledge, skills and social connections with the elected officials in Sala, as well as a clever strategy to bend the local politicians to his will. This is in line with an established MSF hypothesis: "The policy-entrepreneur is more likely to successfully couple the streams during an open policy window, the more access to core policy makers he or she has" (Herweg 2015, 443).

The conditions for the success of the policy entrepreneur in Sala was favourable: the fear of a future response failure strengthened the effect of the focusing event and provided a strong incentive for change, a convergent policy community resulted in consensus around a technical/organizational solution, and a civil servant acting as policy entrepreneur provided a suggestion for a solution which was agreed and decided upon by local politicians without much discussion, after resistance from the county had been overcome. Therefore, both an agenda window and a decision window were opened, but very little political controversy on the local level was involved. Clearly, it was the rarity of the event that gave it the focal power at the local level.

The National Level: Less Focal Power

At the national level the issue came up on the political agenda rather quickly. Immediately after the fire, the national government appointed an independent investigator to evaluate the event (Terms of reference 2014:116). The aim was to evaluate the response operation and other work related to the fire, and give recommendations for improving and strengthening the crisis management system. Thus, an agenda window opened in the problem stream at the national level before the fire was even completely put out. However, after the general election in September 2014, with a new government taking over, a policy window opened in the political stream. The new coalition government decided to considerably delimit the mandate of the independent investigator to providing a description and evaluation of the operative response to the fire (Terms of reference 2015:12). Instead, the new government gave a public national authority, the MSB, with responsibility for the Swedish system of crisis preparedness and management, the mandate to investigate further measures to strengthen and improve the Swedish crisis management system. Both reports (Sjökvist and Strömberg 2015; MSB 2016) pointed towards a need for several national changes and suggestions for increased centralized steering of the crisis management system, and particularly the latter of them, the MSB report, had a considerably larger scope than just improvement of the fire and rescue services. The report suggested eight different measures for strengthening Swedish crisis management generally, and only one of these measures specifically affected fire and rescue services (Public inquiry into the forest fire of 2014, 2015; MSB 2016). Thus, when the forest fire as a focusing event moved from the local to the national level, its focal power seemed to be generalized from firefighting to crisis management generally.

However, even though the problem at the national level became a larger issue of the crisis management system, the issue of the fire and rescue services was still an important part of the investigations. The abovementioned report from the MSB (2016) resulted in several further investigations. One of them, a public inquiry that was launched in 2017, had a focus on organizational and administrative aspects of the Swedish fire and rescue services and published its official report in the spring of 2018 (SOU 2018:54). The report resulted in recommendations to strengthen the capacity of the fire and rescue services by increased standardization, centralization, state supervision, and collaboration in larger units with capacity to uphold 24/7 system command over fire and rescue services.

Thus, the focal power of the forest fire was most visible at the local level, where it opened an agenda window as well as a decision window by drawing attention to the insufficient local capacity to handle the kind of extreme fire that occurred the summer of 2014. However, at the national level the focal power of the fire was limited to opening an agenda window, and to activities within the policy stream. The fire did not lead to decisions or immediate changes in policy. The political stream was involved to a very small extent, limited to discussions in the Swedish Parliament. These discussions did not reflect controversies regarding the content of politics, but rather questions regarding process aspects of the handling of the issue (Parliamentary debate 2014/15: 240). And a decision window was not opened; the event of 2014 did not lead to any political decisions in parliament except initiating investigations. It seems as when debates regarding rare events move from the local to the national level, policy alternatives in the policy stream tend to widen in scope and coverage from firefighting to crisis management. The likely mechanisms may be the involvement of more, and more diverse, actors, and reframing of problems to suit national political interests. Therefore, the wider scope of the MSB (2016) report provided a necessary national context, encompassing the general Swedish system of crisis management, before a national investigation regarding the organization of the fire and rescue services could be undertaken.

Therefore, we propose the following hypothesis:

H1: When a debate based on a rare event moves from local to national level, the focal power of the rare event likely becomes less concentrated and policy alternatives in the policy stream tend to widen in scope.

The Aggregated Events of 2014 and 2018

After the forest fires in 2014 an agenda window had opened at the national level but it was not until after the fires in 2018 that changes were made in the legislation. The major policy change was a demand that all fire and rescue services need to be connected to a command system that have the capacity to practice system command (Civil Protection Act SFS 2003:778). Even if proposals for policy change came after the fire in 2014 it was not until after the events of 2018 that the coupling of all the three streams was made and the subsequent adoption of the changed legislation. Thus, the 2018 fires reopened a policy window in the problem stream at the national level.

The problem that in 2014 was mainly described in terms of a concern for the national level to handle, but still a rare event, was after the fires 2018 emphazied to be of a more acute problem and events likely to occur again. In the investigations made after the fires 2018, and described by our informants, there are two reasons presented as arguments for the need for change. The first reason is climate change and in the government Bill 2019/20:176 it is written that forest fires "... have previously been events that have occurred rarely..." (Government Bill 2019/20:176, 14) but that in the future extreme weather events will occur more often due to climate change which in turn leads to a need for change. The other reason for change is connected to the first but focus on the need for more resources. It is written in the government Bill 2019/20:176 that today's management over the fire and rescue service do not result in a "satisfactory and equivalent protection against accidents throughout the country" (Government Bill 2019/20:176, 17) and that there is a need for a stronger state control. A similar argument is mentioned by our informants who describes that the rescue services did not have enough resources to respond to a large forest fire in 2014 and still lacking in 2018.

> Yes, in 2014 it was... you know, [Sala and the other affected municipalities]. They were too small, they did not have the resources. 2018 was the same with [municipalities affected 2018], the same. "No, now that's enough" says the state. (I2)

Thus, the problem window reopened and the events of 2018 helped to reframe the problem to become an issue of concern for all municipalities. The need of more resources and collaboration was a central lesson learnt after the fires 2014, but it was not generalized to municipalities all over the country; the lack of resources and absence of collaboration were treated as if they were specific conditions in the municipalities affected. The fires of 2018 made it completely clear that this was not a problem only for certain municipalities. By also placing the fires in a wider context of future increasing extreme weather events further gave arguments for the suggested policy changes. Also, informants point out that the fires in 2018 were of great importance for the change to occur.

> But after 2018 and the signals that were then sent from both the Minister of the Interior and the Director General, [...] "No, the level [of command] that generally exists in the country is not enough. There will be a requirement on a system command that must be constantly maintained." This is to say that "municipality, you have not reached the level that we think the law aims at. We therefore adjust the law." (I6)

The focal power of the 2018 event can be attributed to the rare event of the fire of 2014, and something similar occurring once again just a few years later. An isolated event may not lead to change but when it happens several times policy makers learn by the experiences of previous events which may have important implications for policy change (O'Donovan 2017). Our informants highlight the importance of both the event 2014 and 2018 before a change occurs, thus an aggregation of events (cf. O'Donovan 2017). As one of our informants argue it "It's two to three times something needs to happen" (I7) before a change occurs, also discussing a forest fire that occurred before 2014. The two events led to a slightly new emphasis on forest fires as events likely to occur again and something the existing Swedish system of fire and rescue services did not have sufficient capacity to handle. The slightly different framing of the problem helped couple the problem stream with the other streams.

In the policy stream a solution had already been formulated after the forest fires of 2014 but was now further boosted by new investigations. There already existed a solution, i.e., system command, prepared and ready for implementation. What happened now was that the problem and the policy stream was coupled with the political stream.

After the forest fires of 2018 there was an increased pressure for the government to act on the extreme events of forest fires in 2018. With an uncertain outcome of the coming election it was important for the government to show their capability and will to act. On August 16, immediately after the fires and just a few weeks before the election, the government appointed an independent committee to evaluate the event of 2018 (Terms of reference 2018:81). The aim of the evaluation was to take advantage of experiences and gain new knowledge for similar events in the future. The government appointed the same investigator, Jan-Åke Björklund, who had performed the previous investigation (SOU 2018:54). What has been added in the new investigation is mainly a description of the forest fires in 2018. As one of our informants describe:

> Jan-Åke Björklund [..] did an evaluation of the forest fires and came up with a lot. [...] He was then also given the task of reforming the legislation on civil protection.

Björklund himself tells that the Minister of the Interior told him informally "you make sure that what you write now fits in with the investigation you did about the forest fires. (I2)

And as previous literature on MSF states, in parliamentary democracies the political parties play an active role in influencing policy output (Herweg et al. 2015, 441) and the government, here in the role of Minister of Interior, have a specific policy solution in mind when giving the task to the investigator. And there seemed to be a majority in the Swedish Parliament at this point on the need for more resources and increased collaboration to increase the capacity of the fire and rescue services (Persson 2018). In other words, the political stream was ripe since the government coalition was embracing the proposal (Herweg et al. 2015, 439).

The three streams had now been coupled and enabled a so called decision coupling to occur (Herweg et al. 2015, 444). The new investigation (SOU 2019:7) was handed over in February 2019 and concluded that "The most important conclusion is that the investigation SOU 2018:54 proposals for changes in the law and other measures should be implemented." (SOU 2019:7, 16) The new investigation SOU 2019:7 thus resulted in very few new conclusions, but again highlighted the same need for change within the fire and rescue service as the investigation SOU 2018:54. In the government Bill 2019/20:176 the government proposes amendments to the Civil Protection Act (SFS 2003:778) so that the country's municipal fire and rescue services more effectively and coherently can handle future challenges, such as forest fires. In the parliamentary Committee on Defense, consisting of representatives from the parties in proportion to their mandates in the Parliament, that was responsible for preparing the proposal before an adoption in Parliament they stated that they "largely share the government's picture of the problem" (2020/21:FöU3, 14). It is further written that:

This is not least important in light of the extensive Swedish forest fires in recent years. For the reasons stated by the government, the Government bill is therefore approved in its whole. (2020/21:FöU3, 14)

In January 2021 the Civil Protection Act (SFS 2003:778) was changed. The solution that was decided in the legislation was a solution that had been discussed for a long time within the policy area, that is *system command*. In the legislation it is now stated that the municipality must be able to monitor and manage the fire and rescue service 24/7 (SFS 2003:778). This requires in practice a collaboration between different fire and rescue services to manage to maintain this. This was also the solution that was decided at the local level, in the municipality of Sala, after the 2014 event.

Even though there already existed a proposal before the forest fires of 2018, the event gave stronger arguments for policy change. One of the informants points out that it was not until after the fires in 2018 that someone really wanted to invest money in the fire and rescue services:

> There are now completely different requirements for command and coordination within the fire and rescue services. That's really good. But it was something that was known before 2018, but which was not taken care of, because it would cost too much. So then there were a lot of forest fires that were partly due to not having this coordination and plan for early helping each other. So I definitely think that after 2018, measures have been taken. (I4)

After 2018 the three streams were coupled and resulted in policy change. The aggregated focusing event of 2014 and 2018 made the problem stream to be coupled with the policy stream were a policy solution already existed. The policy stream was then ripe since there already existed a policy solution ready to implement (Herweg et al. 2015, 443). And most importantly, in the political stream there was now a willingness in the government for the solution and they were ready to actively engage in coming to a decision. However, the road to political change had been paved long before the fires of 2018. A "softening up" process (Kingdon, 2011) had taken place in the policy stream at the national level since 2014, and a public inquiry with proposals for policy change (SOU 2018:54) was already written when the fires of 2018 occurred. The aggregation of several rare events further strenghened the arguments for policy change, which were afterwards codified by another public inquiry (SOU 2019:7). Thus, due to a combination of the focal power of the aggregated events of 2014 and 2018, and the existing policy proposal that was first developed in the investigation SOU 2018:54, then further lifted in the investigation SOU 2019:7, a decision window opened. In the Swedish parliamentary system the actual policy making is mainly handled in the preparatory stage. The parliamentary committee that prepare the proposal for the Parliament takes a clear position for the proposed changes in the fire and rescue services and refer to the two thorough investigations made after the forest fires 2014 and 2018 (Committee report 2020/21:FöU3:14). The differences between the focal power of the forest fires on the national and local level respectively, is that the event of 2014 was not enough for a coupling of the three streams and a decision window to open at the national level. There had to be an aggregation of events in order for the streams to be coupled.

We summarize our findings in one hypothesis referring to the aggregation of events:

H2: A rare event with a limited impact area may likely lead to policy change at the local level, but in order for policy change to occur at the national level it takes an aggregation of similar events.

CONCLUSION AND DISCUSSION

The aim of this chapter was to investigate the policy changes that occurred after the forest fires that took place in Sweden during the summers of 2014 and 2018. More specifically, the events were examined in order to explain the difference in focal power between the local and national levels and the effects the events had on subsequent policy changes regarding the fire and rescue services at the local and national levels. Our study uses the MSF to provide knowledge on the focal power of a rare event for the local and the national level in the same analysis and also, the effects of a single rare focusing event as well as the effects of the *aggregation* of a chain of similar focusing events.

The focal power of the fires differed between the local and national level. The rare event of 2014 had major consequences in Sala. The framing of the event at the local level focused mainly on specific issues that the municipality had a possibility, and responsibility, to change, i.e., the lack of resources and coordination capacity in the local fire and rescue services. At the national level, the forest fire of 2014 came up on the political agenda but was formulated as a larger issue of changes needed in the crisis management system. The problem had to be reframed to suit national political interests and therefore also included more, and more diverse actors. The event was thus framed in a slightly different way and became a larger issue than as a specific fire and rescue service issue. The focal power of the event was less focused at the national level and did not lead to a decision window to open. Based on these conclusions we can formulate the following hypothesis: *When a debate based on a rare event moves from local to national level, the focal power of the rare event likely becomes less concentrated and policy alternatives in the policy stream tends to widen in scope.*

The effects of the forest fires in 2014 led to policy changes at the local level but not at the national level, even though investigations were initiated. The event had a major impact locally and the problem was framed in a way that something had to be done to make sure this kind of event would not happen again. At the local level the event resulted in changes in the organization of the fire and rescue services. At the national level the event had the effect of opening the agenda window and that investigations were initiated to find appropriate changes for developing the Swedish crisis management system. When the forest fires of 2018 occurred only a few years later and hit several localities at the same time in different parts of Sweden the problem became more acute to handle. The problem was framed as an increasing problem because of climate change and a concern for most municipalities lacking the sufficient capacity to handle this kind of extreme events. Because of extreme forest fires occurring again only a few years later and revealing a vulnerability in the crisis management system the policy window opened again and now actors at the national level managed to couple the three streams in order for a political decision to be made. We can therefore formulate one more hypothesis: A *rare event with a limited impact area may likely lead to policy change at the local level, but in order for policy change to occur at the national level it takes an aggregation of similar events.*

In terms of MSF, the study confirms but also amends the impact of focusing events. Focusing events can indeed concentrate attention and increase the likelihood of witnessing policy changes. But the amendment we propose reveals a scope condition: limited-impact focusing events tend to command less attention as policy shifts up government levels. The implication is that policy entrepreneurial coupling strategies and audience need to shift focus "in flight," meaning within the same issue cycle. As attention disperses when moving from the local to the national, more resources will likely be expended and different networks activated to facilitate policy change. But the skill that is likely to be most valued during this type of coupling effort is framing. To achieve the instensity that commands national attention, focusing events tend to be aggregated. Future research needs to elaborate on the mechanisms of such aggregation. Is coupling under these conditions simply a question of relating disparate events in a logical way or, as prospect theory suggests, an editing process of presenting likely consequences as losses or gains? Answers have significant consequences for MSF theorizing and beyond.

NOTE

1.   We would like to acknowledge funding from FORMAS, Sweden, FR-2019/0002 (Putting out Fires: A Multiple Streams Analysis).

REFERENCES

Albright, Elizabeth A. and Deserai A. Crow. 2021. "Capacity building toward resilience: How communities recover, learn, and change in the aftermath of extreme events." *Policy Studies Journal* 49 (1): 89–122. doi:10.1111/psj.12364.

Birkland, Thomas A. 1996. "Natural disasters as focusing events: Policy communities and political response." *International Journal of Mass Emergencies and Disasters.* 14 (2): 221–243.

Birkland, Thomas A. 1998. "Focusing events, mobilization, and agenda setting." *Journal of Public Policy* 18 (1): 53–74. doi: 10.1017/S0143814X98000038.

Boin, Arjen, Paul t' Hart, and Allan McConnell. (2009) "Crisis exploitation: political and policy impacts of framing contests." *Journal of European Public Policy* 16 (1): 81–106.

Fredholm, Lars and Ann Johansson. 2003. Kommunal samverkan inom räddningstjänsten: Erfarenheter och framtida handlingsvägar [Municipal collaboration within the fire and rescue service: Experiences and future courses of action]. Karlstad, Sweden: Räddningsverket.

2020/21:FöU3. En effektivare kommunal räddningstjänst [More effective municipal rescue services]. Parliamentary Committee on Defense.

Giordono, L., H. Boudet and A. Gard-Murray. 2020, "Local adaptation policy responses to extreme weather events." *Policy Sciences* 53: 609–36. doi: 10.1007/s11077-020-09401-3.

Government Bill 2019/20:176. En effektivare kommunal räddningstjänst [More effective municipal rescue services].

Henstra, Daniel. 2010. "Explaining local policy choices: A multiple streams analysis of municipal emergency management." *Canadian Public Administration* 53 (2): 241–58. doi: 10.1111/j.1754-7121.2010.00128.x.

Herweg, Nicole, Christian Huß, and Reimut Zohlnhöfer. 2015. "Straightening the three streams: Theorising extensions of the multiple streams framework." *European Journal of Political Research* 54 (3): 435–49. doi: 10.1111/1475-6765.12089.

Herweg, Nicole, Nikolaos Zahariadis, and Reimut Zohlnhöfer. 2018. "The Multiple Streams Framework: Foundations, refinements, and empirical applications." In *Theories of the Policy Process,* 4th edition, eds. Christopher M. Weible and Paul A. Sabatier. New York: Routledge.

Jones, Michael D., Holly L. Peterson, Jonathan J. Pierce, Nicole Herweg, Amiel Bernal, Holly Lamberta Raney, and Nikolaos Zahariadis. (2016) "A river runs through it: A Multiple Streams meta-review." *Policy Studies Journal* 44 (1): 13–36.

Kingdon, John W. 2011. *Agendas, Alternatives, and Public Policy.* NewYork: Longman.

Levy, Jack S. 2008. "Case Studies: Types, Designs, and Logics of Inference." *Conflict Management and Peace Science* 25: 1–18.

May, Peter J. 1991. "Reconsidering policy design: Policies and publics." *Journal of Public Policy* 11 (2): 187–206. doi:10.1017/S0143814X0000619X.

MSB (Swedish Civil Contingencies Agency) 2016. Ansvar, samverkan, handling. Åtgärder för stärkt krisberedskap utifrån erfarenheterna från skogsbranden i Västmanland 2014. [Responsibility, collaboration, action. Measures towards strengthened crisis management based on lessons from the forest fire in Västmanland 2014.] Karlstad, Sweden: MSB.

Nilsson, Lars and Håkan Forsell. 2013. 150 år av självstyrelse: Kommuner och landsting i förändring [150 years of self-government: Municipalities and county councils in change]. Stockholm, Sweden: Swedish Association of Local Authorities and County Council.

O'Donovan, Kristin. 2017. "An assessment of aggregate focusing events, disaster experience, and policy change." *Risk, Hazards & Crisis in Public Policy* 8 (3): 201–19. doi: 10.1002/rhc3.12116.

Ordinance 2007:857. Förordning med instruktion för Statens räddningsverk [Ordinance with instructions for the Swedish Rescue Services Agency].

Ordinance 2008:1002. Förordning med instruktion för MSB [Ordinance with instructions for the Swedish Civil Contingencies Agency].

Parliamentary debate 2014/15:240. (Debate on major written questions put to a minister.)

Persson, Fredrik. 2018. Valextra 2018. Så ser partierna på räddningstjänstens framtid, del 1 [Election 2018. This is how the parties see the future of the fire and rescue service, part 1]. *Swedish Firefighters.* September 6.

Petridou, Evangelia. 2017. *Political Entrepreneurship in Swedish: Towards a (Re) Theorization of Entrepreneurial Agency.* Diss. Sundsvall: Mid Sweden University.

Petridou, Evangelia and Jörgen Sparf. 2017. "For safety's sake: the strategies of institutional entrepreneurs and bureaucratic reforms in Swedish crisis management, 2001–2009." *Policy and Society* 36 (4): 556–74. doi:10.1080/14494035.2017.1369 677.

Petridou, Evangelia, Roine Johannsson, Kerstin Eriksson, Gertrud Alirani, and Nikolaos Zahariadis. Forthcoming. *Policy Studies Journal.* "Theorizing Reactive Policy Entrepreneurship: A Case Study of Swedish Local Emergency Management."

Public inquiry into the forest fire of 2014. 2015. Rapport från Skogsbrandsutredningen [Report from the Public inquiry into the forest fire of 2014], Stockholm, Sweden: Justitiedepartementet.

Robinson, Scott E. and Warren S. Eller. 2010. "Participation in Policy Streams: Testing the Separation of Problems and Solutions in Subnational Policy Systems." *Policy Studies Journal* 38 (2): 199–216. doi: 10.1111/j.1541–0072.2010.00358.x.

SFS 1944:521. Brandlag [Fire regulation]. Swedish Code of Statutes.

SFS 2003:778. Civil Protection Act. Swedish Code of Statutes.

SFS 2017:725. Local Government Act. Swedish Code of Statutes.

Sjökvist, Aud, and Ingrid Strömberg. 2015. Rapport från Skogsbrandsutredningen [Report from the investigation of the forest fire]. Ministry of Justice, Stockholm, Sweden.

SOU (Swedish Government Official Reports) 1983:77. Effektiv räddningstjänst. Slutbetänkandet av Räddningstjänstkommittén. [Effective fire and rescue services. The final report of the Fire and Rescue Services Committee]. Stockholm: Swedish Government Official Reports.

SOU (Swedish Government Official Reports) 2018:54. En effektivare kommunal räddningstjänst [More effective municipal rescue services]. Stockholm: Swedish Government Official Reports.

SOU (Swedish Government Official Reports) 2019:7. Skogsbränderna sommaren 2018. [The forest fires 2018.] Stockholm: Swedish Government Official Reports.

Svensson, Stefan, Erik Cedergårdh, Ola Mårtensson, and Thomas Winnberg. 2009. "Tactics, command, leadership". Karlstad, Sweden: Swedish Civil Contingencies Agency.

Swedish Association of Local Authorities and Regions. 2015. Trygghet och säkerhet 2015: Tema kommunal räddningstjänst [Safety and security 2015: Theme municipal fire and rescue service]. Stockholm, Sweden.

Terms of reference (of a commission of inquiry) 2014:116. Skogsbranden i Västmanlands län – lärdomar för framtiden. [The forest fire in Västmanland county – lessons for the future.]

Terms of reference (of a commission of inquiry) 2015:12. Tilläggsdirektiv till Skogsbrandsutredningen. [Additional terms of reference for the commission of inquiry regarding the forest fire.]

Terms of reference (of a commission of inquiry) 2018:81. Utvärdering av operativa räddningsinsatser vid skogsbränder 2018. [Evaluation of response operations regarding forest fires 2018.]

14. Subnational policy windows: Shanghai's grid screening policy

Stephen Ceccoli and Xinran Andy Chen

INTRODUCTION

Since the publication of John Kingdon's *Agendas, Alternatives and Public Policies,* the multiple streams framework (MSF) has provided a useful heuristic for policy process conceptualization. Recognizing the value of "conceptual stretching", this volume's editors contend that MSF "travels" well and that its central concepts remain malleable to governing arrangements beyond its original US federal policymaking scope (See Herweg et al. 2018; 2022). Since national-level policy processes within the domains of North American and European democracies have dominated MSF scholarship (Jones et al. 2016), considerable promise remains for what may be termed downward vertical stretching (i.e., from the national context) to subnational applications.

Early subnational MSF scholarship sought to probe the framework's applicability beyond the central level and establish whether MSF *could* be applied subnationally. Among the first to recognize the spatial importance of the streams, Exworthy and Powell differentiated "big windows" at the central level from "little windows" at the local level (2004, 265; see also Exworthy et al. 2002). Early subnational MSF scholarship generated valuable results, finding that local politics "exhibit unique and differing dynamics from national politics" in the political stream (Liu et al. 2010, 82) and that subnational problem and policy streams lack independence (Robinson and Eller 2010). Others demonstrated successes of subnational policy entrepreneurs (Henstra 2010; Oborn et al. 2011). Collectively, such work put to rest the question of whether the framework had subnational applicability.

By attending to MSF refinements and more deliberately generating testable propositions, subnational MSF scholarship has now entered its second generation. Yet, in contrast to upward vertical stretching, particularly with insightful European Union applications (Ackrill et al. 2013; Herweg 2016; Rietig 2021), subnational MSF scholarship has been slower to advance. Perhaps this is because Kingdon's original agenda setting formulations meant that other phases of the policy process such as implementation – a task often performed by subnational actors and "a subject with which MSF theorists rarely if ever deal" (Howlett 2019, 415) – require even further conceptual stretching. Like other recent subnational applications, this chapter connects policy adoption with implementation (Ridde 2009; Fowler 2022; also see Howlett 2019).

Whether stretching upward or downward, applying MSF beyond its original scope requires first defining the functional equivalents[1] of MSF elements in alternate contexts and then linking such equivalents with causal mechanisms, especially via policy windows and coupling activities (Herweg 2016; Zohlnhöfer et al. 2022). This chapter contributes to subnational MSF literature by focusing on institutional context and coupling's temporal aspects, two policy window elements once identified as "sparingly used" in the broader MSF literature (Jones et al. 2016, 25), but the subject of considerable refinement (Herweg et al. 2015; 2018; Zohlnhöfer et al. 2016; 2022).

In accounting for institutional factors when extending MSF beyond its original scope (Zahariadis 2016; Zohlnhöfer et al. 2016), we first consider how and to what extent the subnational institutional context privileges certain actors over others and therefore circumscribes whose support is needed for successful policy action (Herweg et al. 2018). We seek to demonstrate that the situational context of the policy process, especially the extant institutional configuration, has substantial policymaking implications (Biesbroek and Candel 2020; Koebele 2021). Such context matters greatly as lessons from urban regime analysis confirm that "cities are not the nation state writ small" (Stone 2015, 117). Instead, city-level governing is a "multitiered process" occurring within the context of the wider urban order and featuring "significantly different layers of concurrent activity" (Stone 2015, 109).

Second, we demonstrate the connection between the subnational policy context and policymaking's temporal aspects, particularly via policy windows and coupling processes. The influence of context on policy implementation conditions – here involving local-national interactions – remains critical since MSF accounts "often lack a clear story of the *configurations* of conditions that explain successful policy actions" (Shephard et al. 2021, 526, italics in original). This critique is consistent with recent efforts to incorporate causal processes and mechanism-based accounts into MSF analyses (Kay and Baker 2015; Koebele 2021) and into policy process theorizing more broadly (Capano and Howlett 2021; van der Heijden 2021; Wellstead et al. 2018).

In applying MSF refinements subnationally, we examine the grid screening policy implemented by authorities in Shanghai, China, in March 2022. Under the principle of localized management, Chinese Covid-19 responses are locally administered in following specific prevention and control guidelines authored by central authorities in Beijing. Such efforts, carried out on the ground by specialists, technocrats, and bureaucrats, result in varying thresholds that trigger Covid restrictions and other public health protocols across cities and provinces. Although incentive structures established by the central government prioritize pandemic control over other policy priorities and tend to compel local officials toward risk averse behavior – such as imposing widespread lockdowns to contain local outbreaks – Shanghai officials initially eschewed a citywide lockdown, instead opting for a more targeted grid screening approach following an Omicron subvariant outbreak in early 2022.

Decisions by Shanghai authorities to implement the grid screening policy make it a valuable case for MSF analysis. This chapter examines how local authorities engaged in coupling during an open problem stream window leading to grid screening. Empirically, how did problem stream developments contribute to policy window openings and become ripe for coupling? Further, why did local authorities implement grid screening after initially eschewing stringent lockdowns? The answers, we argue, have broader implications for subnational MSF analyses.

The following section offers several minor MSF adaptations applicable to subnational policymaking, particularly in the Chinese context. Next, we discuss why Shanghai's grid screening policy offers a compelling study and briefly sketch the chapter's research design. Our empirical analysis then demonstrates how problem window openings became ripe for coupling activity. Finally, we offer observations for further applying MSF to other subnational cases.

SUBNATIONAL MSF ADAPTATION: DEFINING FUNCTIONAL EQUIVALENTS

As a system-level framework, MSF conceptualizes the policy process as non-linear and non-rational with policymaking possibilities enhanced when: (a) three metaphorical streams are ready for coupling; (b) a policy window opens; and (c) a policy entrepreneur succeeds in stream coupling (Herweg et al. 2018; Kingdon 2003). These assumptions can be readily mapped to subnational applications as officials at all levels (subnational and otherwise) simultaneously frame problems and pose solutions while confronting political constraints and opportunities.

Recent MSF scholarship offers valuable insights for extending the framework beyond its original scope (Herweg et al. 2018; 2022). A first step requires defining the functional equivalents of MSF elements in alternate contexts. Equivalence challenges have long been central to policy sciences research (van Deth 2009), including translating Kingdon's concepts beyond their original scope. For instance, since political stream elements such as national mood, pressure group campaigns and administrative turnover do not readily translate to a Chinese context, Mu (2018) coins the phrase "political attention" to capture such elements. Short of direct measures, political attention offers a composite of political stream elements, which "can directly tell where policy makers search for solutions and what public values governments pursue" (Mu 2018, 5).

Functional equivalents also need to be linked to MSF causal mechanisms, especially those involving policy windows and coupling activities. MSF refinements bifurcate the coupling process into agenda coupling and decision coupling to differentiate agenda setting from alternative selection (Herweg et al. 2015; Zohlnhöfer et al. 2016). Decision coupling, which refers to "bargaining about concrete design of the policy proposal" (Herweg et al. 2015, 444), necessitates focus on the political stream, magnifies the importance of institutions and "allows for the focusing of attention on circumstances advantageous for adopting a policy" (Herweg et al. 2015, 447). Such emphases also facilitate the generation of testable propositions.

The remainder of this section briefly sketches several functional equivalents aimed at subnational policy processes and actors, particularly in the Chinese context.

The Policy Stream and Subnational Institutional Context

MSF's policy stream captures processes of forming and refining policy alternatives by highlighting the availability of solutions to extant problems within a policy community whose structure and membership vary across differing contexts. A given alternative must satisfy various survival criteria, including technical feasibility, financial viability and value acceptability (Herweg et al. 2018; Kingdon 2003). The policy stream is generally deemed to be ready for coupling when at least one alternative satisfies these criteria.

China's long tradition of policy experimentation, in which local or provincial authorities innovate policies that can later inform national-level policymaking (Heilmann 2008; Teets and Hasmath 2020), offers a useful step toward specifying functional equivalents of concepts such as value acceptability and softening up. Policy experimentation reflects a pragmatism deeply rooted in Chinese policymaking and an enduring characteristic of Chinese policy style predating the People's Republic of China's 1949 founding (Heilmann and Perry 2011). Characterized as "experimentation under hierarchy", Chinese policy style remains distinguished by a "volatile yet productive combination of decentralized experimentation with *ad hoc* central interference" (Heilmann 2008, 2).[2]

"Decentralized experimentation" and "*ad hoc* central interference" provide useful referents for policy stream equivalents. As the policy stream requires "a solution ready to go, already softened up, already worked out" (Kingdon 2003,142), decentralized policy experimentation plays a vital softening up role. Characteristically, the Chinese policymaking process involves "ceaseless change, tension management, continual experimentation, and *ad-hoc* adjustment" (Heilmann and Perry 2011, 3). In softening up equivalence, the central government (more precisely, leading Communist Party officials), establishes both the policy objectives and the all-important ideological parameters, while subnational authorities experiment and innovate policies within those constraints. Successful subnational policies can then be scaled up and diffused nationally, with Deng Xiaoping-era economic reforms reflecting the most prominent example (Heilmann and Perry 2011).

Similarly, ad hoc central interference provides a critical value acceptability proxy tacitly understood with policy experimentation. Such interference connotes consensus among top central level officials – both government and Party – regarding a given policy alternative and can be instructive for signaling policy window openings. Policy experimentation in China is "focused on finding innovative policy *instruments*, rather than defining policy *objectives*, which remains the prerogative of the Party leadership" (Heilmann 2008, 3, emphasis in the original). Such policy instrument emphasis necessitates a closer look at both the institutional context and the subnational policy community operating therein.

Defining subnational policy community functional equivalents is imperative since Chinese Communist Party (CCP) leadership is prevalent at all layers of governance (i.e., national, provincial, county, township) in the Chinese Party-state system. Though national (e.g., president, premier) and subnational (e.g., provincial governor, mayor) governance roles have direct western parallels, the extent of multi-level Party governance – and corresponding decision-making significance – does not. Institutionally, the Party's multilevel pervasiveness remains formally embedded within the CCP Constitution, a separate entity from the state Constitution and one that notably asserts clear, broad, and omnipresent authority in all matters of society, including the state. The Party Constitution declares: "The Party exercises overall leadership over all areas of endeavor in every part of the country" (2017, 10). Moreover, "acting on the principle of guiding the overall situation and coordinating the work of all sides", the Party "assume(s) the role of leadership core among all other organizations at the corresponding levels".

Consequently, Party officials serve in parallel capacity with state officials "at the corresponding levels", effectively creating a dual executive system across the governing spectrum with municipalities (like Shanghai) led by both a mayor (the leading government official) and Party Secretary (the top Party official), just as provinces are led by a provincial governor and a provincial Party Secretary. Per the Party Constitution, however, Party leaders outrank their state counterparts at all governance layers and are the *de facto* leaders of a given jurisdiction. Moreover, as national-level Party institutions, the Politburo and Politburo Standing Committee (PBSC) have direct subnational governance links with Politburo seats reserved for the Party Secretaries of China's four provincial-level municipalities (Beijing, Chongqing, Shanghai and Tianjin). This consequential arrangement inherently fuses the national and subnational in a multilevel governance situation with few comparative parallels.

Multilevel governance (MLG) perspectives, which recognize actor heterogeneity and decision-making competencies "shared by actors at different levels rather than monopolized by state executives" (Marks et al. 1996, 346), can enhance the specification of subnational policy stream processes and be especially relevant in distinct institutional contexts. Beyond the Party-state, for instance, medical professionals in a public health context are akin to epistemic communities – both governmental and non-governmental – and well-positioned to play pivotal policy entrepreneur and problem broker roles (Mukherjee and Howlett 2015). Actor input at varying governance levels, including locally, therefore, is pertinent even in China's autocratic system, where a variety of traditionally excluded actors play increasingly important policy process roles (Mertha 2009).

Consequently, we focus here on defining the functional equivalent of one particular policy community actor – the leading small group (LSG) [or leading group, *lingdao xiaozu*] – a Party organ and collective actor with few direct parallels outside China's Party-state system. Leading groups, which meet multilevel governance criteria with respect to task-specific jurisdictions, intersecting memberships, unlimited jurisdictional levels and flexible design (Hooghe and Marks 2003, 236–38), possess vital policy formulation and implementation authority.

As ad hoc entities dating to the Maoist era, LSGs operate at multiple tiers (from national to sub-municipal) with a scope, structure, mandate and membership determined by high-level CCP officials.[3] Distinct from non-Chinese policy subsystem entities, leading groups enable the Party to focus on coordinating and solving specific and often highly specialized problems while maintaining a form of control as LSGs "integrate the interests and opinions of departments through formal institutional and informal political channels" (Tsai and Zhou 2019, 3). Their significance as policy community actors, especially through combining problem broker and policy entrepreneur roles, cannot be underestimated. Indeed, the LSG system serves as "the most important coordination and decision-making mechanism that the CCP uses to integrate the work of various government departments" (Tsai and Zhou 2019, 21).

Given our primary interest in policy window openings, which enable "opportunities for action on given initiatives" (Kingdon 2003, 177), we now turn to the problem stream, where LSG coupling activities are critical for policy formulation and implementation.

Problem Stream Windows and Consequential Coupling

Applying problem stream logic to the subnational level invites opportunities for further policy window and coupling activity hypothesizing. Policy windows in the problem stream (i.e., problem windows) generally open when a policy-maker's re-election is put at risk (Herweg et al. 2018). In autocratic political contexts, problem windows open when leaders become concerned about threats to the ruling party or to regime stability (Herweg et al. 2022). Van den Dool modifies such theorizing to fit national level Chinese policy processes, contending that a problem window opens "if a condition puts the survival of the Communist Party at risk" (2022, 8) . Recognizing Party pervasiveness across multiple governance layers, this problem window hypothesis can also be applied subnationally. Doing so requires modifying the survival risk from the Party as a whole to the survival of the Party leadership authority at the given subnational level jurisdiction. This leads to the following hypothesis:

Problem window hypothesis: A problem window opens if a condition puts the survival of the relevant Communist Party *leader* (e.g., Party Secretary) or *leadership* (e.g., Party Standing Committee) at risk.

In seeking solutions to a given problem, MSF logic anticipates "consequential coupling" (Zahariadis 2003), where problem framing falls to problem brokers who possess persistence, access and credibility as invaluable political resources (Knaggard 2015). During open problem windows, typically noted for their short duration relative to other policy windows (Herweg et al. 2018), successful problem brokers tend "to come either from the people around the autocratic leader or from the bureaucracy and public officials" (Herweg et al. 2022, 210). In the Chinese subnational context and distinct from other policy subsystems, LSGs serve as a problem broker collective. Comprised of high-ranking local officials, technocrats, and (in this case) medical experts, all Party members, LSGs provide "a scientistic and technocratic bias to the framing of problems and solution s" (Du and Baark 2021, 50).

MSF logic posits that policy entrepreneurs are more likely to experience coupling success during an open policy window if "they have more access to core policymakers" (Herweg et al. 2018, 30). Thus, beyond problem broker-ing, LSGs simultaneously operate as political entrepreneurs seeking support for a particular solution, often not a given with policy experimentation. Here, the political entrepreneur label, rather than policy entrepreneur, is appropriate since the latter: (a) operate "outside the formal governmental system" (Roberts and King 1991, 152); and (b) hold an elected leadership position, a feature incompatible with autocratic settings (Herweg et al. 2022).

Given their credibility resulting from the membership's technocratic, sci-entific or medical bona fides as well as their direct access to high-level Party leadership, LSGs exhibit the functional equivalence of combined problem broker and political entrepreneur roles, a feature with at least two implications. First, problem brokers and political entrepreneurs coexist within the same collective entity, not only unable to maintain distinct roles, but also undermining stream independence. Second, given the direct Party leadership linkages, LSG political entrepreneur roles (e.g., assembling a winning coalition) inherently become subordinate to problem brokering. Thus, in the Chinese subnational context, LSGs serve as the predominant subnational coupling agent in framing conditions as problems and in seeking support for a particular solution.

Coupling hypothesis: During open problem windows, the leading group will utilize problem brokering and political entrepreneurship to couple its preferred solution to the problem.

RESEARCH DESIGN

This chapter employs a disciplined configurative case study (George and Bennett 2005), typically enlisted when utilizing an existing theoretical approach (such as MSF) to explain a given case. Rather than seeking to generalize across individual cases, our within-case research design focuses on Shanghai's grid screening policy, a case with intrinsic importance for illustrating policy windows openings and coupling activities.

Consistent with this approach, the chapter uses causal process tracing (CPT) to identify the temporal order of certain causal conditions (or casual process observations) leading to policy windows openings. Noted for its theory development capacities (George and Bennett 2005), CPT not only offers the policy sciences literature "promise of a more robust method for understanding causality from within-case accounts of policy change" (Kay and Baker 2015, 2), but also the practical benefits of improving policy design (Capano and Howlett 2021) and closing the science-policy gap (Wellstead et al. 2018). Temporal sequencing evidence is drawn from several primary and secondary data sources, including LSG press conference transcripts, Party meeting readouts, policy reports, and newspaper articles as well as participant-observation as one chapter co-author (Chen) was immersed with city's daily prevention and control measures throughout the study period as a Shanghai resident.

POLICY WINDOWS, CONSEQUENTIAL COUPLING, AND GRID SCREENING

Shanghai's "Bespoke" Grid Screening Policy in Brief

With a metropolitan area of nearly 26 million residents, Shanghai experienced remarkable success in stemming Covid transmissions, reporting just 400 cases and seven deaths prior to March 2022 (Zhang 2022). Throughout the pandemic's first two years, Shanghai's exemplary contact tracing capacity – particularly its innovative "2+4+24 principle"[4] – was a primary reason citywide testing and lockdowns could be avoided. In effect, contact tracing teams could be mobilized to arrive on site within two hours of detecting an infection, finish tracing key information within four hours, and complete the initial contact tracing report within 24 hours. Such micro-level precision enabled targeting of specific buildings or residential complexes for containment measures.

Yet, when the highly transmissible (though less deadly) Omicron BA.2 subvariant began ravaging several Chinese cities in China's worst Covid outbreak since the pandemic's onset, Shanghai's precision-guided containment measures were suddenly less effective in preventing community transmission. As a key epidemiological marker, community transmission refers to virus spread breaching a population already under quarantine or some form of control. Consequently, local authorities adopted the grid-based screening approach on March 16 to *broaden* local containment efforts, actually making contact tracing, testing, and isolation measures *less* targeted than prior containment efforts, but (critically) still neglecting citywide testing and lockdowns. With grid screening, the entire city was divided into approximately 44,000 grid units, each consisting of multiple buildings, apartment complexes and blocks. Individuals in each grid were given two nucleic acid tests within 48 hours and those with positive results were quarantined in centralized facilities. With contact tracing conducted with case discovery in each grid, specific lockdown measures ranging from an all-of-grid stay-at-home order to merely discouraging travel outside the grid were imposed. Such remedies were then lifted after a certain number of consecutive days with no new within grid cases.

Primarily due to asymptomatic transmissions, the policy failed to contain the virus and within a matter of two weeks local authorities pivoted to yet another novel approach by announcing a two-phase citywide lockdown on March 27. City dwellers on the Huangpu River's eastern side would be locked down for four days (March 28–March 31) followed by a subsequent lockdown (April 1–5) of the river's western bank residents. Even that approach was short-lived as authorities abruptly placed the entire city on lockdown on April 1, a closure that would endure for two months and inflict a costly toll on city residents.

Policy Context: Grid Screening Building Blocks

Two building blocks established prior to Covid's arrival established the technocratic infrastructure for grid screening while providing valuable technical feasibility and value acceptability signals: an urban grid governance system and a local e-government digital infrastructure (Bernot and Cassiano 2022). Though dating to imperial China, urban grid management (later, urban grid governance) was revived in Shanghai in 2004 as a mobilizational tool for dividing cities, towns and villages into subsections (called zones or grids) serving as the "basic supervision and management unit of digital city management" (Mittelstaedt 2022, 3). In a system replicated across China, each grid is served by a grid manager and grid workers, essentially government-paid community organizers (or "residential community organizers") tasked to "both monitor the grass roots while at the same time providing services to them" (Mittelstaedt 2022, 3).

Complementing urban grid governance, Shanghai's e-government infrastructure provided a second pre-Covid cornerstone. Consistent with its quest to become a global digital hub by 2035, the Shanghai Municipal Government opened the Shanghai Big Data Center in 2018 as a municipal data collection and management entity serving to integrate artificial intelligence, industrial internet networks, and 5G technology. Soon after, the city's "One Netcom Office" portal began offering access to various digital government services; accessibility increased further in early 2019 with the release of the *suishenban* ("services available in pocket") mobile app, enabling city residents to conduct more than 1,200 local government services via smart phones (e.g., obtain marriage or driver's licenses, file tax returns).

Recalling a widely recognized adage from China's Three Kingdom's period, military strategist Zhuge Liang famously advised, "Everything is ready except the east wind" when concluding key battle preparations. With the Shanghai Municipal Government's capacity to integrate 185 subsystems in 50 local agencies across the city's 16 districts (Zhu 2021a), local officials were well-prepared for virus containment work when the 'unknown epidemic' emerged in December 2019.

In February 2020 and shortly following the country's initial Covid-19 outbreak in Wuhan, the PBSC established the Central Leading Small Group for Epidemic Response, operated from Beijing and led by the premier, Li Keqiang, the PBSC's second highest ranking member, behind only General Secretary Xi Jinping. The Shanghai LSG, known formally as the Shanghai Epidemic Prevention and Control Leading Group, formed on December 31, 2019, just days before the city's first identified case. Its leader, then-Shanghai Mayor Ying Yong was soon replaced by incoming Mayor Gong Zheng[5] following Ying's elevation to Hubei provincial Party Secretary after the Wuhan outbreak mismanagement led to several Party sackings. Though typically led by a lone individual, Shanghai Party Secretary Li Qiang was later installed as Shanghai LSG co-leader, despite not being an original LSG member. Li's addition increased the group's credibility and added seriousness to its pandemic control work. Other notable Shanghai LSG members included its director, Gu Honghui, the municipal government's Secretary-General, Wu Jinglei, director of the Shanghai Municipal Health Commission and Dr Zhang Wenhong of Fudan University's Huashan Hospital.

Also in February 2020, the Shanghai health QR code, or *suishenma* digital ID, was integrated into the *suishenban* app and made accessible via popular mini-apps in WeChat and Alipay. Using green, yellow and red colors to classify individual risk levels, the health QR code was later integrated with the itinerary code, used to track individual movements via travel and contact history over a 14-day period through integration with cell phone tower connection data provided by three of China's major state-owned telecommunications companies. In May 2020, Chen Jing, deputy secretary-general of the Shanghai Municipal Party Standing Committee and secretary-general of the municipal government, asserted: "*Suishenma* will lead to such a wide range of applications, which is beyond our expectation. This is a model of seeking opportunities in a crisis" (Song 2020).

Then solely a health code, Chen signaled that *suishenma* could be integrated with other municipal services via the One Netcom Office portal. This proved prescient as Shanghaiese could soon use *suishenma* to visit public swimming pools (May), pay for public transport (July), or make hospital appointments (August). By September, the Municipal Health Commission announced that the codes were being used "as proof of personal identification" (Shen 2020) and their ubiquity expanded in depth and breadth over the following months, used more than 3.7 billion times by 54 million people through July 2021 (Yang et al. 2021). The itinerary code (tied to national databases) was integrated with the Shanghai health QR code and nucleic acid testing sites operated by local officials in August 2021 as an important technocratic step forward for ensuring precision-guided responses (Zhu 2021b).

The current interpretation of Zhuge Liang's wisdom ("Everything is in order except what is crucial") provides an apt MSF depiction of solutions awaiting problems. We now turn to how Omicron-related problems came to the attention of policymakers through various problem stream channels.

Problem Window Opening

Immediately prior to its Shanghai arrival, the Omicron wave rapidly spread across Hong Kong, illustrating a combination of key indicators and a dramatic event for Shanghai officials, especially important developments since Hong Kong – like Shanghai – had reported single-digit daily cases since Covid's onset (Stevenson 2022). First, low vaccination rates among Shanghai's elderly population, simultaneously evident in Hong Kong, became a salient problem stream indicator. While Shanghai resident double-dose vaccination rates (as of May 2022) exceeded 90 percent, just 62 percent of the city's approximately 5.8 million people over age 60 were vaccinated (Zhang et al. 2022). Further, though Chinese-made vaccines were somewhat less effective than western ones, just five percent of Shanghai's Covid deaths to this point involved vaccinated individuals (Zhang et al. 2022). Within just two months, Hong Kong recorded over one million Omicron cases and more than 7,000 deaths (Hale et al. 2022).

As problem stream indicators, however, Hong Kong's rising cases and vaccination figures alone fail to convey the outbreak's true impact as its hospitals and health system were quickly overrun. The Hong Kong outbreak ultimately served as "a dramatic turn of events" (Stevenson 2022) since the new infection spike pushed Hong Kong hospital mortuaries past their capacity. By March 11 health authorities there could no longer effectively treat infected patients and corresponding images of "patients on gurneys…parked outside hospitals" and "body bags…piled up in wards" served to "shock many in the mainland" (Qin and Chien 2022).

Hong Kong's worsening fortunes spilled into Shanghai, where the HuaTing hotel was designated as an emergency quarantine center in February for visitors entering from Hong Kong. A positive test result spike emanating from HuaTing began around March 2 with at least 62 hotel-linked cases, development that directly precipitated the Shanghai LSG's first public reference to grid screening. At its March 7 daily Covid press conference, Wu Jinglei acknowledged, "It is necessary to implement grid and refined management, find out the situation of testing personnel" (117th Press Conference).

Our first hypothesis contends that a problem window opens if a condition puts the relevant Communist Party leader or leadership's survival at risk. As a matter of pure coincidence, the Omicron outbreak was hitting Shanghai while Party Secretary Li and Mayor Gong were in Beijing attending the March 4–11 "Two Sessions" meetings, the back-to-back plenary sessions of the National People's Congress (China's Parliament) and the National Committee of the Chinese People's Political Consultative Conference (the government's top advisory body). As China's most important annual political gatherings, such meetings are renowned for revealing national priorities and setting the overall policy direction.

Central government pressure on Shanghai officials to contain the local outbreak at this point was growing increasingly apparent and palpable. At the March 7 press conference, Wu conceded that Li and Gong "gave instructions and…communicated and guided several times a day…" from Beijing. Li convened "an emergency [LSG] meeting" the following day "to demand more aggressive responses" (Yang 2022, 206). Sharing the same conference room with central government leaders, including Xi Jinping, with their city under Omicron's increasing siege could have been an awkward moment for both Li and Gong, particularly with pandemic control elevated as the top local government priority under the zero-Covid policy.

If the priority hadn't been made clear, Xi Jinping personally chaired a March 17 PBSC meeting days after the "Two Sessions" concluded with the entire meeting readout devoted to pandemic control work. The occurrence and content of PBSC meetings are rarely made public and not since May 2020 had official reporting publicized a PBSC meeting devoted entirely to pandemic management. The rare publication of the March 17 meeting is a strong indicator that pandemic control was top of the mind in the Party leadership's agenda amid the rapidly developing Shanghai outbreak. In the meeting readout, Xi Jinping and the other six PBSC members urged local officials to "conduct pandemic prevention and control strictly and practically...to quickly control local cluster outbreaks. " Xi also personally tied China's prior pandemic management successes to the "outstanding advantage of the Party's socialist system" (Xinhua 2022a).

Shortly after returning from the Beijing meetings, Li and Gong received further central government pressure to get the Shanghai outbreak swiftly under control when the State Council sent an inspection team to Shanghai to meet with the pair on March 22. Thus, clear and multiple signals were sent to both Li and Gong to get the Shanghai outbreak under control.

Further enhancing problem window opening likelihood, Li's position as Shanghai Party Secretary has an unmistakable track record of upward mobility through the CCP's highest ranks. With just one exception, every Shanghai Party Secretary since 1987 later reached the PBSC.[6] With the twice per decade National Party Congress meetings scheduled for November, CCP General Secretary Xi was expected to seek a precedent-defying third term and introduce the new slate of Politburo and PBSC members. Given their close association dating to when the two served together nearly two decades earlier in Zhejiang province, Li's handling of the outbreak figured to have repercussions well beyond Shanghai municipal politics (especially noting his roles as Shanghai LSG co-leader, Shanghai Party Secretary, and sitting Politburo member), substantially increasing pressure on him to contain the virus.

Coupling via Problem Brokering and Political Entrepreneurship

Beyond problem window openings, we now briefly illustrate the LSG's coupling activities. For brevity's sake, we focus simply on problem brokering through the use of imagery and political entrepreneurship through repeated rejections of a viable alternative.

With Li and Gong facing political pressure, other Shanghai LSG members used daily press conferences throughout March to frame the problem using various images and analogies. Expert panel member Dr Wu Fan likened grid screening's precision to clearing mines, suggesting "the potential risks are very critical to clearing the social surface" for protecting citizens (Xinhua 2022b). She later used a cancer screening parallel, explaining "If screening is a 'physical examination' for Shanghai, then 'grid' screening is equivalent to precise 'targeted therapy' implemented on the 'lesions' after a doctor reads the CT scan" (Xinhua 2022c).

Other problem brokering efforts focused on timing and precision. Wu Jinglei conceded the city had "entered a critical stage" requiring adherence "to scientific precision and dynamic clearing…with fast control and meticulousness" (Xinhua 2022b). Another time the group cited the virtues of precise testing, noting: "Antigens are like the 'clothes' worn on the outside of the virus, and nucleic acids are the 'genes' inside the virus" (Xinhua 2022d).

Beyond press conferences, LSG expert panel leader Dr Zhang Wenhong often used the social media platform Weibo to convey candid, data-driven communications. On March 7, he urged against taking "a one-size-fits-all approach" while arguing pandemic control entered a "new stage". Two weeks later, "to keep the city and basic economic activities functioning during the outbreak", he argued, "there should be policy adjustments backed by data" (Zhang 2022). As one observer previously acknowledged about Dr Zhang's public communication style, "We don't often see such a technocrat speak to the public in this way in China" (Ni 2021).

Collectively, such problem brokering underscores the MSF notion that how a problem is defined "substantially affects the solutions that can be coupled to it" (Herweg et al. 2018, 22). In contrast, LSG political entrepreneurship was most clearly demonstrated through the continued rejection of an obvious policy alternative: citywide lockdown. With Omicron waves contemporaneously triggering citywide lockdowns in Dongguan (March 14; 7.5 million people locked down), the entire Jilin province (March 14; 24 million) and elsewhere, the Shanghai LSG continually rejected the approach.

A city of 12.5 million people, Shenzhen's experience provides the closest illustrative parallel. After reporting sporadic Omicron cases in early March, Shenzhen authorities announced a seven-day citywide lockdown on March 13, requiring all residents to stay at home and suspending all public transportation and non-essential businesses. Authorities then carried out three rounds of citywide testing to identify and isolate infected individuals. At the end of the lockdown period, Shenzhen officials announced normal life, work, and production order would be restored and the city soon resumed normal operations. The swift lockdown was so effective, some public transportation and restaurants in low-risk areas re-opened with limited capacity even before the lockdown ended.

Demonstrating political entrepreneurship, LSG officials remained insistent throughout March that Shanghai would not lockdown given the economy's importance and faith in their playbook combatting earlier Covid variants, including Delta. On March 15 with 955 new cases reported since March 1, Shanghai LSG director Gu Honghui cited the city's previous precision-guided results when asked whether stricter measures would be implemented, noting,

"Shanghai has always adhered to...precise prevention and control. At present there is no lockdown and there is no need to lockdown now" (Zhang and Bao 2022).

During the March 22 meeting with the State Council inspection team, Li pledged to strengthen community level management and control measures, but still promoted grid screening as a lockdown alternative. As late as March 26, the day before grid screening was overturned, Dr Wu Fan told reporters that municipal authorities cannot shut down Shanghai because doing so would negatively affect the Chinese and global economies. Yet, the citywide lockdown began days later and the April 2 visit by Politburo and Central LSG member Sun Chunlan, read as "a sign of greater direct involvement from Beijing", indicated the closing policy window (Hale et al. 2022).

Ultimately, LSG members who took pride in the fact that earlier precision-guided control measures were held up as admirable containment examples while minimizing economic disruptions had a hard time adjusting their targeted approach when confronted by Omicron. Their refusal – and disdain – for citywide testing and lockdown measures gave birth to grid screening, but the approach ultimately failed to contain the highly transmissible Omicron variant and, crucially, its asymptomatic spread.

CONCLUSION

As this chapter seeks to demonstrate, MSF is well-positioned to conceptualize subnational policymaking, even in China's autocratic system. Since expanding MSF's scope to subnational policymaking requires several conceptual adaptations, the chapter identifies various institutional structures and policy community actors as functional equivalents of MSF elements, essential for establishing causal mechanisms via policy windows and coupling activity.

Examining Shanghai's March 2022 grid screening policy, we focus on the Shanghai leading group's problem brokering and political entrepreneurship as officials engaged in policy experimentation, advocating for precise testing and contact tracing measures while avoiding the stringent lockdowns deployed elsewhere throughout China. While Shanghai's success in utilizing precision-guided control measures repeatedly won praise over the pandemic's first two years, the Omicron variant's emergence posed stern problem stream challenges to the Shanghai LSG, particularly its co-leaders, Party Secretary Li Qiang and Mayor Gong Zheng, suggesting a problem window opening.

This case's empirical features shed insight into the timing and conditions favorable for policy window openings and are consistent with prior subnational MSF scholarship suggesting that "policy windows need to be 'wedged' open at national and local levels" (Exworthy et al. 2002, 93). In recognizing national and subnational linkages, moreover, our results offer somewhat of a counter to the critique that MSF "struggles to account for policy change resulting from governance processes across multiple governance levels" (Rietig 2021, 57).

Although an innovative attempt to avoid disruptive lockdowns, grid screening ultimately failed to contain the fast-evolving Omicron outbreak. Ultimately, the policy likely will be remembered as one of the major policy failures of China's "dynamic zero clearing" (or zero-Covid) strategy. The failure paved the way for the subsequent two-month citywide lockdown that fueled public resentment and accelerated a messy transition toward the 'living with covid' strategy.

NOTES

1. Defined here, functional equivalent is a different entity or structure that performs the same or similar tasks. As a parallel reflecting Kingdon's metaphorical language, functional equivalence remains critical in translation studies where conveying meaning necessities the combination of precise terminology, cultural context and deviation from original textual wording (Nida 2001).
2. As a core Chinese policy style stratagem, "advice derived from theory and abstract models is not to be trusted; instead, new methods of action are derived from pilot efforts and practical experience in concrete settings" (Heilmann and Perry 2011:13). Qian (2018) describes China's policy style and Mei (2020) and Ceccoli (2022) provide a Covid-19 application.
3. Featuring an interlocking nature of appointments and often secretive agendas and memberships (Miller 2017), leading groups are organized around three main actors – group leader (*xiaozu zuzhang*), head of the lead department (*qiantou bumen shouzhang*), and office director (*bangongshi zhuren*).
4. Reflecting local-national policy experimentation, Shanghai's 2+4+24 principle was later incorporated into the National Health Commission's (NHC) official "COVID-19 Prevention and Control Guide." Demonstrating NHC praise, Central LSG member Wu Liangyou, noted "we have learned from the experience of Shanghai and other places in handling the epidemic, and taken effective measures in grasping small problems early and quickly controlling the epidemic" (107th Press Conference).
5. Chinese LSGs underscore the multiplicity of policy milieu actors and roles. For example, Shanghai mayor Gong Zheng wears three distinct Covid policymaking hats: (1) mayor; (2) Deputy Party Secretary of the Municipal Party Standing Committee; and (3) Co-Leader of the Municipal Leading Group for Epidemic Prevention and Control.
6. The group includes Xi Jinping, former president Zhang Zemin, and former premier Zhu Rongji. The sole exception, Chen Liangyu, was later jailed on corruption charges. Ironically, Chen was credited for his "visionary thinking" in establishing Shanghai's urban grid management system in 2004 (CMP Staff 2021).

REFERENCES

Ackrill, Robert, Adrian Kay and Nikolaos Zahariadis. 2013. "Ambiguity, Multiple Streams, and EU Policy." *Journal of European Public Policy* 20 (6): 871–87.

Bernot, Ausma and Marcella Siqueira Cassiano. 2022. "China's COVID-19 Pandemic Response: A First Anniversary Assessment." *Journal of Contingencies and Crisis Management* 30: 10–21.

Capano, Gilibert and Michael Howlett. 2021. "Causal Logics and Mechanisms in Policy Design: How and Why Adopting a Mechanistic Perspective Can Improve Policy Design." *Public Policy and Administration* 36 (2): 141–62.

Ceccoli, Stephen. 2022. "Policy Styles and the Chinese COVID-19 Response." In *Policy Styles and Trust in the Age of Pandemics: Global Threat, National Responses*, eds. Nikolaos Zahariadis, Evangelia Petridou, Theofanis Exadaktylos and Jörgen Sparf, 41–58. London: Routledge.

CMP Staff. 2021. "Grid Based Management." *The China Media Project*. April 16. https://chinamediaproject.org/the_ccp_dictionary/grid-based-management/.

Constitution of the Communist Party of China. 2017. Revised and adopted at the 19th National Congress of the Communist Party of China on October 24, 2017. http://www.xinhuanet.com//english/download/Constitution_of_the_Communist_Party_of_China.pdf.

Du, Coco Dijia and Erik Baark. 2021, "The Emergence of Environmental Policy in China: Multiple Streams and the Shaping of a Technocratic Bias." *China: An International Journal* 19 (4): 32–51.

Exworthy, Mark, Lee Berney, and Martin Powell. 2002. "'How Great Expectations in Westminster May Be Dashed Locally': The Local Implementation of National Policy on Health Inequalities." *Policy & Politics* 30 (1): 79–96.

Exworthy, Mark and Martin Powell. 2004. "Big Windows and Little Windows: Implementation in the 'Congested State'." *Public Administration* 82 (2): 263–81.

George, Alexander and Andrew Bennett. 2005. *Case Studies and Theory Development in the Social Sciences*. Cambridge, MA: MIT Press.

Hale, Thomas, Andy Lin and Primrose Riordan. 2022. "Shanghai Lockdown Tests the Limits of Xi Jinping's Zero-Covid Policy." *Financial Times*. April 3.

Heilmann, Sebastian. 2008. "From Local Experiments to National Policy: The Origins of China's Distinctive Policy Process." *The China Journal* 59: 1–30.

Heilmann, Sebastian and Elizabeth Perry. 2011. "Embracing Uncertainty: Guerrilla Policy Style and Adaptive Governance in China." In *Mao's Invisible Hand: The Political Foundations of Adaptive Governance in China*, eds. S. Heilmann and E. Perry, 1–29. Cambridge, MA: Harvard University Press.

Henstra, Daniel. 2010. "Explaining Local Policy Choices: A Multiple Streams Analysis of Municipal Emergency Management." *Canadian Public Administration* 53 (2): 241–58.

Herweg, Nicole. 2016. "Explaining European Agenda-Setting Using the Multiple Streams Framework: The Case of European Natural Gas Regulation." *Policy Sciences* 49 (1): 13–33.

Herweg, Nicole, Christian Huß and Reimut Zohlnhöfer. 2015. "Straightening the Three Streams: Theorising Extensions of the Multiple Streams Framework." *European Journal of Political Research* 54: 435–49.

Herweg, Nicole, Nikolaos Zahariadis, and Reimut Zohlnhöfer. 2018. "The Multiple Streams Framework: Foundations, Refinements, and Empirical Applications." In

Theories of the Policy Process, 4th edition, eds. Christopher Weible and Paul Sabatier 17–53. New York: Westview.

Herweg, Nicole, Nikolaos Zahariadis and Reimut Zohlnhöfer. 2022. "Travelling Far and Wide? Applying the Multiple Streams Framework to Policy-Making in Autocracies." *Polit Vierteljahresschr* 63: 203–23.

Hooghe, Liesbet and Gary Marks. 2003, "Unraveling the Central State, But How? Types of Multi-Level Governance." *American Political Science Review* 97(2): 233–43.

Howlett, Michael. 2019. "Moving Policy Implementation Theory Forward: A Multiple Streams / Critical Juncture Approach." *Public Policy and Administration* 34 (4): 405–30.

Jones, Michael et al. 2016. "A River Runs Through It: A Multiple Streams Meta-Review." *Policy Studies Journal* 44 (1): 13–36.

Kay, Adrian and Phillip Baker. 2015. "What Can Causal Process Tracing Offer to Policy Studies? A Review of the Literature." *Policy Studies Journal* 43 (1): 1–21.

Kingdon, John. 2003. *Agendas, Alternatives, and Public Policies*. 2nd edition. Longman Classics in Political Science. New York: Longman.

Knaggård, Åsa. 2015. "The Multiple Streams Framework and the Problem Broker." *European Journal of Political Research* 54 (3): 450–65.

Koebele, Elizabeth. 2021. "When Multiple Streams Make a River: Analyzing Collaborative Policymaking Institutions Using the Multiple Streams Framework." *Policy Sciences* 54: 609–28.

Liu, Xinsheng, Eric Lindquist, Arnold Vedlitz, and Kenneth Vincent. 2010. "Understanding Local Policymaking: Policy Elites' Perceptions of Local Agenda Setting and Alternative Policy Selection." *Policy Studies Journal* 38 (1): 69–91.

Marks, Gary, Liesbet Hooghe, and Kermit Blank. 1996. "European Integration from the 1980s: State-centric v. Multi-level Governance." *JCMS: Journal of Common Market Studies* 34 (3): 341–78.

Mei, Ciqi. 2020. "Policy Style, Consistency, and the Effectiveness of the Policy Mix in China's Fight Against COVID-19." *Policy and Society* 39 (3): 309–25.

Mertha, Andrew. 2009. "Fragmented Authoritarianism 2.0: Political Pluralization in the Chinese Policy Process." *The China Quarterly* 200: 995–1012.

Miller, Alice. 2017. "The CCP Central Committee's Leading Small Groups." In *Critical Readings on the Communist Party of China*, eds. K. E. Brodsgaard, 279–303. Leiden: Brill.

Mittelstaedt, Jean Christopher. 2022. "The Grid Management System in Contemporary China: Grass-Roots Governance in Social Surveillance and Service Provision." *China Information* 36 (1): 3–22.

Mukherjee, Ishani and Michael Howlett. 2015. "Who Is a Stream? Epistemic Communities, Instrument Constituencies and Advocacy Coalitions in Public Policy-Making." *Politics and Governance* 3 (2): 65–75.

Ni, Vincent. 2021. "'China's Dr Fauci': How Dr Zhang Wenhong Became the Face of Beijing's Covid Battle." The Guardian. September 13. London: Guardian News & Media Limited.

Nida, Eugene. 2001. *Contexts in Translating*. Amsterdam and Philadelphia: John Benjamins Publishing.

Oborn, Eivor, Michael Barrett, and Mark Exworthy. 2011. "Policy Entrepreneurship in the Development of Public Sector Strategy: The Case of London Health Reform." *Public Administration* 89 (2): 325–44.

Qian, Jiwei. 2018. "Policy Styles in China: How to Control and Motivate Bureaucracy." In *Policy Styles and Policy Making*, eds. Michael Howlett and Jale Tosun, 201–21. New York: Routledge.

Rietig, Katharina. 2021. "Multilevel Reinforcing Dynamics: Global Climate Governance and European Renewable Energy Policy." *Public Administration* 99 (1): 55–71.

Robinson, Scott and Warren Eller. 2010. "Participation in Policy Streams: Testing the Separation of Problems and Solutions in Subnational Policy Systems." *Policy Studies Journal* 38 (2): 199–216.

Shen, Xinmei. 2020. "Shanghai Adds Personal ID to its Covid-19 Health Codes." *South China Morning Post*. September 5. https://www.scmp.com/abacus/tech/article/3100270/shanghai-adds-personal-id-its-covid-19-health-codes-joining-new.

Shephard, Daniel D. et al. 2021. "Kingdon's Multiple Streams Approach in New Political Contexts: Consolidation, Configuration, and New Findings." *Governance* 34 (2): 523–43.

Song, Qibo. 2020. "Suishenma Will Be Associated with Various Convenience Services." *SOHU Morning News* May 26. https://www.sohu.com/a/397658343_120044982.

Stevenson, Alexandra. 2022. "Hong Kong's Overwhelmed Hospitals are Keeping the Dead in Wards with Covid Patients." *New York Times* March 11. https://www.nytimes.com/2022/03/11/world/asia/hong-kong-hospitals-covid.html.

Stone, Clarence. 2015. "Reflections on Regime Politics: From Governing Coalition to Urban Political Order." *Urban Affairs Review* 51 (1): 101–37.

Teets, Jessica and Reza Hasmath. 2020. "The Evolution of Policy Experimentation in China." *Journal of Asian Public Policy* 13 (1): 49–59.

Tsai, Wen-Hsuan, and Wang Zhou. 2019. "Integrated Fragmentation and the Role Of Leading Small Groups in Chinese Politics." *The China Journal* 82 (1): 1–22.

van den Dool, Annemieke. 2022. "The Multiple Streams Framework in a Nondemocracy: The Infeasibility of a National Ban on Live Poultry Sales in China." *Policy Studies Journal*.

van Deth, Jan. 1998. "Equivalence in Comparative Research: Staying in the Middle of the Road." In *Comparative Politics: The Problem of Equivalence*, ed. Jan van Deth, xii-xxvii. Essex: ECPR Press.

Wellstead, Adam, Paul Cairney, and Kathryn Oliver. 2018. "Reducing Ambiguity to Close the Science-Policy Gap." *Policy Design and Practice* 1 (2): 115–25.

Xinhua News Agency. 2022a. "The Standing Committee of the Political Bureau of the CPC Central Committee held a meeting presided over by Xi Jinping." March 17. http://www.gov.cn/xinwen/2022–03/17/content_5679571.htm.

Xinhua News Agency. 2022b. "Shanghai Epidemic Prevention and Control Has Entered a Critical Stage Experts: Grid Screening is to Eliminate 'Mines'." March 20. http://sh.news.cn/2022–03/19/c_1310520970.htm.

Xinhua News Agency. 2022c. "Implementing 'New Play' of Sliced and Gridded Screening." March 25. http://www.news.cn/2022–03/25/c_1128504642.htm.

Xinhua News Agency. 2022d. "Ten Q &A about Zoning and Grid Management in Shanghai Pudong." April 2. http://www.xhby.net/index/202204/t20220402_7488893.shtml.

Yang, Dali. 2022. "China's Zero-COVID Campaign and the Body Politic." *Current History* September.

Zahariadis, Nikolaos. 2003. *Ambiguity and Choice in Public Policy*. Washington, DC: Georgetown University Press.

Zahariadis, Nikolaos. 2016. "Delphic Oracles: Ambiguity, Institutions, and Multiple Streams." *Policy Sciences* 49 (1): 3–12.

Zhang, Phoebe. 2022. "Official Policy Faces Test as Shanghai Outbreak Traced to Quarantine Hotel." *South China Morning Post* March 12.

Zhang, Shufan and Zhiming Bao. 2022. "Shanghai Has More Than 100 New Infections for Three Consecutive Days, and the Government Says It Will Not Lockdown." March 15. *Caixin* https://www.caixin.com/2022–03–15/101856255.html.

Zhang, Xinxin, Wenhong Zhang and Saijuan Chen. 2022. "Shanghai's Life-Saving Efforts Against the Current Omicron Wave of the COVID-19 Pandemic." *The Lancet* May 28. Vol. 399, Issue 10340, 2011–2012.

Zhu, Shenshen. 2021a. "Shanghai Services to Become More Intelligent." *Shine* June 7. https://www.shine.cn/biz/tech/2106070266/.

Zhu, Shenshen. 2021b. "Anti-Epidemic App with Essential Tracking Makes Debut on City Platform." *Shine* August 6. https://www.shine.cn/biz/tech/2108063234/.

Zohlnhöfer, Reimut, Nicole Herweg, and Christian Huß. 2016. "Bringing Formal Political Institutions into the Multiple Streams Framework: An Analytical Proposal for Comparative Policy Analysis." *Journal of Comparative Policy Analysis: Research and Practice* 18 (3): 243–56.

Zohlnhöfer, Reimut, Nicole Herweg, and Nikolaos Zahariadis. 2022. "How to Conduct a Multiple Streams Study." In *Methods of the Policy Process*, eds. Christopher Weible and Samuel Workman, 23–50. New York: Routledge.

15. The Multiple Streams Framework and Multilevel Reinforcing Dynamics: The case of European and international climate policy

Katharina Rietig

INTRODUCTION

How can the Multiple Streams Framework (MSF) (Kingdon 1995) be applied to analyze policymaking at the international level? How can we better understand the linkages and interactions between levels of governance, especially over a longer period of time, and including the international level? This chapter expands upon the MSF as central policy theory with its far-reaching popularity and applicability (Cairney and Jones 2016) while drawing upon key conceptual advances and updates (e.g., Jones et al. 2016, Zohlnhöfer et al. 2015, Zohlnhöfer 2016). The MSF has been widely and dominantly applied at the national level or single governance level context such as the local level or regional levels (e.g., Carter and Childs 2018, Goyal et al. 2021, Heaphy 2022, Ridde 2009, Robinson and Eller 2010, Sanjurjo 2020), or in transnational governance between, e.g., two countries and relevant local levels (Koebele 2021). A recent theoretical advancement in the MSF allows the framework to tackle dynamic interactions between governance levels, especially the national or regional (i.e., European Union/EU) level and the international level in the form of Multilevel Reinforcing Dynamics (MRD) (for a more thorough discussion, see Knaggård and Hildingsson 2023, Rietig 2021a). MRD are interactions between governance levels that, in aggregate form, increase in the level of policy ambition over time.

This expansion to the MSF is useful because in many empirical areas, policies do not emerge from within a national context and remain limited to one jurisdiction. Instead, there is an increasing number of policy fields that seek to address problems that are not of a purely local or national nature but interact with the regional and/or international governance levels. These are also influenced by decisions taken at other governance levels (Bolleyer and

Börzel 2010, Hooghe and Marks 2003, Hooghe 2012). These problems are cross-boundary in nature and either not limited to one jurisdiction or require the cooperation of several countries within global governance institutions for their resolution. Subsequently, political interests and actors are also spread across multiple jurisdictions and governance levels with their interactions not limited to their countries of origin. They also tend to interact regularly, rather than only once, as suggested by game-theoretical or two-level game approaches (Putnam 1988). Policy areas where the original single-level conceptualizations of the MSF may be expanded upon to take into account interactions with other governance levels over time include, for example, biodiversity loss, climate change, development, the environment, human rights, migration, political economy and globalization, security and technology, as well as coordinated approaches towards achieving the Sustainable Development Goals.

These MRD are illustrated through the empirical example of climate policymaking between the 1970s and 2020, tracing key interactions between the regional EU level and the international level in the form of negotiations within the United Nations Framework Convention on Climate Change (UNFCCC). The time frame covers several stages in the international outlook on climate change including: (i) early concern about climate change in Europe in the 1970s; (ii) the inception of the UNFCCC in 1992 as part of the Rio Conventions; (iii) early experimentation in EU Member States with climate policies; (iv) the 1997 Kyoto Protocol of the UNFCCC; (v) the need to implement international commitments in the form of EU climate policy together with increasing leadership ambitions of the EU on the international level (Elgström and Skovgaard 2014, Schreuers and Tiberghien 2007); (vi) the conclusion of the 2015 Paris Agreement by the UNFCCC and its rapid adoption in 2016; and finally (vii) the increasing international ambition led by the EU and Member States towards the adoption of net-zero targets by 2050. The empirical analysis applies the theoretical framework by process-tracing (Rohlfing 2012) the development of climate policy by the European Commission between the 1990s and 2017, as well as MRD with the UNFCCC negotiations between 1997 and 2015. It is based on Rietig (2021a), Rietig (2019) and Rietig (2021b) drawing on over 60 interviews with key policymakers from across policy levels and is supplemented with the analysis of various policy documents.

In the section below, I introduce key aspects of the MSF and how they are linked to MRDs between levels of governance. The MRD extension to the MSF is then illustrated at the case of the evolution of climate policy since the early 1990s in interaction between the national (Member State) level, the regional (EU) level and the international (UNFCCC) level. The chapter concludes with a discussion of the findings and avenues for further research.

THE MULTIPLE STREAMS FRAMEWORK AND MULTILEVEL REINFORCING DYNAMICS

The MSF by John Kingdon (Kingdon 1995, Zahariadis 2007) is based on the assumption that policy change is a chaotic, complex process. It includes a problem stream, policy stream as well as a politics stream, while policy entrepreneurs and policy windows play a central role (for more details and background on the MSF, see Herweg et al. 2018, Jones et al. 2016, Zohlnhöfer et al. 2015 as well as the introduction to the volume).

The MSF's scope can be widened to account for the interdependence among global dynamics influencing the problem, policy and politics streams as well as policy entrepreneurs' ability to couple the streams during a policy window. At the same time, regional (EU)-level problems and policies can also open windows of opportunity for policy change at the international level if they motivate policy entrepreneurs to seek solutions in appropriate global venues such as the United Nations or World Trade Organization. Integrating the international level into the MSF is important as national policy developments are frequently tied to international agreements – they may act as inspiration, proof of concept or implementation. National- or regional-level problems and their related policy solutions can motivate policy entrepreneurs to use windows of opportunity at the international level. This can in turn result in international agreements that need to be implemented at the national and regional levels.

These *multilevel reinforcing dynamics* (Rietig 2021b) form a complex picture and increase ambiguity (Ackrill, Kay and Zahariadis 2013, Copeland and James 2014, Zahariadis 2016), especially when different issues (i.e., policy domains such as environment and energy) are interlinked through feedback mechanisms in the problem stream. For example, renewable energies were developed as alternative energies in the 1970s to improve energy security. Due to their low carbon dioxide emissions, they were re-framed as a policy solution to the climate change problem in the 1990s and 2000s.

Developments in each of the three streams at one level can influence the streams at other policy levels, both during *agenda coupling* and *decision coupling* (Herweg et al. 2015, Rietig 2021b). This enables policy entrepreneurs to attach solutions from one governance level to problems from another governance level, e.g., solutions from the national level to problems from the international level, which in turn further increases complexity and ambiguity (Zahariadis 2016). Subsequently, policy entrepreneurs that are sufficiently skilled and experienced can make use of windows of opportunity across two or more levels of governance by engaging in more than one policy venue. Policy entrepreneurs can thus increase their international reputation and address national-level or international level problems at the same time when they exploit such MRD strategically. Policy ambition can increase or decrease depending on the success of policy entrepreneurs and socio-economic framework conditions that may elevate or reduce an issue's position on the policy-making agenda (Rietig 2021b).

The modified MSF for empirical applications taking into account MRD is visualized in Figure 15.1. The upward arrows symbolize agenda coupling and the downward arrows symbolize decision coupling, while there are also interactions between streams across one or more levels. The next section applies the modified MSF to the development of climate policy in the European Union and international climate governance through the UNFCCC to illustrate the theoretical contribution of the concept of MRD.

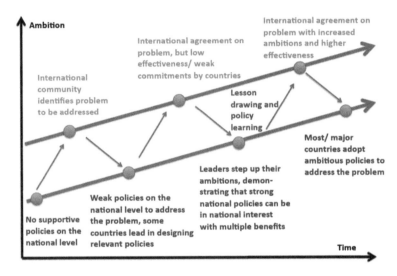

Figure 15.1   Multilevel reinforcing dynamics across time and policy levels. Based on Rietig 2021b, p. 61

EUROPEAN CLIMATE POLICY AND MULTILEVEL REINFORCING PROCESSES WITH THE UNFCCC (1970–2020)

Context

European climate policy is based on a number of key directives and has evolved in its level of ambition since the early 2000s. Central policy elements are the 2001 Renewable Electricity Directive (EU 2001), the 2003 Biofuel

Directive (EU 2003a), the 2003 EU Emission Trading Scheme including subsequent revisions (EU 2003b) and the Climate Package consisting of the "20–20–20" targets to be achieved by 2020 (EC 2008). These include a greenhouse gas emission reduction by 20 percent from the 1990 baseline, improving energy efficiency by 20 percent, and achieving a 20 percent share of renewable energies based on the 2009 Renewable Energy Directive (EU 2009). The 2001/2003 Directives were prepared as an implementation of the 1997 Kyoto Protocol, while the comprehensive 2009 Climate Package served as implementation as well as a way to demonstrate Europe's leadership in preparation of hosting the 2009 UNFCCC COP15 Summit in Copenhagen that was earmarked to conclude a post-2012/post Kyoto Protocol Agreement. While COP15 did not deliver a comprehensive climate agreement, it served as a departure point for the negotiation of the 2015 Paris Agreement (Rietig 2019). In the meantime, the EU developed its 2050 Roadmap and greenhouse gas emission reduction targets, aiming for a 80–95 percent reduction by 2050 and interim targets for 2030, which were revised in 2019/20 towards net-zero by 2050 and 50 percent greenhouse gas emission reductions by 2030 (EC 2019).

1970s-early 1990s: Early National-Level Policy Experimentation and International-Level Agenda Coupling

Climate governance at the international level dates to the 1972 UN Rio Earth Summit, which drew global attention to the deterioration of the environment and the necessity for international collaboration to solve environmental concerns of a cross-border nature (Jänicke and Quitzow 2017). This marks early agenda coupling for European Economic Community (EEC)-level environmental policies and the national level of EEC Member States. In the 1970s and 1980s, the amount of scientific evidence documenting the effects of greenhouse gas emissions on climatic change increased and entered the international problem stream. This coincided with the 1973/74 OPEC oil and 1979 energy crises that made clear to policy makers that it was important to improve energy security through alternative energy sources – other than fossil fuels. Countries such as the UK, Germany, Denmark, and Austria began to experiment with policies supporting alternative energies including wind, solar and biomass.

Early EU-level climate policies originate in these 1970s/80s alternative energy policies of Member States that were primarily focused on improving energy security. Only later, when climate change entered the international agenda, were they re-framed as climate policies with the objective to reduce greenhouse gas emissions based on the assumed synergies for achieving both policy objectives. Following the announcement of first targets to reduce greenhouse gas emissions by European countries, a phase of experimentation that included carbon taxes and feed-in tariffs followed (Schreurs and Tiberghien 2007, Jänicke and Quitzow 2017, Rietig 2021b). This decision coupling at the national level supported agenda coupling on the EEC level in support of the 1991/92 Carbon Tax proposal. Despite the failure of the Carbon Tax proposal in the face of industry opposition and a lack of sufficient EEC Member State support, these early policy ambitions allowed the EEC to play a central role in the Rio Earth Summit in 1992, of which one central output was the establishment of the UNFCCC (Jordan et al. 2012, Rietig 2021b).

Mid-1990s: Agenda Coupling in the National and Local-Level Politics Streams

Additional impetus to raise national-/EEC-/international policy ambition emerged from the local level in the 1990s. Throughout Europe, a large number of cities and local communities enhanced public transportation and installed biomass, solar/PV and wind turbines. This facilitated agenda and decision coupling. The Directorate General for Energy of the European Commission (DG Energy) also encouraged the uptake of renewable energies at the sub-national level, which became the origin for the converging policy communities in the EU-level policy stream. This was primarily motivated by the need to implement UNFCCC commitments and marks a preparatory step for agenda coupling in the EU-level politics stream. The purpose was to influence the national mood and political acceptability of renewables as the favored policy solution (Rietig 2021a). The UNFCCC provided an avenue to involve cities and local communities as key partners for implementation through the inclusion of an article that encouraged civil society participation. To deliver on the UNFCCC civil participation article, DG Energy engaged with mayors across Europe from the early 1990s onwards and set up several networks promoting renewable energies and energy efficiency (Hildingsson et al. 2012). Prominent members of these networks include, among others, the Greater London Energy Efficiency Network, the global network ICLEI (Local Governments for Sustainability) and the Covenant of Mayors. DG Energy also helped to set up programs raising awareness among citizens, companies and Member States and promoting the uptake of renewable energies (e.g., European Community program ALTENER) and energy efficiency improvements. Overall, DG Energy activities facilitated decision coupling at the local level and enabled subsequent agenda coupling at the EU level (Rietig 2021b).

Late 1990s/early 2000s: Agenda Coupling on the International Level, and in the European-Level Problem and Policy Streams

European-level climate policy and renewable energy policy in the early 2000s emerged as an opportunity to address a number of increasingly pressing, yet not directly related policy problems across Europe and results from over 30 years of policy development and experimentation at the national and local levels. There was a growing need to find solutions to the policy problems of energy security with regards to political instability in the Middle East and unreliable natural gas and oil supply from Russia, addressing climate change, furthering the integration of the energy market in an enlarged EU and strengthening economic development in rural areas (Rietig 2021b). The European Commission developed the capacity to address the policy problem of energy security following the external motivation of the 1970s oil shocks and the resulting desire to increase energy independence from countries outside Europe. It set up a policy unit dedicated to developing policies in support of 'alternative energies' (later renamed to renewable energies) and increased funding for research and development. Yet, the indicators for the uptake of renewables such as biofuels/biomass, solar/PV, hydropower, geothermal heat, and onshore/offshore windfarms (Haggett and Toke 2006) remained low across most Member States.

Through the policy entrepreneur Vice President Al Gore, the US assumed a leadership role in negotiating the 1997 UNFCCC Kyoto Protocol, a central international treaty requiring specified emission reductions from industrialized "Annex-1" countries. The Kyoto Protocol entered into force in 2005 and expired in 2012. Following the US' withdrawal from the Kyoto Protocol under the Bush Administration, Europe increasingly assumed a leadership role in international climate policy (Schreurs and Tiberghien 2007, Wurzel and Connelly 2011). This increased the pressure to deliver on the international commitments.

Agenda coupling in the policy stream at the international level, especially the need to implement the Kyoto Protocol targets of reducing greenhouse gas emissions by 8 percent (as compared to 1990) across the European Community by 2005, was a central motivating factor for agenda-coupling at the European level to save face and deliver on these commitments. The leadership ambitions resulted in a consultative process with stakeholders across the national and local levels that fed into the 2000 European Climate Change Programme (EC 2000) proposed by the European Commission (Schreuers and Tiberghien 2007). This underpinned subsequent agenda coupling at the European Council Summit of EU Member States in Gothenburg (June 2001) requesting the European Commission to prepare policy measures facilitating the implementation of the Kyoto Protocol.

2000s: Agenda Coupling in the Problem and Politics Streams at the European Level, and in the Politics Stream at the International Level

EU Member States increasingly developed ambitious climate and renewable energy policies to both comply with internal burden sharing agreements and to implement the Kyoto Protocol as a consequence of various reinforcing dynamics across the policy and politics streams at the national level. Examples include the German feed-in tariff to support the uptake of renewable energies (Jordan et al. 2012) and the 2003 UK Emission Trading Scheme (EU 2003b). This national-level implementation underpinned by burden sharing with higher commitments by, e.g., Germany, Sweden and the UK, encouraged and facilitated decision coupling on the European level.

The European Commission engaged in a number of outreach activities at the local level. Together with the pressure to implement the Kyoto Protocol commitments, this facilitated the opening of a policy window resulting in the 2001 Renewable Electricity Directive (EU 2001). It was also made feasible by personnel turnover in the form of a new European Commissioner for Energy and Transport, including a new cabinet. These new individuals subsequently introduced new beliefs into the politics stream and created a shared optimism that the right time had come to make progress on European climate policies (Rietig 2021a).

The resulting 2001 Renewable Electricity (EU 2001) and 2003 Biofuels (EU 2003a) Directives provided the basis for developing the 2009 Renewable Energy Directive (EU 2009) from 2005 onwards. In compliance with its institutional mandate, the Renewable Energy Unit of the European Commission raised the profile of heating and cooling in renewable energies. This coincided with the window of opportunity to place climate mitigation-related decisions on the European Council's agenda. The subsequent 2005 European Council called for policies to address climate change through targets to reduce greenhouse gas emissions (Council 2005, Rietig 2021a). Policy entrepreneurs in the European Commission were subsequently acting strategically to create the political mandate for the pre-determined policy solution of increasing the share of renewable electricity and to prepare the groundwork for strengthening renewable energy policy in a feedback-supported round of policy reforms later on (Rietig 2021a, Rietig 2021b). A resolution was passed by the European Parliament that requested the European Commission to offer a proposal for legislation by July 31, 2006 detailing measures on renewable energies for heating and cooling (European Parliament 2006). The European Commission subsequently developed the Renewable Energy Road Map (EC 2007) which included key targets that were adopted by the European Council in March 2007 (Council 2007). The European Commission communicated the policy proposal and discussed it with the policy communities in the Member States, the European Parliament, and related stakeholders. There was high value acceptability, as renewable energies were considered useful in addressing different policy problems simultaneously. As little details on how to achieve the target had been discussed in favor of emphasizing the overall desirability of the policy, technical feasibility and resource adequacy were widely accepted following the publication of the Renewable Energy Roadmap Impact Assessment by the Commission.

This support within the European Institutions coincided with overall strong cross-party support for renewable energies and climate policies across national-level politics streams between 2004 and 2007, which further facilitated decision coupling at the European level. Public concern on climate change increased, together with environmental NGOs' lobbying activities in support of climate action, thus creating a balance of interests that met with the political objectives of key governments. Across the EU, there was a consensus among key actors, including political parties, in support of climate action (Carter and Jacobs 2014).

The favorable public mood was influenced by a window of opportunity at the international level, especially through the politics stream. A significant event was the release of the 4th Assessment Report by the Intergovernmental Panel on Climate Change (IPCC), which contained alarming scientific findings (IPCC 2007), and was accompanied by strong communication of the impacts of climate change through the media. Al Gore's documentary movie "An Inconvenient Truth" (Guggenheim 2006) also made an important contribution to raising public awareness about climate change through its accessible and emotional presentation of the emerging climate crisis. This facilitated an increased willingness also among policymakers to address climate change, both out of a personal sense of urgency and in reflection of strong public concern.

The 2007 European Council conclusions on targets to reduce emissions by 20 percent (from 1990), increase the share of renewable energies to 20 percent and improve energy efficiency by 20 percent, all by 2020, were strongly supported by the UK, Germany and France (Council 2007, Council 2008). The politics stream at the European level was softened by the reframing of renewable energies as serving multiple purposes, catering to the majority of party interests and offering solutions for a variety of policy problems, including addressing climate change as a primary focus (Hildingsson, Stripple, and Jordan 2010), while also supporting energy security and rural economic development.

DECISION COUPLING IN THE POLICY STREAM AT THE EUROPEAN LEVEL

A window of opportunity and strong policy entrepreneurial drive from a number of national-level actors and European-level actors allowed the 2008 Climate Package, including the Renewable Energy Directive, to pass unusually quickly in the European Parliament and Council. This decision coupling on the European level was made possible by a number of factors. Renewable energy policy was re-framed as climate policy in the policy stream, which fit with the overall pressure in the politics stream from the international level to develop an ambitious European climate policy ahead of the global summit of the UNFCCC hosted in Copenhagen, as well as an overall conducive public mood in favor of climate action in the politics stream.

The UNFCCC climate summit in Copenhagen in December 2009 was a major focusing event and opportunity for decision coupling on the European level, thus opening up a policy window for actors at the European Commission. The objective to be achieved at the 15th Conference of the Parties of the UNFCCC (COP15) was to agree on a comprehensive post-Kyoto climate agreement to replace the Kyoto Protocol, which was expiring in 2012. The European Commission identified COP15 as a major chance for the EU to adopt a leadership role on the global level (Elgström and Skovgaard 2014, Rietig 2021b). This resulted in a shared objective by the President of the European Commission and other key leaders to have an agreed European position in Copenhagen based on an adopted ambitious European Climate Package.

There was also an added sense of urgency for the policymakers as this window of opportunity was beginning to close in reaction to the growing financial crisis of 2008 and the resulting widespread economic crisis. Policy entrepreneurs who pushed for the climate package were not only within the European Commission, but also part of the German and French presidencies. Both understood the urgency of the issue, wanted to demonstrate leadership, and leave a legacy of advancing climate policy at the European and subsequently the national levels (Rietig 2021a).

DECISION COUPLING IN THE POLITICS STREAM AT THE INTERNATIONAL LEVEL

These multilevel reinforcing dynamics continued beyond the Copenhagen summit to the 2015 Paris Agreement on climate change. One central interim step was the European Commissions' 2050 Roadmap (EC 2011), which set out the long-term objective to reduce emissions by 80–95 percent by 2050 compared to 1990 greenhouse gas emission levels. Mutual exchange of experiences with national climate policies increasingly took place at the "margins" of the UNFCCC negotiations where government representatives engaged with each other and nongovernmental actors in stakeholder dialogues between 2011 and 2014. Both developed and developing countries increasingly set up climate change policies on a voluntary basis (Nachmany et al. 2014). The EU moved into a mediator role (Elgström and Skovgaard 2014) to facilitate information exchange at national-level climate change policies via activities conducted at the international level. The focus was on diffusing experiences at the national- and EU-level climate and energy policies via policy-network members, which included representatives of governments from across the world, EU Member States, European Commission officials (mostly from DG Environment/Climate Action), academics, NGOs, cities and regional governments. At the 2011 UNFCCC negotiations in Durban, South Africa, the European Commissioner for Climate Action convinced the Indian Prime Minister in the final hours of the negotiations to agree to a follow-up agreement to the Kyoto Protocol that would also include commitments from developing countries to address climate change, entering into force by 2020 (Rajamani 2012). This opened up the space for the EU to agree on a second commitment period for the Kyoto Protocol for 2013–19 to avoid an expiration of the Kyoto Protocol without a replacement. This constitutes a central moment of decision coupling in the international-level politics stream that enabled broad political momentum and subsequently progress on what was later referred to as the "Road to Paris". This public commitment at the international level provided the necessary political pressure for European governments to adopt a similar emission reduction trajectory. At the international level, DG Climate Action continued to act as policy entrepreneur by pursuing strategies at the intersection of mediation and leadership. The international level negotiations resulted in the Durban Platform on Enhanced Action, which in turn allowed for the 2014–15 Lima-Paris Action Agenda, the High Ambition Coalition between the EU and developing countries, and ultimately the Paris Agreement (Christoff 2016).

DECISION COUPLING AT THE EUROPEAN LEVEL

Following the success of negotiating the Paris Agreement, the treaty was adopted quickly by the necessary majority and entered into force in 2016. This again increased the pressure on the EU and member states to implement the ambitious target to keep global temperature increases well below two degrees Celsius. The change from the European Commission under President Barroso to the European Commission led by Jean Claude Juncker in 2014–15 came with a comprehensive reform that introduced powerful vice-presidents, who acted as a filter for initiatives by lower-level policy entrepreneurs. The Juncker

Commission's focus was on addressing the multiple crises of the EU including the Euro Crisis and the Migration Crisis, which resulted in a downgrading of climate action ambitions from the agenda (Rietig and Dupont 2021). As a result, 2030 targets remained behind ambitions and were partly voluntary such as the 30 percent renewable energy target (Bürgin 2015, Čavoški 2015). By 2019, the climate crisis re-gained higher priority on the EU policymaking agenda. This was a result of exacerbating climate change impacts such as devastating floods and fires, as well as the political pressure of the *Fridays for Future* and other climate-related movements across Europe and the world, which reflected a major concern about climate change in the public mood. Ursula von der Leyen took over as President of the European Commission in 2019 and, together with the lead candidate from the social democratic parties in the European Parliament, Frans Timmermans, declared climate action a major priority of the European Commission and thus policymaking at the European level (Rietig 2021c).

At the same time, an increasing number of countries discussed and adopted more ambitious climate targets. As host of the 2020 Glasgow UNFCCC summit, which was considered a major stock-taking milestone summit five years after the Paris Agreement, the UK was one of the first countries to declare an objective of achieving carbon neutrality by 2050. This was a step up from the 80–95 percent greenhouse gas emission target and was reframed as net-zero to allow for carbon sinks such as forests to compensate remaining carbon emissions from e.g., agriculture or transport. The EU quickly followed in adopting a 2050 net-zero target and a 50 percent greenhouse gas emission reduction target by 2050 as part of a revised roadmap and the subsequent European Green Deal, Europe's man-on-the-moon-moment (Rietig, 2021c) that was characterized by a major collective effort to decouple economic prosperity from carbon emissions. This resulted in decision coupling in a large number of countries to implement the ambitious net-zero targets.

DISCUSSION

This chapter focused on illustrating the multilevel reinforcing dynamics between the European and international level through the lens of the MSF, while also taking into account the national and local levels. It served as illustrative case for modifying the MSF to include multilevel reinforcing dynamics between different governance levels and in particular the international level, which allows for a higher precision in policy fields where policymaking at one level is influenced by other governance levels.

The climate change case illustrated how ambition can increase over time, especially if taken in the aggregate, i.e., the ambition at the international level is higher than that of only one region (the EU), and the ambition on the

European level is higher than any individual country. Between the 1970s and 1990s, countries such as Germany, Sweden and the UK took on a leading role in experimenting with initial climate policies that at the time were predominantly framed as policies supporting the development and deployment of "alternative energies". These renewable energies supported energy independence following oil crises. As the issue of climate change emerged and entered policy agendas in the 1980s and 1990s, renewable energies and energy efficiency were re-framed as climate policies as they offered the co-benefit of reducing greenhouse gas emissions from fossil fuels. This agenda coupling at the national level facilitated agenda coupling at the European level in the form of early policy initiatives such as the (failed) 1992 carbon tax and developing EEC/EU internal burden sharing agreements for emission reductions in the lead up to the 1997 Kyoto Protocol negotiations and the increasing ambition for taking on an international leadership role on the issue of climate change. This facilitated agenda coupling at the international level in the form of adopting the Kyoto Protocol with its binding greenhouse gas emission reduction commitments for developed countries.

Following the adoption of the Kyoto Protocol, the European Commission faced increasing internal and external pressure to implement the international commitments, which resulted in decision coupling at the European level and thus key policies. Also faced with the prospect of an expiring Kyoto Protocol in 2012, the EU was motivated to continue with its leadership role and consider more ambitious emission reduction targets especially in the run-up to the Copenhagen climate change summit in 2009. This facilitated decision coupling at the European level for one of the globally most ambitious climate policy packages at the time. It included the objective to reduce greenhouse gas emissions by 20 percent by 2020 especially through the European Emission Trading Scheme (EU 2003b) and its revisions, increasing the share of renewable energies to 20 percent across the EU through the Renewable Energy Directive (EU 2009a), and to improve energy efficiency by 20 percent. This was made possible by policy entrepreneurs across the EU and national levels making use of policy windows that presented themselves especially through the influence of the international level and their perception of a supportive public mood (Carter and Jacobs 2014). This in turn necessitated decision coupling at the national level to implement the European level directives within burden sharing agreements, i.e., allowing some countries to maintain or even increase their emissions while other countries took on more ambitious targets of up to 40 percent emission reductions within the overall 20 percent target. This was facilitated by experimentation at the level of cities, communities and local authorities. There were also some direct interactions among the local, and European and international levels in the form of networks such as the Covenant of Mayors and ICLEI. This local and national level experimentation demonstrated the feasibility of technologies and encouraged a scaling up of policies.

Although a post-Kyoto Agreement did not emerge at COP15 in Copenhagen 2009, the Copenhagen Accords and the perceived failure of COP15 allowed for Europe to suggest and agree to a second commitment period of the Kyoto Protocol from 2012 to 2019 to gain time for the negotiation of a more ambitious agreement in the meantime. The European Commission enabled agenda coupling through the publication of its 2050 roadmap (EC 2011) providing a longer-term vision of reducing emissions by 80–95 percent by 2050 with subsequent indicative interim targets for 2030 and related carbon budgets. Difficult EU-internal negotiations in the face of the Euro crisis nevertheless resulted in 2030 targets through the 2030 EU Energy & Climate Framework with a revision to improve the effectiveness of the European Emission Trading Scheme, increased energy efficiency and voluntary renewable energy targets of 30 percent (Bürgin 2015).

This agenda coupling at the EU level towards more ambitious medium- and longer-term targets contributed to decision coupling at the international level at the UNFCCC negotiations in Lima/Peru 2014 and especially Paris 2015. Europe was able to deliver on its leadership and mediator ambitions (Elgström and Skovgaard 2014) especially through the French presidency's central role in achieving a common landing zone (Rietig 2019) for the Paris Agreement. This was also facilitated by a number of other factors such as civil society and public pressure (Jacobs 2016) culminating in a window of opportunity.

The ambition of the Paris Agreement to limit global temperature increases to below two degrees Celsius necessitated a review of the initial 2030 and 2050 targets. Following a period of closed policy windows given Europe's pre-occupation with internal crises such as the Euro crisis, the migration crisis and Brexit, the European Commission under the new leadership of European Commission President Von der Leyen reacted to changes in the public mood demanding more ambitious climate action and implementation (Rietig 2021c). This opened a new policy window allowing for decision coupling to revise the 2050 target towards net-zero ambitions, and subsequent 50 percent greenhouse gas emission reductions by 2030, in the form of the European Green Deal. Together with the UK's early adoption of a net-zero target, the EU was thus able to maintain an early-mover role. The majority of key greenhouse gas emitting countries followed with similar net-zero targets by 2050 especially in the run-up to the 2020 (delayed to 2021 due to Covid) Glasgow summit of the UNFCCC with the primary objective of raising global climate action ambitions. Table 15.1 summarizes the key factors within each MSF stream/policy window and Figure 15.2 illustrates these multilevel reinforcing dynamics with a focus on the European and International level between the 1990s and 2010s

Table 15.1   Key factors within each MSF stream/policy window

	Problem stream	Policy stream	Politics stream	Policy window
EU level	Need to address climate change and energy security	Climate action and renewable energies: per cent target; type of policy instrument, e.g., feed-in tariff	Public mood supporting action on climate change, no objection to renewables (local level networks)	Favorable economic and security situation in early/mid-2000s, no crowding out of energy/climate politics, policy window closing in 2009, larger climate package helped to push RED through;
Multilevel reinforcing dynamics on the global level	Need to implement Kyoto Protocol and maintain leadership in UNFCCC, avoid loss of face	EU 20–20–20 by 2020 Climate Package: good fit of 20% renewables target, bargaining space for 30% target	Strong public demand for action on climate change, influence of global policy entrepreneurs	Coincided with 'deadline' negotiations of 2009 (UNFCCC Copenhagen Climate Change Summit); Further pressure to maintain leadership and mediator role for Paris Summit 2015 and need to implement Paris Agreement while increasing ambitions towards net-zero by 2050 in the run-up to the UNFCCC Glasgow summit in 2020/21.

(for a more detailed version spanning the 1970s to 2020s as well as including the local and national levels, see Rietig 2021b, 68).

The case of energy and climate policy multilevel reinforcing dynamics between the regional EU level and the international level (and taking into account MRD from the local and national level) illustrated how the MSF can be expanded to reflect complex multilevel governance interactions. As the richness of empirical research on the MSF, also evidenced in this book (see also Jones et al. 2016) has demonstrated, there are policy fields and cases where the key MSF elements of streams, policy windows and policy entrepreneurs do not all occur on the same governance level. Especially when analyzing policy change over a longer time frame and beyond a single case/ instance of agenda setting and/or decision-making, it is increasingly likely that dynamics from other governance levels are influential. This means that cases can rarely be analyzed in isolation within one governance level alone without sacrificing accuracy and possibly missing important explanations for specific aspects of policy change.

However, the more governance levels are taken into account and the longer the timeframe of analysis, the more complex MRDs get. This requires careful

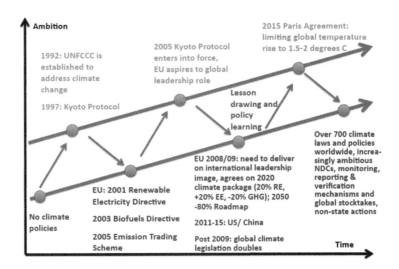

Figure 15.2   Multilevel reinforcing dynamics in climate action between the regional/EU and international levels between the 1990s and 2010s. Based on/for more details, see Rietig (2021b, 68)

methodological planning and analysis, in most cases within a process-tracing approach that allows to identify the key instances of agenda and decision coupling within governance levels, as well as how policy, politics and problem streams, policy entrepreneurs and open/closed policy windows on one level influenced other MSF elements on the other governance levels. Especially when taking into account the international level, there is no single regional and national level, but possibly a handful of regional levels and possibly hundreds of national and local levels (i.e., >190 countries and the corresponding number of local levels within each country). This high level of complexity requires careful research decisions on how parsimony can be maximized by, e.g., explicitly focusing on the most relevant local/national/regional levels and clearly specifying the research question to allow for a targeted analysis.

CONCLUSION

This chapter illustrated how multilevel reinforcing dynamics can increase the precision of the MSF in a policy context where policies are not limited to decision-making at one governance level. This is the case for climate policy, but also a number of other policy fields where national and/or regional levels interact with the international level and either need to implement decisions they contributed to on the international level, or want to influence other countries' policies to address major global, cross-boundary challenges that impact countries through interdependencies either in the economic, social, security or environmental arenas.

The empirical findings suggest that multilevel reinforcing dynamics from the international level need to be considered in such policy areas to increase the precision of the MSF and to better understand the underpinning reasons why windows of opportunity open, and why they stay open for as long as they do. In many cases, a central explanatory factor can be based on agenda and/or decision coupling in streams that occur on other governance levels. Avenues for further research point towards applying the MRD extension to the MSF to other policy areas than climate change and to other geographical areas beyond Europe.

REFERENCES

Ackrill, R., A. Kay and N. Zahariadis. 2013. "Ambiguity, multiple streams, and EU policy." *Journal of European Public Policy* 20 (6): 871–87.

Bolleyer, N. and T. Börzel. 2010. "Non-hierarchical policy coordination in multilevel systems." *European Political Science Review* 2 (2) 157–85.

Bürgin, A. 2015. "National binding renewable energy targets for 2020, but not for 2030 anymore: why the European Commission developed from a supporter to a brakeman." *Journal of European Public Policy* 22 (5): 690–707.

Cairney, P. and M. Jones. 2016. "Kingdon's Multiple Streams Approach: What Is the Empirical Impact of this Universal Theory?" *Policy Studies Journal* 44 (1): 37–58.

Carter, N. and M. Childs. 2018. "Friends of the Earth as a policy entrepreneur: 'The Big Ask' campaign for a UK Climate Change Act." *Environmental Politics* 27 (6): 994–1013.

Carter, N. and M. Jacobs. 2014. "Explaining Radical Policy Change: the Case of Climate Change and Energy Policy Under the British Labour Government 2006-10." *Public Administration* 92 (1) 125–41.

Čavoški, A. 2015. "A post-austerity European Commission: No role for environmental policy?" *Environmental Politics* 24 (3): 501–05.

Christoff, P. 2016. "The promissory note: COP 21 and the Paris Climate Agreement." *Environmental Politics* 25 (5): 765–87.

Copeland, P. and S. James. 2014. "Policy windows, ambiguity and Commission entrepreneurship: explaining the relaunch of the European Union's economic reform agenda." *Journal of European Public Policy* 21 (1): 1–19.

Council. 2005. "Presidency Conclusions", 7619/05 CONCL 1. 23.3.2005. *Journal of the European Communities*, Brussels.

Council. 2007. "March Council Conclusions Requesting Proposals for 20-20-20 Climate Strategy", 7224/1/07. REV 1, CONCL 1. 8/9.3.2007. *Journal of the European Communities*, Brussels.

Council. 2008. "20-20 by 2020. Europe's Climate Change Opportunity", COM(2008) 30 final. *Journal of the European Communities*, Brussels.

Elgström, O. and J. Skovgaard. 2014. "Previewing Paris 2015: The EU's 'Leadiator' Role in Future Climate Change Negotiations. " Georgetown Journal of International Affairs Online, December 16, 2014.

European Commission (EC). 2000. Towards a European Climate Change Programme (ECCP). Brussels: European Commission. COM(2000)88. 8.3.2000, Brussels.

EC. 2007. "Renewable Energy Road Map, Renewable Energies in the 21st century: Building a more Sustainable Future", COM(2006) 848 final. 10.01.2007. Brussels.

EC. 2008. "20-20 by 2020. Europe's Climate Change Opportunity", COM(2008) 30 final. Brussels.

EC. 2011. "Energy Roadmap 2050", COM(2011) 885 final. 15.12.2011. Brussels.

EC. 2019. "The European Green Deal", COM(2019) 640. Brussels.

European Parliament. 2006. "European Parliament Resolution with Recommendations to the Commission on Heating and Cooling from Renewable Sources of Energy", 2005/2122(INI). 14.02.2006. *Journal of the European Communities*, Brussels.

EU. 2001. "Renewable Electricity Directive", Directive 2001/77/EC. L283. *Journal of the European Communities*, Brussels.

EU. 2003a. "Biofuels Directive", Directive 2003/30/EC. L123/43. *Journal of the European Communities*, Brussels.

EU. 2003b. "European Emission Trading Scheme", Directive 2003/87/EC OJ L 275. *Journal of the European Communities*, Brussels.

EU. 2009. "Renewable Energy Directive", 2009/28/EC. L140/16. *Journal of the European Communities*, Brussels.

Goyal, N., M. Howlett, and A. Taeihagh. 2021. "Why and how does the regulation of emerging technologies occur? Explaining the adoption of the EU General Data Protection Regulation using the multiple streams framework." *Regulation & Governance* 15 (4): 1020–34.

Guggenheim, Davis. 2006. *An Inconvenient Truth*. United States. http://www.imdb.com/title/tt0497116/.

Haggett, C. and D. Toke. 2006. "Crossing the Great Divide – Using Multi-Method Analysis to Understand Opposition to Windfarms." *Public Administration* 84 (1): 103–20.

Heaphy, J. 2022. "British counterterrorism, the international prohibition of torture, and the multiple streams framework." *Policy and Politics* 50 (2): 225–41.

Herweg, N., C. Huß and R. Zohlnhöfer. 2015. "Straightening the Three Streams: Theorising Extensions of the Multiple Streams Framework." *European Journal of Political Research* 54 (3): 435–49.

Herweg, Nicole, Nikolaos Zahariadis, and Reimut Zohlnhöfer. 2018. "The Multiple Streams Framework: Foundations, Refinements, and Empirical Application." In *Theories of the Policy Process*, eds. Christopher M. Weible and Paul A. Sabatier, 17–54. Boulder, CO: Westview Press.

Hildingsson, R., J. Stripple and A. Jordan. 2012. "Governing Renewable Energy in the EU: Confronting a Governance Dilemma." *European Political Science* 11 (1): 18–30.

Hooghe, L. 2012. "Images of Europe: How Commission Officials Conceive Their Institution's Role." *JCMS: Journal of Common Market Studies* 50 (1) 87–111.

Hooghe, L. and G. Marks. 2003. "Unravelling the Central State, but How? Types of Multi-level Governance." *American Political Science Review* 97 (2): 233–43.

IPCC. 2007. *Climate Change 2007: Synthesis Report*. Geneva.

Jacobs, M. 2016. "High Pressure for Low Emissions: How Civil Society Created the Paris Climate Agreement." *Juncture* 22 (4): 314–23.

Jänicke, M. and R. Quitzow. 2017. "Multi-level Reinforcement in European Climate and Energy Governance: Mobilizing economic interests at the sub-national levels." *Environmental Policy and Governance*, 27 (2): 122–36.

Jones, M., H. L. Peterson, J. J. Pierce, N. Herweg, A. Bernal, H. L. Raney and N. Zahariadis. 2016. "A River Runs Through It: A Multiple Streams Meta-Review." *Policy Studies Journal* 44 (1): 13–36.

Jordan, A., H. Van Asselt, F. Berkhout, and T. Rayner. 2012. "Understanding the Paradoxes of Multi-level Governing: Climate Change Policy in the European Union." *Global Environmental Politics* 12 (2): 43–66.

Kingdon, J. 1995. *Agendas, Alternatives, and Public Policies*. New York: Longman.

Knaggård, A., and R. Hildingsson. 2023. "Multilevel influence and interaction in the MSF: A conceptual map". In *The Modern Guide to the Multiple Streams Framework* (this volume).

Koebele, E.A. 2021. "When multiple streams make a river: analyzing collaborative policymaking institutions using the multiple streams framework." *Policy Sciences* 54 (3): 609–28.

Nachmany, M., S. Fankhauser, T. Townshend, et al. 2014. *The GLOBE Climate Legislation Study: A Review of Climate Change Legislation in 66 Countries*. 4th edition. London: GLOBE International and LSE.

Putnam, R. 1988. "Diplomacy and Domestic Politics: The Logic of Two-level Games." *International Organization* 42 (3): 427–60.

Rajamani, L. 2012. "The Durban Platform for Enhanced Action and the future of the climate regime." *International & Comparative Law Quarterly* 61 (2): 501–18.

Ridde, V. 2009. "Policy Implementation in an African State: An Extension of Kingdon's Multiple-Streams Approach." *Public Administration* 87 (4): 938–54.

Rietig, K. 2019. "Leveraging the power of learning to overcome negotiation deadlocks in global climate governance and low carbon transitions." *Journal of Environmental Policy and Planning* 21 (3): 228–41.

Rietig, K. 2021a. *Learning in governance. Climate policy integration in the European Union*. Cambridge: MIT Press.

Rietig, K. 2021b. "Multilevel reinforcing dynamics: Global climate governance and European renewable energy policy." *Public Administration* 99 (1): 55–71.

Rietig K. 2021c. "Accelerating low carbon transitions via budgetary processes? EU climate governance in times of crisis." *Journal of European Public Policy* 28 (7): 1018–37.

Rietig, K. and C. Dupont. 2021. "Presidential leadership styles and institutional capacity for climate policy integration in the European Commission." *Policy and Society* 40 (1): 19–36.

Robinson, S.E. and W. S. Eller. 2010. "Testing the separation of problems and solutions in subnational policy systems." *Policy Studies Journal* 38 (2) 199–216.

Rohlfing, I. 2012. "Varieties of Process Tracing and Ways to Answer Why-Questions." *European Political Science* 12: 31–9.

Sanjurjo, D. 2020. "Taking the multiple streams framework for a walk in Latin America." *Policy sciences* 53 (1): 205–21.

Schreurs, M. A. and Y. Tiberghien. 2007. "Multi-Level Reinforcement: Explaining European Union Leadership in Climate Change Mitigation." *Global Environmental Politics* 7 (4) 19–46.

Wurzel, R. and S. Connelly.2011. *The European Union as a Leader in International Climate Change Politics*. London: Routledge.

Zahariadis, N. 2007. "The Multiple Streams Framework: Structure, Limitations, Prospects", In *Theories of the Policy Process*, ed. P. Sabatier, 65–92. Boulder, Colorado: Westview Press.

Zahariadis, N. 2016. "Delphic Oracles: Ambiguity, Institutions, and Multiple Streams." *Policy Sciences* 49 (1) 3–12.

Zohlnhöfer, R., N. Herweg and F. Rüb. 2015. "Theoretically refining the multiple streams framework: An introduction." *European Journal of Political Research* 54: 412–18.

Zohlnhöfer, R. 2016. "Putting Together the Pieces of the Puzzle: Explaining German Labor Market Reforms with a Modified Multiple-Streams Approach." *Policy Studies Journal* 44 (1): 83–107.

16. The challenge of applying the Multiple Streams Framework to non-decisions and negative decisions

Annette Elisabeth Töller

EXPLAINING NON-DECISIONS AND NEGATIVE DECISIONS AS CHALLENGE

Most studies applying the MSF, aim to explain the occurrence of decisions actually made (i.e., positive decisions).[1] These are then interpreted as the result of the coupling of mature streams. For example, Ackrill and Kay explain the emergence of the 2005 EU sugar reform (Ackrill & Kay 2011), Zohlnhöfer explains the emergence of the 2003 German labor market reform (Zohlnhöfer 2016), and Bollmann and Töller explain the adoption of a purchase premium for electric vehicles in Germany in 2016 (Bollmann & Töller 2018). In these and many other cases, the authors ultimately show how the respective decision came about, in that the coupling of the streams occurred. This is the case after a window of opportunity opened and the streams were ripe. In stark contrast, the analysis of failures of decisions to materialize, or cases in which decisions are made but turn out negative with respect to some aspect have been the stepchild of MSF research so far. Few exceptions can be found, for example in the study by Zahariadis (1996) on the privatization of British Rail, a study on education policy in Minnesota (Stout & Stevens 2000), the study of EU economic reform (the first attempt at the Lisbon Strategy) by Copeland and James (2014), the study by Cooper-Searle et al. (2018) on UK regulations regarding GHG emissions of cars, as well as in the analysis of policy diffusion of energy conservation policies in India (Goyal 2022).

Not without reason, however, the authors of one of the studies mentioned criticize that the MSF itself offers little help in applying it to such cases:

> It is fairly easy to recognize that a window is open or was open when a significant policy initiative does get enacted. It is much more difficult, however, to determine whether or not a real window of opportunity was missed and an initiative failed

because of poor timing and partial coupling, or whether the policy was a nonstarter to begin with because there was no open window. (Stout & Stevens 2000, 353)

The authors conclude that "the window of opportunity feature of the model functions best as a metaphor for capturing the sense of opportunity that must exist in order for policies to be enacted" (Stout & Stevens 2000, 353).

Although it is quite common in every day politics that decisions are just not made over a period of time, or are made but turn out negatively with regard to certain aspects, policy research is predominantly interested in positive (i.e., actually adopted) policies and pays little attention to the phenomena just mentioned (e.g., t'Hart & McConnell 2019, 646). Therefore, answering the question of whether and, above all, how non-decisions and negative decisions can be explained with the help of MSF, is important not only for the conceptual development of the MSF, but also for policy research more generally.

In addressing this question, this chapter proceeds as follows: The first section turns to the conceptual challenges that arise when applying the MSF to non-decisions and negative decisions. Second, two contributions that have been devoted to explaining non-decisions or negative decisions are examined in more detail in terms of how they deal with the issues raised earlier. Third, a case study dealing with the non-consideration of bioplastics is presented to apply the considerations raised in the earlier parts of the chapter.

CONCEPTUAL CHALLENGES

When it comes to using the MSF to explain non-decisions and negative deci-sions, three conceptual challenges arise: First, the phenomenon to be explained must be characterized more precisely. Second, it must be worked out which explanatory elements the MSF provides for such cases. And third, methodo-logical issues also arise.

Phenomena to be Explained

In their 1963 paper, Peter Bachrach and Morton B. Baratz coined the term non-decision, which they defined as "the practice of limiting the scope of actual decision-making to 'safe' issues ..." (Bachrach & Baratz 1963, 632). The authors concede that a non-decision itself may be difficult to detect, but that the process of non-decision-making is observable and analysable just like the process of decision-making (Bachrach & Baratz 1963, 641). On closer inspec-tion, different variants of non-decision-making can and must be distinguished. When Bachrach and Baratz coined the term, they had in mind those situations in which decisions do not even reach the agenda because they do not appear to be politically viable. In this context, the reasons for inaction can be diverse and include strategic, ideological, or inadvertent inaction (t'Hart & McConnell 2019: 651). Bachrach and Baratz, for example, thought of anti-poverty policies in Baltimore (Bachrach & Baratz 1970). Crenson (1971), in his study of the "unpolitics of air pollution", showed how in Gary, Indiana, the problem of air pollution was not addressed in city policies for decades – unlike in other cities with similar air problems. Kingdon points out that, when an administration defines its political priorities, this implies identifying major political issues as well as putting "other subjects that could be prominent agenda items in different administrations" "on the shelf for the time being". He concludes that the "blocking of an issue is at least as important an agenda-setting effect as positively promoting an issue" (Kingdon 2003, 69).

Relevant examples in Germany are the abolition of the "Ehegattensplitting" (an outdated tax rule that privileges male breadwinner constellations) or the adoption of a speed limit. Both concepts have been discussed again and again but have so far not made it onto the political agenda due to manifest opposition or, in any case, lack of political support in the governing majority. These types of non-decision can be called *latent non-decision*. They are difficult to identify because the measures may be discussed on and off over a long period of time, but no decision is formally proposed or made.

From these constellations we can distinguish *manifest non-decisions* where a project was proposed and expected to be adopted. Only in the political decision-making process, or sometimes only during the final steps of the decision, does it become apparent that political support is insufficient. In German environmental policy, this, for example, applies to the Environmental Code, an act that was supposed to bundle the fragmented federal environmental legislation into one set of rules but could not be passed even in the second attempt in 2009.

A third category are decisions that are adopted, but do not include certain elements. These can be called *negative decisions*. However, it is not random or off-topic issues that are missing. Instead, we talk about negative decisions when there is conscious neglect of an issue of a certain relevance that could just as well be part of the decision. A neglect is conscious, for example, when the issue was included in a prior proposal or is being debated. An issue could potentially be part of the decision when it is on other administrations' agenda (see the Kingdon quote above), pursued elsewhere under similar circumstances or recommended by experts as a relevant solution to an acknowledged problem. There is certainly a subjective element in identifying negative decisions, resulting from the interest of an author in, let's say, material recovery bins, energy efficiency, or bio-plastics. This does not mean, however, that negative decisions are arbitrary or that any issue not included in a policy constitutes a negative decision. But certainly, if you start searching for them, many decisions may include negative decisions with regard to specific aspects, as defined above. The question is if MSF can be useful to explain them.

In political reality, non-decisions and negative decisions can occur in combination, including over time. A case in point is the so-called "Wertstoffgesetz" (material recovery act): In Germany, over the period of 12 years (between 2005 and 2017), several governments intended to adopt a circular economy act that would – among other things – allow for all recyclable material to be collected together in one bin, the so-called "Wertstoff-Tonne" (material recovery bin). This would help to increase the share of recycled material that had been stagnant for years but touched on the established demarcation of tasks and resources between public and private waste management companies (Stroetmann & Below 2016), a highly sensitive issue in German waste management policy. Various drafts went through lengthy negotiations but could not be passed due to resistance from various stakeholders. Instead, the Packaging Act was passed in 2016, which contained various previously planned regulations, but not a binding regulation on the material recovery bin (Bruckschen 2017, 44). Thus, until 2017 we saw a number of manifest non-decisions which then turned into a negative decision – with regard to the introduction of the material recycling bin. This crucial element, which had been at the core of 12 years of controversial debate, was left out consciously.

Since the MSF in the Kingdon variant aims at explaining the agenda setting, only latent non-decisions can be explained with it, while in the case of manifest non-decisions and negative decisions the agenda setting has already taken place, but the sticking point is the decision. Only recent work provides for the application of the model in a second loop to the actual decision as well (Herweg et al. 2015).

Explanations Offered by MSF

Although the MSF has been applied predominantly to explain positive measures and why they got on the agenda, Kingdon's initial question by no means restricts the framework to explain successful agenda-setting only. Rather, in the same breath, Kingdon also asks "why some potential issues and some likely alternatives never came to the focus of serious attention" (Kingdon 2003, 1). However, specific conditions are mentioned only for the positive choices, with regard to the conditions for an issue to get on the decision agenda, where authoritative decisions are then made (Dolan & Blum 2023, 4): For a measure to get on the agenda, the three streams must be coupled. This is likely if three conditions are met (Herweg et al. 2015, 443):

• A policy window must open in the problem or politics stream.
• All three streams must be mature.

• Finally, there must be entrepreneurs who have strategies to couple the streams, with policy entrepreneurs often playing an important role (Dolan & Blum 2023).

Policy windows represent "an opportunity for advocates of proposals to push their pet solutions, or to push attention to their special problems" (Kingdon 2003, 165). They usually open for only a short time in the problem stream or the politics stream (Herweg et al. 2015, 443). In the problem stream, policy windows (also called problem windows) can open especially when there are problems that threaten re-election (Herweg et al. 2015, 437). Windows in the politics stream open primarily as a result of elections (Herweg et al. 2015, 443).

The problem stream is *ripe* when conditions become problems in public attention through focusing events, indicators, or feedback (Herweg et al. 2015, 436). The politics stream can be understood as ripe when the government majority supports a project (Herweg et al. 2015, 439) or a key policy-maker like the relevant minister or an influential member as a political entrepreneur, actively supports the idea in question and is willing to stitch together a majority for it (Herweg et al. 2018, 26). This should be related to partisan issue ownership, but can also be an effect of changing public opinion or interest group campaigns, and in turn also has to do with re-election (Herweg et al. 2015, 439–41). The policy stream is mature when there is at least one policy that meets the selection criteria (Herweg et al. 2015, 443). These are that policies are compatible with the ideologies of the ruling parties and also meet the requirements of technical feasibility, normative acceptability and implementability (Herweg et al. 2015, 442–43).

If at the same time a pressing policy problem enters the political agenda, a suitable policy is at hand and the politics stream is ripe, then there is a good chance for agenda change (Kingdon 2003, 165). However, coupling of the streams is needed.

In a policy window, the problem stream, the policy stream, and the politics stream can be *coupled*. Policy entrepreneurs (any type of individual or corporate actor with expertise, institutional power, or decision-making authority) have an important role in coupling the streams. Often, they first advance their project in the policy stream and then, when an agenda window opens, try to couple the solution with the other two streams: "Entrepreneurs must be not only persistent but also skilled at coupling. They must be able to attach problems to their solutions and find politicians who are receptive to their ideas [...]" (Herweg et al. 2018, 28). Yet, the type of window has implications for the coupling process: If a window opens in the problem stream, then a solution to a problem should be sought (consequential coupling). In contrast, if a window opens in the politics stream, then the focus is on the solution (doctrinal coupling) (Zahariadis 2003, 139) and a problem may be sought for the solution (Ackrill & Kay 2011, 77). Finally, in the case of political coupling, a version that was introduced by Blum (2018, 111), a policy decision is rather the result of a political situation like the national mood than of a more-or-less objective problem. The nature of the coupling should have an impact on the policy output. Whereas non-decisions are the result of non-coupling and non-coupling can be explained by referring to the three possible reasons for this, negative decisions appear as the result of a specific way of coupling.

Methodological Aspects

In qualitative studies as well as in quantitative research, methods ensure that analysis does not consist only in telling stories that may have been one way or another. In this paragraph I elaborate on aspects that can possibly ensure causal inference when applying MSF to single-case studies. In their study on the methodology of MSF studies, Zohlnhöfer et al. (2022, 6) recommend formulating hypotheses even for single-case studies. I argue here that this is a good approach when non-decisions are to be explained, but less so when it is about explaining negative decisions.

Turning the abovementioned condition for an agenda change into the opposite, latent non-decisions (i.e., issues that did not make it onto the agenda) and manifest non-decisions (proposals that were finally not adopted) can be attributed either:

- to the fact that no policy window opened;
- or one opened but not all streams were ripe;
- or a window opened and the streams were ripe but there was no policy entrepreneur to successfully couple the streams (see also Zohlnhöfer et al. 2022, 23).

Since there are clear statements as to the possible reasons of non-decisions, it seems advisable to translate these theoretical expectations into competing, testable hypotheses on why coupling did not occur. These hypotheses can be tested – depending on the number of cases among other things – either by applying qualitative or quantitative methods (see, e.g., Goyal 2022, 645–49).

If, as it seems, the occurrence of negative decisions is the consequence of the nature of the coupling process, explaining negative decisions is a more explorative exercise than explaining non-decisions. For this exploration the different variants of coupling that have been identified can guide the analysis, but they are ill-suited to serve as hypotheses in the strict sense.

Both, hypotheses-testing research and explorative research in the context of case studies and comparative case studies can and possibly should be complemented by a further technique for securing results in qualitative research designs, counterfactual reasoning. When working with combined explanatory approaches, as is the case with the MSF, there is fundamentally the problem of securing causal interference (Steinberg 2007, 182). The technique of counterfactual reasoning is to imagine what the outcome would have been if the factors had been different (Levy 2008), ultimately critically testing the assumed causal effect. In any case of positive decisions, this kind of a thought experiment can help to test whether they would have turned out negative if certain conditions had been different (e.g., Töller 2021, 500). And it can equally allow for imagining if a negative result would have been positive, if certain conditions defined in the MSF would have been met.

HOW OTHER STUDIES HAVE DEALT WITH THE ISSUE SO FAR

As mentioned at the outset, there are only a few MSF studies that are primarily, or partly, devoted to explaining non-decisions or negative decisions. Except for Stout and Stevens' critique mentioned above, however, none of these studies explicitly addresses the challenge of explaining negative outcomes with the MSF. In what follows, I consider two of these studies in more detail. With respect to the nature of the decision, I have selected two examples that address latent non-decisions (Zahariadis 1996) and negative decisions (Cooper-Searle et al. 2018). I then consider these in more detail with respect to the questions of how the decision is explained using the MSF and how this is methodologically ensured.

Phenomenon Under Analysis

With regard to the nature of the decision, in Zahariadis' study we find the analysis of several latent non-decisions: beginning in the late 1970s, Zahariadis identifies a number of latent non-decisions: situations in which a decision to privatize British Rail could have occurred but did not, as well as a final positive decision, which was finally taken in the early 1990s (Zahariadis 1996, 401).

Cooper-Searle et al., on the other hand, are concerned with negative decisions. They wonder "why material efficiency solutions are currently only a limited part of the UK policy agenda to reduce GHG emissions from cars" (Cooper-Searle et al. 2018, 55). This would include measures to reduce the mass of material inputs, re-using material without melting, extended product lifetimes and other approaches which (in the absence of rebound effects) should lead to a reduction in material demand and thus GHG emissions (Cooper-Searle et al. 2018, 52). So here the question is why a specific solution was not chosen for a problem in various instances. However, the authors do not distinguish between non-decisions and negative decisions in their study. Moreover, they do not identify the precise decisions in which material efficiency does not play a role. While they devote maximum attention to data collection and analysis as well as to the analysis of streams (Cooper-Searle et al. 2018, 55), the phenomenon to be explained thus remains largely vague, i.e. largely limited to measures mentioned in a table to which no concrete political processes can be assigned (Cooper-Searle et al. 2018, 58).

Explanation

Zahariadis identifies four windows in the politics stream and two windows in the problem stream (Zahariadis 1996: 408). However, privatization of British Rail did not take place in various situations, such as in the late 1970s, because political intervention by the Department of Transport (DOT) prevented a coupling of privatization as a solution to BR's existing financial problems (Zahariadis 1996, 410) or because (in the early 1980s) rail union strikes put the company in a bad light for potential investors (p. 411). Not even the Thatcher Government's major privatization program of 1987 was able to put the privatization of BR on the agenda; since due to successful privatization in other areas there was enough money in the public budget and thus the problem had been "lost" (p. 412). Privatization remained on the (ideologically determined) agenda as a solution, but a coupling of streams continued to appear "unattainable" (p. 414). Even the serious train accidents in 1988 and 1989 could not be coupled as a quality problem of BR with privatization (p. 415).

Ultimately, the privatization decided in 1992 appears as a solution that was first favored and for which a suitable problem was then sought (a typical case of doctrinal coupling), with the situation of the fresh election and the person of the new transport minister playing an important role in the successful coupling (Zahariadis 1996, 417–18).

In conclusion, non-decisions with regard to privatization in the British case appear as either a consequence of misfit between (perceived) problems and (prioritized versions of) privatization as a solution, or as the result of a deliberate action to prevent a coupling (sort of a negative entrepreneurship).

Cooper-Searle et al. state that in the problem stream, attributing GHG emissions to material flows is technically challenging, not standardized, and therefore not easily communicated politically – especially given the constraints of political decision makers on their time and understanding of complex issues (Cooper-Searle et al. 2018, 58). Because issues compete with each other and policy makers work in "sector or thematic silos", material efficiency was not prioritized as a problem. In addition, the diesel scandal strongly focused public attention on emissions as a problem. It is a "lack of capacity, interest and certainty that prevented material efficiency from being defined as a problem" (Cooper-Searle et al. 2018, 59). In the policy stream, there were indeed a number of possible solutions to increase material efficiency. But in addition to an inconsistent understanding of what should be included, the problem proved to be that the overall political line favored climate change mitigation measures that entailed economic co-benefits. However, such solutions are poorly identified for material efficiency, partly so because efficiency implies a reduction of material which might not be compatible with economic co-benefits. Furthermore, the precise GHG reductions that can be achieved have not yet been identified (p. 60). Finally, in the politics stream, the authors primarily identify a waning interest in climate issues, especially in a situation where UK environmental policy needs to be reorganized post-Brexit (p. 61). Addressing the requirement of policy entrepreneurs, the authors realized that they could find "no dedicated community of entrepreneurs promoting material efficiency improvements as a solution to reduce life-cycle GHG emissions from cars, apart from a few actors promoting car sharing as one option" (p. 61).

Overall, the study provides a number of interesting indications – such as the lack of available data, the complexity of the matter or the lack of political support for very specific solutions – that are typical for environmental policy decision-making processes.

Methods

While Zahariadis gives precise reasons for his case selection, we learn – quite in line with the times – little about the methods the author uses to establish causal relations. Zahariadis does not use hypotheses, but in his detailed and comprehensible process analyses he makes the theoretical implications of the empirical relationships he describes very clear at all points. Without mentioning it, he also works punctually with the technique of counterfactual reasoning, when he writes – with regard to the privatization that finally took place – "... had Labour won, BR's sale would not have been announced. This would have caused a radical change in the political stream. Which would have precluded a coupling of all streams" (Zahariadis 1996, 415).

The Cooper-Searle et al. study does not analyze specific decision-making processes but asks in interviews for the assessment of those involved in the decision-making processes. In doing so, it identifies problems in all three streams plus the widespread absence of potential policy entrepreneurs. The authors thus undertake an MSF-inspired interpretation of the failure to consider material efficacy solutions. This is very insightful but does not offer a concrete explanation of the failure to consider these solutions in specific policy decisions. It is not clear in individual cases whether the consideration of material efficiency failed due to the lack of data on potential GHG savings, the lack of measures with economic co-benefits, the lack of political capacity due to Brexit, or the lack of a policy entrepreneur. Thus, the high expectations of the study are not fully met. Nor are the questions of causal inference critically reflected upon and examined, despite elaborate data collection and analysis.

Which lessons can we learn from presenting these examples? First, it is obviously possible to explain non-decisions, and arguably also negative decisions with the help of MSF. Second, when explaining either non-decisions or negative decisions with the help of MSF, the dependent variable needs to be a specific (non-)decision in a specific case or a number of such (non-) decisions and cases. There is little analytical benefit in analyzing the causes of negative decisions by drawing on an undefined number of policies which are neither defined as such nor with regard to the policy processes that precede their adoption. It should hardly be possibly to identify the reason why streams have not been coupled or coupled in a specific way with negative outcome, if no specific policy process is being analyzed. To identify overall characteristics of a policy that make it unlikely to be adopted, MSF is not necessarily needed.

Second, it is not absolutely necessary to work with hypotheses when explaining non-decisions. A thick description with MSF in the researcher's mind, as in the British-Rail example, works fine. However, working with hypotheses helps to formulate clear expectations and to structure empirical analysis accordingly. It makes life easier for researchers, but also for readers of the analysis.

Next, I would like to turn to a case of negative decisions to further explore if and how this can be analyzed by applying MSF.

THE CASE OF BIOPLASTICS

Global plastics production has increased twentyfold since 1960 (European Commission 2018a, 4). In 2015, 332 million tons of plastic were produced worldwide, and this figure is expected to double in the next 20 years (European Commission 2018a, 4). On the one hand, plastics have a number of positive properties such as malleability, stability, low weight and manufacturing costs (OECD 2018, 2). On the other hand, the production and disposal of conventional plastics pose a number of environmental problems. First, the energy intensive production using fossil raw materials releases large quantities of climate-damaging greenhouse gases. Second, plastics have so far only been recycled and returned to the cycle for the manufacture of new products to a limited extent. Instead, they are mainly disposed of by incineration, which in turn leads to significant climate gas emissions. And third, improper disposal, including in the oceans, causes significant ecological damage to marine ecosystems, particularly due to the longevity of plastics (Jambeck et al. 2015; OECD 2018; Loges & Jakobi 2020, 1006). When it comes to reducing these negative environmental effects of plastics, the substitution of conventional plastics with bioplastics (in the sense of biobased[2] or biodegradable plastics[3]) is a relevant option (Fraunhofer UMSICHT 2018, 7), which is also discussed under the heading of *bioeconomy* (Töller et al. 2021; Vogelpohl et al. 2021). However, such bioplastics only have a market share of less than one percent worldwide so far. Political measures to promote bioplastics have largely failed to materialize until now – at least on the EU level – in contrast to China, for example. In so far, we are confronted with a *variety of negative decisions* that do not reflect bioplastics as a solution in a variety of plastics policies. As a case in point, I will present a study on the adoption of the Single-Use Plastics Directive in the EU in 2019. In the European multi-level system, a broad range of issues is decided at the EU-level. If MSF is applicable to parliamentary systems of EU Member States, there is no reason why MSF should not be applied to EU-policy-making, since institutional settings are not fundamentally different from those of EU Member States (Ackrill & Kay 2011; Herweg & Zohlnhöfer 2022).

The Single-use Products Directive: A Negative Decision for Bioplastics[4]

In May 2019, the EU adopted the so-called Single-Use Products Directive (Dir. 2019/904, OJ No. L 155/2019), which represents a concretization of the European Commission's European Plastics Strategy (European Commission 2018a; Vogelpohl et al. 2021). In addition to requirements for product design, labeling obligations, producer responsibility measures, separate collection, and consumption minimization, the Directive stipulates in particular that, from July 2021 on, single-use plastic products may no longer be sold in areas where affordable alternatives are available. This applies to cotton swabs, cutlery, plates, drinking straws, stirrers and balloon wands made of plastic, as well as polystyrene food packaging (Annex B). In addition, PET plastic bottles must consist of 25 percent recyclates from 2025 and 30 percent from 2030. Member States must transpose this into national law in good time. The Directive was celebrated as "a positive example of the impact of transformative alliances" (Schröder & Chillcott 2019, 52).

It is now noteworthy that the Directive treats bio-based and biodegradable plastics in the same way as conventional plastics produced from fossil raw materials (11th recital). This can be substantiated by two points: first, and in particular, the Directive does not contain any exemptions for biodegradable plastics in the product bans. This is remarkable in that certain biodegradable plastics largely decompose in the ocean in about one year, whereas this can take several hundred years for conventional plastics (Burgstaller et al. 2019, 7). Thus, for the problem of ocean pollution, bio-degradable plastics could definitely bring an improvement, even though waste management improvement would be a first choice (Calabrò & Grosso 2018). France had decided on a ban on single-use plastic cutlery and cotton swabs, effective from 2020, but explicitly excluded biodegradable plastics (Burgstaller et al. 2019, 8). China decided in early 2020 to ban a number of single-use plastic products, including disposable cutlery, but also explicitly excluded biodegradable plastics from this ban. It also decided to expand research on biodegradable plastics and explicitly promote their use (Nova Institute 2020, 4). Second, the Directive contains rules for the review of its impact, among other things, in the context of a report at the end (Article 15). The Commission proposal had foreseen an opt-out for bioplastics in the future (European Commission 2018b). Accordingly, the report should also include information on whether

> sufficient scientific and technical progress has been made and criteria or a standard for biodegradability in the marine environment have been developed for single-use plastic articles falling within the scope of this Directive and their single-use substitutes, in order to determine for which products, if any, marketing restrictions are no longer necessary. (European Commission 2018b: 31)

However, this relatively open wording was significantly restricted by the intervention of the European Parliament (European Parliament 2019). The Directive therefore states in a much more restrictive manner that such an assessment of scientific and technical progress for the biodegradability of single-use plastic articles in the marine environment is foreseen, but under the condition "that the plastics break down completely into carbon dioxide (CO_2), biomass and water within such a short time that they do not harm marine fauna and flora ..." (Article 15 paragraph 3d). The fact that no exceptions from the product bans were made for bio-degradable plastics is identified as a negative decision – and not as one issue of an uncountable quantity of irrelevant aspects coincidently not included in the Directive. This is the case because the Commission's plastic strategy had mentioned this option (see below) and the Commission proposal had included at least an opt-out for bioplastics in the future; because not only China but also France had adopted such exceptions; and finally because there are good scientific reasons to at least discuss biodegradable plastics as a solution to the problem of marine pollution (e.g., Schröder & Chillcott 2019, 51).

The Political Process from and MSF-Perspective

Looking at the political process that led to this negative decision (and the Directive more broadly), the first remarkable aspect is that the process was "incredibly quick" (Int_BP_3) from the Commission's official proposal in May 2018 to its adoption in May 2019 just before the European elections at the end of May 2019.

The *problem stream* developed very dynamically since 2017 as a result of two focusing events (Vogelpohl et al. 2021, 6–7). In July 2017, China announced an import ban on plastic waste starting in early 2018 (Brooks et al. 2018). This measure represented a first focusing event, through which plastic waste was increasingly perceived as a problem in Europe. At the same time, it initially remained vague what exactly the problem was: Was it that plastic waste is no longer recycled in China and instead exported to other countries with less reliable infrastructure for recycling or that it is incinerated in Europe (Schröder & Chillcott 2019, 50)? That there is so much plastic waste in the first place? That it is not possible to recycle relevant quantities of plastic and then use the recyclates in production (OECD 2018)? That this leads to greenhouse gas emissions? In October 2017, the BBC's feature on plastic pollution in the oceans in the series Blue Planet reached an audience of millions – and not just in the UK. This episode, with its images of a Whale calf choking on a plastic bag was the second focusing event and led to a further increase in attention and a specification of the plastic problem: This was now seen primarily in terms of marine pollution from plastic waste (Science Focus 2019; Schröder & Chillcott 2019, 45; Int_BP_03), which had also previously been known as a problem to a scientific audience (e.g., Jambeck et al. 2015).

While the European Commission's Plastic Strategy, developed during 2017 and published in January 2018, still defined the lack of recycling of plastics and the resulting GHG emissions as a priority problem, and while marine litter was addressed more as a complementary issue (European Commission 2018a, 3–6; Vogelpohl et al. 2021, 6–8), this perception changed in the first months of 2018, a phenomenon that one of our interviewees coined the "Blue Planet effect": Now marine litter was perceived as the major problem (Int_BP_03). The problem stream was thus definitely ripe as a result of two focusing events in the first half of 2018: Plastic was defined as a problem, with the dominant problem definition changing and narrowing down over time.

The European Commission based the draft European Directive presented in May 2018 largely on the problem of marine litter:

> The amount of plastic marine litter in oceans and seas is growing, to the detriment of ecosystems, biodiversity and potentially human health, and causes widespread concern. At the same time, valuable material that could be brought back into the economy is lost, once littered. Plastic makes up 80–85% of the total number of marine litter items, measured through beach counts. (European Commission 2018b: 1)

A whole range of possible measures were underway in the *policy stream* at the beginning of 2018, with the focus primarily on measures for better, i.e., more recyclable, product design (for example, within the framework of the Ecodesign Directive), but also an increase in capacities for separate collection and for recycling, as well as the improvement of market conditions for recyclates (European Commission 2018a, 6–16). For the problem of marine litter, especially from single-use plastic articles, only comparatively vague measures were under discussion at that time. Thus, measures analogous to the regulation on lightweight plastic bags were suggested (European Commission 2018a, 14). Here, the EU had adopted decreasing per capita use values binding for the Member States, whereas the measures to achieve them could be determined by the member states themselves (OJ 2015 No. L 115/11). Among the possible solutions to the problem of plastic inputs into the environment, the promotion of biodegradable plastics was explicitly present at that time, even though clarification was still needed (European Commission 2018a, 15; Vogelpohl et al. 2021, 7). In this respect, the policy stream was clearly ripe when a whole series of ideas for measures of different levels of concretization were on their way. What was not recognizably present in the policy stream at that time was a product ban (European Commission 2018a). Product bans are usually rather unpopular because they interfere very strongly with the freedom of both producers and consumers and also leave the Member States no leeway. The European Commission in particular tends to prefer measures that leave the Member States degrees of freedom in implementation (cf. Loges & Jakobi 2020: 1012).

For the *politics stream*, it was crucial that the European Parliament elections were coming up in May 2019. On the one hand, this meant that the draft Directive would either have to be adopted by then, or its fate would be uncertain. It thus seemed sensible to exclude complicated and potentially controversial issues from the outset. On the other hand, in view of widespread criticism of European regulations and often rather low voter turnout in European elections, the Directive appeared to be a good opportunity to attract positive attention with a measure that was responsive to voters' concerns. Also, both the Council and European Parliament got on board with this issue (EP 2018; Vogelpohl et al. 2021, 7–8). Thus, it can be said that the political stream was also ripe, insofar as the majority of the European Parliament and the Council stood behind the issue.

The intriguing question, which is not easy to answer at first glance, is: In which stream did the policy window open? Was it opened in the problem stream by the Blue Planet issue? Or in the politics stream by the window of opportunity that opened for a short time at the end of the legislative period for the adoption of a Directive that met with acceptance among the electorate? Both, data gathered in our interviews (in particular Int_BP_3; cf. Vogelpohl et al. 2021, 6) and the speedy nature of the process strongly aiming at adopting the Directive in this election period let the last option (politics window) appear more probable. It was the political opportunity that existed for a very short time that constituted the politics window. The nature of this politics window was decisive for how the streams were coupled and the Directive was shaped in terms of content.

The European Commission acted as a *policy entrepreneur*. To succeed in getting a Directive adopted in the unlikely time of one year, it had to present a proposal that enjoyed high support among those who had to make political decisions, while offering few points of attack. Of all the problems of plastic, some of them complicated to communicate, the Commission therefore coupled the one that had entered the European electorate's consciousness of the problem through Blue Planet: marine pollution from plastic. The Commission cleverly narrowed this problem down by the results of a study that identifies the ten single-use plastics mostly found on European beaches, accounting for 86 percent of all single-use plastics found and 43 percent of all marine litter on European beaches. This problem, now simplified once again, demanded strong, unambiguous, and also symbolic measures because of its perception as urgent (Crolly & Grassmann 2018). The Commission thus coupled the problem with (apart from some other things like recycling quota for plastic bottles etc.) a solution that had not even been present in the policy stream before: a product ban for exactly these 10 products. Bans not only no longer allow certain behavior, but also mark it as socially undesirable at a symbolic level (Böcher & Töller 2019). Such a measure was also worthy of support by political decision-makers, such as the European Parliament, especially during election campaigns, where they have to repeatedly prove that "Europe" does good things for its citizens.

This kind of coupling finally also explains why biodegradable plastics were not considered as an option to reduce marine pollution from plastic waste. This is because the question of whether biodegradable plastics are advantageous over conventional plastics is complicated (Int_BP_5). First, plastic products should be recycled, or at least disposed of in a regulated manner, and in any case should not end up in the oceans. Therefore, the question of how they should be made so that they cause as little damage in the environment as possible is in itself somewhat problematic. In addition, there is a wide variety of biodegradable plastics, which not only differ greatly among themselves, but whose degradation behavior can be quite different in different environments (Napper & Thompson 2019), making it difficult to design biodegradable plastics for unregulated disposal, which can vary greatly precisely because of the lack of regulation. In addition, there is still a considerable need for research on the behavior of these plastics in different contexts (Burgstaller et al. 2019). Thus, it can be said that policies for bioplastics were not yet sufficiently mature. Moreover, with a market share of less than one percent, the bioplastics industry leads a niche existence and is also not very assertive in the landscape of interest representation, while the conventional plastics industries, for example, and especially the waste management industry, have an interest in ensuring that as little as possible changes in the current material constellations (Calabrò & Grosso 2018).

The *type of coupling* is ultimately decisive for the result. This appears neither as a consequential coupling, where the problem determines the choice of solution, nor a doctrinal coupling, where the solution is fixed, and the problem is sought to match it. Rather, the political situation of limited time and the political need to decide something that appeals to the electorate determines that problem and solution were coupled in this sense – a process that can best be described as "political coupling" (Blum 2018, 110–111).

Using a counterfactual reasoning perspective, one can critically examine this finding: Had the outcome been different, would there have been an exception for biodegradable plastics from the ban, if the window had opened in the problem stream? Here, the window terminology does seem somewhat abstract. However, if the process had taken place earlier during the election period, it would have been less shaped by political needs ("political coupling") and more by the problem definition ("consequential coupling"). The European Commission would probably have anticipated less of the time pressure and would not have placed such a high value on public acceptance. It would still have used marine litter as a hook, but probably in a broader problem context. If it had proposed a product ban because of the high urgency that the public would have attributed to the problem in this case as well, an exemption for bio-degradable plastics would have been more likely to get on the agenda because a delay in the discussion, possibly including referral to the mediation commit-tee, would not have jeopardized the overall project. The probability that such an exemption for bioplastics would have been included in the final Directive is nevertheless not very high. This is because the question of whether and under what conditions bioplastics can be a solution to the marine problem is complicated and has not yet been definitively answered scientifically (Calabrò & Grosso 2018, 801;Int_BP_5). Furthermore, among organized interests there is also a lack of influential actors who could act as entrepreneurs, attempting to couple bioplastics as a solution to problems deemed relevant. This is because on the one hand, bioplastics industries still represent a niche-business and thus were little influential in the policy process (Int_BP_5). On the other hand, environmental NGOs would not support such a solution because they prefer fundamental changes in attitudes and behaviors (less plastics, better manage-ment) to changes in materials (Int_BP_2; 4 and 5; Crolly & Grassmann 2018)). Thus, there are interesting parallels here to the study on the non-adoption of material efficiency measures discussed above.

CONCLUSION

Non-decisions and negative decisions can certainly be explained with the help of the MSF – just like the positive decisions that have been frequently addressed so far. In doing so, it is important to precisely define the phenomenon to be explained. Sound analysis cannot be done in a global approach addressing a policy issue without identifiable policy results and corresponding policy processes (as the energy efficiency study demonstrates). Rather, in a case study (or comparative cases studies) analyzing the occurrence of the specific decision (or non-decision), it must be analyzed why in the case of non-decisions the coupling failed to materialize. For doing so, hypotheses are not absolutely necessary (as the British-Rail-example demonstrates) but they definitely help to clarify theoretical expectations and structure empirical research. In the case of decisions that materialized but turned out negative with respect to a certain issue, it is the type of coupling that has to be considered in more detail. Here, explorative instead of hypothesis testing research seems to make more sense.

The case study on the non-consideration of bioplastics in the EU Single-Use Plastics Directive demonstrates first that negative decisions are a relevant, identifiable category. Second, negative decisions can be fruitfully analyzed in an explorative way. Third, identifying the nature of coupling can help to explain why a certain, relevant aspect has been omitted in a specific policy. For the area of environmental policy we can conclude that negative decisions with regard to specific solutions to environmental problems are highly probable, when these solutions have not yet been exhaustively researched, are technical and complicated in nature so they cannot be easily simplified for policy-makers, and there are few and little influential supporters among interest associations and environmental groups that could help to successfully couple this solution with a politically defined problem. If at all, such solutions may have a chance for a positive decision in cases of consequential coupling, when the process can be characterized by searching for a solution to a defined problem with little political or time pressure. Such solutions are unlikely to be the positive result of doctrinal coupling, because they simply do not have sufficient political appeal. Furthermore, they have no chance in cases of political coupling – as demonstrated above – because they are too complicated for public sentiment and perception and not compatible with speedy decision-making.

Applying MSF, either to positive or to negative decisions, remains a challenging exercise: How do you separate complex realities into three different streams? How do you determine in which stream the policy window opened? This chapter aimed at facilitating the analysis of negative decisions, which so far have been the stepchild of MSF research. Further studies will have to show whether this is helpful and in which respects more conceptual clarification is needed.

NOTES

1. I would like to thank Nicole Herweg and Reimut Zohlnhöfer and the participants of the T01P12 Session 3 (Multiple Streams Framework) at ICPP 5, Barcelona, July 2021, in particular Nikolaos Zahariadis, for their very helpful comments on earlier versions of this chapter. Thanks to Hanno Hahn for valuable research assistance.
2. Bio-based plastics are mainly derived from starch-rich plants such as corn, wheat, or sugar cane.
3. Some plastics are both, biobased and biodegradable.
4. The case study is based on a research project on bioeconomy policy conducted from 2017–2021, funded by the Federal Ministry of Research (BMBF) (FKZ 031B0227), in which bioplastics policies were studied alongside bioenergy and biofuel policies (Töller et al. 2021; Vogelpohl et al. 2021). Various policy decisions at different levels (EU/federal/local) with regard to regulation, promotion, etc. of bioplastics were analyzed, based on the evaluation of sources as well as 13 interviews with actors from politics, administration, business and environmental associations, as well as municipal companies which were conducted between August 2018 and February 2019. For the EU-level case studies, four interviews are relevant (see References and Vogelpohl et al. 2021, 6).
5. Interviews:
    Interview with a German Environmental NGO (Int_BP_2)
    Interview with a European Research Agency (Int_BP_3)
    Interview with the German Environmental Agency (Int_BP_4)
    Interview with the European Bioplastics Industry Association (Int_BP_5).

REFERENCES[5]

Ackrill, R., and A. Kay. 2011. "Multiple Streams in EU Policy-Making: The Case of the 2005 Sugar Reform." *Journal of European Public Policy* 18 (1): 72–89.

Bachrach, P., and M. S. Baratz. 1963. *"Decisions and Nondecisions: An Analytical Framework."* American Political Science Association 57 (3): 632–42.

Bachrach, P., and M. S. Baratz. 1970. *Power and Poverty: Theory and Practice*. Oxford: Oxford University Press.

Blum, S. 2018. "The Multiple-Streams Framework and Knowledge Utilization: Argumentative Couplings of Problem, Policy, and Politics Issues." *European Policy Analysis* 4 (1): 94–117.

Böcher, M., and A. E. Töller. 2019. *Umweltpolitik in Deutschland. Eine politikfeldanalytische Einführung*, 2nd edition. Hagen: FernUniversität in Hagen.

Bollmann, A., and A. E. Töller. 2018. "Lösungen auf der Suche nach Problemen? Instrumentenwahl in der deutschen Elektromobilitätspolitik." *Zeitschrift für Umweltpolitik & Umweltrecht* 41 (2): 105–42.

Brooks, A. L., S. Wang, and J. R. Jambeck. 2018. "The Chinese import ban and its impact on global plastic waste trade." *Science advances* 4 (6): eaat0131.

Bruckschen, A. 2017. "Diskussion zum Verpackungsgesetz auf den Berliner Abfallrechtstagen – Vom Wertstoffgesetz zum Verpackungsgesetz." *Zeitschrift für das Recht der Abfallwirtschaft* 16 (1): 44–46.

Burgstaller, M., A. Potrykus, and J. Weißenbacher. 2019. "Behandlung biologischer abbaubarer Kunststoffabfälle in Deutschland." *Zeitschrift für Abfall- und Ressourcenmanagement* 51(1): 4–13.

Calabrò, P.S., and M. Grosso. 2018. "Bioplastics and waste management." *Waste Management* 78: 800–01.

Cooper-Searle, S., F. Livesey, and J. M. Allwood. 2018. "Why are Material Efficiency Solutions a Limited Part of the Climate Policy Agenda? An application of the Multiple Streams Framework to UK policy on CO2 emissions from cars." *Environmental Policy and Governance* 28 (1): 51–64.

Copeland, P., and S. James. 2014. "Policy windows, ambiguity and Commission entrepreneurship: explaining the relaunch of the European Union's economic reform agenda." *Journal of European Public Policy* 21 (1): 1–19.

Crenson, M. A. 1971. *The Un-Politics of Air-Pollution. A Study of Non-Decisionmaking in the Cities*. Baltimore and London: The Johns Hopkins Press.

Crolly, H., M. Grassmann. 2018. "Das sind die entscheidenden Fehler in Brüssels Plastik-Strategie." Die Welt, 28 May 2018. Available at: https://www.welt.de/wirtschaft/article176764551/Neue-Verbote-Das-sind-die-entscheidenden-Fehler-in-Bruessels-Plastik-Strategie.html. (Accessed: 10 January 2023).

Dolan, D. A., and S. Blum. 2023. "The Beating Heart of the MSF: Coupling as a Process." *The Modern Guide to the Multiple Streams Framework*, (this volume).

European Commission. 2018a. *Communication from the Commission to the European Parliament, the Council, the European Economic and Social Committee and the Committee of the Regions*. COM(2018) 28 final. Brüssel. Available at: https://eur-lex.europa.eu/legal-content/EN/TXT/?uri=CELEX%3A52018DC0028 (Accessed: 28 June 2021).

European Commission. 2018b. *Proposal for a Directive of the European Parliament and of the Council on the reduction of the impact of certain plastic products on the environment*. COM (2018) 340 final. Brüssel. Available at: https://eur-lex.europa.eu/legal-content/EN/ALL/?uri=CELEX%3A52018PC0340 (Accessed: 28 June 2021).

European Parliament. 2018. *Report on the proposal for a directive of the European Parliament and of the Council on the reduction of the impact of certain plastic products on the environment (COM (2018)0340 – C8–0218/2018 – 2018/0172(COD))*. Available at: https://www.europarl.europa.eu/doceo/document/A-8-2018-0317_EN.pdf (Accessed: 28 June 2021).

European Parliament. 2019. *Position of the European Parliament adopted at first reading on 27 March 2019 with a view to the adoption of Directive (EU) 2019/... of the European Parliament and of the Council on the reduction of the impact of certain plastic products on the environment* (EP-PE_TC1-COD (2018) 0172). Available at: https://www.europarl.europa.eu/doceo/document/TC1-COD-2018-0172_EN.pdf (Accessed: 28 June 2021).

Fraunhofer UMSICHT. 2018. "Recycling von Biokunststoffen. Fraunhofer UMSICHT nimmt Stellung. Lassen sich Biokunststoffe recyclen?" *Pressemitteilung*. Available at: https://www.umsicht.fraunhofer.de/de/presse-medien/pressemitteilungen/2018/recycling-biokunststoffe.html (Accessed 29 June 2021).

Goyal, N. 2022. "Policy Diffusion through Multiple Streams: The (Non-)adoption of Energy Conservation Building Code in India." *Policy Studies Journal* 50 (3) 641–69.

Herweg, N., C. Huß, and R. Zohlnhöfer. 2015. "Straightening the Three Streams: Theorising Extensions of the Multiple Streams Framework." *European Journal of Political Research* 54 (3): 435–49.

Herweg, N., N. Zahariadis, and R. Zohlnhöfer. 2018. "The Multiple Streams Framework: Foundations, Refinements and Empirical Applications." In *Theories of the Policy Process*, eds. C.M. Weible and P.A. Sabatier, 17–54. New York: Routledge.

Herweg, N., and R. Zohlnhöfer. 2022. "Analyzing EU policy processes: applying the multiple streams framework." In *Elgar Encyclopedia of European Union Public Policy. Political Science and Public Policy Collection 2022*, eds. P.R. Graziano, and J. Tosun, 484–494. Cheltenham, Edgar Elgar.

Jambeck, J. R., R. Geyer, and C. Wilcox. 2015. "Plastic waste inputs from land into the ocean." *American Association for the Advancement of Science* 347 (6223): 768–71.

Kingdon, J. W. 2003. *Agendas, Alternatives, and Public Policies*, 2nd edition. New York: Longman.

Levy, J. S. 2008. "Counterfactuals and case studies." In *The Oxford handbook of political methodology*, eds. J. M. Box-Steffensmeier, H. E. Brady, and D. Collier, 627–644. Oxford, Oxford University Press.

Loges, B. and A. P. Jakobi. 2020. "Not more than the sum of its parts: de-centered norm dynamics and the governance of plastics." *Environmental Politics* 29 (6): 1004–23.

Napper, I. E., and R. C. Thompson. 2019. "Environmental Deterioration of Biodegradable, Oxo-biodegradable, Compostable, and Conventional Plastic Carrier Bags in the Sea, Soil, and Open-Air Over a 3-Year Period." *Environmental Science & Technology* 53 (9): 4775–83.

Nova Institute. 2020. "Opinions of the Chinese National Development and Reform Commission and the Ministry of Ecology and Environment concerning the further reinforcement of measures against plastic pollution." Available at: http://bio -based.eu/downloads/opinions-of-the-chinese-national-development-and-reform -commission-and-the-ministry-of-ecology-and-environment-concerning-the-further -reinforcement-of-measures-against-plastic-pollution/ (Accessed: 28 June 2021).

OECD. 2018. "Improving Plastics Management: Trends, policy responses, and the role of international co-operation and trade." Paris, *OECD Environment Policy Papers* 12.

Schröder, P., and V. Chillcott. 2019. "The Politics of Marine Plastics Solution." In *The Circular Economy and the Global South*, eds. P. Schröder, M. Anantharaman, K. Anggraeni, and T. J. Foxon, 43–56. London: Routledge.

Science Focus. 2019. "Has Blue Planet II had an impact on plastic pollution?" *BBC Science Focus Magazine*. Available at: https://www.sciencefocus.com/nature/has -blue-planet-ii-had-an-impact-on-plastic-pollution/. (Accessed: 28 June 2021).

Steinberg, P. F. 2007. "Causal assessment in small-N policy studies." *The Policy Studies Journal* 35 (2): 181–204.

Stout, K. E., and B. Stevens. 2000. "The Case of the Failed Diversity Rule: A Multiple Streams Analysis." *Educational Evaluation and Policy Analysis* 22 (4): 341–55.

Stroetmann, C., and M. Below. 2016. "Verpackungsverordnung, Wertstoffgesetz, Verpackungsgesetz?" *Umwelt- und Planungsrecht* 9: 321–25.

T'Hart, P., and A. McConnell. 2019. "Inaction and public policy: understanding why policymakers 'do nothing'." *Journal of Policy Sciences* 52 (4): 645–61.

Töller, A. E. 2021. "Driving bans for diesel cars in German cities: The role of ENGOs and Courts in producing an unlikely outcome." *European Policy Analysis* 7: 486–507.

Töller, A. E., T. Vogelpohl, K. Beer, and M. Böcher. 2021. "Is bioeconomy policy a policy field? A conceptual framework and findings on the European Union and Germany." Journal of Environmental Policy & Planning 23 (2): 152–64.

Vogelpohl, T., K. Beer, and B. Ewert. 2021. "Patterns of European bioeconomy policy. Insights from a cross-case study of three policy areas." Environmental Politics 31 (3): 386–406.

Zahariadis, N. 1996. "Selling British Rail. An idea whose time has come?" *Comparative Political Studies* 29 (4): 400–22.

Zahariadis, N. 2003. *Ambiguity and Choice in Public Policy. Political Decision-making in Modern Democracies.* Washington DC: Georgetown University Press.

Zohlnhöfer, R. 2016. "Putting Together the Pieces of the Puzzle: Explaining German Labor Market Reforms with a Modified Multiple Streams Approach." *The Policy Studies Journal* 44 (1): 83–107.

Zohlnhöfer, R., N. Herweg, and N. Zahariadis. 2022. "How to conduct a Multiple Streams Study." In *Methods of the Policy Process*, eds. C. M. Weible and S. Workman, 23–50. New York: Routledge.

17. Multiple Streams in the public policymaking processes of the European Union

Theofanis Exadaktylos

INTRODUCTION

The Multiple Streams Framework (MSF) as an approach to investigate public policymaking processes in the European Union (EU) has gained traction, not only in terms of the agenda-setting side, but also in other stages of the policy cycle and spans many areas of policymaking that either emanate from the EU itself or originate from other processes of European integration. The framework is the centerpiece of other contributions in this volume and for the purposes of this chapter it suffices to highlight the importance of the coupling of streams with the goal to produce a policy output (Cairney and Jones 2016; Cairney and Zahariadis 2016; Herweg and Zahariadis 2018).

From an analytical point of view, in the context of public policymaking research within the three streams, we are looking at specific elements to help guide the empirical data collection and assessment of findings. The definition of the problem itself in terms of specific indicators, focusing events and feedback, alongside the political environment in terms of the national mood, pressure group activity and political fermentations, become constitutive elements in the construction of a policy window coupled with an assessment of different policy solutions in terms of their value added and their feasibility (Zahariadis 2016; Zohlnhöfer, Herweg and Huß 2016). In the wider conceptualization of MSF, solutions are developed in response to identified problems (within the *problem stream*), they are produced within a specific rationale within the confines of the political debate (*politics stream*) and they are brought forward by policy entrepreneurs (informed by the *policy stream*). The role of policy entrepreneurs should not be underestimated because of their ability to affect the selection of a policy based on access, resources and different political strategies that are utilized based on their skills. All elements taken together affect the availability and utilization of a policy window through which the streams are filtered through to create the policy output.

When looking at EU public policymaking processes, it is important to consider both how such processes are informed by European integration theories and that the EU as a political system in its own right has the capacity to produce public policy at the European, domestic, and international levels. In other words, EU public policy affects political actors, their identity, and their preferences on the one hand, and on the other it becomes a space for deliberation, socialization, and learning, as well as policy diffusion. The impact of the EU can be found at every stage of the policy cycle, from agenda-setting to policy formulation, to decision-making, to implementation and monitoring, and to evaluation (Exadaktylos and Graziano 2022). The empirical studies involving EU public policymaking have consequently explored not only pivotal policy areas and policy actors, but also the way the process itself affects inter- and intra-institutional relations, policy implementation mechanisms, policy mainstreaming, bureaucratic politics and interest group input, policy feedback, compliance mechanisms, as well as on the creation of policy styles both at the domestic and EU level, within this unique public policy sphere with common elements and mentalities.

One of the main focal points of EU public policymaking literature has traditionally been the impact that policies originating from the EU have on the domestic policies of the Member States. EU institutions and various agencies have increased their competence in a number of policy areas, and through the EU's multilevel system of governance, influence the outlook of domestic policymaking processes. To that end, we need to consider that the EU has a policy framework for policies under the wider "community" approach (such as economic policy, agriculture and cohesion or environmental policies), and that frequently spills over into areas that remain largely in the domestic domain of policymaking (including pensions and employment, foreign policy, and development policy to name a few). The main interest there is the degree of adaptation of the Member States in terms of responding to pressures coming from the EU, and equally the presence or absence of coalitions and constellations of actors supporting or opposing certain policymaking outcomes (for instance, in terms of compliance and implementation monitoring). To that extent, it is equally interesting to explore how even signals of policy intent at the EU level may affect the trajectory of policymaking at all levels and policy domains.

The objectives of this chapter are to review the scholarship on the utility of MSF in EU-related public policy events and processes, explore notions of Europeanization as relevant to the MSF convergence (problem, politics, policy), and reflect on the methodological and research design challenges of using MSF concepts (such as policy windows and policy entrepreneurs) to study EU public policy phenomena as part of the discussion on the wider research agenda of MSF. The chapter also reflects on crises as focusing events taking inspiration from three recent EU-wide crises: the financial crisis of 2009, the pandemic in 2020 and the outbreak of war in Ukraine in 2022.

THE EU AS A PRODUCER OF PUBLIC POLICY

The EU as a political system producing public policy (Exadaktylos and Graziano 2022), alongside the complexity of its public policymaking processes, the involvement of a host of different local, regional, national and transnational interests, the presence of a diversity of solutions to common problems within the EU space and the plurality of policy entrepreneurs presents the perfect natural laboratory to explore policy outcomes through the lens of MSF (Zahariadis 2008).

The EU has historically been notoriously slow in the production of public policy (Copeland and James 2014) and therefore, despite being faced with slow-burning or fast-burning crises (Seabrooke and Tsingou 2019), the response time to a problem has not always been prompt. Delays built into the way the EU policy-making system is constructed are intentional or have served to satisfy the direction of travel of European integration. Therefore, problems can become apparent as crises evolve, or they may take time to emerge considering any differences between the priorities of the EU itself, the Member States and various other actors in the policymaking system.

Looking at the agenda-setting stage, the plurality of access points to decision-makers, which is part of the multilevel governance approaches to EU public policy, served the purpose of ensuring that the EU acted as a platform for various political actors to bypass their national political systems and reach out to the EU for solutions to problems. However, the side-effect of this is a delay in the way the agenda may be set. Similarly, the across-the-board involvement of domestic and transnational interest groups can also slow down agenda-setting (Herweg 2016a; Rozbicka and Spohr 2016) precisely because of the general mindset of finding consensus or building in compromises. In this case, the European Commission can be seen as the driver of the EU agenda (Schmitt 2000; for a reassessment cf. Kreppel and Oztas 2017; Oztas and Kreppel 2022) considering its initiation powers. Yet, individual Member States can drive the direction of travel of the EU agenda (see for instance the nexus between France and Germany in pushing initiatives (Saurugger and Terpan 2016, Degner and Leuffen 2019) or the policy priorities of the EU presidencies (Tallberg 2004, Panke 2010).

The policy formulation stage is closely related to the agenda-setting stage (Leppänen and Liefferink 2022). This is linked to the exclusive power of the Commission to initiate policy (Zahariadis 2008) but also to the role of the European Parliament, especially in light of its enhanced role within the EU policymaking system. In the context of policy formulation, actors present themselves as policy entrepreneurs with the ability to frame problems, prime action, and present and advocate for certain narratives. In the context of collective actors such as institutions, the Commission is a key entrepreneur at this stage, as it is the one presenting the first draft of any proposals (Copeland and James 2014; Schön-Quinlivan and Scipioni 2017). Yet, other choices such as the scope, criteria and budget can be influenced by other actors.

Once the policy has reached the decision-making stage, MSF lenses can help reconstruct the policy window. The solutions have been developed in response to specific problems (as identified in the previous stages), the rationale behind the policy has been calibrated and the policy entrepreneurs have brought in their skills to promote a particular version of the policy itself. The EU decision-making requirements, bouncing between the Parliament and the Council, and the actual negotiations, bargaining and persuasion processes, create a vibrant environment where consequential or doctrinal coupling logics are at play. MSF literature makes three assumptions at this stage: (1) that policy makers are constrained by time and therefore the policy output cannot be optimized; (2) that the means to achieve a policy goal and the actual solution are not necessarily well connected in terms of appropriateness; and (3) that ambiguity or lack of defined preferences allow political manipulation of the output by those who have access to information, policy venues and timetables – the latter linked to the first assumption (Ackrill, Kay and Zahariadis 2013).

The implementation stage is a fruitful locus for MSF approaches, especially in relation to the attainment of the stated policy goals (Zahariadis 2008). Despite the existence of conflict and the complexity of the EU's institutional environment, decisions are still implemented – and here, it is the domestic political context that plays an important role as domestic political actors are responsible for carrying out implementation of EU-level decisions (leading to compliance, or not). It is true that although the EU may decide the policy goals, it is up to the Member States to reach those goals, and that is a creative process (Zahariadis and Exadaktylos 2016). This becomes even more complex in decentralized systems, where constituent authorities have to transpose directives locally (for an interesting example see Sager and Thomann (2017), and create their own implementation strategies.

The one element that characterizes the EU policy implementation process is complexity (Zahariadis 2012). In turn, this effectively means that despite the presence of policy windows following the decision on a particular policy, its implementation can be impaired by certain structural features. Clear job descriptions in terms of responsibility are not always present and the domestic institutional architecture may not be appropriately constructed to cope with the pressures of implementation (Bursens 2002). That can lead to conflict between implementing institutions, agencies or actors within the same polity.

If we scale it up however, the complex nature of a problem and the differing approaches within each Member State's administrative context can be accentuated in the case of transnational/transboundary issues, for instance, environmental policy (Knill and Liefferink 2013), pandemics or refugee inflows, on which the chapter will reflect at a later section. Pressures to adapt the national context in terms of allocation of resources or reorganization of administrative structures as a result of EU policy implementation have been the essence of Europeanization studies, reflecting on issues of policy compliance or adaptational change. Thus, implementation is possible when ambiguities are minimized and the coping mechanisms to change are adaptable and flexible to the new conditions set out by the policy goals.

Considering the iterative process for policy making, the evaluation stage closes the loop and leads again to the agenda-setting side of things. The policy output is evaluated against the problem it was called out to resolve in terms of key performance indicators, and the feedback from: (a) those implementing it; and (b) those affected by it. The political actors are also assessed against the outcomes, in terms of their ability to solve the problem itself. Equally, the policy itself is assessed in terms of amendments, corrections, and redesigning. The evaluation stage then can present a new policy window out of which a novel policy output may stem as it sheds more light on a previously defined problem and solution. This is particularly important when targets move because of evolving phenomena, such as climate change (Cooper-Searle, Livesey, and Allwood 2018) or a change of practice. For instance, the EU's approach to evaluation changed in its shift from "Better Regulation" to "Smart Regulation" in 2010 (Smismans 2015) to account for the whole policy cycle. This effectively links the ex-post evaluation into the ex-ante assessment for new policy intervention and is applied on all EU-originating policy with the purpose of closing the feedback loop in policymaking. This goes back to ideas of policy learning for future decision-making and increase of transparency and involvement of more actors in the learning process (Borrás and Radaelli 2011).

Turning to the political elements of public policy making, we need to explore the points of formation, aggregation, and representation of different interests and how policy discourses emerge. The politics stream is informed by the alignment of interest groups and the presence of new political actors in the system, following the rise of nationalism and populism in European politics both at domestic and EU levels (see Monteleone, 2021; Hettyey, 2021; Dimitrova, 2021) which alters the "national mood" (Ackrill, Kay and Zahariadis 2013; Zahariadis 2014; Cairney and Zahariadis 2016). The politics stream was particularly evident in the context of the European financial crisis and the orientation of policy making towards austerity (e.g., Afonso, Zartaloudis and Papadopoulos 2015 on Greece and Portugal; for an extensive discussion, cf. Caiani & Graziano 2021).

The role of interest groups within the EU politics stream has been widely acknowledged in the literature (Herweg 2016b; Rozbicka and Spohr 2016). Interest groups and policy communities are affected within new political opportunity windows in terms of inclusion and representation (Coen 2007; Beyers, Eising and Maloney 2008). Hence, lobbying both at the national level and the European arena become important and groups can be transformed into policy entrepreneurs depending on the level of access, the resources they have and the skills they acquire in coupling their interest to that of the political actors within decision-making – for instance if they are attached to business or civil society interests makes a difference in their success (Eising, Rasch and Rozbicka 2017).

How does the EU politics stream create opportunities for new and old actors, such as national governments, parliaments, and bureaucracies? The EU as a producer of public policy has the capacity to change the organizational government structures at the domestic level. In other words, the production of public policy at the EU level may alter job descriptions, hierarchies, and salience of different actors in the domestic context. New political opportunity windows at the EU level may empower non-institutional actors, including regional-level actors with institutional and policy functions (López and Tatham (2018) present this case in a comparative study of Spain, Italy, and the UK). Symbolic institutions may also acquire elevated status because of their country's participation in EU policy implementation processes. For instance, as a result of the Swedish and Finnish accession to the EU, the Sami Parliament upon implementation of EU minority rights acquired a more than symbolic monitoring role especially in light of EU climate change policy (Atikcan 2010; Coates and Holroyd 2020). Thus, part of the EU public policy effect on domestic governance structures has implications for networked governance, for the implementation of national reform programs such as in taxation emanating from the European Commission (Cacciatore, Natalini and Wagemann 2015) and for transferring competences to or via the EU.

Finally, we should not underestimate the effects of the EU as a global actor or producer of international public policy on associated countries and non-Member States. As part of the wider research of EU public policy this concerns the ability of the EU to project public policy norms and governance agendas beyond its own borders, alongside policy beliefs and ways of doing things (Iusmen 2013; Spohr 2016). Findings from such research suggest that the effect of conditionality as a mechanism for EU membership does not only impact all streams but it also alters the conditions for the construction of policy windows by enabling different and new policy entrepreneurs to participate in the policy process. The same effect applies to non-Member States in their interactions with EU policies, such as Switzerland (Sager and Thomann 2017) or Norway (Farstad et al. 2022), and in the context of democracy promotion and external governance in the countries of the Southern and Eastern Neighborhood (Catalano and Graziano 2016; Freyburg et al. 2009).

METHODOLOGICAL AND RESEARCH DESIGN CHALLENGES

The epistemological challenge of isolating the EU effect from other competing processes – either domestic politics or globalization – is significant, precisely because of the complexity of policymaking at the EU level and the participation of a host of different institutional and non-institutional actors, alongside the entanglement of the EU dimension in domestic policy contexts. One of the merits of public policy analysis is its eclectic methodological nature (see Sil and Katzenstein (2010) for a discussion of "analytic eclecticism") allowing the use of both qualitative and quantitative methods of evidence collection and analysis. Frequently, studies combine the two sides as the evidence can range from hard economic data to semi-structured elite interviews. Public policy has also been a field of experimentation with mixed methods (for instance, using fuzzy set analysis by Maggetti (2007) or Thomann, Trein and Maggetti (2019)). However, policy analysis is partly descriptive and partly normative. This is a blessing and a curse: as a blessing it is pragmatic in terms of being policy-relevant but as a "curse" the findings can be easily reduced to a simple reconstruction of facts and timelines or into a narrative. Hence, beyond strong theoretical underpinnings, any public policy analysis work must present a methodical and systematic way of studying evidence that renders the research analytical in tandem with the complex nature of policy making (Dunn 2015; Fischer 2019).

What does this mean for the application of MSF as a theoretical and analytical framework in the study of EU public policy-related questions? Considering the demand for methodological rigor in mainstream political science and the turn to theoretical precision, MSF research cannot be a *sui generis* literature. Hence, looking at the models for MSF, there are methodological and theoretical challenges in the case of its application to EU-related public policy making by the *sui generis* and complex nature of the EU itself. Due to the wealth of its applications and impacts the opportunities for methodological pluralism are immense. The first challenge focuses on the way we study our research object, the second challenge concerns the subfields and frameworks it links to, and the third challenge regards the focus on the individual streams with the framework in terms of prioritization of causal/interpretive effects.

The way we study the EU public policymaking ecosystem requires awareness and explicit mention of research design, primarily in the way the choice of policy cases, countries, institutions/actors and time periods is justified. Here for instance, time as a variable may help us determine critical junctures, watershed moments and other focusing events but also talk about timing of the three streams and tempo of policy change. Second, the interdisciplinary nature of MSF in studying EU public policy requires the blending of concepts and ideas from other subfields (for instance, political psychology, political sociology, political economy, other behavioral sciences, but also political theory and international relations). Hence, the researcher may need to extend into the constraints that those other fields may present. This is both an opportunity and a challenge; the former being on the capacity to eclectically select elements from various toolkits and the latter being the compatibility of concepts among different disciplines ontologically and epistemologically.

Finally, the focus on problems, politics or policies becomes a challenge as the policy output itself is a compound variable (Exadaktylos 2012) and it stretches our research object in terms of actors, instruments, procedures, and paradigms followed. Considering the nature of EU public policy there is a plurality of actors involved: European, domestic, international, and transnational. Therefore, tracing the change across those explicit statements on research design becomes imperative. This helps avoid the pitfall of simple storytelling or rendering the analysis a narrative.

Within MSF applications of EU public policy there is a strong preference for qualitative methods, justified by the fact that it is overlapping with the wider EU studies field of research which is driven by a strong qualitative tradition (Jupille 2006). In that sense, there is also a preference for single case studies which add to our deeper knowledge of specific policy areas, policy outputs or countries missing from the literature. The temporal aspect is usually part of these studies, considering the moving goalposts of both a set of "living" policies, an institutional architecture that is everchanging, and the influence of current affairs, political circumstances and changing preferences of EU Member States. However, the causal impact of time, timing and tempo is missing, with the temporal effect frequently presented in a narrative mode.

If we consider the three streams as our independent variables and the policy output as our dependent variable, there are studies that focus on the causal path or the reconstruction of the policy window leading to a policy output and there are others that try to measure policy change. In terms of the individual streams, the literature focuses on the dynamics that develop between the European Commission, the Council, and other EU institutions and national/subnational executives and other domestic actors. It also brings light into the policy options available, as well as the way different problems become salient and others less prominent. But most importantly, it examines change in specific policy areas.

Returning to the original puzzle of this section, the demarcation of the research object is imperative. This is linked to the conceptualization and theoretical developments within MSF itself and the operationalization of its theoretical constitutive elements. As a policy-driven subfield it struggles with comparative politics, single cases, and comparative analysis, precisely because of the diverse nature of different countries and policy areas and their respective intricacies in terms of institutional arrangements. Therefore, the pitfall MSF applications must avoid is to become navel-gazing exercises rather than systematic studies of EU public policymaking. Finally, the moving target element requires the incorporation of time as a variable and perhaps the introduction of process tracing as a method to capture longer-term processes.

To close the discussion on the methodological and research design challenges of applying MSF into EU public policy making questions, the field affords itself the opportunity to cut across methodological and theoretical traditions giving the opportunity of innovative research outputs. Yet, it is still difficult to isolate the EU effect on the policy outputs from other parallel processes of domestic or international origin, which is a wider challenge of EU-related studies. Nonetheless, the consciousness of methodological and research design choices supports the selection of cases and the construction of alternative pathways to the policy output, it adds transparency and contextualizes the findings better within the MSF. Accepting the liquescent nature of the beast itself, i.e., the EU, as a producer of public policy, not only helps align the application of MSF at the EU public policymaking level with other applications described in this volume, but also leads to methodological innovation.

CRISES AS FOCUSING EVENTS ON EU PUBLIC POLICYMAKING

The literature on EU public policymaking has been burgeoning in the past decade with pieces detailing the many crises that the EU as a political system has faced, alongside their impact on the EU's inter- and intra-institutional relations and their effects on the Member States (Rhinard 2019). The concept of "crisis" has therefore become central in researching developments in EU politics. As a recurrent element, the EU has faced the European financial crisis, a refugee crisis that is still ongoing, the departure of an EU Member State, only to be followed by a global public health crisis and pandemic, and aggression and war in its doorstep. As Massetti and Exadaktylos (2022) suggest, crises "are now so numerous and overlapping that is has become impossible even to characterize a solar year by attaching it to a specific crisis". From an MSF perspective, a crisis becomes an intervening variable on all constitutive elements within the framework.

In terms of the problem stream, a crisis can be seen as a focusing event and can cause the prioritization or reprioritization of existing problems and at the same time, the emergence of new foci of public policy at the EU level. Problems arising at the Member-State level can be projected upwards to become EU-level problems. On a similar vein, crises can uncover problems of transboundary nature that affect Member States in a more horizontal fashion or the EU itself as a supranational system. Crises can also present themselves as external shocks that have the capacity of changing the direction of travel of the EU as a political entity (affecting integration). Finally, crises can create not only knock-on effects on existing policies (in terms of channeling attention and resources) but they can accentuate the lack of action in existing problems.

In terms of the politics stream, crises affect the national mood and create new points of political polarization, they affect the strategies of political actors and interest groups, and they can frequently lead to a change of the balance of power within national and supranational organizations. Considering that policies are made with certain rationale in mind, the politics stream during a crisis can present more affective reasoning than cognitive/rational ones for policy intervention or choice. At the same time, crises create a sense of urgency of response by the politics stream to problems as described above. In essence, political actors need to be seen at least as taking some form of action. Thinking about the slow-moving beast that the EU political system is, it is evident that the politics stream at the EU-level needs to maintain its ability for consensus building on the one hand, and its capacity to react on the other.

Finally, in terms of the policy stream, a crisis could affect the value behind a policy as well as the capacity of the political system to deliver the policy. From that perspective, a crisis affects the organizational elements of the policy, it renders some instruments of policymaking obsolete and may require a complete turnaround of procedures and beliefs on how the policy can affect change and achieve its goals. In the EU environment, this is a significant blow, as the majority of policies at the EU-level require long periods of deliberation, assessment of different options, fairness and equity, and balance between EU and national interests. To that extent, Member States are likely to prioritize their interests over those of the EU, even though this prioritization in terms of the policy itself may disproportionately affect their EU partners or become a process of knocking the can further down into the future. The concept of path dependency becomes useful in this case, as in the latter case, the reconfiguration of policies may present them with additional problems in the future.

In times of crisis, there is scope for new policy entrepreneurs to emerge. They may either bring forth an innovative solution or take advantage of certain opportunity structures to push forward certain agendas or capture specific decision-making agents. When it comes to the EU-level, the plurality of points of access to the decision-making process further complicates the selection of a solution. Policy entrepreneurs may defend older paradigms and previous ways of doing things in an effort to cause minimum disruption to the status quo. Hence, in times of crisis, policy entrepreneurs can both hinder and facilitate the coupling of the streams at the EU level.

When examining the policy window while taking into account the slow-moving nature of the EU and the complexity of its own public policy making system, opportunities to react may be missed in times of crisis. During those times, uncertainty is rising, especially as new information may come to light as the crisis unfolds, ambiguity increases, and job descriptions may get blurred. At the EU-level for instance, those policy windows may become "make or break" moments akin to critical junctures, or the output may end up not addressing the problem itself. Therefore, as crises have the ability to change power dynamics, agendas and schedules of preferences, the EU policy output may end up not offering sustainable solutions or even revert to older paradigms – ones that the EU may feel safe in, yet ones that hinder innovation and effective tackling of the problem at hand.

The remainder of this section will focus on three crises, i.e., the euro-crisis (starting from the Greek financial crisis of 2009), the Covid-19 public health crisis in 2020 and the crisis in Ukraine in 2022, and their manifestation in the context of EU public policy responses. The sequencing here is important as lessons learned from one crisis should ideally create a mechanism of learning for policymaking for the next one and can ensure the appropriate policy output to reflect the policy choices, the political balance and the tackling of the problem – leading effectively each crisis to be seen as a policy window that moves integration to a desired direction. This in practice may be far from ideal. Of course, for crises to have an analytical value, the literature makes the distinction between slow- and fast-burning crises as able to trigger different mechanisms of policy responses (Seabrooke and Tsingou 2019; Schmidt 2022). Learning mechanisms become essential in developing policy solutions and in bringing together actors with the politics stream. As Radaelli (2022) points out, different mechanisms of learning exist, differentiating between inferential and contingent mechanisms; yet the continuous overlap between crises may bring about both mechanisms at the same time, affecting resource allocation, interests, and ideas of various actors and, by extension the setting in which public policymaking takes place. As a focusing event then, a crisis can change the parameters of policymaking at the EU level as a result of crisis management policies and the political interplay, as well as the will to identify an event as a crisis.

The European financial crisis emanated from the global financial crisis of 2008. By 2009–10, it had turned into a crisis on the sustainability of the Greek economy and eventually by 2012 it turned into a crisis on the survival of the Euro (Capelos and Exadaktylos 2017). Thinking about the problem, the concern revolved around the ability of the EU to tackle the practical bankruptcy of a Eurozone economy without having the appropriate institutional arrangements within the Eurozone architecture to be able to support a Eurozone partner financially through the European Central Bank (ECB). As plenty of studies focusing on the new policy instruments that emerged out of this crisis suggest (Saurugger and Terpan 2016; De Rynck 2016; Schön-Quinlivan and Scipioni 2017; Copeland and James 2014), the politics of the day had created camps between the countries of the European South and the so-called frugal countries of the European North.

The balance of power within the affected countries (see for instance Vasilopoulou, Halikiopoulou and Exadaktylos 2014) but also the inability of some of those countries to successfully respond to the pressures for reform coming from the EU (Exadaktylos and Zahariadis 2014) did not lead to a solid rationale behind the choice of policy. In fact, the pressures from the unfolding crisis itself managed to silence policy entrepreneurs with innovative ideas and allowed others who were serving an older policy paradigm (e.g., austerity) to emerge in the forefront. Policy windows were missed on several occasions, for instance in the way transfers could be made from one Member State to another, the creation of central EU protection mechanisms in the form of Eurobonds and the arming of supranational institutions who were being bound by national preferences such as the ECB with political agency. Delays in responding to the crisis had long-lasting effects on the countries mostly affected by it, such as Greece. In fact, coming up with a new institutional architecture to safeguard against future crises of sovereign debt took years to materialize.

Turning to the global pandemic of Covid-19, which began in 2020, the crisis coincided with the aftermath of the Brexit negotiations and the solidarity that the EU-27 showed in dealing with the UK's departure (Laffan 2019). In the context of the first few weeks of the pandemic, the Commission and national governments within the EU struggled to understand the complexity of the challenge: there was panic in terms of the uncertainties ahead, alongside a degree of ambiguity as to who had the mandate to do what and therefore there were delays in creating a coordinated response (Zahariadis et al. 2022; Lynggaard, Jensen and Kluth 2023). In fact, initial responses with the closing down of national borders indicated that prior policy paradigms were very much still active in EU policy making. However, the EU was eventually able to coordinate a response centrally, change the hierarchy of previously low standing agencies (e.g., the European Center for Disease Control and the European Medicines Agency), but also coordinate national efforts in terms of both pharmaceutical and non-pharmaceutical interventions.

Beyond the efforts to develop quickly a safe and effective vaccine, the EU created a set of policy outputs targeting the impact of the pandemic on the European economy and prioritized the responses over other policy interests (Ladi and Wolff 2021). It also managed to keep afloat promises regarding the European Green Deal (that materialized despite the Covid-19 attention). Policy entrepreneurs in the form of experts in public health were incorporated in the daily workings of EU institutions (Forman and Mossialos 2021) and despite differences in national responses and policy styles (Zahariadis et al. 2023), the EU managed to keep itself depoliticized despite the high contestation of the measures (Chatzopoulou and Exadaktylos 2021). Policy outputs and instruments at the EU level, such as the suspension of the Stability and Growth Pact, the creation of the Pandemic Emergency Purchase Program by the ECB, the Next Generation EU and the Recovery and Resilience Facility were aimed at facilitating long-term recovery taking only a few months to complete and be agreed upon.

Finally, looking at the most recent EU crisis, i.e., the blatant invasion of Ukraine by Russia in February 2022, the EU was hit by the energy crisis, raising concerns about energy security and the sustainability of the Green Deal. This clearly posed a new challenge for the EU's policy output, creating a policy window of the "make or break" type. The EU was either going to respond to this new challenge or face the consequences against its own survival. Coming from the lessons of the previous crises and only just emerging from the peak of the Covid-19 public health crisis, the EU took only a few weeks to address the invasion and provide diplomatic and military assistance to Ukraine. To paraphrase Radaelli (2021), crises have not only become the new (empirical) normal of EU policy making but a key explanatory variable in the policy output of the EU. Policy outputs at the EU level have started to speed up as a result of consecutive crises.

In the emotional climate that crises create, consultation processes, evaluation procedures and meticulous assessment of information are bypassed or reduced to simple box-ticking exercises (Boin, Lodge and Luesink 2020). They expose leadership points of vulnerability. Despite their short-term and abrupt nature, they can have long-lasting impact and threaten values for policy making. They test political systems and social fabrics. They can create longer-term emotional feedback loops that can linger within the national and European-level politics creating affective polarization (Chatzopoulou and Exadaktylos 2021; Exadaktylos 2020). So how can we incorporate the concept of crises within the MSF approach? Certainly, crises can create natural critical junctures through which we can compare the way the problem, politics and policy streams come together under normal circumstances and under conditions of pressure, urgency, and uncertainty. Comparing the old with the new normal can thus give us valuable insights in public policymaking and how policy windows are constructed, including the variation in roles of different actors within the EU political system itself (for a discussion on experts for instance, see Lynggaard et al. 2023).

CONCLUDING REMARKS

The purpose of this chapter was to review the scholarship around the use of MSF in EU public policy events and processes. It embarked on a journey of reviewing how the different streams converge in the context of EU public policymaking, borrowing some conceptual elements from Europeanization studies, reflecting on the methodological and research design challenges and take stock of how the concept of "crisis" can be incorporated in the context of MSF-related studies of the EU, commenting in an illustrative manner on the Eurozone crisis, the Covid-19 pandemic and the war in Ukraine.

Becoming evident from the discussion is not only the traction that the MSF approach has gained in examining EU public policy events, but most importantly the versatility of the framework to be applied at different stages of the policy process and its adaptability to incorporate constellations of actors, interests, and strategies across numerous policy areas. From an analytical point of view, MSF approaches to EU public policymaking provide a useful platform to look at issues of problem definition, incorporation of focusing events and feedback; describe and analyze the political environment and the power dynamics between actors; and review the solutions available to tackle problems. In that sense, MSF approaches allow us to reconstruct the policy windows, successfully bringing in the host of policy entrepreneurs within the EU public policy space to analyze well the policy outputs.

Certainly, EU public policymaking is informed by theories of European integration, and we can claim that the slow-moving nature but also the complex properties of the EU political system have an intricate role to play in the development of policy outputs. But in essence, the EU becomes a natural laboratory for the study of complex phenomena of policymaking, as it becomes a space for deliberation, socialization and learning, as well as policy diffusion. Such complexities certainly pose certain methodological and research design challenges in terms of moving goalposts, demarcation of the research object and pathways to causality. However, the illustrative cases of the three crises add on one more element to the MSF model, i.e., the incorporation of "crises" as intervening variables that have the capacity to change not only the parameters of policy production, but also the direction of travel of public policymaking at both the EU level and the national context of countries participating within the EU institutional architecture or are simply associated with it.

REFERENCES

Ackrill, Robert, and Adrian Kay. 2011. "Multiple Streams in EU Policy-Making: The Case of the 2005 Sugar Reform." *Journal of European Public Policy* 18 (1): 72–89.

Ackrill, Robert, Adrian Kay and Nikoloas Zahariadis. 2013. "Ambiguity, Multiple Streams, and EU Policy." *Journal of European Public Policy* 20 (6): 871–87.

Afonso, Alexandre, Sortirios Zartaloudis, and Yannis Papadopoulos. 2015. "How Party Linkages Shape Austerity Politics: Clientelism and Fiscal Adjustment in Greece and Portugal During the Eurozone Crisis." *Journal of European Public Policy* 22 (3): 315–34.

Atikcan, Ece. O. 2010. "European Union and Minorities: Different Paths of Europeanization?" *European Integration* 32 (4): 375–92.

Bache, Ian. 2013. "Measuring Quality of Life for Public Policy: An Idea Whose Time Has Come? Agenda-Setting Dynamics in the European Union." *Journal of European Public Policy* 20 (1): 21–38.

Beyers, Jan, Rainer Eising and William Maloney. 2008. "Researching Interest Group Politics in Europe and Elsewhere: Much we Study, little we Know?" *West European Politics* 31 (6): 1103–28.

Boin, Arjen, Martin Lodge and Marte Luesink. 2020. "Learning from the COVID-19 Crisis: An Initial Analysis of National Responses." *Policy Design and Practice* 3 (3): 189–204.

Borrás, Susan, & Claudio M. Radaelli. 2011. "The politics of Governance Architectures: Creation, Change and Effects of the EU Lisbon Strategy." *Journal of European Public Policy* 18 (4): 463–84.

Bursens, Peter. 2002. "Why Denmark and Belgium have Different Implementation Records: On Transposition Laggards and Leaders in the EU." *Scandinavian political studies* 25 (2): 173–95.

Caiani, Manuela and Paolo Graziano. 2021. *Varieties of Populism in Europe in times of Crises.* Abingdon, Routledge.

Cairney, Paul and M. D. Jones. 2016. "Kingdon's Multiple Streams Approach: What is the Empirical Impact of This Universal Theory?" *Policy Studies Journal* 44 (1): 37–58.

Cairney, Paul and Nikolaos Zahariadis. 2016. "Multiple Streams Approach: A Flexible Metaphor Presents an Opportunity to Operationalize Agenda Setting Processes." In *Handbook of public policy agenda setting.* Cheltenham, Edward Elgar Publishing.

Capelos, Tereza and Theofanis Exadaktylos. 2017. "Feeling the Pulse of the Greek Debt Crisis: Affect on the Web of Blame." *National Identities* 19 (1): 73–90.

Catalano, Serida L and Paulo R. Graziano. 2016. "Europeanization as a Democratization Tool? The Case of Morocco." *Mediterranean Politics* 21 (3): 364–86.

Chatzopoulou, Sevasti and Theofanis Exadaktylos. 2021. "Whose Opinion is it? Public Debates and Repertoires of Action in Greece During the First Covid-19 Lockdown Period." *Javnost-The Public* 28 (2): 185–201.

Coates, Kenneth S. and Carin Holroyd. 2020. "Europe's North: The Arctic Policies of Sweden, Norway, and Finland." *The Palgrave Handbook of Arctic Policy and Politics* 283–303.

Coen, David. 2007. "Empirical and Theoretical Studies in EU Lobbying." *Journal of European Public Policy* 14 (3): 333–45.

Cooper-Searle, Simone F. Livesey and Julian M. Allwood. 2018. "Why are Material Efficiency Solutions a Limited Part of the Climate Policy Agenda? An Application of the Multiple Streams Framework to UK Policy on CO2 Emissions From Cars." *Environmental Policy and Governance* 28 (1): 51–64.

Copeland, Paul and Scott James. 2014. "Policy Windows, Ambiguity and Commission Entrepreneurship: Explaining the Relaunch of the European Union's Economic Reform Agenda." *Journal of European Public Policy* 21 (1): 1–19.

De Rynck, Stefan. 2016. "Banking On a Union: The Politics of Changing Eurozone Banking Supervision." *Journal of European Public Policy* 23 (1): 119–35.

Degner, Hanno and Dirk Leuffen. 2019. "Franco-German Cooperation and the Rescuing of the Eurozone." *European Union Politics* 20 (1): 89–108.

Dimitrova, Antoaneta L. 2021. "Understanding Europeanization in Bulgaria and Romania: Following Broader European Trends or Still the Balkan Exceptions?" *European Politics and Society* 22 (2): 295–304.

Dunn, William N. 2015. *Public Policy Analysis*. Abingdon, Routledge.

Eising, Rainer, Daniel Rasch and Patryja Rozbicka. 2017. "National Interest Organisations in EU Policy-Making." *West European Politics* 40 (5): 939–56.

Exadaktylos, Theofanis. 2012. "Europeanization of Foreign Policy Beyond the Common Foreign and Security Policy." *Research design in European studies: Establishing causality in Europeanization* 195–220.

Exadaktylos, Theofanis. 2020. "Them and Us: The Politics of Exclusion in Greece in Times of Polarisation." In *The Emerald Handbook of Digital Media in Greece*, 275–88. Emerald Publishing Limited.

Exadaktylos, Theofanis and Nikolaos Zahariadis. 2014. "Quid pro Quo: Political Trust and Policy Implementation in Greece during the Age of Austerity." *Politics & Policy* 42 (1): 160–83.

Farstad, Fay M., Erland A. T. Hermansen, Bard S. Grasbekk, Kristiane Brudevoll and Bob van Oort. 2022. "Explaining Radical Policy Change: Norwegian Climate Policy and the Ban on Cultivating Peatlands." *Global Environmental Change* 74: 102517.

Fischer, Frank. 2019. *Politics, Values, and Public Policy: The Problem of Methodology*. Abingdon, Routledge.

Forman, Rebecca and Elias Mossialos. 2021. "The EU Response to COVID-19: From Reactive Policies to Strategic Decision-Making." *Journal of Common Market Studies* 59 (S1): 56.

Freyburg, Tina, Sandra Lavenex, Frank Schimmelfennig, Tatiana Skripka and Anne Wetzel. 2009. "EU Promotion of Democratic Governance in the Neighbourhood." *Journal of European Public Policy* 16 (6): 916–34.

Herweg, Nicole. 2015. "Against All Odds: The Liberalisation of the European Natural Gas Market—A Multiple Streams Perspective." *Energy Policy Making in the EU: Building the Agenda* 87–105.

Herweg, Nicole. 2016a. "Explaining European Agenda-Setting Using the Multiple Streams Framework: The Case of European Natural Gas Regulation." *Policy Sciences* 49: 13–33.

Herweg, Nicole. 2016b. "Clarifying the Concept of Policy-Communities in the Multiple-Streams Framework." *Decision-making under ambiguity and time constraints: Assessing the multiple-streams framework* 125–145.

Herweg, Nicole and Nikolaos Zahariadis. 2018. "The Multiple Streams Approach." *The Routledge handbook of European public policy* 1: 32–41.

Herweg, Nicole and R. Zohlnhöfer. 2022. "Analyzing EU Policy Processes: Applying the Multiple Streams Framework." In *Elgar Encyclopedia of European Union Public Policy*, 484–494). Cheltenham, Edward Elgar Publishing.

Hettyey, Andras. 2021. "The Europeanization of Hungarian Foreign Policy and the Hungarization of European Foreign Policy, 2010–18." *Journal of contemporary European studies* 29 (1): 125–38.

Iusmen, Ingi. 2013. "Policy Entrepreneurship and Eastern Enlargement: The Case of EU Children's Rights Policy." *Comparative European Politics* 11: 511–29.

Jupille, Joseph. 2006. "Knowing Europe: Metatheory and Methodology in European Union Studies." *Palgrave advances in European Union studies* 209–32.

Knill, Christoph and Duncan Liefferink. 2013. "Environmental Politics in The European Union: Policy-Making, Implementation and Patterns of Multi-Level Governance." In *Environmental politics in the European Union*. Manchester, Manchester University Press.

Kreppel, Amie and Bucket Oztas. 2017. "Leading the Band or Just Playing the Tune? Reassessing the Agenda-Setting Powers of the European Commission." *Comparative Political Studies* 50 (8): 1118–50.

Ladi, Stella and Sarah Wolff. 2021. "The EU Institutional Architecture in the Covid-19 Response: Coordinative Europeanization in Times of Permanent Emergency." *Journal of Common Market Studies* 59 (S1): 32.

Laffan, Brigid. 2019. "How the EU27 Came to Be." *JCMS: Journal of Common Market Studies* 57 (S1): 13–27.

Leppänen, Taru and Duncan Liefferink. 2022. "Agenda-setting, Policy Formulation, and the EU Institutional Context: The Case of the Just Transition Fund." *European Policy Analysis* 8 (1): 51–67.

López, Facundo A. S. and Michael Tatham. 2018. "Regionalization with Europeanization? The Rescaling of Interest Groups in Multi-Level Systems." *Journal of European Public Policy* 25 (5): 764–86.

Lynggaard, Kennet, Theofanis Exadaktylos, Mads D. Jensen and Michael F. Kluth. 2023. "Between Depoliticization and Politicization: The Role of Expertise in Covid-19 Politics in Europe." *Policy & Politics* (forthcoming).

Lynggaard, Kennet, Mads D. Jensen and Michael F. Kluth. 2023. *Governments' Responses to the Covid-19 Pandemic in Europe: Navigating the Perfect Storm*. Basingstoke, Palgrave Macmillan.

Maggetti, Martino. 2007. "De facto Independence after Delegation: A fuzzy-set Analysis." *Regulation & Governance* 1 (4): 271–94.

Massetti, Emanuele and Theofanis Exadaktylos. 2022. "From Crisis to Crisis: The EU in Between the Covid, Energy and Inflation Crises (and War)." *Journal of Common Market Studies* 60(S1): 5–11.

Monteleone, Carla. 2021. "Foreign Policy and de-Europeanization under the M5S–League Government: Exploring the Italian Behavior in the UN General Assembly." *Journal of European Integration* 43 (5): 551–67.

Oztas, Buket. and Amie Kreppel. 2022. "Power or Luck? The Limitations of the European Commission's Agenda Setting Power and Autonomous Policy Influence." *Journal of Common Market Studies* 60 (2): 408–26.

Panke, Diana. 2010. "Small States in the European Union: Structural Disadvantages in EU Policy-making and Counter-strategies." *Journal of European Public Policy* 17 (6): 799–817.

Rhinard, Mark. 2019 "The Crisisification of Policy-making in the European Union." *Journal of Common Market Studies* 57 (3): 616–33.

Rozbicka, Patrycia, and Florian Spohr. 2016. "Interest Groups in Multiple Streams: Specifying Their Involvement in the Framework." *Policy Sciences* 49: 55–69.

Sager, Fritz and Eva Thomann. 2017. "Multiple Streams in Member State Implementation: Politics, Problem Construction and Policy Paths in Swiss Asylum Policy." *Journal of Public Policy* 37 (3): 287–314.

Saurugger, Sabine and Fabien Terpan. 2016. "Do Crises Lead to Policy Change? The Multiple Streams Framework and The European Union's Economic Governance Instruments." *Policy Sciences* 49: 35–53.

Schmidt, Vivien A. 2022. "European Emergency Politics and the Question of Legitimacy." *Journal of European Public Policy* 29 (6): 979–93.

Schmitt, Susanne K. 2000. "Only an Agenda Setter? The European Commission's Power over the Council of Ministers." *European Union Politics* 1 (1): 37–61.

Schön-Quinlivan, Emmanuelle and Marco Scipioni. 2017. "The Commission as Policy Entrepreneur in European Economic Governance: A Comparative Multiple Stream Analysis of the 2005 And 2011 Reform of the Stability and Growth Pact." *Journal of European Public Policy* 24 (8): 1172–90.

Seabrooke, Leonard and Eleni Tsingou. 2019. "Europe's Fast-and Slow-Burning Crises." *Journal of European public policy* 26 (3): 468–81.

Sil, Rudra and Peter J. Katzenstein. 2010. *Beyond Paradigms: Analytic Eclecticism in the Study of World Politics*. London, Bloomsbury Publishing.

Smismans, Stijn. 2015. "Policy Evaluation in the EU: The Challenges of Linking Ex Ante and Ex Post Appraisal." *European Journal of Risk Regulation* 6 (1): 6–26.

Spohr, Florien. 2016. "Explaining Path Dependency and Deviation by Combining Multiple Streams Framework and Historical Institutionalism: A Comparative Analysis of German and Swedish Labor Market Policies." *Journal of Comparative Policy Analysis: Research and Practice* 18 (3): 257–72.

Tallberg, Jonas. 2004. "The Agenda-Shaping Powers of the Council Presidency." In *European Union Council Presidencies*, 27–46. Abingdon, Routledge.

Thierse, Stefan. 2019. "Policy Entrepreneurship in the European Parliament: Reconsidering the Influence of Rapporteurs." *Journal of European Public Policy* 26 (2): 267–85.

Thomann, Eva, Philipp Trein and Martino Maggetti. 2019. "What's the Problem? Multilevel Governance and Problem-Solving." *European Policy Analysis* 5 (1): 37–57.

Vasilopoulou, Sofia., Daphne Halikiopoulou, & Theofanis Exadaktylos. 2014. "Greece in Crisis: Austerity, Populism and the Politics of Blame." *Journal of Common Market Studies* 52 (2): 388–402.

Zahariadis, Nikolaos. 2008. "Ambiguity and choice in European Public Policy." *Journal of European Public Policy* 15 (4): 514–30.

Zahariadis, Nikolaos. 2012. "Complexity, Coupling and Policy Effectiveness: the European Response to the Greek Sovereign Debt Crisis." *Journal of Public Policy* 32 (2): 99–116.

Zahariadis, Nikolaos. 2014. "Ambiguity and Multiple Streams." In *Theories of the policy process*, eds. Paul Sabatier and Christopher M. Weible, 25–58. Boulder: Westview Press.

Zahariadis, Nikolaos. 2016. "Delphic oracles: Ambiguity, Institutions, and Multiple Streams." *Policy Sciences* 49: 3–12.

Zahariadis, Nikolaos and Theofanis Exadaktylos. 2016. "Policies that Succeed and Programs that Fail: Ambiguity, Conflict, and Crisis in Greek Higher Education." *Policy Studies Journal* 44 (1): 59–82.

Zahariadis, Nikolaos, Evangelina Petridou, Theofanis Exadaktylos and Jorgen Sparf. 2022. *Policy Styles and Trust in the Age of Pandemics: Global Threat, National Responses*. Abingdon, Routledge.

Zahariadis, Nikolaos, Evangelina Petridou, Theofanis Exadaktylos and Jorgn Sparf. 2023. "Policy Styles and Political Trust in Europe's National Responses to the COVID-19 Crisis." *Policy Studies* 44 (1): 46–67.

Zohlnhöfer, Riemut, Nicole Herweg and Christian Huß. 2016. "Bringing Formal Political Institutions into the Multiple Streams Framework: An Analytical Proposal for Comparative Policy Analysis." *Journal of comparative policy analysis: research and practice* 18 (3): 243–56.

Index